Theory and Practice of Community Social Work

Theory and Practice of Community Social Work

Edited by SAMUEL H. TAYLOR and ROBERT W. ROBERTS

COLUMBIA UNIVERSITY PRESS   New York

Columbia University Press
New York   Guildford, Surrey
Copyright © 1985 Columbia University Press
All rights reserved

Printed in the United States of America

Library of Congress Cataloging in Publication Data
Main entry under title:

Theory and practice of community social work.

    Includes bibliographies and index.
    1. Social service—Addresses, essays, lectures.
2. Community organization—Addresses, essays, lectures.
I. Taylor, Samuel H.   II. Roberts, Robert W.
HV37.T465   1985   361.8   84-15628
ISBN 0-231-05368-1 (alk. paper)

c 10 9 8 7 6 5 4 3

DEDICATED TO THE BOARD OF DIRECTORS, RANCH EHRLO SOCIETY
OF REGINA, SASKATCHEWAN, CANADA, FOR THEIR COMMITMENT TO,
AND ENDURING SUPPORT FOR, THE DEVELOPMENT AND DISSEMINATION
OF KNOWLEDGE FOR THE BETTERMENT OF SOCIAL SERVICES

Contents

viii   Contents

Contributors

Kenneth L. Chau, Associate Professor, Department of Social Work, California State University, Long Beach. [At the time his article was written, Professor Chau was Senior Lecturer, Department of Social Work, University of Hong Kong.]

Carel B. Germain, Professor, School of Social Work, University of Connecticut.

Charles F. Grosser, Professor, School of Social Work, Columbia University.

Peter Hodge, Professor and Head, Department of Social Work, University of Hong Kong.

Bruce S. Jansson, Associate Professor, School of Social Work, University of Southern California.

Paul A. Kurzman, Professor, School of Social Work, Hunter College, City University of New York.

Ben Lappin, Professor, School of Social Work, Bar-Ilan University, Israel; Visiting Professor, Sir Wilfred Laurier University, Canada.

Jacqueline Mondros, Assistant Professor, School of Social Work, Columbia University.

Abraham Monk, Brookdale Professor of Gerontology, School of Social Work, Columbia University.

Geoffrey L. Pawson, Executive Director, Ranch Ehrlo Society, Regina, Saskatchewan, Canada.

Robert W. Roberts, Dean and Professor, School of Social Work, University of Southern California.

Jack Rothman, Professor, School of Social Work, University of Michigan.

Terry Russell, Director of Child and Youth Services, Regina Mental Health Region, Saskatchewan, Canada.

Ramon Salcido, Associate Professor, School of Social Work, University of Southern California.

Barbara B. Solomon, Professor, School of Social Work, University of Southern California.

Madeline R. Stoner, Assistant Professor and Assistant Dean, School of Social Work, University of Southern California.

Samuel H. Taylor, Associate Professor, School of Social Work, University of Southern California.

Mayer N. Zald, Professor and Chair, Sociology Department, University of Michigan.

Preface

Virtually every author who has completed a major work on community practice for social workers has commented on the rudimentary nature of theory underlying this approach as compared with other social work methods. The reasons for the underdevelopment of theory to guide community work practice are many and complex: some experts believe that the development of appropriate theory is imminent; others worry that premature development will hinder the growth of practice and limit consideration of alternative conceptual frameworks; while others contend that the development and adoption of practice theory are either irrelevant or not likely to appear for some time to come.

Despite the absence of well-formulated theories, a careful review of the literature convinced us that distinct approaches do exist and that these can serve as a springboard for organizing more cogent conceptual frameworks that would be of value to practitioners and researchers. As we struggled with trying to organize the knowledge that has developed out of community work, however, we discovered that much of the literature does not have a theoretical orientation; instead, it focuses on the historical development and pragmatic realities of community work in specific fields or with particular problems or populations.

Fields of practice are important and to exclude them would seem to be a serious deficiency, especially in a book on community practice. Therefore, unlike *Theories of Social Casework* (University of Chicago Press, 1970) and *Theories of Social Work with Groups* (Columbia University Press, 1976), we decided on a dual rather than a singular focus for this volume: one group of authors would address the major theoretical models or approaches, while another group would survey and deal with community work as it is actually practiced in various fields of practice.

In order to assist contributors in designing and developing their essays, we prepared separate topical outlines for the two perspectives. To the extent that authors followed these outlines, readers will be able to make comparisons and analyses of community work across approaches to, as well as in, selected fields of practice. The outlines represented our understanding of these approaches to community work; they were not "conceptual straitjackets," and authors were not bound to cover the suggested topics.

One of the more rewarding aspects of a project such as this is derived from the opportunity for contributors to meet together for an exchange of ideas. After all initial drafts were completed, each person received copies of the contributions of the others and then gathered in Regina, Saskatchewan, Canada, where energetic discussions took place in general sessions as well as informally over coffee and in hallways. The final versions of the articles in this book are the product of those exchanges and the willingness of contributors to grapple with issues, accept well-intended criticisms and suggestions, and advance the development and dissemination of knowledge for social work community practice.

Throughout the stages and processes associated with the completion of this book, we were all keenly aware of our sincere debt of gratitude to the Ranch Ehrlo Society of Regina, Saskatchewan, Canada, for their generous support of the project. Their Board's encouragement and commitment, especially during times when allocations to the human services were declining, was noteworthy and commendable.

A deep personal sadness for all the contributors to this book was our sudden and surprising loss of Charles Grosser, of the School of Social Work, Columbia University and Peter Hodge of the Department of Social Work of the University of Hong Kong. Their sustained efforts within social work and community practice in general, as well as in our deliberations, were keenly recognized and appreciated. As fate would have it, their articles are their final written contributions to the profession. They will be missed by all who were fortunate enough to have been associated with them.

As in any enterprise such as this, there are many who helped to make this book possible. Our special thanks to Ruth Britton, librarian at the Arlien Johnson Social Work Library at the University of Southern California, whose patience and diligence in locating resources were particularly helpful; to Rebecca Amescua, Gloria Byrd, Ramona Hernandez, Angela Lee Thomas, and Nettie Mowery for their typing of the manuscripts; to George Wolkon and Wilbur Finch whose early suggestions served to guide our work; and our deep appreciation for the patience and care that Dorothy M. Swart devoted to the manuscript.

We wish to record a note of appreciation to our wives, Sue Taylor and Helen Roberts, who encouraged us and supported our work in innumerable ways. Finally, our thanks to each contributor and to those social work practitioners and academicians whose interest in books such as this both stimulated and sustained us through numerous revisions.

Samuel H. Taylor
Robert W. Roberts

PART ONE

The State of Community Practice Theory

1

The Fluidity of Practice Theory: An Overview

Samuel H. Taylor and Robert W. Roberts

The task of describing community social work practice would have been substantially easier if it had been done before the 1960s. Social work's efforts then were based on a strong problem-solving orientation, and it was taken as a matter of faith that problems of clients and neighborhoods were amenable to solution by rational interventions based upon this ideological perspective. Starting from a common philosophical premise, community practitioners fashioned principles and techniques that revolved around two primary approaches: (1) the sociotherapeutic approach, which had strong ties to direct services and clinical practice (Lippitt, Watson and Westley 1958); and (2) the rational planning approach (Kahn 1963) which had ties to community and agency councils. Social action was a familiar concept that was comfortably accommodated within both the sociotherapeutic and planning approaches, even though its characteristics varied considerably when applied. From the planning perspective, social action most often related to improving the social environment by providing needed services or organizing citizens and professionals to press for social reforms. In the sociotherapeutic approach, social action involved enabling community groups to become active participants in the democratic processes of society so that they could engage in problem-solving activities or reform efforts that were intended to change societal organizations and institutions.

Harper and Dunham (1959:281) acknowledged the broad, often vague and pervasive quality of social work's use of the term social action and suggested that it involves the quality of unfreezing a static situation in order to achieve particular objectives. It was not until the seminal work of Rothman (1968) that social work formally acknowledged the more activist, confrontive, grass-roots efforts which had emerged as a unique approach and were claiming exclusive right to use of the label social action (Haggstrom 1964; Grosser 1965; Brager and Purcell 1967; Erlich 1966).

By the mid 1970s, however, many sponsors and agencies began to withdraw funding and sanction of this newly defined approach. The confrontive and disruptive tactics used by social actionists were sufficiently embarrassing and uncomfortable that long before the profession began to recognize its demise, social action had been replaced by citizen participation. If carried on at all as Rothman described it, social action was usually implemented by neighborhood self-help groups and oppressed populations (such as racial and ethnic minorities, gay liberation groups, the women's movements, the aged) rather than by professional social workers. Though social workers might consult or collaborate with such groups, the new model of social action was given a subsidiary position within the profession's traditional concern for both cause and function. Following historical patterns, the certitudes of function were emphasized, and less priority was given to cause as a basis for practice roles supported by social agencies.

This discussion of the development and decline of the social action model is but one example of the fluid nature of community practice and its sensitivity to the winds of social change inherent in the perpetual flux of society's social, political, and economic institutions. As such, it illustrates the quaking ground upon which community practice has been built and why, unlike casework and group work, it has not yet been included in the "royal family of received social work methods" (Schwartz 1977:210).

Although many factors have been identified as possible causes for this exclusion, there is agreement that a principal obstacle has been the near absence of theory development. Kramer and

Specht (1975:2) contend that the more refined efforts to build theory have been handicapped by equivocation while the more ideologically oriented authors have not been able to justify their optimism. Practitioners, on the other hand, tend to identify a need for theory development only when they are overwhelmed by the complexities of situations that fail to yield to their interventive efforts. At other times they seem to enjoy the challenges and excitement of improvisation and the eclectic use of a randomly constructed repertoire of strategies and techniques.

Much of the interest in theory development emerges from academicians who have sought to construct theories as a basis for educating students and designing empirical research. At times this effort has seemed to proceed from the premise that any theoretical formulation is better than none at all, because even an invalid theory can be tested, and if disproved, the search can begin anew. In contrast to the theory-first approach, there have been a few efforts to conduct research that might lead to practice theory (Lebowitz 1961; Olshansky 1961; Rainman 1962), but this has not been a sustained line of inquiry. For instance, Rothman (1974) surveyed and compiled the social science and professional research literature that had potential for improving theory development, but this ambitious project has not stimulated correspondingly rigorous effort by others.

Practice in Search of Theory

This volume is in the tradition of earlier attempts at describing and analyzing practice theory for social casework (Roberts and Nee 1970) and social group work (Roberts and Northen 1976). It is similar to these earlier efforts in that social work scholars were commissioned to write essays defining what the editors considered to be the major theoretical models of community practice. It differs in that this effort was approached from a two- rather than a one-dimensional perspective. Thus, in addition to those who were invited to describe generic models of community social work practice, other scholars were commissioned to report on community social work as it has been practiced in designated fields of practice or with designated client populations. Added to these were requests for an article on community social work in developing countries and another on the place of community practice within the generic eco-systems approach to practice.

In a spirit that now seems unduly optimistic and ambitious, an outline was prepared for the contributors of the papers on generic community practice theory. In the hope that the outline would provide a structure that would facilitate the identification of salient aspects of each approach to community practice, each author was asked to address ten separate but admittedly interrelated topics:

1. Basic characteristics of the model
2. Major historical developments
3. Assumptions regarding the nature of society and processes of change
4. Political, social, economic, and behavioral science foundations
5. Goals and objectives
6. Recruitment and selection of participating groups and individuals
7. Processes and structures
8. Principles, methods, and techniques
9. Linkages to practice with individuals and groups
10. Unsolved problems.

The charge to the contributors was to cover each topic according to their respective theoretical approaches to practice. The models of community practice and the authors are as follows:

1. Community development: Ben Lappin
2. The political action approach; pluralism and participation: Charles F. Grosser and Jacqueline Mondros
3. Program development and coordination: Paul A. Kurzman
4. Planning: Jack Rothman and Mayer N. Zald
5. Community liaison: Samuel H. Taylor

What became clear early on in the process was that our expectations were unrealistic. Not only did each of the theoretical approaches have submodels and permutations, only some of which had been reported in the literature, but in addition, the parameters of each approach were hazy and varied according to the settings of practice and the goals subscribed to by sponsors and practitioners. Some of the major aspects of the overlaps will be identified in this essay when the major features of each of these models are discussed.

MAJOR FEATURES OF MODELS OF COMMUNITY SOCIAL WORK PRACTICE

It has been argued that only stylistic differences separate community practitioners regardless of the model they adhere to or the population they work with, since the basic nature of the processes and tasks they utilize are more alike than different (Kramer and Specht 1975:8). Other authors have identified a range of differences varying according to goals (Brager and Specht 1973:46–49). As Schwartz noted:

Patterns and relationships between lumping and splitting tendencies in a process as complex as the development of social work education and theory are not easily determined and can appear in the eye of a beholder as swings of a pendulum, oscillations, spiralling, dialectical, synergistic, or other effects. (1977:208)

It is in that spirit that we attempt to trace and highlight the differences and similarities among the theoretical approaches to practice described in this volume.

Rothman and Zald in their discussion on planning describe an approach that relies heavily on research and technological competencies that are utilized in the service of comprehensive, systematic activities that will produce a plan or forecast future conditions. Striving for neutrality and objectivity, social planners use formal structures and processes to guide themselves and those they collaborate with in the pursuit of outcomes that are logical, rational, and, it is hoped, beneficial. While they acknowledge the emergence of more people-oriented (transactive) and political (advocacy) streams within planning, to account more realistically for sponsors' and constituencies' expectations, the hallmark of the planning approach is a set of technical skills which have transferability whether the practitioner is functioning at the national level or in the planning department of a community social agency.

Kurzman acknowledges that the program development and

coordination orientation at times resemble planning. In fact, agencies responsible for these functions may also engage in social planning, and they often use the term to describe themselves to the public; but more important, they engage in the mediative and political processes that bring about actual implementation. Incrementalism (Lindblom 1959) is not only a submodel on the way to finding out what works and what does not, but is in fact the *raison de être* of program development. Change is conceived of as a process that engages the full range of political and organizational interests that may revolve around a particular problem, issue, or decision. While selected community representatives may be invited to participate, and neighborhoods or special populations may be surveyed, or may even collectively petition such organizations, the professional worker's primary allegiances are to the service agencies, sponsors, funding sources, and political systems of the community. Whether lodged in the voluntary sector (a federation or council) or in the public sector (an area council on aging), the worker's primary constituency is composed of professionals and agencies. Indeed, the task forces, committees, and commissions of coordinating agencies often serve as arenas for community liaison activity by representatives from the direct-service agencies. Originally conceived as a means of identifying needs and stimulating the development of programs and services, program developers frequently serve public relations functions on behalf of the functional communities of interest they represent (developmentally disabled, aged). When consensus is achieved on the desirability of attaining a particular goal, program developers can be a significant force at the community or state level, especially when engaged in publicity campaigns, political lobbying, or efforts to educate the public.

Lappin approaches community development by focusing on the concept of enabling, which over the years has been conceived of as both means and goal, and at times has symbolized the style and the distinctiveness of social work in a way that could bring unity when differences threatened the fabric of the profession. Carefully delineating enabling as a process that is separate from facilitating, Lappin differentiates community development from program development and coordination, which frequently describe its activities at the community council level as enabling.

Community development is characterized by dual emphasis

on growth of the individual and the group, neighborhood, or community. The worker's constellation of practice principles (begin where the client is, help people to help themselves) center on practice roles that encourage participation and social involvement as vehicles for personal and group enhancement even more than as embodiments of democracy in action. In tracing community development's path from the settlements to its use in Third World colonies as a bridge to independence and then back again as a means of helping selected urban neighborhoods improve their poverty-ridden condition, it becomes clear that this practice approach is seen as an opportunity system for self-help, aided by a professional worker who is sensitive to cultural nuances and skilled in educating. Regardless of sponsorship and whether it is practiced in rural or urban neighborhoods, the emphasis is on developing local leadership and organizing structures that will permit residents to improve their socioeconomic circumstances. Cooperation, collaboration, and conflict resolution are the principal strategies used for achieving change.

Community development's focus on participation of all the people in a neighborhood or village documents its integrationist goals and its preoccupation with community self-determination. Lappin argues that these values are especially attractive to professionals utilizing other community practice approaches. This has led to a wholesale borrowing of terminology and techniques from the community development approach in order to gain acceptance by local residents for goals predetermined by vertical systems. At times, community development workers themselves seek to deny the role that sponsors' expectations play in the processes of consensus-building and decision-making at the local level.

Grosser and Mondros' description of the political empowerment approach, while somewhat similar to community development, emphasizes participation and involvement, but with an important difference. They assume that in every community there is a plurality of interests that frequently compete with each other, but within that process, some groups are consistently excluded from decision-making. Struggle and conflict are ever-present, and practitioners must understand and use power in its varied forms in order to achieve desired outcomes. Practice roles include serving as an educator, resource developer, or agitator, with the self-determined interests of the disadvantaged group serving as the primary guide for decisions related to goals and means. Though individual participants and groups are assumed to grow and develop and learn new skills in the process of organizing to achieve improvements in their situation, a more proximate goal is to make democracy work for the interests of those who have been excluded or ignored.

Empowerment activities can take place through legally mandated approaches such as citizen participation on boards and client advisory bodies, but more important, they can be self-generated, as in neighborhood and minority rights associations. This last feature is an important distinction from the community development approach in that self-determination is an inherent aspect of the group's fundamental autonomy and control over its decision-making prerogatives. This is observed most clearly when function-transfer strategies are employed: when frustrated by a lack of, or inadequate, services from existing institutions, groups can design, implement, and manage their own alternative programs, whether these be food co-ops, information and referral services, or self-help groups such as Parents Anonymous, composed of actual and potential child abusers. While social workers are typically involved in the formal aspects of this approach, as in agency-sponsored advocacy and clients' rights programs, organizational forms that eschew external sponsorship and/or rely on confrontive strategies often function without social work community practitioners, except when they collaborate as consultants or part-time volunteers apart from their agency roles.

Taylor's discussion of the community liaison approach contends that the prevailing models of community practice do not attend to the goals, limits, roles, and special purposes that characterize efforts by the staff and administration of direct-service agencies to engage in community practice. Although acknowledged by community practice authors over the years, this practice approach has been largely ignored by authors and researchers who are more dedicated to describing and analyzing community practice in settings where it is a primary rather than a secondary function. There is some confusion over its purpose since in one form administrators carry out activities commonly perceived to be part of community practice (such as interorganizational, boundary spanning; community relations; environmental, reconnaisance, and support activities) as routine aspects of their administrative role. On the other hand, clinical practitioners often engage in program development, need determination, and client advocacy as part of their direct-service role. In recent years the trend toward generalist practice by clinicians and the tendency to integrate forms of macro-practice (administration, community, policy) are both viewed as potentially productive for theory development (Schwartz 1977:224). More important, this approach to community practice proceeds from a more holistic perspective that recognizes social work's need to assess and intervene at both environmental and intrapersonal levels. As generalist practice authors (Germain 1979; Pincus and Minahan 1973; Compton and Galloway 1975) move to integrate and incorporate the community within their formulations, this approach to practice has gained a new legitimacy.

While the preceding discussion of characteristics of the five approaches to community practice does not do justice to the authors' contributions, it does serve to call the reader's attention to selected differences among these orientations. When authors refer to historical antecedents of key stages in the evolution of practice, there is a strong sense of a shared perception of key trends and developments. Each orientation acknowledges that the settlement house movement and/or the charity organization societies were progenitors, except for the community liaison approach which claims linkage to the earliest voluntary and church-sponsored societies and social agencies which sought to mobilize support for improving the care of disadvantaged groups such as orphans and paupers.

The question posed in the beginning stage of planning this book—Are there two or three or five or more models of community practice within social work?—remains largely unanswered, though hotly debated. In recent years new orientations have emerged that utilize a social development framework (Spergel 1982:21) and a Marxist perspective toward practice (Burghardt 1982). There is in all of these approaches the opportunity to find both similarities and differences, but in the spirit of Schwartz's (1977) discussion of macro-theory development there is reason to ask whether the differences are in degree or kind. By a strict interpretation, such as that applied to a comparison of theories of personality (Urban and Ford 1963), we would have to conclude that none of these orientations or approaches is sufficiently articulated or differentiated to allow practitioners to follow them as models that prescribe a complete course of action. Rather they can be viewed as stages in the development of practice theories. As working papers toward theory development they are rich resources that suggest clusters of roles, functions, and objectives that trace the elements of paradigms not yet fully developed.

Clients and Sponsors

While the charity organization societies devoted some attention to societal conditions in their recognition of poverty and social conditions, their primary emphases were on the development of elaborate procedures to determine need and efforts to avoid duplication of services. This, plus their early opposition to outdoor relief, suggests that they were more allied with the sponsors of services than with the families in need. Interestingly, the settlement house movement, which obtained its early leaders from society's elites, adopted a much more client-oriented perspective. This may well have derived from the firsthand experience its volunteers gained when living in the neighborhoods of the poor and observing the effects of environmental factors that were beyond the residents' control.

Over a hundred years later it is possible to rank each of the approaches to practice in this book along a continuum ranging from a client-centered to a sponsor-centered approach.

If one uses the extent to which both sponsors and clients determine: (1) the parameters of practice; (2) the alternative strategies that can be considered; and (3) the extent to which decisions are influenced by clients or sponsors, figure 1.1 suggests the extremes and the points between. Rothman (1968), in order to highlight the differences in his three models of practice, presented clear lines of demarcation in terms of each model's orientation toward power structures and conceptions of the client role, while encouraging social workers to mix and phase in order to match their practice to the needs of particular situations. For the practitioner still struggling to understand and decide which formula to apply, this figure may help in comprehending the tugs of client and sponsor influence.

In program development and coordination and in political

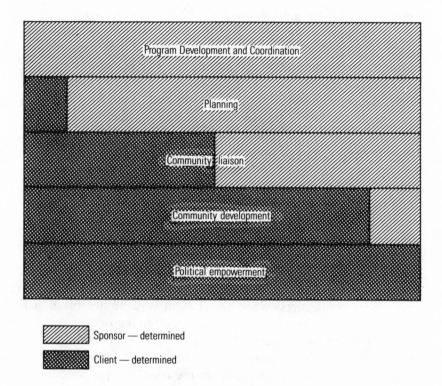

Sponsor — determined

Client — determined

FIGURE 1.1. Client and Sponsor Determination of Practice Decisions

empowerment, the practitioner is rarely caught in a marginal status except as the tenets of those approaches to practice are consciously redirected in order to accommodate momentary pressures or circumstances that seem to compel such adjustments. For example, a planning council, whose primary relationships and allegiances are to member agencies, may make a special effort to reach out to a client group or a neighborhood in order to effect a compromise or reach a working agreement between the two groups. Similarly, a community group such as an association of welfare mothers may cooperate with a public assistance agency in order to achieve needed changes in policies or procedures. However, in both instances these are strategies employed to gain limited goals and in no way alter the more basic values, goals and allegiances of the respective parties. Recognition of diversities of interest need not block all efforts at accommodation in order to gain objectives or changes which have value to both sides. Agency councils regularly adjust their recommendations in order to neutralize the opposition of, or gain support from, powerful or vocal community interest groups and vice versa.

The continual tension or practitioner ambiguity is more apparent in the community liaison, planning, and community development aproaches to practice. In planning, the predominant orientation is the use of rational procedures and analytic techniques that ostensibly produce objective solutions and forecasts. Recent reliance on some degree of input from groups that will be most affected by the plans, and advocacy planning (not widespread) wherein disadvantaged or oppressed groups or neighborhoods are able to use planning technology to come up with competing or alternative plans from those developed by government or private organizations, allow some client groups a measure of influence. In community liaison, the situation is more fluid, with clients' and sponsors' interests converging in a partnership which subjects the practitioner to role stress when he is caught between organizational and client interests that are not congruent. Community development relies heavily on the participation and involvement of community or client groups, but for all its rhetoric, as Lappin and Chau and Hodge point out, the sponsors who support the community development worker do have expectations and will withdraw their resources if they are not satisfied with the processes used or the outcomes.

In recognition of the central role that sponsorship plays in determining what the practitioner can or cannot do and what outcomes are acceptable or unacceptable to sponsors or client or constituency groups, Brager and Specht have devoted two chapters of their book (1973:171–212) to the strain and struggle which often characterize the role and change strategies employed by practitioners.

This raises a critical question concerning the development of theory in social work community practice. To what extent is the seeming proliferation of "submodels" within each theoretical approach more than stylistic or goal differences? Are they rather the efforts of social workers to mediate between, and navigate through, the contending expectations of sponsors and clients, each rooted in a particular field and influenced by the particular differences among the organizational and community contexts within which practitioners function? This thorny question will be dealt with again in the final section of this essay, but that consideration may be illuminated by some consideration of authors' efforts to describe and analyze practice within various fields and with selected populations. Before discussing these, however, consideration of Germain's ecological perspective is appropriate since it focuses on the generic practice approach which deals with the issue of community practice's relationship and linkage to the other methods of social work.

Generic Perspectives: Macro-Micro Continuum

The social worker who adopts an ecological or generic perspective is expected to develop a multifaceted approach which allows practice to occur on a micro-level (individual, family) or a macro-level (environment, organizations, community) or on both levels simultaneously. The social worker cannot be content with acknowledging or making mental note of the fact that, for example, there are few adequate child care facilities for working mothers. The expectation is that the client will receive the worker's direct help and steps will be taken to improve conditions at the community level. Reminiscent of the early settlement approach, but reinforced by theories such as human ecology, general systems, and exchange, the ecologically trained professional is expected to focus on total problem configurations, including the identification of stressors and the mobilization of interventions that serve to remedy person:environment problems. The growth-oriented, developmental approach specifically encourages social workers to assess presenting situations from a transactional perspective which mandates the necessity for working to achieve change at both the individual and community levels.

At the present time this approach seems to be directed primarily to clinical practitioners, encouraging them to expand their roles, functions, and skills, and there is an absence of generic or practice formulations from the opposite end of the continuum. Germain, in her article, pointedly notes that although students of the community (Park, Burgess, and McKenzie 1925; Hawley 1950) have a long tradition of using ecological tenets to understand community life, social work community practice authors have not explicitly used ecological terms that might guide the development of appropriate practice roles or strategies of intervention. Germain calls attention to the fact that this development in theory is one-sided. Community practice authors have not been as diligent in their effort to chart conceptual paths toward direct service, except as they note the purpose and define community practice as an interest in "influencing social problems" (Brager and Specht 1973:27) or engaging in "social problem-solving" (Perlman and Gurin 1972:61). Rothman suggests that one of the dilemmas of social work community practice is whether it should "stress the delivery of services to individuals in need or the modification of social conditions" (1979:274). While this raises the historic question of whether the profession's primary mission is cause or function, to reform society or to help people in need, it also suggests that the closest efforts at linkage to other methods of direct practice relate to the development, coordination, and delivery of services to clients by group workers and caseworkers.

Germain refers back to the settlement house movement to lay claim to the profession's dual concern with people in need and reform, but community practice authors relate to that tradition only in terms of social action, progressive reform, and empowerment of disadvantaged groups. Whether this imbalance is attributable to the nascent nature of theory development for community practice, or is reflective of community work's uneasy integration under the broad umbrella of the profession, is unanswerable.

A second critical aspect of Germain's contribution is her emphasis on moving toward problem, population, or institution specializations. This radical departure from social work's traditional reliance on method specialization assumes that professionals will develop knowledge and skills that will facilitate their ability to work with individuals, groups, organizations, or communities in relation to problems (such as delinquency) or populations (such as the aging). Such an integrated methods approach requires a reconceptualization of practice roles and functions, restructuring of the majority of social agencies, and a new and as yet unattained synthesis of macro- and micro-practice. While critics have suggested that this might dilute practice competency and effectiveness, at precisely the time when other professions are becoming more method-specific, Germain's ideas pose a substantial challenge to customary approaches to model- and theory-building for practice. Germain's proposals offer a stimulating perspective for our consideration of the articles that endeavor to describe and analyze community practice with populations or in problem areas.

Areas of Practice

Our initial thoughts about the development of this book were limited to what seemed to be an already challenging assignment: to describe schools of thought that seemed to hold promise for theory formulation for community practice. The decision to add specific areas of practice was undertaken in order to capture some of the unique structural and organizational differences that might be found in various fields and to see if and to what extent there might be a range of different orientations or approaches within each field. Authors charged with the responsibility of describing these areas were aware of the theoretical orientations which were to be discussed by other authors, but they were free to mention or not the extent to which particular theoretical orientations or approaches to practice were utilized or present within their arena.

Our outline for the authors suggested that they consider community practice in terms of:

1. Issues and problems
2. Sponsors, participants, and goals
3. Models of practice
4. Successes and failures
5. Recommendations.

Our hope was for an elaboration of predominant goals, tasks, needs, problems, and issues rather than an encyclopedic listing. It was expected that there would be significant variation within each area based to some extent on sponsorship, participants, levels of practice (neighborhood or national), and the constellations of participants involved. In selecting the fields of mental health, aging, child welfare, and health we were guided by two considerations: (1) social work's consistent and historical involvement in each of these fields; (2) the specific community practice mandates issued by both governmental and voluntary private sponsors. For the readers who miss or resent our not including their particular sphere of interest, we assume full responsibility for our decisions, which in the final analysis represented our best judgment of which fields would yield the richest returns and stimulate thought among students, researchers, theoreticians, and, most of all, practitioners.

Our inclusion of community practice in developing countries and in oppressed minority communities emerged from distinctly separate lines of reasoning. Our interest in developing countries was influenced by awareness that especially since World War II, students from foreign nations have attended American graduate schools of social work and then returned to practice and provide social welfare leadership in their homelands. Further, we anticipated that developing countries, because of their particular socioeconomic and political arrangements, would be formulating community practice in ways that are quite different from those on the American scene.

Inclusion of a contribution on minorities stemmed from the recognition that although social work has a long history of efforts to reduce discrimination and offer help to the victims of societal and personal prejudice, the profession has also overlooked some of the unique aspects of practice in minority communities. Moreover, although social work has acknowledged that race and ethnicity are factors that must be considered by practitioners, the profession has not been as diligent in articulating or recognizing new forms of practice that are responsive to the needs and aspirations of minority groups.

The following sections consider some of the issues raised by the papers on the practice of community work in selected areas, especially their relevance to theory development.

DIRECT AND INDIRECT PRACTICE

A recurring debate among social work theorists has centered on the distinction between direct practice with clients and indirect practice such as administration, research, and policy development. Historically, indirect practice has been viewed as supportive and complementary to the principal mission of the profession, namely, providing skilled help and services to troubled individuals, families, and groups. Prior to the Lane Report (Lane 1939), some community practitioners argued that community organization was a field of practice linked to the broadly defined goals of social welfare rather than to the profession of social work. As the profession and its graduate schools moved to embrace community work as one of its three methods of practice, this debate receded but did not disappear. One of the pivotal distinctions between those from other disciplines who organized in communities and those who classified themselves as social work community practitioners was the relationship to those agencies, clients, problems, and populations wherein social work's values and competencies were established, or defined by society through institutional and organizational structures. At the risk of oversimplification, when social workers were offering direct services to clients with particular problems, community work was perceived to be a part of the profession's response. Thus, it is no surprise that the authors have identified community practice as integral to the effective conduct of social work activities in the areas surveyed in this volume.

A partial listing of such activities includes population and problem advocacy, identifying unmet needs, influencing legislation, organizing constituencies, planning, outreach, prevention, coordination of services, action research, evaluation, fundraising, building community and public awareness, and developing needed programs. With such a long list of identified professional activities it might be expected that community social workers can be found at every geographic level (neighborhood, community, state, and national) and in nearly every aspect of social work practice. The truth, however, is that in every area of practice surveyed there are constellations of supportive functions and a myriad of problems, issues, and needs which cry for attention, intervention, and efforts to bring about change. Work on these challenges is deterred by disagreements about the appropriate function of community social work. In some instances, community work is conceived of as a means of enhancing or supporting direct practice with clients, such as in program coordination or fund raising; in other instances, the goal is to influence the policies of organizations and governments so that they are more responsive to unmet needs or quicker to identify new problems. Summing up these descriptions could lead to the conclusion that the community worker is an all-purpose utility player who functions as a boundary or linkage agent between direct-service workers and agencies and the wider environment. Whether referring to social conditions which require remedial change in order to reduce individual and family breakdown or the establishment of policies and procedures which will assure adequate allocations of resources for those in need, the community worker is perceived by the authors to be a multipurpose change agent.

If this scenario were applied literally it would be realistic to expect the numbers of community practitioners to exceed those who provide direct services to clients. Such is not the case. In fact, the reverse obtains. In each field of practice, the majority of community-level needs and problems were being neglected or ignored. Jansson and Salcido, for instance, note that health agencies deemphasize community practice in relation to health education, outreach, reform, and community involvement in planning and decision-making. Pawson and Russell note the scant attention paid to establishing neighborhood day care centers for the children of working parents; the establishment of community-based group homes and a network of local services for children released from residential institutions; or the need for improving child protective services. Monk reports that despite the increase in the frail elderly as a proportion of our population, services are being reduced, local planning and service coordination have been cut back, and community service networks are not being developed to maintain the elderly in their homes, not even those with major physical handicaps and modest financial resources. Stoner describes the earlier work of community practitioners in community and program development, coordination of service with other community agencies, consultation and education, and building bridges of communication and involvement between local citizen groups and mental health centers. Stoner also notes the atrophy of these important functions in favor of more delimited direct services to identified patients.

What is clear is that within each field of practice there is a bewildering array of special problems, situations, and needs that call for attention by professionals skilled in community practice; what is equally clear is that these needs are not being attended to by trained practitioners. While some of these activities are limited functions (fund raising, education), others require a problem-solving approach that includes assessment, goal development, strategy, and action for change (Cox et al. 1974:425–29).

The Lane Report (1939) conceptualized community work as a complete social work method rather than a constellation of community-type functions in the service of the profession's direct-service methods. Although the historic debate as to whether community practice is a social work method or a field of practice is not currently waged, issues associated with the argument remain. For many in the profession, community social work is still seen as an auxiliary service to the profession's mission of providing direct and clinical services. For these people, the tradition (which began with the charity organization societies) of linking direct and indirect service is compatible with the more contemporary field-of-practice approach; to a large extent, community practice is defined by them as a complement, supplement, or extension of agency-based direct services. When such arrangements prevail, community practitioners may feel like the "hired gun" who enlivens so many cowboy movies: they are called in to set up or promote a program, to solve service delivery problems, to establish a constituency of interested and supportive citizens to lobby government, or to manage and improve community relations. These activities are far different from the community development and social reform agendas initially set forth during the settlement house movement. The emphasis then was not on initiating a process, but on achieving particular goals related to a population in need or at risk. In some instances the target of these change-oriented activities are social institutions that are not aware of particular problems (or choose to ignore them) or that favor the needs of some at the expense of others. For instance, a community that offers telephone and emergency services to teenage drug abusers but does not offer counseling or social and recreational programs for its youth probably has not engaged in a process of deliberately assessing its human service needs and alternative means of dealing with those needs. Instead, it has decided, consciously or by default, to initiate programs that enjoy support from funding sources such as the federal government, foundations, or local funding bodies.

This state of affairs, in turn, encourages professionals and citizens with special interests to launch campaigns that will bring their concerns to center stage. The outcome is that community practice is viewed by many sponsors and direct-service professionals in purely instrumental terms, as a means of enhancing their prospects in the marketplace. In such situations, social work community practitioners may well find that decisions about who is to be recruited or involved, what goals are to be set, and what strategies and tactics are to be employed, are substantially influenced by their sponsor's preferences. As Pawson and Russell's example of the formation of a residential treatment program in a Canadian province illustrates, such a process may involve an informal coalition of sponsors and the impression that community practitioners have considerable autonomy and latitude. Such freedom continues, however, only if previously conceived goals are pursued. As Ross (1958:24–26) noted, however, such goal pursuit leads to a deemphasis on the processes of community involvement and self-determination. The community worker who "wants a strong team that will be able to implement sound technical plans . . . must move in directions defined by the law and professional interest" (IBID.:21) even if this is achieved without helping broad sectors of the community to become involved in discovering their problems and the means of solving them.

In reviewing the articles dealing with areas of practice we came to the conclusion that in many instances community practice is less an end in itself—a deliberate and defined process of community growth, empowerment, and learning—and more a means of obtaining specific changes, reforms, and responses to clearly identified needs. In such circumstances, community practice often becomes an instrumentality of the profession's direct service to clients.

INNOVATION AND IMPROVISATION: SUBMODELS?

Although theoreticians attempt to force practice into discrete categories, most workers seem more eclectic in their approaches to situations. There is reason to believe that they may borrow from many models to deal with a given situation at a particular time and may adopt or utilize quite different models at different times or in various circumstances. This state of affairs might be necessary when community practitioners must function within and across an entire field of practice, dealing with planning and coordination at one juncture and advocacy or enablement at another. It might be assumed also that, in the real world, individual workers opt for an eclectic stance and position themselves along a continuum between pure theoretical models according to their values, talents, the expectations of their employers, the nature and sophistication of the groups they are involved with, and the particular goals that they are striving to achieve.

The marginality and ambiguity inherent in the role of community workers suggest that an infinite array of combinations is possible, and this indeed appears to be the situation. Stoner's description of the mental health centers' multiple responsibilities to clients, local, state, and federal governments, other agencies, minorities, poverty groups, mental health professionals, citizens' groups, and the organizations and citizens located within defined geographic catchment areas portrays an overwhelming web of accountability. Within this confusing state of affairs, practitioners actually have considerable latitude, and this enables them to adopt widely varying constellations of goals and strategies. Stoner's discussion also suggests that within a given metropolitan area there is an array of community practitioners whose styles barely resemble one another. Pawson and Russell call attention to the fact that community workers from different agencies see the question of institutional care for children from widely varying perspectives and in the process of campaigning for their particular position, employ a series of different strategies and tactics on each other. Jansson and Salcido report that community work is deemphasized in health settings, but where it occurs, it is usually at the initiative of individual staff rather than an organizationally mandated or supported service.

Chau and Hodge note that in the developing countries social workers were not a significant presence until after World War II, and then they were utilized in remedial programs aimed at dealing with a limited range of carefully delineated clientele such as orphans or deliquents. Community practice emerged out of the roots of colonialism and the values of the missionaries, but at present the various national governments of Asia and Africa restrict the manifestations of community practice because of its potential contribution to economic development and the establishment of politically desired goal consensus. The emphasis on consensus and collaboration highlights the political goals associated with citizen participation and self-help, and governments limit the role of community practice to avoid organized conflicts which might upset the balance of power or threaten national stability. The outcome is a plethora of "models" of community development depending on the interests of particular governments and sponsors and the unique societal and cultural factors in each nation.

In minority neighborhoods and communities, Solomon observes, social work, with its emphasis on services and practitioners associated with agencies and organizational networks, has not enjoyed widespread acceptance and has not been effective because its approaches have not been seen as relevant to the concerns and aspirations of minority communities. At the neighborhood level, charismatic leaders have had more credibility and visibility than social work professionals; the styles and approaches of these indigenous leaders have varied widely because they have proceeded from pragmatic and personalized orientations to achieving change. Minority social workers, who voluntarily involve themselves in efforts to secure programs or empower neighborhoods, most often function independently and without relying on established approaches that are more relevant to the wider community.

As we reviewed the variations in practice, it seemed clear that submodels have been developed to meet the special needs of particular fields of practice, national situations, and the unique cultural and psychological configurations of oppressed minorities (Erlich and Rivera 1979:493). There is reason to question whether theory development can maintain the pace.

New Issues and Syntheses for Community Practice

Our conclusions regarding the state of theory development in community work are similar to the conclusions reached in the preceding volumes on casework (Roberts and Nee 1970) and group work (Roberts and Northen 1976) in that there is great diversity among the various schools of thought and approaches to practice. This diversity seems greater in community work, however, and eclecticism, pragmatism, and the practice wisdom of professonals foster a turbulence and diversity that makes categorization and model building especially difficult tasks.

The absence of a tradition of case recording reduces the empirical base of the study process, while most research on community practice has been flawed by an incomplete consideration of the influences exerted by other actors who have their own conceptualization of what strategies and outcomes are to be preferred. It has been documented that in clinical practice, congruence of goals set by the social worker and the client often leads to effective practice (see, for instance, Maluccio, 1979); there is reason to expect that this holds true for community practice as well. Lappin points out, however, that the achievement of such congruence is made difficult in community work by the paternalistic or traditional goals of sponsors, who legitimate the role and provide the resources that allow community workers to function. The goals of sponsors are often at variance with the goals of particular neighborhood groups, client groups, or oppressed minorities, and the social worker's reliance on professional values, such as self-determination, may not be enough to bridge or reconcile such differences.

THE FEDERAL STIMULUS: CITIZEN PARTICIPATION

Beginning in the 1960s with the Model Cities legislation, the Economic Opportunity Act, community mental health legislation, and the public welfare amendments, the federal government developed a series of policies and programs intended to remedy many of the social problems of the nation. Although regulations, funding, and philosophical guidelines emanated from the federal level, implementation was at the state, city, and neighborhood levels through intermediary structures empowered to develop programs and services appropriate to particular local needs. To assure that these programs would be responsive to the needs of targeted populations, various mechanisms were devised to involve local citizens and consumers in policy determination and program implementation. The intent was that these new programs would either change or bypass present patterns of state and local policy relating to human services. Citizen participation was the mandated vehicle to assure organizational responsiveness; unfortunately, operational definitions did not accompany these philosophical imperatives (Vandervelde 1979). Although the ambiguity may have been purposeful to allow for local differences and initiative (Yin et al.: 1973), the outcome was that poverty groups, special populations, and racial and ethnic minorities saw this as their opportunity to shape community and societal decisions so that they were related to their own problems and needs.

Agencies and social work professionals were at a loss, at least initially, about how to reach out to and include these newly enfranchised groups who heretofore had been the recipients of the charity of a paternalistic system. As agencies prepared to offer new services and newly created agencies were formed in response to the federal government's priorities, community practice attained an importance and status it had not enjoyed in earlier years. Schools of social work created or expanded their community-oriented programs in response to agency demand for trained practitioners. Even when the political empowerment and community development thrust of the War on Poverty began to wane, community practitioners remained in demand in those fields of practice where community-based programming was being conducted. Citizen advisory groups were linked to both public and voluntary agencies by the U.S. Department of Health, Education, and Welfare's 1972 decision to "devolve to citizens a greater measure of power of DHEW programs [and] to reduce feelings of alienation and estrangement from government" (Yin et al. 1973:6).

While this was not true political empowerment, the policy did require agencies in the fields of health, mental health, and aging to provide formal avenues of communication with community groups that had been neglected in the past. This sustained the emphasis on community practice until well into the late 1970s when the emphasis of the federal government shifted toward evaluation, efficiency, and management, with a consequent tapering off of the demand for community practitioners in favor of administrators.

While many critics argued, with justification, that citizen participation in policy and program implementation was almost as monumental a failure as the War on Poverty's efforts to empower the poor, an interesting consequence has been a renewed awareness on the part of many populations that they must organize themselves if they are to promote their own interests effectively in a pluralistic society. The net result has been the emergence of neighborhood associations, the politicalization of the elderly, the gay rights movement, associations of former mental patients, and inner-city coalitions of Asians, Hispanics, and blacks. The goal of these new self-help groups has been to force society to respond to their demands in ways that it has not done in the past.

In this relatively new state of affairs, these groups often seek to remain independent of government and established networks of health and welfare agencies. They do not usually have the resource base to hire full-time professionals. While they will form alliances with agencies to advocate for services they value and want, they will also publicly criticize or attack organizations or programs that they feel are irrelevant, inadequate, or unresponsive to their perceived interests and needs. While on the one hand this development is seen as troublesome to the established roles of social workers, it offers promise of new syntheses of practice and theory, almost before we have had a chance to learn from our mistakes.

Clearly, there is as yet no overarching theory of social work community practice. There are orientations and schools of thought, but the practitioner searching for a theory of community practice by which to guide and evaluate practice must still be patient. This volume may well be a step forward in the development of such theory.

References

Brager, George A. and Francis P. Purcell, eds. 1967. *Community Action Against Poverty: Readings from the Mobilization Experiences.* New Haven, Conn.: College and University Press.

Brager, George A. and Harry Specht. 1973. *Community Organizing.* New York: Columbia University Press.

Burghardt, Stephen. 1982. *The Other Side of Organizing: Resolving the Personal Dilemmas and Political Demands of Daily Practice.* Cambridge, Mass.: Schenkman.

Compton, Beulah and Burt Galloway. 1975. *Social Work Processes.* Homewood, Ill.: Dorsey Press.

Cox, Fred M. et al., eds. 1974. *Strategies of Community Organization.* 2d ed. Itasca, Ill.: Peacock.

Erlich, John L. 1966. "Bibliography: Organizing the Poor." *Poverty and Human Resources Abstracts* (December), 1(6):167–72.

———— and Felix Rivera. 1979. "The Challenges of Minorities and Students." In Fred M. Cox et al. eds., *Strategies of Community Organization*, pp. 491–96. 3d ed. Itasca, Ill.: Peacock.

Germain, Carel B., ed. 1979. *Social Work Practice: People and Environments.* New York: Columbia University Press.

Grosser, Charles F. 1965. "Community Development Programs Serving the Urban Poor." *Social Work* (July) 10(3):15–21.

Haggstrom, Warren. 1964. "The Power of the Poor." In Frank Riessman, Jerome Cohen, and Arthur Pearl, eds., *Mental Health of the Poor: New Treatment Approaches for Low Income People*, pp. 205–23.

Harper, Ernest and Arthur Dunham. 1959. *Community Organization in Action.* New York: Association Press.

Hawley, Amos. 1950. *Human Ecology: A Theory of Community Structure.* New York: Ronald Press.

Kahn, Alfred J. 1963. *Planning Community Services for Children in Trouble.* New York: Columbia University Press.

Kramer, Ralph M. and Harry Specht, eds. 1975. *Readings in Community Organization Practice.* 2d ed. Englewood Cliffs, N.J.: Prentice-Hall.

Lane, Robert P. 1939. "The Field of Community Organization." In *Proceedings of the National Conference of Social Work, 1939*, pp. 495–511. New York: Columbia University Press.

Lebowitz, Milton. 1961. "The Process of Planned Community Change: A Comparative Analysis of Five Community Welfare Council Projects." DSW dissertation, Columbia University.

Lindblom, Charles E. 1959. "The Science of 'Muddling Through.'" In *Public Administration Review* (Spring), 19(2):79–88.

Lippitt, Ronald, Jeanne Watson, and Bruce Westley. 1958. *The Dynamics of Planned Change.* New York: Harcourt Brace.

Maluccio, Anthony. 1979. *Learning from Clients: Interpersonal Helping as Viewed by Clients and Social Workers.* New York: Free Press.

Olshansky, Bernard. 1961. "An Approach to Evaluating Research in Social Planning." Ph.D. dissertation, Brandeis University.

Park, Robert, E. Burgess, and R. McKenzie. 1925. *The City.* Chicago: University of Chicago Press.

Perlman, Robert and Arnold Gurin. 1972. *Community Organization and Social Planning.* New York: Wiley.

Pincus, Allen and Anne Minahan. 1973. *Social Work Practice: Model and Methods.* Itasca, Ill.: Peacock.

Rainman, Eva Schindler. 1962. "Community Organization: Selected Aspects of Practice." DSW dissertation, University of Southern California.

Riessman, Frank, Jerome Cohen, and Arthur Pearl, eds. 1964. *Mental Health of the Poor: New Treatment Approaches for Low Income People.* Glencoe, Ill.: Free Press.

Roberts, Robert W. and Robert Nee. 1970. *Theories of Social Casework.* Chicago: University of Chicago Press.

Roberts, Robert W. and Helen Northen. 1976. *Theories of Social Work with Groups.* New York: Columbia University Press.

Ross, Murray G. 1958. *Case Histories in Community Organization.* New York: Harper.

Rothman, Jack. 1964. "An Analysis of Goals and Roles in Community Organization Practice." *Social Work* (April), 9(2):24–31.

———. 1968. "Three Models of Community Organization Practice." *Social Work Practice, 1968,* pp. 16–47. New York: Columbia University Press.

———. 1974. *Planning and Organizing for Social Change: Action Principles from Social Science Research.* New York: Columbia University Press.

———. 1979. "Macro Social Work in a Tightening Economy." *Social Work* (July), 24(4):274–81.

Sanders, Daniel, ed. 1982. *The Developmental Perspective in Social Work.* Honolulu: School of Social Work, University of Hawaii.

Schwartz, Edward. 1977. "Macro Social Work: A Practice in Search of Some Theory." *Social Service Review* (June), 51(2):207–27.

Spergel, Irving A. 1982. "The Role of the Social Developer." In Daniel Sanders, ed., *The Developmental Perspective in Social Work.* pp. 12–30.

Urban, Hugh and Donald Ford. 1963. *Systems of Psychotherapy: A Comparative Study.* New York: Wiley.

Vandervelde, Maryanne. 1979. "The Semantics of Participation." *Administration in Social Work* (Spring), 5(1):65–77.

Yin, Robert et al. 1973. *Citizen Organizations: Increasing Client Control Over Services.* Santa Monica, Calif.: Rand.

2

The Place of Community Work Within an Ecological Approach to Social Work Practice

Carel B. Germain

Ecological ideas are making their way into social work practice, although more into practice with individuals, families, and groups than with communities. Why this should be so is not entirely clear, especially since the earliest developments in "human ecology" appeared in the work of urban sociologists (Park, Burgess, and McKenzie 1925; Park 1952; Hawley 1950), who used ecological ideas to explain community structure, development, and functioning. Perhaps the general shunning of biological ideas by social scientists, after the destructive impact of Social Darwinism, accounts for the absence of further applications of ecology to the study of community life. Because the social sciences have been influential underpinnings of community practice by social workers, biologically derived ideas may have also been similarly rejected in the development of community organization as a method. But where community is regarded as the environment of individuals and primary groups, it has entered the ecologically oriented social worker's attention as an environmental force to be understood and worked with.

Among the ways in which ecological ideas are reshaping social work practice with individuals, families, and groups are the following:

1. The unit of client(s)-worker attention expands to include the total life space (including the community) of the individual, family, or group, thus demanding greater knowledge and skill of the practitioner in determining with clients the pertinence and salience of many variables, and their accessibility to social work intervention.

2. Social work processes of engagement, assessment, contracting, problem or need definition, goal-setting, action, and evaluation of outcomes are reoriented to two complementary social work functions of releasing people's capacities for growth, health, and adaptive social functioning, *and* increasing the responsiveness of social and physical environments to their needs, rights, aspirations, and capacities.

3. People's problems, needs, or predicaments are defined in transactional terms, that is, as outcomes of maladaptive person:environment relationships. They are viewed as problems in living that involve personal, environmental, and transactional features.

4. The focus of help shifts to the transactional phenomena of adaptedness, stress, and coping as expressions of people:environment relationships. This includes a focus on such transactional outcomes as competence, self-direction, self-esteem, and human relatedness—as these are defined in the particular cultural context. It also includes a focus on such maladaptive transactional outcomes as oppression and other injustices derived from the misuse of power and from technological and social pollutions of the environment.

5. A framework for primary prevention and growth promotion at the clinical and community levels is provided.

6. Method distinctions or specializations practiced by agencies or assumed by practitioners, and reinforced by social work's educational programs, give way to a reconceptualized, integrated method of practice with people—whether as individuals, families, groups, networks, neighborhoods, organizations, or communities. My own bias is to view specialization as professional competence in providing service in a given substantive area (which might involve a social problem, a population group, or a social institutional base) based upon knowledge of pertinent research findings and methods,

social policy, and program developments. Social workers educated for practice with people using the service should be able to work across all levels of human organization, as the felt need or the situation demands. (I also believe that ecological ideas have implications for social workers who practice in policy and planning, research, and administration, but they are beyond the scope of this essay.)

A conceptual and practical problem must be noted at the outset. The community, like the family or the group as environment for its individual members, may be regarded as environment for its component parts. Community interventions are made on behalf of individuals and primary and secondary groups within the community. Or the community itself may be the user of the service, so that interventions are made on behalf of the community as an entity, and for the well-being of all. Whether the community is regarded sometimes as environment and sometimes as client is not only a conceptual issue, it may affect practice processes as well.

Pushed to the extreme in its emphasis on people:environment relationships, ecology might suggest that only relationships exist and that entities have no reality beyond their relationships to one another. Hence the community, with its web of internal relationships among individuals, families, and other collectivities, and its complex of relationships to the world outside itself, should always be the focal point of the social worker's attention. Without going to that extreme, the ecological metaphor does suggest that the community is an integral part of the life space of individuals and collectivities that we serve. Hence it must be part of assessment, intervention, prevention, and other practice processes. Reciprocally, when the client is the community, or some segment of it, then individuals and collectivities within the community must also be in the foreground of attention throughout the processes of assessment, intervention, and prevention.

Such a position echoes the traditions of the settlement house movement, one of the forerunners of social work. The stance is re-emerging as the social context of social work practice changes, and practice itself moves more and more into the life space of people. This is already observable in rural social work, school social work, child welfare, industrial social work, and social work in health care.

The implications for social work education are examined in the concluding section of this article.

To accomplish its task of examining the place of the community in ecological social work, elements of the perspective will be reviewed. Next, certain adaptive and maladaptive outcomes of person:environment transactions will be specified, and, finally, implications for practice will be suggested.

The Ecological Perspective

Historically, social work has been committed to the person-situation conception as its central, common feature across the diversity of fields of practice, agency settings, methods, roles, and tasks. Rather than uniting the profession, however, the conception frequently left us at odds with one another, depending on whether we viewed the social work function as changing the person(s) or changing the situation(s). The historical reasons for such divisiveness are many and have been frequently commented upon. It is noteworthy, however, that the profession—in addition to lack of unity about its function in society—did not have a conceptual framework for viewing person and situation as a unitary system.

Contemporary social work seems to be moving toward some agreement on the general dimensions of its purpose or function in society (*Social Work* 1981; 1977). The reach toward agreement is expressed differently by different social workers. As described by Gordon (1969), social work's purpose is "the matching of people's coping patterns with the qualities of impinging environments for the purpose of producing growth-inducing and environment-ameliorating transactions." I would enlarge that idea to include releasing people's potential for continued growth, health, and satisfying social functioning.

Such a statement of purpose suggests that all social workers have two simultaneous, complementary functions: helping to release people's adaptive potentialities *and* helping them to improve their environments. The two functions may be carried out in many ways, depending on whether one is working with an individual, family, group, or community, and on their objectives and definitions of needs or predicaments. Methods include helping people mobilize and sustain their internal resources, improve the quality of their exchanges with the environment, and increase the responsiveness of their environments to their adaptive needs. In some situations the worker may remove environmental obstacles to adaptive functioning, mobilize environmental resources and supports, and eliminate environmental stressors or minimize their impact. Social work is uniquely positioned to carry out the complementary simultaneous functions, and their multiple tasks, by its location in the transactional domain where people:environment exchanges take place. Admittedly, the knowledge and skill for carrying them out are still limited.

One conceptual framework that offers promise for the further development of such knowledge and skill is the ecological perspective. Ecology is the study of organisms: environment relations. Its use as a metaphor for social work has been described elsewhere (Germain 1979). Here I shall only describe its central concepts, but before doing so it is necessary to distinguish between the ideas of transaction and interaction.[1] The difference is between viewing person and environment as a unitary system in which each affects the other, and viewing them as separate and independent of each other. The first view is transactional; that is, person and environment are engaged in constant circular exchanges in which each is reciprocally shaping and influencing the other over time. The key words are *reciprocal, circular,* and *exchange.* The second view is interactional; that is, person and environment are engaged in one-directional action and reaction. In a given interaction, the action of one is antecedent to the reaction of the other. The one causes an effect on the other, while leaving itself unchanged. The key words are *cause, effect,* and *one-directional.*

If we think interactionally, we tend to see linear chains of cause and effect, essentially predictable, even deterministic in their outcomes, and occurring in discrete intervals of time. If we think transactionally, we tend to see a continuous flow of psychological, physiological, and environmental processes and events, all influencing and reshaping one another in a continuous flow of time (Coyne and Lazarus 1980; Pervin and Lewis 1978). Outcomes are not predetermined by what has gone before, and therefore are not predictable. What is cause may sometimes be effect and what is effect may sometimes be cause, tracked all around the circular loop of feedback processes (Powers 1973; Maruyama 1963). This is not to say that linear chains of cause and effect do not exist in some simple behavioral phenomena, but rather that the transactional view explains more complex phenomena, such as those that enter the social work domain.

The distinction between transaction and interaction is important because it affects our notions of causality and hence of professional action to be taken. The consequences of the operations of any one part of the person:environment system on the operations of other parts are the focus rather than one-directional, interactive processes involving an independent variable acting on a dependent one. The ecological concepts to be described are all transactional in nature. They do not refer to person(s) alone or to environment(s) alone, but they express a relationship between them. The concepts are adaptedness, stress, and coping; and competence, self-direction, relatedness to others and to the world of nature, and self-esteem.

Put simply, adaptedness refers to the fit between person and environment, the adaptive balance between needs, capacities, rights, and goals, *and* the qualities of the social and physical environment within a given culture. The fit is never fully achieved because people change and environments change, and each such change calls for further adaptations by the human being (Dubos 1968). People's adaptive processes include changes in the self (physiological or psychological) to fit environmental pressures or opportunities; changes in the environment to make it fit human needs and requirements; or migration to new environments.

Since these changes require further adaptation on the part of the human being, adaptation is a continuous process. It involves reciprocal shaping of both person and environment over time, and hence is transactional and not interactional. People do react to the environment, but they also act upon it. People's attitudes, goals, values, needs, and so forth influence the ways in which they use their environments; properties of the environment, often internalized, influence the development and social functioning of the people within them. When these transactions go well, people grow and develop, and environments flourish and are able to support human growth and functioning. When the transactions do not go well, people's development, health, and functioning may be impaired, and environments may be polluted technologically and by injustice and oppression, all of which increase people's adaptive burdens. Adaptedness expresses a relationship between people and environment. The absence of adaptedness or the lack of person: environment fit also expresses a relationship between people and environments but of an opposite kind.

Such negative or maladaptive outcomes of people:environment transactions can be conceptualized as stress. Psychiatric epidemiologists have equated stress with the lack of perceived control over events because of insufficient internal and external resources, and with threats to self-esteem arising from devaluation and rejection by others, especially by intimate partners (Wills and Langner 1980). Poverty, unemployment, loss, and devaluation by others are examples of stressors likely to have long-term consequences because they undermine self-esteem, are outside the individual's control, and exceed personal and environmental coping resources. Over time, such experiences can lead to discouragement, feelings of helplessness, incompetence, and depression. Thus stress begets more stress in a circular loop or vicious cycle of internal and external messages.

Stress theorists have developed a perceptual model of stress (Cox 1978). In this model, stress is experienced subjectively at the point when the person recognizes a discrepancy between a perceived demand and perceived internal and external resources for dealing with the demand. Such perceptions are presumably mediated by age, sex, culture, experience, and physical and emotional states. The emotional experience of stress sets in motion the physiological, psychological, and behavioral responses that we call coping. If coping is effective, stress is reduced or eliminated or its impact mastered. When severe stress is unrelieved, it can lead to physical illness, emotional disturbance, or disruptions in family or community life—thus creating still further stress. Stress is a transactional phenomenon. It expresses a particular relationship between person and environment.

Since stress represents harm or threat of harm, it is important to recognize that it is often generated by incongruences between people's adaptive capacities and the qualities of environments actually created by human beings. The pollution of air, water, and food affects the health and well-being (adaptedness) of the total population and future generations. But in many instances such incongruences fall heaviest on the poor and other powerless groups. The presence of toxic waste in working class communities, lead paint in slum dwellings, and asbestos in old inner-city schools affects lower socioeconomic groups more than middle-class populations. The presence of hazardous materials in factories and mines affects the working class and their families more than others.

Similar observations can be made of social pollutions of the environment. Poor housing, inferior schools, inadequate health care, poor systems of income security, and inadequate juvenile and criminal justice systems tax personal, familial, and community resources beyond system limits. Nevertheless, the abuse of power and the oppression of population segments based on race, ethnicity, gender, sexual orientation, disablement, and age affect adversely the quality of life (adaptedness) for the total population in our society and around the world. The stresses of pollutions and oppression are created by society and require societal solutions.

Still other major stressors in modern society are also less amenable to individual coping efforts because of their complexity. They require collective solutions (Mechanic 1974). But institutional responses often lag far behind new demands created by rapid social change. For example, many aged persons depend on the help of adult daughters and daughters-in-law in order to avoid institutionalization. As women continue to enter the labor force, they will be less available for care of elderly family members. Yet alternative services and supports are not being developed despite this trend and the rapid aging of the population. Other common stressors respond more readily to group solutions than to individual coping efforts. The growing prevalence of self-help groups, and the recognition of the effectiveness of rural and urban natural helping systems, reflects the importance of groups in effective coping with stress. Research findings suggest that social networks protect people from stress or mediate the effects of stress (Cobb 1976; Cassel 1974).

Effective coping, then, requires personal capacities such as problem-solving skills, managing negative feelings, and maintaining self-esteem. But it also requires environmental resources and supportive societal structures. Resources include motivation and incentives and rewards for sustaining motivation and coping efforts; information about the stressor, coping tasks, resources, and so on; social and emotional supports to help regulate the negative feelings aroused by the stress; training in problem-solving; adequate time and space to develop coping strategies; and concrete resources such as money and services (White 1974; Mechanic 1974). Because coping capability rests on both personal skills and external resources, it too expresses a particular person:environment relationship.

Reference has been made here to adaptive transactions that lead to human growth, development, and social functioning and to the expansion of the environment's capacity for supporting such outcomes. Four clusters of qualities involved in adaptive outcomes appear to be competence, self-direction, relatedness, self-esteem and a sense of identity. These qualities have received special attention in ego psychology (Bettelheim 1969; Erikson 1959; Hartmann 1958; White 1959; Will 1959). But they are also concepts used by biologists (Dubos 1968; Dobzhansky 1976), and to some extent they are illuminated by the findings of cultural anthropologists (Stack 1974; Valentine and Valentine 1970; Valentine 1978) and social workers (Shapiro 1970). All organisms must take effective (competent) action on their environments if they are to survive. All organisms have some degree of autonomy from their environments, and some species have relative independence from their internal or genetic limits to the degree that they are capable of learning. All organisms, except those that reproduce asexually, maintain some degree of relatedness to other members of the species for protection, reproduction, and, in some, care of the young. So they recognize conspecifics, a form of identity. The four qualities seem to be universal life processes. They are more fully developed in mammals, especially the primates, and reach their highest development in human beings including self-esteem.

All four qualities appear to be relatively free of cultural bias, which we would expect to be true of universal life processes. They may have different substantive content in different societies and cultures or subcultures. But all groups seek to promote competence in fulfilling culturally defined roles; to develop self-direction—although in our society and others, one's autonomy, options, and freedom of choice are severely constrained by one's location in the social-economic structure, so that self-direction is related to power.

Since relatedness to others is a biological and social imperative in the human being, all cultures seek to support it, although kinship rules, and the norms governing rights and obligations in social relationships, may be differently defined across cultures and subcultures. Self-esteem and the sense of identity may be individual, familial, or tribal—and may be attached to community as well—but respect for one's self and/or one's group seems to be a universal concern (Germain 1979).

Environmental nutriments that release and sustain people's potentialities are varied indeed. Such nutriments must include biological, cognitive, sensory-perceptual, emotional, and social stimuli of the appropriate quality and quantity at the appropriate time, and in a form congruent with various dimensions of the culture. Among the social nutriments are the environmental properties of opportunity, social respect, and power (Smith 1968) which influence the availability and quality of environmental nutriments. These three properties are differentially allocated by our society, however, depending on the physical, social, and cultural characteristics of the individual, family, group, or community.

Opportunity provides the context for the development of biological, cognitive, perceptual, emotional, and social competence, and influences the development of relatedness. Social respect is the foundation for self-esteem and the sense of identity and for competence; it also influences the development of relatedness. Power represents objective control over what affects the individual's or the collectivity's destiny. Having no, or too few, options means being powerless and deprived of many opportunities for self-direction thereby negatively influencing competence, relatedness, and self-esteem and identity. Clearly, the four qualities, as potentialities in the genetic structure of the human species, are interdependent.

The Community and Transactional Outcomes

While adaptation and adaptedness are observable in individual human beings, in the science of ecology these processes actually refer to units of organisms as they are organized in a biotic community, or even to whole species as they achieve a fit with the environment over evolutionary time. Thus adaptedness and adaptation are appropriate concepts to use in considering the community or any other human collectivity. Indeed, for Hawley, "adaptation to environment is a population rather than an individual problem," to which he applied the term communal adaptation (1950:31). "The community . . . is in the nature of a collective response to the habitat" (*ibid.:* 66). Thus for the ecologically oriented social worker, the community's exchanges with its external environment (the physical and the social worlds in which it is embedded), as well as its internal culture, social structure, and physical setting are part of the unit of attention.

It is probably inappropriate to say that the community experiences stress. But individual members do. When the number of members experiencing a shared stress is proportionately large, we do refer to a high level of community stress. Such stress may be the outcome of the community's transactions with the larger environment that produce poverty, exploitation, or inadequate services. Or, it may come about through intracommunity conflict or through community crises in response to the shutdown of a hospital, the closing of an industrial plant, a natural disaster, or the search for energy that creates a rural boom town.

Similarly, it is probably inaccurate to say that a community copes or fails to cope with stress. It is the individual members who cope with their individually experienced stress. But when most of the members have the personal and environmental resources to cope successfully with individual or shared demands perceived as stressful, then we say the community has been able to meet the demand or handle the stress effectively. When that is not the case, we are apt to say the community is demoralized, alienated, helpless, or disorganized. In some instances, however, needed resources available to other communities may have been withheld by the larger environment. In other instances, members' coping efforts may be viewed as problematic behaviors because the observer's personal and professional value orientations act either to obscure the cultural base of members' coping styles or to block recognition of the coping strengths in the context of a harsh environment. Two ecological concepts, habitat and niche, shed light on these issues.

HABITAT

In ecology, habitat refers to the place where the organism is found, the dwelling place, home range, and territory. In the case of human beings, the physical and social settings within a cultural context are the habitat. Physical settings such as dwellings, buildings, rural villages, and urban layouts must support the social settings of family life, social life, work life, religious life, and so on, in ways that fit with life styles, age, gender, and culture. Habitats that do not support the health and social functioning of individuals and families are likely to produce or to contribute to feelings of isolation, disorientation, and despair. Such stressful feelings may interfere further with the basic functions of family and community life.

Within the habitat, both public and private housing may be poorly located in relation to public transportation. In rural areas, transportation may be lacking altogether, thereby limiting access to health care, shopping, workplaces, and so forth. In poor neighborhoods and rural villages such amenities as parks, recreation centers, libraries, and museums may be absent, negatively affecting the quality of life in the community.

Time is an important dimension of the habitat. It takes time to grow and develop, and time to learn. One must have time for solitude and time for interaction, and time to develop ways of coping with stress. Yet in some communities time may be a scarce resource. This is the case where public transportation is inadequate, needed human services and workplaces are outside the community, or the community is comprised of a large number of working mothers, one-parent families, families caring for frail elderly members or developmentally disabled children, or workers on evening, night, or swing shifts. Such populations have few opportunities for respite from their continuous caring or child rearing tasks; and their work arrangements isolate them temporarily from members of their families and social networks.

Habitat, then, is a critical arena for all practice with individuals, families, groups, and the community or one of its segments. Practitioners must have the knowledge and skill to work in new ways to help improve habitats. For example, the social worker may provide help to families in housing projects to form stairwell societies to control the conditions of their shared habitat, replace lost networks, and develop mutual-aid systems for the exchange of child care, information, and other resources. Such work with project tenants as a community has positive consequences for individual, family, and group life (Glaser 1972). It may sometimes begin with an individual or family and move to the collective level; or it might begin with the collective, that is, all the families on the stairwell, and move in some instances to concurrent work with individuals or a family.

Improving the habitat also involves advocacy at the community level and the mobilization of group efforts to influence the design, location, and policies of public urban and rural housing; to secure better transportation and traffic control (urban) or to develop transportation resources (rural); to develop the use of urban or rural school facilities as community centers for after-school services, recreation programs, family life education, and community forums (Janchill 1979); to develop rural cooperatives for solving energy-related problems (Marlett 1979); and to develop respite services and quality day care for urban and rural children, the elderly, and disabled residents. Habitat as workplace also suggests community-based work to influence the work organization(s) on matters of health and safety, flexitime, shared jobs, temporal arrangements such as shift work that interfere with family life, and so on.

From a transactional point of view, the habitat as a physical environment evokes spatial and temporal behaviors that help create a social environment (Germain 1976; 1978). Such behaviors are shaped also by culture, age, sex, personality, experience, and so forth. They are commonly used by individuals, families, and groups to regulate distance intimacy within the collectivity or in other interpersonal processes. They also serve to define and maintain role expectations and functioning, and authority and/or decision-making hierarchies in family and organizational life. They therefore seem pertinent to understanding and dealing with particular issues in community life as well. Altman (1975) has constructed a paradigm that may be helpful in understanding some community issues. He suggests that people regulate their interpersonal boundaries by: (1) distancing behaviors based on personal space (Hall 1966), or what Kinzel (1970) has called body-buffer zones; (2) territorial behaviors (Esser 1971; Stea 1970); (3) verbal behaviors (Draper 1979); and (4) nonverbal behaviors, including the use of such environmental props as fences, hedges, doors and locks, uniforms, badges, signs, and even weapons. When boundary-maintenance activity results in more social interaction than is desired, the individual or collectivity experiences a sense of crowding or intrusion (not to be confused with density of persons in a given space which may or may not be associated with crowding, depending on personal and cultural factors). When boundary-maintaining activity results in less than the desired level of social interaction, then the individual or collectivity experiences a sense of social isolation.

An analysis of family life (Kantor and Lehr 1975) identifies a range of temporal behaviors that also help regulate internal closeness-distance among members. They also help maintain synchrony with external events and processes such as the temporal requirements of work, school, shopping, health care, religious affiliation, and other components of community life. These behaviors include orienting members to past, present, and future time; regulating the sequence, frequency, duration, and pace of experienced events; synchronizing or regulating the family's total use of time through monitoring, priority setting, programming, coordinating, and reminding. Some families or some members may feel discomfort with temporal arrangements that force members apart or force them to interact; or personal orientations to time may generate conflict as one member is preoccupied with past time and another with future time. Pacing of events and processes may suit some members and not others. Communities, too, may find sources of comfort or stress in community "time tables" governing activities.

It is likely that stress will be aroused in members of the community when there are violations of biologically based spatial needs and temporal rhythms, cultural orientations to space and time, or psychologically based need for, or experience of, space and time exerted by the spatial and temporal arrangements of the community's institutions. The spatial location and arrangement or design, and the fixity of hours in health care and other community services and facilities, may not fit the spatial and temporal orientations and needs of community residents. This is true especially of working parents, the elderly, and ethnic groups whose values and norms regarding space and time are different from those of "outside" providers and purveyors of services and goods.

In impoverished communities, the spatial-temporal dimensions of the habitat may not provide opportunities for individuals, families, and groups to regulate closeness-distance and to make role relationships explicit. Constricted access to public space may, for example, lead to generation conflicts between teenage and elderly residents, or to conflict between racial, ethnic, or religious groups. In such instances territoriality is manifested by hostile aggression rather than by social organization. Public space such as parks, streets, and sidewalks may be taken over by predators, adversely affecting the spatial and temporal needs of women and the elderly. In-migration and out-migration may upset established spatial and temporal patterns of social interaction, creating stress for old and new community members.

Intrusions into individuals' and groups' psychological, physical, or social space can generate stress by interfering with community customs, status hierarchies, and natural support systems. The social or emotional isolation from others in communities that is often experienced by the elderly, one-parent families, and unattached, divorced, or widowed individuals produces loneliness and stress (Weiss 1973). In rural areas such isolation may be brought on by, or intensified by, geographic (spatial) isolation.

These and other conditions related to space and time in the habitat are experienced by individuals and primary groups, but they may require intervention at the community level. Practitioners working with individuals and primary groups on personal, interpersonal, and environmental issues may need to examine shared habitats and to undertake interventions designed to improve conditions on behalf of all those similarly afflicted. Programs to bring elders and teens together in mutually satisfying exchanges and activities; group services for newcomers; respite centers; horticultural projects for young and old; efforts to promote more flexible and responsive temporal and spatial arrangements at the organizational and/or institutional level; help in devising environmental props as physical buffers for more satisfying regulation of social relations in housing projects and neighborhoods—these are but a few examples of community work on behalf of individuals and families. They also strengthen the community's own development and enhance the quality of rural and urban life.

NICHE

In ecology, niche refers to the position in the biotic community that is occupied by a species of organisms, that is, their place in the web of life. In the case of human beings, niche refers metaphorically to the status occupied in the social structure by a particular group or individual and is related to issues of power and oppression. What constitutes a growth-supporting, health-promoting human niche is defined differently in various societies and in different historical eras. In our own society, the assumption is generally held that such a niche is shaped by a set of rights, including the right to equal opportunity (DeLone 1979). Yet, in our society, millions of children and adults are forced to occupy niches that do not support human needs and goals—often because of sex, age, color, ethnicity, social class, life style, or some other personal or cultural characteristic devalued by society. Many communities are laced by such marginal or destructive niches as "deinstitutionalized patient," "hard-to-place foster child," "AFDC mother," "hard-core unemployed," "school drop-out," "project tenant," "minority poor," "migrant laborer," "old woman," "homosexual," and so on. These and similar niches are shaped by our political and economic structures, and by our systems of education, health and mental health care, child welfare, juvenile justice, welfare, work, and the media.

Niche, then, is a critical element in the context of all social work practice. It suggests that neither social workers nor agencies can remain aloof from efforts to influence local, state, and federal policies through professional associations, political coalitions with other concerned groups, skilled use of the popular press and other media to heighten public understanding, and activity as individual, concerned citizens. When working at the community level, the ecologically oriented social worker must specifically deal with issues of community empowerment (Solomon 1976), supporting community strengths and reshaping nonsalutary niches, to the degree that present knowledge and skill allow. Our avowed values lead to such a commitment.

From an ecological point of view, the four adaptive outcomes of people: environment transactions—competence, self-direction, relatedness, and self-esteem—can be considered also as community strengths or capacities paralleling those of individuals. Since they have been fruitful to practitioners in developing preventive and restorative interventions and new entry points in work with individuals and primary groups, they may yield useful principles in reshaping niches, improving habitats, and promoting health and social functioning at the community level. Cottrell (1976), out of his interest in helping communities to upgrade their capacities for dealing with a wide range of problems, developed the concept of community competence.

The competent community is one in which its component parts "1. are able to collaborate effectively in identifying the problems and needs of the community; 2. can achieve a working consensus on goals and priorities; 3. can agree on ways and means to implement the agreed-upon goals; and 4. can collaborate effectively in the required actions" (Cottrell 1976:197). Such a community will be competent in dealing with the problems of its collective life. Its members will have problem-solving skills such as verbal, writing, and listening skills; skills in managing conflict, including collaboration, negotiation, and bargaining; skills in public speaking and in leading discussions; and technical skills in locating, obtaining, and using resources. When working with a community, the social worker's tasks include the teaching and modeling of such skills and encouraging and facilitating their development and use.

An autonomous community does not exist, especially in today's electronically wired-together society. But, in contrast to the so-called alienated or apathetic community, the community that strives toward balanced self-direction maintains connections with its larger social, economic, political environment so that a flow of needed resources into the community can be sustained. As an ideal type, the self-directed community will value and seek to mobilize the active participation of all members in matters that concern them individually and are pertinent to the well-being of the community as a collective. Its members will be committed to, and engaged in, protecting the community against threats posed by external forces of power. Reciprocally, however, the self-directed community will concern itself with achieving and maintaining internal strengths as the community itself defines them: mutual-aid systems, folk or natural support systems—and dealing with internal threats posed by the loss or absence of mutual concern or respect among the community's component parts.

The issue of community self-direction is parallel to issues of empowerment, especially as a sense of power and influence can move individuals and communities from a stance of passivity and despair to a stance of action in areas of life that are important to the individual and the cultural group. For the social worker, the essence of community self-direction goes beyond the community's ability to use the practitioner's knowledge and skill as resources, to its maintaining control of its own destiny. Thus the social worker's function is to help community members take control over meeting their own needs, goals, and aspirations as they define them, with respect to housing, education, health care, and other aspects of community life. This requires helping people rediscover their own capacities and collective resources, energies, and commitment—and helping provide the conditions under which such attributes can flourish. Without self-direction and self-power, any community is in danger of internal disorganization or of external tyranny and social neglect.

The sense of community identity is a knotty issue, tied as it is to matters of definition. The concept of community is an ambiguous one, ranging across such collectivities as the global community of all human beings, the therapeutic community of an institution, the community of scholars in a university, a housing project with a thousand tenants or an SRO hotel with a hundred, an ethnic community, a rural village or urban neighborhood, or a gay or lesbian community. Avoiding definitional issues, the content of this paper is directed primarily to a local urban or rural area, but the ideas will apply to any community however defined. Even the social work profession as a community must itself deal with issues of professional competence, professional self-direction, professional identity and self-esteem, and professional relatedness.

The matter of community boundary, even around an urban neighborhood or rural village, remains a troublesome one. Cottrell suggests that a local community can be regarded as the "population living in a local area and conducting overlapping and interdependent life activities that are perceived to bind the residents into a collective entity with which they are identified and to which they give a name" (1976:198). While the boundary may be clear in a self-aware or an homogeneous community, even there it can be a trouble-some matter depending on whether the residents view themselves as a community entity.

Where the boundary is drawn bears on community identity and pride (self-esteem in individual terms). Without a sense of iden-tity, the community will find it difficult to develop commitment to its self-defined needs and goals. In today's rapidly changing society, people frequently move in and out of local communities. What was once a homogeneous rural village becomes a "boom town"; what was once a clearly defined ethnic neighborhood may be broken up as one group moves out and several new groups move in. Genera-tional changes in the community's composition may be a complicat-ing factor in reaching toward a sense of identity as the young people of one group move out, leaving the elders behind. In such instances, internal conflict or anomie may develop as old folkways and mores yield to a multiplicity of life styles, values, and norms. Time is required to develop a new sense of community identity based on recognition and pride in the new and rich diversity.

The social worker must seek to help such diverse groups within the community develop a sense of reciprocity and mutuality through active personal involvement in significantly "real" ac-tivities. Cottrell suggests that people become genuinely committed to a community when "1. they see that what it does and what hap-pens to it has a vital impact on their own lives and values they cherish; 2. they find that they have a recognized significant role in it; and 3. they see positive results from their efforts to participate in its life" (1976:198). A sense of community identity and pride, then, is interdependent with community competence and self-direction.

Community competence, self-direction, and identity also rest on human relatedness, on the sense of belonging, and of being "in place." Relatedness is the essence of community. Relatedness to others and to the physical setting evokes the reciprocity of caring and being cared about. Many communities transcend the harshness of their conditions by the operations of their natural networks (Stack 1974; Valentine 1978; Shapiro 1970), shared pleasure in music, lan-guage, laughter, and the shared commitment to religion, social club, or other affiliations (Valentine and Valentine 1970; Draper 1979; Mizio 1974). Here the social worker's functions include helping the community to keep open the channels of communication between disparate groups, perhaps through community forums on such issues as housing, schools, welfare, or transportation; street fairs, health fairs, art shows, music festivals; and even the town meeting that still works well in the villages and towns of rural New England.

The social work functions in relatedness also include locating, supporting, and encouraging rural and urban natural helpers (Patterson 1977; Collins and Pancoast 1976; Delgado 1980). It includes mobilizing natural social networks (Swenson 1979; Attneave 1976) and support groups for newcomers, deinstitutionalized persons, refugees, isolated elderly, women—indeed, all who can benefit from being esteemed and valued, and from being involved in a mutual exchange of emotional support, learning, and other resources. A community laced with natural support systems is more likely to be a community that is competent, self-directing, and has a firm sense of its identity. It may not be able to reshape its marginal niches but it can reduce their impact in the short run and may gain empowerment for reshaping them in the long run.

Primary Prevention

Although much of what has been included here refers implicitly to primary prevention in helping communities to extend their strengths and capacities for supporting the health and well-being of all members, an explicit framework may be helpful. The life model approach to practice (Germain and Gitterman 1980), derived from an ecological perspective on people and environments, views people's predicaments as outcomes of stress-producing exchanges between people and environments. Such transactions can arise in three connected realms of the life space. They are: (1) life transitions (including developmental stages, changes and/or conflicts in statuses and roles, and intensely problematic or crisis events); (2) interpersonal processes in collective life; and (3) environmental issues.

Because these three areas are also the contexts in which human growth and adaptive functioning take place when person:environment transactions go well, they afford a framework for developing programs of primary prevention. At the clinical level, practitioners can be alert to early warning signals of potential destructive stress, and initiate appropriate client-worker efforts at *preventing negative outcomes*. Presumably, also, good practice also *promotes positive outcomes* in general; that is, we hope that people emerge from social work encounters with enhanced competence, self-direction, relatedness, and self-esteem, and a firmer sense of identity.

At the community level, the framework suggests entry points for programs directed to promoting health and adaptive functioning among all community members and preventing negative outcomes for members in at-risk situations. These include, for example, programs directed to developmental stages such as puberty, status changes such as first-time parenthood or retirement, role conflicts such as those involved for working mothers, crisis events such as a natural or man-made disaster. They include programs directed to promoting adaptive interpersonal processes in families, groups, social networks, and other social structures. They include programs to improve the environment in all the ways heretofore mentioned, on the assumption that a caring community is more likely to have fewer families, groups, and individuals suffering from painful and destructive stress, and more members whose adaptive capacities contribute to, and reflect the strengths of, their community.

Implications for Social Work Education

Ecologically oriented social workers carrying out the simultaneous complementary functions related to people:environment exchanges or transactions will need to draw upon an integrated method of practice. Such a method, in contrast to what is often called a generalist method, is not a little bit of casework, group work, and community work put together. An integrated method is based on a reconceptualization of practice that rests on a more extensive knowledge base, and social work skills that are common to working with people as individuals, groups, families, communities, and informal organizations. Social work values and ethics, of course, are fundamental and uniform across all social work practice. The knowledge base for an integrated method must cover: (1) the structures, functions, and dynamics of individuals, families, groups, communities, and organizations within varying cultural contexts; (2) the structures, functions, and dynamics of physical and social settings within varying cultural contexts; and (3) the nature and consequences of transactions between (1) and (2).

The skills common to all levels of human organization, and hence basic to an integrated method, include skills in listening, observation, relationship and empathy, skills in interviewing and other means of communication, skills in assessment, contracting, coaching and teaching, mediating, advocacy, and problem solving, as well as in planning, evaluation, and management of one's practice demands. Many more could doubtless be identified, and each probably has several components that might be further specified. What is important is the commonality across work with different levels of human organization. What is also important is that their effective use depends on differential knowledge concerning each level. This means that school curricula must be ready to provide the theoretical underpinning, and provide it in an integrated way to support the teaching of an integrated method. Field education must be ready to provide opportunity for skills development through practice experience across the various levels. A close partnership between field and school with greater reciprocity and mutual enrichment of each by the other is required so that education can be more responsive to the practice demands of the 1980s and beyond.

The movement away from the methods specializations to specializations on other grounds, such as social problems, population groups, or social institutional bases, is both a challenge and an aid to the continued development of an integrated method of social work practice. This is because an assumption of substantive area specializations is that the social worker will be able to provide effective services to individuals, families, groups, and communities in the area of, let us say, health or mental health, child welfare, and so on. In addition, the practitioner will understand the policy issues, research implications, and systems of service provision within the specialized area or field. Many social workers are already practicing in this way. They report that it fits the real world. Many schools are already educating students in this way, with the partnership of field agencies and training centers. Professional development requires lifelong learning, and further study following completion of professional education is available to all through continuing education, staff development, institutes, and personal efforts.

The empowerment of those we serve requires a caring society that provides options for people: jobs for those who wish to work, especially minority youth; income security; adequate housing; schools that educate; accessible health care that provides equitable quality care while teaching people how to live in healthful ways; and environments free of oppression, pollution, and the threat of nuclear war. Whether one chooses to remain a method specialist or to adopt an integrated method, all social workers require the knowledge and politically oriented skills for influencing the direction of social and economic policy toward a caring community and a caring society. This is the meaning of our traditional person-situation commitment, cast in a new form.

Note

1. This discussion draws on Carel B. Germain, "Using Social and Physical Environments," in Rosenblatt and Waldfogel, eds., *Handbook of Clinical Social Work,* pp. 110–33.

References

Altman, Irwin. 1975. *The Environment and Social Behavior.* Monterey, Calif.: Brooks/Cole.

Attneave, Carolyn. 1976. "Social Networks as the Unit of Intervention." In Guerin, ed., *Family Therapy: Theory and Practice,* pp. 220–32.

Bettelheim, Bruno. 1969. *The Informed Heart.* Glencoe, Ill.: Free Press.

Cassel, John. 1976. "Psychosocial Processes and 'Stress': Theoretical Formulation." In Kane, ed., *Behavioral Sciences and Preventive Medicine: Opportunities and Dilemmas,* pp. 53–62.

Clausen, John, ed. 1978. *Socialization and Society.* Boston, Mass.: Little, Brown.

Cobb, Sidney. 1976. "Social Support as a Moderator of Life Stress." *Psychosomatic Medicine,* 38 (5):300–314.

Coelho, George V., David A. Hamburg, and John E. Adams, eds. 1974. *Coping and Adaptation.* New York: Basic Books.

Collins, Alice and Diane Pancoast. 1976. *Natural Helping Networks.* Washington, D.C.: NASW.

Cottrell, Leonard. 1976. "The Competent Community." In Kaplan, Wilson, and Leighton, eds., *Further Explorations in Social Psychiatry,* pp. 195–209.

Cox, Tom. 1978. *Stress*. Baltimore: University Park Press.

Coyne, James and Richard S. Lazarus. 1980. "Cognitive Style, Stress Perception, and Coping." In Kutash and Schlesinger, eds., *Handbook on Stress and Anxiety*, pp. 144–58.

Delgado, Melvin. 1980. "The Indigenous Healer as a Professional: Social Worker or Charlatan?" *Ethnomedicine*, 6 (2):283–304.

DeLone, Richard. 1979. *Small Futures: Children, Inequality, and the Limits of Liberal Reform*. New York: Harcourt Brace Jovanovich.

Dobzhansky, Theodosius. 1976. "The Myths of Genetic Predestination and Tabula Rasa." *Perspectives in Biology and Medicine* (January) 19 (2):156–70.

Draper, Barbara Jones. 1979. "Black Language as an Adaptive Response to a Hostile Environment." In Germain, ed., *Social Work Practice: People and Environments*, pp. 267–81.

Dubos, René. 1968. *So Human an Animal*. New York: Scribner's.

Erikson, Erik. 1959. "Growth and Crises of the Healthy Personality." In Erikson, *Identity and the Life Cycle*, pp. 50–100.

——, ed. 1959. *Identity and the Life Cycle*. Psychological Issues, Monograph I. New York: International Universities Press.

Esser, Aristide. 1971. *Behavior and Environment*. New York: Plenum.

Germain, Carel B. 1976. "Time, an Ecological Variable in Social Work Practice." *Social Casework* (July), 57 (7):419–26.

——. 1978. "Space, an Ecological Variable in Social Work Practice." *Social Casework* (November), 59 (9):515–22.

——. 1983. "Using Social and Physical Environments." In Rosenblatt and Waldfogel, eds., *Handbook of Clinical Social Work*, pp. 110–33.

—— ed. 1979. *Social Work Practice: People and Environments*. New York: Columbia University Press.

Germain, Carel B. and Alex Gitterman. 1980. *The Life Model of Social Work Practice*. New York: Columbia University Press.

Glaser, John S. 1972. "The Stairwell Society of Public Housing." *Comparative Group Studies* (August), 3 (3):159–73.

Gordon, William E. 1969. "Basic Constructs for an Integrative and Generative Conception of Social Work." In Hearn, ed., *The General Systems Approach: Contributions Toward an Holistic Conception of Social Work*, pp. 5–11.

Guerin, Philip J., ed. 1976. *Family Therapy: Theory and Practice*. New York: Gardner Press.

Hall, Edward T. 1966. *The Hidden Dimension*. New York: Doubleday.

Hartmann, Heinz. 1958. *Ego Psychology and the Problem of Adaptation*. New York: International Universities Press.

Hawley, Amos. 1950. *Human Ecology: A Theory of Community Structure*. New York: Ronald Press.

Hearn, Gordon, ed. 1969. *The General Systems Approach: Contributions Toward an Holistic Conception of Social Work*. New York: Council on Social Work Education.

Janchill, Sr. Mary Paul. 1979. "People Can't Go It Alone." In Germain, ed., *Social Work Practice: People and Environments*, pp. 346–62.

54　C. B. Germain

Kane, Robert L., ed. 1976. *Behavioral Sciences and Preventive Medicine: Opportunities and Dilemmas.* Washington, D.C.: GPO.

Kantor, David and William Lehr. 1975. *Inside the Family.* San Francisco: Jossey-Bass.

Kaplan, Berton, Robert N. Wilson, and Alexander H. Leighton, eds. 1976. *Further Explorations in Social Psychiatry.* New York: Basic Books.

Kinzel, August. 1970. "Body-Buffer Zone in Violent Prisoners." *American Journal of Psychiatry,* 127 (1):59–64.

Kutash, Irwin L. and Louis B. Schlesinger, eds., 1980. *Handbook on Stress and Anxiety.* San Francisco: Jossey-Bass.

Lazarus, Richard S. and Raymond Launier. 1978. "Stress-Related Transactions Between Person and Environment." In Pervin and Lewis, eds., *Perspectives in Interactional Psychology,* pp. 287–327.

Marlett, Ron. 1979. "Easing the Energy Crunch—a Strategy for Rural America." *NASW News* (October), 24(9):6–7.

Maruyama, Magoroh. 1963. "The Second Cybernetics: Deviation-Amplifying Mutual Causal Processes." *American Scientist,* 51(2):164–79.

Mechanic, David. 1974. "Social Structure and Personal Adaptation: Some Neglected Dimensions." In Coelho, Hamburg, and Adams, eds., *Coping and Adaptation,* pp. 32–44.

Mizio, Emelicia. 1974. "Impact of External Systems on the Puerto Rican Family." *Social Casework* (February), 55(2):76–83.

Park, Robert E. 1952. *Human Communities: The City and Human Ecology.* Glencoe, Ill.: Free Press.

Park, Robert E., Ernest W. Burgess, and Roderick McKenzie. 1925. *The City.* Chicago: University of Chicago Press.

Pastalan, Leon A. and Daniel H. Carson, eds. 1970. *Spatial Behavior of Older People.* Ann Arbor, Mich.: University of Michigan and Wayne State University Institute of Gerontology.

Patterson, Shirley, 1977. "Toward a Conceptualization of Natural Helping." *Arete* (Spring), 4(3):161–73.

Pervin, Lawrence and Michael Lewis. 1978. "Overview of the Internal-External Issue." In Pervin and Lewis, eds., *Perspectives in Interactional Psychology,* pp. 1–22.

———, eds. 1978. *Perspectives in Interactional Psychology.* New York: Plenum.

Powers, William T. 1973. "Feedback: Beyond Behaviorism." *Science,* January 26, pp. 351–56.

Rosenblatt, Aaron and Diana Waldfogel, eds. 1983. *Handbook of Clinical Social Work.* San Francisco: Jossey-Bass.

Shapiro, Joan. 1970. *Communities of the Alone.* New York: Association Press.

Smith, M. Brewster. 1968. "Competence and Socialization." In Clausen, ed., *Socialization and Society,* pp. 270–320.

Social Work. 1977. Issue on "Conceptual Frameworks." (September), 22(5).

———. 1981. Issue on "Conceptual Frameworks II." (January), 26(1).

Solomon, Barbara B. 1976. *Black Empowerment: Social Work in Minority Communities.* New York: Columbia University Press.

Stack, Carol. 1974. *All Our Kin: Strategies for Survival in a Black Community.* New York: Harper Colophon.

Stea, David. 1970. "Home Range and Use of Space." In Pastalan and Carson, eds., *Spatial Behavior of Older People,* pp. 138–47.

Swenson, Carol. 1979. "Social Networks, Mutual Aid, and the Life Model of Practice." In Germain, ed., *Social Work Practice: People and Environments,* pp. 213–38.

Valentine, Betty Lou. 1978. *Hustling and Other Hard Work.* New York: Free Press.

Valentine, Charles A. and Betty Lou Valentine. 1970. "Making the Scene, Digging the Action, and Telling It Like It Is: Anthropologists at Work in a Dark Ghetto." In Whitten and Szwed, eds., *Afro-American Anthropology,* pp. 403–18.

Weiss, Robert S. 1973. *Loneliness, the Experience of Emotional and Social Isolation.* Cambridge, Mass.: M.I.T. Press.

White, Robert W. 1959. "Motivation Reconsidered: The Concept of Competence." *Psychological Review* (September), 66 (5):297–333.

———. 1974. "Strategies of Adaptation: An Attempt at Systematic Description." In Coelho, Hamburg, and Adams, eds., *Coping and Adaptation,* pp. 47–68.

Whitten, Norman and John Szwed, eds. 1970. *Afro-American Anthropology.* New York: Free Press.

Will, Otto. 1959. "Human Relatedness and the Schizophrenic Reaction." *Psychiatry* (August), 22(3):205–23.

Wills, Thomas A. and Thomas S. Langner. 1980. "Socioeconomic Status and Stress." In Kutash and Schlesinger, eds., *Handbook on Stress and Anxiety,* pp. 160–73.

PART TWO

Theoretical Orientations to the Practice of Community Social Work

3

Community Development: Beginnings in Social Work Enabling

Ben Lappin

In the 1950s, community development arrived on the North American continent from the Third World as a fresh and promising answer to the problem of widespread poverty. Social workers greeted the new approach with an inquiring interest that expressed itself in the form of anecdotal, descriptive, and analytical comparisons with their own form of community work.

The reception that community development received in America may have been symptomatic of a disenchantment with community practice as carried out by social workers who, in an earlier era, were themselves hailed as holding the answer to widespread poverty and human need. Comparisons with community work in developing countries also reflected a striving within the social work profession for an accommodation with the adherents of this approach who functioned as national and regional planners, generalists, administrators, subject matter specialists, and village-level workers, and who were trained in institutions that bear little or no relationship to professional schools of social work (Dunham 1960:37).

An unanticipated outcome of the importation of community development strategies was that it provided a comparative perspective (Chekki 1979:3) which has evolved into a manageable framework for subjecting multiple approaches to simultaneous evaluation. More than a hundred countries are currently sponsoring various types of development programs (Berger 1981:29) based on conceptions that differ as widely from one another as do present-day theories on economics or political science. Concurrently, community practice as it developed in a social work context remains in wide use. In this discussion a comparative approach will be used to examine the practice roles of these two approaches. Thus, community practice will be viewed as a two-level system: (1) embodying a direct form of work with community residents; and (2) indirect community work, carried out by representative bodies or community surrogates which function in the areas of social service planning, coordination of services and programs, setting priorities with respect to community needs, and establishing standards of service among local social agencies.

By contrast, community development is basically a one-level system of direct community work concerned with the total needs of residents whether in rural villages or in urban neighborhoods. Its origin goes back to the 1920s although it came into massive use after World War II as a way of helping societies long dependent on colonial administrations to cope with drastic changes which followed the dissolution of European imperialism. Hence, its emphasis on self-reliance and on social animation that stresses the raising of the consciousness of the people, the building up of their inner resources, and the encouragement of collective participation as prerequisites to lifting rural populations out of conditions of absolute poverty.

The initial results produced by the community development approach were impressive. For example, by 1951 community development (frequently referred to as CD) workers had reached 272,000 of India's villages and affected the lives of 149,000,000 people; 53,000 new cooperatives had been started, and 5,000,000 acres of land were brought under irrigation (Dunham 1960:3–36).

Similarly, when it moved to the United States, CD achieved high visibility as a strategy against rural poverty. In 1956, development projects were under way in approximately 25 counties within several states. Four years later, 210 counties across the nation were involved in community development with more than 2,000 projects designed to improve farms, build new industries and train people for the labor market (Canada Department of Agriculture 1961). Subsequently, urban communities joined the trend; new groups such as Action for Boston Community Development were started, and long-established organizations such as the Save the Children Federation (Biddle and Biddle 1965:281–96) began to apply the philosophy and methods of CD to their operating programs.

In Canada, CD took on the characteristics of crisis intervention in response to the census of 1956 which revealed that 21 percent of the country's farms had an annual production valued at less than $1,200 (Canada Department of Agriculture 1961). In 1960 the Agricultural Rehabilitation Development Act made it possible for the Federal Government of Canada to enter into agreements with the provinces to improve the productivity of the land and develop income and employment opportunities in rural agricultural areas. Within this national scheme, the French-speaking "social animators" and the English-speaking CD workers shared similarities in concepts and techniques even though they were motivated by different aspirations.[1] In Quebec, community development became tied to the thrust for national independence, particularly when CD was used as an antipoverty strategy in the urban neighborhoods of Montreal. In the other provinces of Canada, community development was deployed as a means of reducing dependence of the rural poor on public assistance (Camfens 1979:202).

Community Development and Its Source in Enabling

The people responsible for the day-to-day work and achievements of community development are known by different names, such as CD workers, community developers, encouragers, nucleus-level workers, and instigators (Biddle and Biddle 1965:281–96). Those in community organization are referred to as community welfare organization workers, community organization workers, intergroup workers, and neighborhood development workers. But the practitioners in both methods share one descriptive label in common, namely, community workers (Smith 1979:47), which will be used here as a generic name. More important, both approaches are rooted in a common orientation described as enabling.

Biddle and Biddle (1965:82) equate enabling with the role of an encourager whose involvement is most intense in the early stages and tapers off as the confidence and capabilities of the residents come to the fore. Others writing on CD mention the term enabling in passing. For example, Lotz (1977:122) speaks of the animator/ enabler as the basic CD role in helping the community develop its own capacity to engage in problem-solving. Similarly, Smith (1979:50) holds that the role of the enabler (rather than the organizer) is the best practice approach if a community is to arrive at the point where it is able to judge its own needs.

Enabling in the context of community welfare organization has been subjected to considerable analysis. Articulated as a concept in the 1940s and 1950s, enabling has been taken for granted by successive generations of community practitioners as the established orientation for the indirect leadership role within social work. Pioneers in CD, perhaps without realizing it, were acting as enablers when they sought to transform dependent impoverished village populations in the Third World into self-reliant communities, while striving at the same time to prevent change through violent revolution. They were, in effect, adopting the approach that the Charity Org nization Society (COS) had urged in nineteenth-century England. The aim of the COS had been to reduce poverty among the pauperized masses and simultaneously circumvent a class struggle with its threat of revolution and bloodshed (Woodroofe 1966:12).

Social change through rational and peaceful means became a permeating value, an aim, and a role at the same time. The term "enabling" in community work was introduced by Pray in 1947 to distinguish the community social worker from the community organization manipulator (Dunham 1959:467). For Newstetter, a contemporary of Pray, enabling was the core of the role structure he conceptualized in an effort to develop community welfare organization as a legitimate intervention within the profession of social work.

Newstetter (1947:14–16) discarded the then prevalent term "community organization" in favor of "intergroup work" as more accurately descriptive of the structured relationship between the community as a natural system and its surrogate, the council, which he saw as the typical operative setting of community welfare organization. The intergroup addresses itself to the problems of the community rather than the personal needs of the representatives who serve on it. He conceived of a "from-and-to" relationship that provides ongoing communication between the natural community and the intergroup. In this way, the day-to-day issues which preoccupy residents can guide the work of their representatives and the professionals who determine which problems should be given priority.

This emphasis on rational problem-solving assumes that harmonious interrelationships can prevail among the representatives who serve on the intergroup. The worker relates in specific ways to the various representatives who bring different mandates from their respective community groups. The worker was described by Newstetter as enabling: (1) the intergroup to develop a suitable structure and operating policies for the purpose of goal attainment; (2) individuals to function adequately as members of the intergroup in relation to the interests of the parent organizations they represent; and (3) the community groups, through their representatives, to participate appropriately in the intergroup process.

This three-part role was composed of forty-three enabling functions listed under seven different headings. These were basically practice skills in mediation, indirect leadership, and administrative tasks related to the surrogate body wherein the intergroup process takes place.

Newstetter's model emphasized reliance on democratic processes. In his view, the version of community practice he had propounded placed it within the social work profession, parallel to other forms of social work practice. What he did not take into account was the fact that his model dealt solely with indirect or community welfare organization. This placed the worker in a role and task structure distinctly different from the other forms of social work. As Sieder (1959:140) points out, the intergroup or council members are simultaneously the worker's employers, constituents, and clients. In contrast, the worker engaged in neighborhood development has a clientele that is separate and distinct from the agency's sponsors who legitimate the practitioner's role.

ROLE LEGITIMATION OF THE ENABLER IN DIRECT COMMUNITY WORK

Dillick traces "two distinct processes . . . which provide the bases for two methods of social work—social group work and intergroup work" (1953:19). Neighborhood development, in social work terms, goes back to the settlement movement, which originated in latter nineteeth-century England. According to a definition quoted by Dillick:

A settlement . . . is a colony of members of upper classes, formed in a poor neighborhood . . . The settler comes to the poor as man to man in the conviction that it means a misfortune for all parties and a danger for the nation if different classes live in complete isolation of thought and environment. He comes to bridge the gulf between the classes. (1953:19)

This sentiment is echoed in the views expressed by COS contemporaries in a quotation by Woodroofe:

The rich, in seeing something of the distress of the poor, will have forced upon their minds the responsibility attaching to wealth and leisure. . . . The poor will . . . have the comfortable assurance that if the day of exceptional adversity should come, they will not be left to encounter it without a friend. (1966:49)

The settlement movement and the Charity Organization Society (COS), seeking to humanize the harshness of the Poor Law guardians in their treatment of the pauperized masses, reinforced each other in their efforts to draw the affluent and the poor into mutual accountability. The former were summoned to attest to a "class consciousness of sin" (Webb 1929:47), and the poor were encouraged to regard poverty as a failing of their own character. This grand design called for a tilting of the wall between the two classes and transforming it into a negotiable ramp which the deserving poor could, if properly motivated by friendly visitors and settlement workers, mount to begin the climb into the promised land of the middle class.

The paternalism that colored both the COS and the settlement movement was transferred intact when these methods of fighting poverty were exported to former colonies and then again crossed the Atlantic to the North American continent in the 1950s. Moreover, the paternalism went largely unquestioned within the social work profession until the 1960s. Despite their paternalistic nature, these movements introduced approaches to the needy that represented marked improvements over the existing treatment under the Poor Law philosophy. This new outreach by the privileged class to the disadvantaged masses embodying the beginnings of the enabling orientation is illustrated in figure 3.1.

Voluntarism

Charity Organization Society
1869

Government Responsibility   Settlement Movement
1601-1869   1884

Poor Law Guardians	The Affluent Class
No accountability to the poor Harsh treatment No rehabilitation	
Impoverished masses	

Friendly Visitors Settlement Workers	The Affluent Class
Trained humanizers of the Poor Law Class harmony, noblesse oblige, The "ramp" as upward striving incentive	
Deserving poor	Undeserving paupers

FIGURE 3.1. Contrast Between the Poor Law and the Enabling Orientations

Under the Poor Law orientation, the barrier separating the affluent and the poor was maintained and reinforced by the Poor Law guardians who were accountable solely to the government.

The enabling outlook reflected the more humanized approach of the friendly visitors of COS and the settlement house workers. Although authority remained with the power structure, the new spirit of mutual accountability between the two classes was reflected in the "ramp" or opportunity system aimed at enabling the poor to move up from dependence to self-sufficiency. While the needy individual was expected to become upwardly mobile, the gap between the rich and the poor classes remained much the same as in the past. The aim was to reduce individual need rather than eliminate the causes of poverty.

The practice role pioneered by caseworkers also stems from the process depicted in figure 3.1. Fashioned after the doctor-patient model (Woodroofe 1966:53; Richmond 1930:100), the interaction between practitioner and the client as instituted and legitimated by an agency and its sponsors is not based on a symmetric relationship between equals. In other words, the worker is recipient of an assigned status, which puts him or her above the client.[2]

Structurally, the sponsorship and the clientele of the traditional casework or group work agency constitute two distinct subsystems within the overall institution. The leadership is that part of the agency that legitimates the role and assigns the status to the neighborhood development worker, the caseworker, or the group worker.

However, there is a fundamental difference in structure between traditional casework and group work agencies which deal directly with clients, and central councils (or community surrogates) which function indirectly through representatives. This difference received little attention from those writing on community practice in the 1940s and 1950s. The stress on similarities between community welfare organization and the other agencies was probably seen as facilitating the acceptance of community welfare organization as a method of social work practice. Hence, the articles in this vein, as already noted, by Pray, Newstetter, Johnson, and others. Ross, writing in the 1950s when community development was in the early stages of its move to the industrialized nations of the West, was not concerned with bridging the differences between community welfare organization and the social work profession. Instead, he sought to formulate a set of practice roles that would be applicable to both community development and community organization. In this respect, he is acknowledged for his contribution not only within social work but in the field of community development as well (Clinard 1970:134).[3]

The concept of direct and indirect community work formulated by Lindeman (1921:145) and Steiner (1925:327) was well known to Ross. In his restatement of their formulations, Ross speaks about his version of direct community work—the need to get the community as a whole to identify and mobilize itself to deal with its own problems. His indirect approach is aimed at a well-balanced program of welfare services planned and organized by what he refers to as "a team" (Ross 1958:18).

Ross relies on the enabling tradition for a role set to meet the needs of the community worker. The guide helps the community establish the means of achieving its goals. The enabler helps by awakening and focusing discontent about existing conditions that are harmful to sound community living whether in the social welfare sector or elsewhere. The expert provides information and advice in his field of competence to the leaders of the community who have the ultimate say as to the use of the information proffered. The social therapist helps the leadership gain understanding of latent divisiveness and conflicts that may block or deflect representatives or indigenous leaders from constructive decision-making with respect to the community's needs and well-being (Ross and Lappin 1967:214–31).

Ross's enabler, as Rothman points out (1979:35), has a procedural focus having little to do with concrete tasks or problems. The same may be said of the guide, expert, and social therapist. However, the intention of the entire role set, as conceived by Ross, was not to describe a set of techniques but to provide principles that would help a worker choose the particular role most appropriate to the demands of a particular situation. A range of tasks and skills considered generic to all of these roles is: (1) system maintenance; (2) planning activities; (3) developing enabling relationships; (4) mobilizing initiatives; (5) innovative tasks; (6) educational and interpretive tasks (see figure 3.2).

FIGURE 3.2. Enabling Orientation

Neighborhood Development (direct community work)	Community Welfare Work (indirect community work)
Agency sponsors and clients as separate constituencies	Agency sponsors and clients as one constituency
Assigned status, constant asymmetric relationship	Variable relationships between worker and council members
Role mastery	Absence of role mastery

Task Roles

System Maintenance	Planning Activities	Enabling Relationships	Mobilizing Initiatives	Innovative Tasks	Interpretation and Education
Implementing tasks: regulations, policies, administrative procedures	Social welfare program design	Interactional tasks: mediating, promoting, brokerage, intergroup process	Organizing	Leadership development	Public relations: contact with public media
	Priority rating of community needs		Fund raising	Developing new program directions based on new knowledge	Publications
Managing tasks: fiscal aspects, funding, budgeting, physical facility	Standard-setting for social services	Individualized relationships with council members and subgroups	Social action	Contributing to theory development	Publicity
			Community participation		Orientation to various publics associated with the agency
Archival tasks: files, records, historical material, information retrieval	Planning strategies of change	Catalyst for decision-making and problem-solving processes	Interagency coordination	New approaches to practice	
	Research as an aid to problem-solving	Expertise and social therapy		Keeping staff and sponsors abreast of new methodology	Education via institutes, workshops, and conferences
Arrangement tasks: Meetings and conferences	Evaluation of services and programs				Volunteer training
	Preventive and trend aspects of planning				Prevention of social pathology through mass education

THE ENABLER AND THE PROBLEM OF ROLE MASTERY

Although Ross had provided a series of role characteristics that are generic to both direct and indirect community work, the specifics of the indirect community practitioner or enabler remained undescribed. Caseworkers usually modeled their role on the doctor-patient relationship in which the patient's attributes of power, influence, and prestige are residual to the treatment relationship with the doctor. The situation remains analogous in the client-worker relationship within group work *and* direct community work, but the analogy does *not* hold for indirect community work.[4]

Although the council member symbolizes community needs, his or her self-image is not one of a person coming to the council as a client but as one who is an acknow'¬dged community leader or a representative of a particular agency or constituency in the community. Objectively, power and prestige are properties of the representative and the leadership function, and they cannot be suspended in the working relationship with a social work enabler.

Again the problem of the power, influence, and prestige of the community leader or representative in the relationship with the community worker was barely dealt with in the 1940s and 1950s since that too might have brought community welfare organizations into conflict with the social work practice value system. For example, the view that Lippitt, Watson, and Westley (1958:31) take of the change agent's role obliges them to eliminate from their study of planned change much material on participation in power struggles as a basis for change. Sieder (1959:139), one of the writers who did refer to this problem, perceived power as corrupting and leading to "abuses of good professional practice." She also noted the tendency of some community workers "to identify with volunteer leaders . . . and to dissociate from professional social workers as having a lower status" (140).

Despite the pioneering efforts of Pray and Newstetter to give the enabler an ethical base of practice which is consistent with social work values, many social workers remain skeptical that such factors as power and prestige can be brought under sufficient control to yield to the enabler the measure of role mastery or role autonomy prevailing in other areas of social work practice. The problem goes beyond the manipulative behavior of some, or even many, community workers. The essential question is whether the community worker's intervention has the structural features that provide for a needed measure of role mastery.

Manipulative behavior becomes an integral part of the relationship between the social worker and the council membership *if* professional intervention is directly tied to the members' status attributes and to their function as sponsors and legitimators of the worker's role. Conversely, role mastery in accordance with social work values is only possible when the worker's relationship with the council members is sufficiently autonomous from their status attributes as well as from their function as sponsors and legitimators of the worker's role.

A condition crucial to the enabler's role autonomy is that the central body responsible for social planning and community welfare organization is discerned by its members as an objective neutral forum for intergroup participation. This condition makes it possible for the social work enabler to relate to the vested interests brought by the members to the intergroup process from a position of perceived neutrality. Thus the posture of the central planning structure itself is basic in providing the practitioner with the ethical means to deal objectively with power symbols without being unduly influenced or corrupted by the politics that often accompany the intergroup process.

Indeed, the challenge to transform the idea of centralization into a community surrogate capable of planning and coordinating social welfare services from a position of neutrality in relation to its member agencies preceded the enabling concept. When the COS took root in the United States it became clear that this organization could not fulfill the role of such a centralizing body. Structurally, the COS lacked the conditions of objectivity with respect to its peer agencies. The solution to this problem is attributed by Bruno to Francis H. McLean, associate director of the charity organization department of the Russell Sage Foundation, and one of the pioneers in community work on the American scene. It was most likely McLean who proposed the new organization to be called a "central council of social agencies" Bruno states, and was to be "composed of representatives of social agencies that wished to unite in a common project of establishing and improving standards, thereby taking the ungracious and impractical responsibility of setting standards away from a single agency and placing it upon the entire group." (Bruno 1964:193).

Predictably, the suggestion of such councils was initially resisted by some COS groups which felt threatened by McLean's approach. The wisdom of his thinking prevailed, however, and the central council idea caught on. These councils, weak at the outset, and with less prestige than many of their member agencies, proceeded in community after community to enlarge and deepen their base of authority. The constituents of the councils did not view this development as competition with them or at their expense. Indeed, the representatives of the direct-service social agencies endowed the council with increasing influence in the community as they used it as an intergroup forum to coordinate local social services, to set standards of social work practice, and to rate community needs in accordance with agreed-upon priorities. The source of the councils' authority for carrying out such tasks was embedded in the dynamics of the intergroup process in which the agency representative engaged and not in external tactics aimed at competing with member agencies for power in the community.

Neighborhood Development and Role Sponsorship as a Problem

Although the sponsors of the settlement houses and community centers legitimated the role of neighborhood development workers, this was frequently perceived by social workers to be a mixed blessing. Their uneasiness is conveyed in Steiner's sixty-year-old description of the social settlement movement:

One of the outstanding features of the settlement movement . . . is its direct concern with the people themselves rather than with the various agencies that are working in their behalf . . . The social settlement, however, possessed features . . . colored by its early beginnings. . . . The initiative for the organization of the settlement as well as its financial support came from outside the neighborhood in which it was located. This tinge of paternalism in its origin, however, was never permitted to dominate its neighborhood policy and program. The settlement residents always considered themselves an integral part of the neighborhood in which they lived. Their neighbors were regarded as social equals . . . their counsel sought in all matters pertaining to welfare of the neighborhood. . . . The social settlements never accepted the traditional idea that leadership was a divine right of the upper class. (Steiner 1925:113–14)

Steiner's description of the settlement movement and the workers' struggle to save it from becoming an "uplift movement" is substantiated in the records and minutes of decisions that are preserved in the archives of many of these agencies. However, the thinly veiled paternalism that the sponsors brought to the settlement house and the social work value of self-determination could not be easily bridged. For the most part, the professionals (many of them trained group workers) viewed this paternalism as a fact of life from which the neighborhood residents needed to be shielded as much as possible.

The chronic problem of role sponsorship became the focus of attention anew when community development workers, functioning outside the social work profession, began moving from the rural to the urban scene in the United States and Canada. Outside sponsors with values of their own, whether paternalistic or otherwise, constituted an intrusion into the community's autonomy in their effort to have local people shape its fate through their own decisions. Yet, despite the fact that community development workers are by no means free of sponsors, the entire issue of CD and sponsorship remains murky. Kramer (1975:184), for instance, speaks of a CD mystique that masks issues growing out of the role of the sponsoring organization. Perhaps CD workers have purposely avoided discussion of sponsorship; they certainly have reason to be discreet about the auspices under which they function. This is especially true in developing countries where the worker, coming as an appointee of an overseas aid foundation or an international aid project and anxious to develop good relations with the local population, would naturally want to avoid drawing attention to his auspices in case it might awaken suspicions associated with a colonial past.

Often, workers with a CD orientation attempt to minimize the nature of their auspices in order to maximize their accountability to the people undergoing development. But the reality is such that the workers themselves appear to the villagers to be external agents (Ross and Lappin 1967:8) sent to motivate, to engender heightened skills and new techniques, with aims attached to ideas of self-reliance that are, often as not, outside the villagers' life experience. To be sure, little can be accomplished without the community's will to help itself. At the same time, many village-level workers have realized that without externally aided self-help, community development efforts amount to no more than a therapeutic exercise that falls far short of raising the standard of living.

By the time CD was adopted in the West, the "aided self-help" concept was an established fact in the Third World (Dunham 1960:34). The prevalence of intervention from without is confirmed by Batten: "We see a worker trying to encourage and help members of some local community . . . to undertake a project . . . which he or his agency thinks will be of benefit to them" (1965:6).

Sponsorship: Differing Outlooks in Social Work and Community Development

Although social workers have paid a price for their sponsorships by prestigious and influential elements in society, their overseeing stewards can also be credited with some positive achievments. For instance, some sponsors were committed to raising professional standards and played a pioneering role in demonstrating to the larger society the value of research-based planning for social welfare.

The comparatively invisible sponsor in CD has become important to practitioners in their attempt to distinguish themselves from social workers for whom sponsorship and its visible relationship to role legitimation have been taken for granted as part of the profession's tradition (Clinard 1970:101–8). This rather insistent differentiation may be an effort to proclaim distinctions that are not substantive from the standpoint of methodology.

One international conference, convened to study the respective features of the two approaches, arrived at the conclusion that the methods of social work community practice and CD were interchangeable (Kindelsperger 1961:35). Social work is acknowledged by Brokensha and Hodge (1969:25) as one of the two roots (the other being education) from which CD sprang. This is borne out in their discussion of the CD process, beginning with the initial contact in which rapport with the community members is created, followed by the encouragement of systematic discussion beginning with the first request for the worker's help. Communication is maintained and broadened through the planning and execution phases of the project; the worker moves with the community through these developments until the concluding celebration-evaluation stage is reached.

Throughout the process, the worker functions very much in the spirit of Ross' guide-enabler-expert-social therapist role set. However, the development worker's manner and style of encountering people are rather more casual than those of traditional social work community organizers. The development worker's presence is ubiquitous, and his contacts with people are informal. Often as not, they occur by happenstance,

[patterned on] a habit of being around and accessible in a community meeting place—a coffee shop, a bench under some trees in the market square or wherever people gather to gossip, to watch the passersby and enjoy their company, until such time as both curiosity and familiarity prompt the first exchange of greeting or inquiry. (Biddle and Biddle 1965:224)

Plainly evident in the CD worker's entire deportment is the readiness to move at the client's pace and a disposition to change from passive to active interest, and from active interest to initiatives leading toward action. Although many social work community practitioners have done much to cultivate this type of stance, there is no doubt that the presence of an agency and a visible sponsor create pressures of timing that are frequently geared to the sponsor's desire to see results rather than the need to move in accordance with the client's readiness to forge ahead.

CD literature dealing with community welfare organization and social work neighborhood development seems to follow a pattern in which its closeness to social work is readily acknowledged as, for example, the Biddles' observation that both fields seek "to discipline efforts by the use of social scientific thinking. Both work through the concepts of community and neighborhood" (1965:224). However, there is a definite parting of the ways and quite different outlooks on the issue of sponsorship.

Equally interesting are the distinctions which are discernible in the exploration of the practice role within these two approaches to community work. Social work community practice is still not on the level of conceptual explication achieved by clinical practice, and theoretical developments in practice with individuals, families, and groups have spurred community workers to elaborate their practice roles conceptually. For example, social work community practitioners have borrowed a well-developed approach to record writing in which social processes and interactions among people are captured in narrative form as a basis for evaluation, supervision, and identification of developing appropriate forms of intervention. In comparison to social work's use of records as a teaching and learning tool, however, the CD case record is still in a formative stage.

Elements of teaching and learning and of social protest tend to be intermingled in CD case records. This is a problem that goes beyond the question of skill in knowing what to select for narration. The difficulty may be traced back to a certain ambivalence with respect to the four characteristics attributed to CD by Sanders (1958:407): *process* entails the phases that a community goes through in reaching the point where the people have acquired the capacity to make decisions about problems of common interest; *method* is a means to an end; *program* constitutes the relevant activities; and *movement* stresses the emotional aspect, or the image that CD aspires to communicate to the larger society. The intense nature of the last-named characteristic is attested to by Dunham (1960:37) when he describes some practitioners as having "a sense of commitment to the aims of CD which is akin to a religious dedication." This may explain the ambivalence one senses in the record writing. Concern with scientific thinking and the desire to communicate the symbolism of a people's movement vie for dominance within the same case records.

When CD and social work community practitioners functioned in two different parts of the world, their respective attitudes toward the question of agency sponsorship and conceptual elaboration of practice roles were largely academic issues. But with the shift of CD from the developing countries to the industrialized societies, and the drawing together of practitioners from both approaches within urban neighborhoods, these questions become real. Take the instance of the Hong Kong Council of Social Services which has a community development division (Mok 1980:1–9). It would be interesting to know whether there is a visible difference in the response to the agency's role as sponsor between the workers active in the CD division and those functioning in the other sections of Hong Kong's Council of Social Services.

The 1960s and Their Effect on Community Work

When CD joined community work as a model for use in urban areas, the convergence was not only in the neighborhood. To all intents and purposes, social welfare became the core preoccupation of both helping approaches. For social work community practice, social welfare has always been the central concern. For CD it became a practical necessity because institutions such as education and economics, which are usually within the scope of the CD worker's intervention, cannot be tackled meaningfully at the neighborhood level. Despite the possibilities envisaged by proponents of urban CD, the neighborhood as locus for changing the educational, economic, and political systems of an urban area in highly urbanized and industrially advanced societies has limited potential (Clinard 1970:114–35).

As the two approaches competed for acceptance in urban communities, symbolic distinctions gained prominence. Hence, the fact that CD paid minimal attention to its establishment sponsor and stressed its people's movement aspect provided it with very good credentials for work in poor neighborhoods. At one time, social work community practice was also very much in the movement phase of its development. By the 1920s, however, the populist stir that social work reformers created in philanthropic circles, among church groups and voluntary organizations, subsided, and the movements were transformed into practice settings for group work, neighborhood development, community welfare organization, and social planning. Also, the effort expended by community practitioners to be accepted into the social work profession has had a good deal to do with their switch from the type of intense deportment, often described as idealistic, to a posture of objectivity and emotional neutrality more in keeping with the self-image of what is deemed to be a professional approach.

Ironically, the professional status sought by community workers coincided with the arrival of a turbulent era in which professionalism became a stigma in the eyes of radicals who had come to work with poor people residing in urban neighborhoods. The new breed of activists insisted on calling themselves community organizers, a label that some neighborhood-based social workers avoided since they did not cherish being lumped together with labor union organizers.

In turn, radical workers in the black ghettos and inner-city slums scorned the professional social work community and the elite members of the community who sponsored their work in government and voluntary agencies. What helped the radicals and CD workers (and, for that matter, many a social worker active in the neighborhoods and seeking to break the connection with establishment sponsorship) defy the power structure were the storefront social agencies that sprang up in the 1960s. These modest institutions were started with the aid of church funds, individual philanthropists, and foundations which were receptive to the idea of enhancing the power of the poor by giving them a sponsorship role over new forms of social agencies designed to serve their immediate needs. This was seen as part of the strategy of power redistribution between the affluent and the needy.

The struggle against the established authorities for greater responsiveness to neighborhood residents might have been a good deal more difficult were it not for the enactment of maximum feasible participation as an aspect of the Economic Opportunity Act of 1964. Initially, this legislative action was meant to advance the CD concept of self-help. As it turned out, poor people in the neighborhoods used the concept of maximum feasible participation as an aid and battle cry in their confrontations with the establishment.

This turn of events brought significant consequences for community welfare organization. Traditionally, social action strategies initiated by a community's central planning bodies would be organized by social workers and carried out by indigenous volunteer leaders acting on behalf of the disadvantaged. Maximum feasible participation policies supported by grants encouraged the recruitment of trained manpower and other resources needed "to help local groups participate. . . in the social issues—encouraging residents to choose issues, frame them in their own terms, and act within their legal rights to deal with problems they encounter daily" (Cloward 1964:1). This meant that the leaders of the central planning bodies, instead of being the spearheads of social action, as in the past, were themselves transformed by the residents of inner-city neighborhoods into targets of social action.

Transfer of citizen action efforts from the establishment to deprived communities resulted in situations which often brought boards and administrators face to face with defiant radical organizers, CD workers, and community social workers engaged in neighborhood development. The relocation of social action also brought a militant outlook into community work which did not easily fit with the traditional tactics of consensus building devised by skilled, neutral mediators conditioned to use the enabling approach.

The Shift from the Neutral Enabler to the Partisan Activist

Social work has evolved as a subsystem of the social welfare society. The profession's methods of intevention range in their application from the privacy of the individual and family to the intermediate public level of neighborhood and community, and beyond that to the more impersonal cosmopolitan public welfare sector. The relationships entered into between client and worker on all of these planes bring to bear values common to all social workers, in which self-regulation of the individual, group, and community is an assumption as well as a core ethic.

Social work intervention is carried out within a network of interrelated institutions. The felt need that comes to the surface in a direct service agency, or in a neighborhood, often becomes an identified need by the process of direct referral or indirect follow-up through research by planning bodies. There is in this agency interrelatedness an ethical implication for the right of the indirect planning and coordinating body to initiate services. What happens in councils may, in fact, be an extended involvement of an intervention begun in the direct service social agency.

Such a systems approach to intervention runs counter to the principles of community development. According to the CD approach, the neighborhood or village that allows itself to be caught up in a web of social agencies surrenders its self-accountability to demands set up at different points in the system, outside the immediate relationship between the worker and the community undergoing development. It follows from this that standard-setting by a body such as a social planning council produces external criteria that are likely to interfere with "community development as a spontaneous, self-generating process of attitude change" (Brokensha and Hodge:129).

Whereas community development workers and social work community practitioners differed in their interpretation of community autonomy, the radical organizers of the 1960s opposed community workers on ideological not methodological grounds. They rejected outright a "situational approach" that focused on problems isolated from the larger condition of society. This reproof, directed specifically at social work, had come from C. Wright Mills (Horowitz 1963:534–5). Mills died in the early 1960s, but his radical view of society continued to influence the decade. Social workers were not the only ones who were on the defensive. Harrington's *Other America* revealed widespread poverty in the midst of the world's richest nation, evolving a sense of collective embarrassment within affluent America that was reminiscent of England's response to poverty at the time the COS emerged as a movement. At the close of the 1860s, British middle-class guilt was responsible for the COS launching a campaign against individual poverty, and in the mid-1960s the same mood gave rise to President Johnson's war against community poverty. This government-sponsored program, coupled with the public response brought about by Harrington's exposé, emboldened the antiestablishment forces which had taken up the struggle on behalf of the disadvantaged.

This was not a time for impartiality or neutrality by those who chose to serve the poor. The mediations of the community workers, who sought to protect the local residents from the paternalism of the agency sponsors, were no longer enough to evoke the cooperation or sympathy of neighborhood people. Nor were the impartial enablers in the central planning bodies acceptable to the needy. Their neutrality was seen as a ploy to keep the establishment at the helm of decision-making. They were held responsible for the decisions of agency sponsors who were far removed from the slum communities, yet had the ultimate say in defining needs and assigning services to impoverished slum dwellers.

Understandably, many social workers, driven by the compelling mood of the times, began to assert a militant partnership in their identification with the people in the neighborhoods. Needless to say, this was at odds with the prevailing social work view that the client system is a totality of interdependent parts in which the practitioner remains neutral toward each part (Lippit, Watson, and Westley 1958:155). The enabler's mediating role, based on nonpartisanship, had made it possible for community welfare organizations to gain entry into the social work profession. Nevertheless, from a moral standpoint, partisan intervention was seen as a more appropriate strategy in the struggle to right the wrongs faced by residents of slum neighborhoods.

As one-sided champions of the poor, many social workers tried to put themselves on even terms both with their colleagues trained in non-social work methods of community development and with the radical organizers. The changed outlook called for tasks and roles appropriate to the new approach and, above all, a rationale that was not to be found in the traditional enabling orientation. These new techniques acquired a hardened militance appropriate to forms of interaction based on direct confrontation. The descriptions of these tasks are often as much concerned with communicating the ardor needed to carry them out as with the nature of the tasks themselves.

Perlman and Gurin (1972:25, 45–46) discuss a number of such roles, among them: (1) the agitator, whose ceaseless prodding brings about something new in the community, be it an institution, a program, or a legal provision; (2) the broker and the advocate, perhaps the most prominently discussed roles that the partisan community worker is called upon to perform; (3) the activist, whose one-sided allegiance in the cause of poverty is symbolic of the rejection of the neutralist passive stance. Terrell (1971:358) combines both terms in his description of the broker-advocate as functioning on behalf of the client to remedy injustices stemming from action initiated by government authorities, voluntary organizations, or influential individuals.

In Grosser's view, the broker is a type of seeing-eye guide who connects those groping for services with the sought after social welfare programs hidden in the complexity of modern urban society. But according to Grosser, the experience of workers engaged in neighborhood development revealed that the broker role lacked direction. Hence, advocacy was adopted from the field of law. The worker's role among the community's residents and their representatives is avowedly that of advocate of the client group's point of view:

> The worker is not an enabler, broker, expert, consultant, guide, or social therapist. He is in fact a partisan in a social conflict, and his expertise is available exclusively to serve the client interests. The impartiality of the enabler and the functionalism of the broker are absent here. (Grosser 1965:17–18).

As an example of how partiality and emotionalism serve to ready the neighborhood for confrontation, a short excerpt by Mary Rabagliati and Ezra Birnbaum is presented:

> The basic attitude is that we were out to attack the inequities in the welfare system, at least at first winter clothing. Anything as far as I was concerned was fair game. This meant attacking the investigators, attacking the Welfare Department . . . attacking almost anybody if it was in the best interests of the client and . . . of the immediate situation. . . . One of the things that became apparent at the very first meeting was that the investigator was seen as the villain, and even though the investigator in reality is not the key villain, at the early stage of organizing this is unimportant. . . . If from the beginning you point to the welfare system or the police department as the enemy, the people will nod their heads and say yes, yes, yes, but then they'll go home and start saying, "I don't give a damn about the policy system. It's that bastard cop on the corner that I want to get rid of, and why doesn't he [social worker] ever talk about that?". . . . We wanted to keep things very personal, very immediate, very emotional and build a spirit around that. If you are personalizing your audience, you have to personalize the target also. . . . We feel that we are being neglected—especially since many of our investigators haven't even been in touch with us to find out about the seriousness of the situation. . . . In most years, many of us have had to wait until December, January, or even later to buy our winter clothing. This year we're not willing to wait that long and see our children have to wear thin summer clothing when it gets below freezing. (1969:108–10)

Grosser, along with others, positions the advocate role within the framework of advocacy much as Ross specifies the enabler in the context of enabling. Looked at in this light, advocacy, like enabling, is more than just a role or role characteristic; it is, in fact, an orientation or rationale for partisan community practice or neighborhood development, in vivid contrast to the neutralist, enabling orientation. However, unlike enabling, advocacy was subjected from the outset to two differing theoretic modalities. Brager (1968) viewed the advocate as a "political tactician" and reformer. Grosser drew on the practice of law for his model. In the latter's view: "If advocacy is compromised in the interests of social reform . . . it is no longer advocacy" (Grosser 1973:199).

Social work traditionalists found both conceptualizations problematic. The advocate as "political tactician" was objected to on grounds perhaps best expressed by Gilbert and Specht in "Advocacy and Professional Ethics," wherein they state that a role urging "the conscious rearrangement of reality to induce a desired attitudinal or behavioral outcome" bears what the writers term "troubling Machiavellian connotations" (1979:98).

The rationale for advocacy based on the legal model brought with it problems of another sort. Once again, social work community practitioners had departed from the traditional medical model in their introduction of a practice role to the profession. By turning to law, they had drawn on a precedent from another major profession for legitimating partisanship and social conflict. It is the model of advocacy adopted from the legal profession that has come to be adopted within social work.

Of the practice roles examined, ideologically motivated radical organizing was alluded to as a phenomenon that came and went, by and large, with the 1960s. Its influence is still present in activist forms of community work. Curiously, a major beneficiary of the radicals' organizing skill has been the very establishment they used to taunt with their bold acts of confrontation. Many former radicals now pursue successful business careers and the militance they brought to the neighborhoods during the 1960s is left, in the 1980s, to the nostalgic recall of social critics, who in hindsight ponder that turbulent era.

Community Development

The rural village of the Third World remains a classical setting for community development workers and social animators. This locus is the base of the first of three models of community development conceptualized by Dasgupta, who views the village community as microscopic compared to the macroscopic societies of the West which underwent the profound changes wrought by the Industrial Revolution.

Western industrial nations have relied on vast resources in raw materials, technology, and managers who have guided massive work forces in the production and distribution of goods and services. The developing countries have had to look to inner resources. As Dasgupta points out: "'People' and 'relationships' at home, rather than 'raw materials' and 'markets' of distant lands were their main assets" (1979:63). CD in the impoverished lands was not intended to be an end in itself. Its aim has been the eradication of absolute poverty, and in the early stages it was responsible for bringing about visible changes in the developing countries. In actuality, however, it amounted to "a general stir in the stagnant societies of the third world, a rise in the aspiration of people and the actual achievement of a high standard of living for a small coterie of the elite" (73).

This observation raises a basic and unresolved question: Is community development primarily economic or social? The issue arose at the National Conference on Social Welfare as far back as 1958, where Dunham delivered an address on "The Outlook for Community Development." Dunham reported difference of views among the forty-two leaders in the field who submitted opinions. Some considered CD as primarily economic, and others took the position that it is basically social. For instance, Albert Mayer insisted "that improvement of the economic base must be the core of community development," while E.R. Chadwick, a former community development officer in the British Colonial Service, insisted that "economic improvement is a by-product of the urge to social improvement" (Dunham 1960:34). Looked at from the economic standpoint, the bleak picture conveyed by Dasgupta is evident. From the social perspective, the situation as reported by the United States Technical Cooperation Mission to India in the late 1950s seems much more hopeful (Dasgupta 1979).

There is also reason to wonder whether the community development role does not carry a bias favoring the social dimension. The insistence on social animation as an autonomous process that must remain free of criteria coming from outside support systems must inevitably have a self-limiting effect on a village society's potential for development. The United Nations, in the third of its Ten Principles of Community Development, sought to integrate the "self-help" and "aided self-help" approaches: "Changed attitudes in people are as important as the material achievements of community projects *during the initial stages of development*" (emphasis added) (Sanders 1958:408).

But it is with the initial stages of CD that the social animator seems to be predominantly concerned. By virtue of a philosophy of education and an outlook reinforced in the field of practice, the worker may not be readily disposed to bring the needs felt in the village to the materialistic ends associated with industrial development. Once the local population moves beyond process and method onto Sanders' other two planes of CD, namely, program and movement, certain perils become apparent. For instance, his conception of movement is explicitly linked to the idea of progress. This is a philosophical precept that from the outset narrows the view of growth to the Western notion of success. Lures beckoning the individual to join the race leading to the top have produced anxiety of epidemic proportions among the societies committed to the idea of progress.

Presumably, if CD remains bound to method and process, the problems inherent on the program and movement levels can be avoided. The tendency toward such a view seems to be implicit in an approach that stresses self-help programs founded on local consensus and allegiance to one's immediate environment. Geographic mobility is minimized, occupational differentiation and specialization are not encouraged, nor is the formation of large-scale organizations promoted. Under such conditions there is likely to be little use for complex organizations and the range of experts needed in modern community living, including technical specialists in community planning (Austin 1970:101).

Such intracommunity preoccupation, unaccompanied by an intercommunity process of coordination among neighboring localities undergoing development, could play into the hands of those bent on misusing development for their own ends. Something akin to such a situation is reflected in a study which reveals that many rural communities in the Third World are not benefiting from international aid programs. The funds earmarked for remote villages are reaching unrepresentative elites that control the resources in those lands (Penketh 1980).

Significantly, the differences between micro- and macro-development are identified through indicators that are basically economic. As Gunnar Myrdal stated, "economic development is a task for governments and that governments must prepare and force a general economic plan containing a system of purposively applied controls . . . to get development started and keep it going" (Austin 1970:98). It also means a process of deliberately altering certain social and cultural patterns at the community level to facilitate economic growth (101).

What all of this points to is conflicting values, especially as they apply to CD in developing nations. Methods and process lend themselves to its early stages and are implicitly micro, stressing the social; while program and movement are explicitly economic, and macro in scope.

Social Work Neighborhood Development

Community development came to the West as a postwelfare phenomenon aimed at the pockets of poverty which the welfare state had failed to eliminate. In the Third World, CD did not manage to play the major role envisaged for it as a catalytic agent in the industrialization of the impoverished lands. In the industrially developed countries, CD did not have to deal with industrialism as an issue. Further, just as the community development workers held out a promise of solving absolute poverty and had to be content with delivering micro-development to the rural villages of the Third World, so the radical organizers in American urbanized neighborhoods used the ominous rhetoric of macro-revolution and settled for a redistribution of power needed by the poor to exert a greater influence over the social agencies in their neighborhoods. Instead of a class struggle, there were localized skirmishes: rent strikes by tenant associations; sit-ins organized by neighborhood residents at welfare agencies for better delivery of services and for more prompt payment of social assistance allowances; consumer organizations formed to bring unconscionable merchants to terms; demonstrations launched for more comprehensive day care, and so forth.

Paradoxically, these militant actions were no less integrationist in nature than the programs that served the neighborhoods earlier in the century. A moderate form of activism was appropriate in Steiner's day because the impoverished hopefuls, entering into the spirit of competition in America of the 1920s, came from the millions of immigrants who made their way to the New World from different European societies. Settlement house workers receiving Irish, Italian, Scandinavian, Jewish, and Polish newcomers used the settlements as the low end of the "opportunity ramp" for beginning the upward socioeconomic climb. But the racial minorities that came to the fore in the 1960s were not newcomers. Sealed off from middle America, they had been down in "the hold" of the society for generations, and the only way they saw of moving into it was by blasting their way upward. This meant a break with the established approach that called for acceptance of the rules imposed by the white middle class as a condition of upward mobility.

It also called for a revision of the traditional middle-class definition of poverty as pathology. The poor had achieved sufficient clout to redefine poverty as society's self-perpetuating moral wrong that needed to be righted instead of treated. Social work traditionalists tended to overlook the fact that the profession was being summoned not to produce a new therapy, but to develop a new practice role that would aid the disadvantaged demanding social justice from the established power structure.

Advocacy in the guise of political tactics seemed to lack a conceptual elaboration of the structural restraints that would keep conflict from being transformed into violence (Brager 1968). The containment of violence was not the unquestioned virtue in the 1960s that it had been within the enabling orientation of the previous era. The uncertainty surrounding this issue gave rise to many polemics. Specht (1969), for example, saw disruption as the outer ethical limit of social work militance. Similarly, Thursz (1971) saw in disruption and civil disobedience, partisan social work involvements that fell short of insurrectionist activities.

Conceptually, advocacy, founded on the legal model, embodies the safety features meant to avert violence; social conflict becomes a process that is analogous to litigation. Irrational elements, such as vendettas between quarreling parties, are barred so that each side of the conflict is freed from violent feuding to pursue relentlessly the justice of its claims (Simmel 1955:36-37). The work in adapting social advocacy from the legal model was pioneered by Grosser, and the concept has been enriched by others. Interestingly, advocacy drifted into community development, much as did enabling in an earlier period.

As is frequently the case, the impoverished sector serves as a proving ground for experimentation in social services and social welfare programming. The advocates, having demonstrated their effectiveness among the poor during the 1960s, became increasingly useful in the 1970s to middle-class clients, helping them right specific wrongs suffered by unsuspecting consumers, organizing tenants to press for their rights, assisting the elderly to lobby for improved services, and so on. The shift from the concept of political tactician to the legal model advocated by Grosser has had the effect of bringing the advocate back to the depoliticized posture of the enabler. It has also made it safer for the affluent to deploy the services of the advocate. Thus, those workers who were so militant during the 1960s in their disavowal of the establishment are now increasingly back in its fold.[5]

Unfortunately, roles not infrequently fail to meet the diverse objectives of the legitimators, of the clients, the practitioners, and the larger society. In this respect social advocacy is no exception, being subject to the problems that affect legal advocacy. For instance, in both situations the practitioners are often prey to the temptations of resorting to tactics aimed at snatching a victory for one's client rather than serving the ends of justice. However, in one sense advocacy has proved to be a boon. Neighborhood development workers, whether hailing from CD or social work, now can use the concept of advocacy as a means of entering into partisan client-worker relationships without feeling quite as encumbered by the sponsor's sense of paternalism.

Community Welfare Organization

The assertion that CD and community welfare organization skills are interchangeable is true up to a point, but there are also divergences, so that skills and roles cannot always be readily carried over from one approach to the other. This becomes clearer when one examines some of the community practice skills identified by Johnson. She speaks of the need for the worker to have a cultivated sense of timing in bringing different groups into interaction with respect to goals that the community is striving to reach. She stresses the worker's ability to maintain multiple relationships with leaders, group representatives, and organizations simultaneously but independently of one another, since they may be at odds despite their desire to solve common problems. Further, the worker must be skilled in distinguishing between primary and secondary group relationships (Johnson 1959:82).

The first skill mentioned by Johnson is palpably interchangeable. The second is partly so. Aside from indigenous leaders, the village society is not likely to have a wide range of organizations nor a large core of representatives who serve to link institutions to the general community. Finally, the practitioner's skill in distinguishing between primary and secondary group relationships cannot be realistically developed in a village community; secondary relationships call for a wide diversity of specialized interests socially, economically, and vocationally.

The preoccupation of workers with the geographic community is not limited to rural villages in developing countries. It applies, as well, to the urban neighborhood. In Israel, for example, community work is to a very large extent confined to the poor inner-city areas and small urban communities known as development towns. The leadership that the workers are instrumental in producing remains neighborhood-bound, and for the most part these leaders lack the capacity to forge links with regional or national centers of influence, either governmental or voluntary. This excessive localism has been a factor in preventing the disadvantaged from gaining status as a national constituency and securing greater influence in representing the interests of the needy.

In the Third World, social welfare and social work are seen as limited and specialized activities which are contributory to, and proceeding within the context of, national plans for social and economic development (Austin 1970:104). But in the West, urban CD is confined to the neighborhoods, and the task of linking the locality to the metropolitan, regional, and national levels of social welfare is within the orbit of community welfare organization. This role derives from a primary concern with the development of the individual and family and with linking this clientele directly to national social insurance and other social security schemes. As a result, the function of the local community as an intermediate support system has been subjected to erosion (Warren 1963:53–154). On the other hand, CD, concerned essentially with locality development, may, as Austin indicates, "take as its objective the maintenance and stabilization of traditional communities, while the goal of national development requires changes in those communities" (Austin 1970:101). If the experiences in the industrialized West and in the developing countries are at all indicative insofar as change is concerned, it is because individuals and families are more easily moved in the direction of nationally determined goals than is the much larger social phenomenon of community.

The diverging concerns of the social animators in the CD framework, and of community workers in the context of social work, make interesting contrasts. The former, committed to micro-development, are ranged against influences from the outside that tend to deflect the locality from its self-selected course. The latter, bent on dealing with the larger problems of the metropolitan society, rebel against the more limited planning outlook of their agency affiliates. Frustration with this situation initially led the councils to break their ties with the local federated fund-raising organizations to which the council staffs used to devote much time, aiding in the annual money-raising campaigns and providing services related to budgeting and allocations to beneficiary agencies.

Subsequently, there was the struggle to cut loose from the tight controls exerted by the social agencies, on the grounds that central planning should be based on urban social problems that transcend the immediate interests of the constituent agencies. This development gave rise to a general change in outlook that resulted in the councils of social agencies becoming social planning communities throughout the United States and Canada.

In the 1970s, community workers bent on transforming social planning councils into independent local services at the metropolitan level began to press for what became known as advocacy planning (Gluskin and Rose 1979:314). The need to be free of the direct service agencies as controlling affiliates was reinforced by the rough passage many social planning councils experienced at the hands of the confronting poor, mobilized by various militants in the neighborhoods. The lesson learned in the 1960s about the high visibility of a central social welfare organization as an exposed target for social action was not lost on community workers. That, combined with the long-held aspiration of community work practitioners to see social planning applied as an independent form of social work intervention led to the final break with the coordinating role of some fifty councils in the United States and Canada.

The School Planning Council of Metropolitan Toronto is an example of this trend. It is sponsored by an independent board made up of volunteers knowledgeable in various aspects of planning and includes individuals connected with the social services. However, the latter do not function on the board as agency representatives. The responsibility for selecting research projects dealing with community needs, problems, and issues is in the hands of the board and the professional staff. Furthermore, the board and the professionals determine the approach to be taken in interpreting the findings to the community and in promoting or advocating recommendations for action leading to needed social change.

Should this trend become more generalized, community councils may succeed in becoming independent social agencies offering a direct service to a growing number of metropolitan areas on the North American continent. At the micro-end of the urban spectrum, community development workers remain committed to their work in the neighborhoods. In either case, the need to deal with social services left uncoordinated will become an issue in communities where the social planning councils have abandoned this role and CD workers have never accepted it. The ironies of history are such that the 1980s may conceivably see a return to the challenge of centralization prompted by gaps and duplication in uncoordinated services, which, in the first place, brought about the formation of the COS movement more than a century ago.

Notes

1. Social animation was the process by which community consciousness was raised as an initial step leading to planning and joint participation by the people, who were to put into effect various enterprises recommended by experts who had made comprehensive studies of

the resources and the potential of the different areas that had been earmarked for development in Quebec. The social animator's pervasive concern with processes of communication as a prerequisite to community participation is not, generally speaking, pursued with the same intensity by development workers. For further discussion see: Michel Blondin, *Animation Sociale* and Marc Morency, *Animation Sociale: The Experience of the BAEQ.*

2. The term ascribed status, used by sociologists to characterize a prior rank brought by an individual to the relationship with other actors, does not quite convey the social worker's role mastery in relation to the client. Assigned status describes more accurately a standing that is directly endowed by the practitioner's agency. The social worker's status is less autonomous than the physician's. The latter does not depend so much on the hospital or clinic as on external settings to provide the status the physician brings to the relationship with the patient, whereas the social worker's dependency on the agency for legitimation is much greater.

3. Clinard, in *Slums and Community Development,* points out that "Ross, a writer in the field of social work, uses the term 'community organization' in much the same way as 'community development' is used. Ross approaches community work from the perspective of the community as a natural system rather than as a rational model in the form of council structures" (Clinard 1970:134).

4. With the emergence of "scientific charity" under the COS, training took the place of "good intentions." Charles Lock, a leader of the COS movement, compared the trained helper to what he called, "the social physician" (Woodroofe 1966:55). In the United States, Mary Richmond continued to look to the medical profession as a model for social work in her pioneering efforts to lay the foundations for present-day casework. (Richmond 1930:100).

5. One of many such success stories is that of Muriel S-V reported in the *Toronto Globe and Mail,* January 27, 1981. Muriel, a former activist who battled oil companies and various government-sponsored agencies in Edmonton, Alberta, was head of Native Outreach, a job-finding agency for native people. She fought to secure compensation for native trappers whose livelihoods were threatened by oil and gas explorations. She is now community relations officer of Bechtel Canada, Ltd., a subsidiary of the American giant energy corporation.

References

Austin, David J. 1970. "Social Work's Relation to National Development in Developing Nations." *Social Work* (January), 15(1):97–106.

Batten, T. R. 1965. *The Human Factor in Community Work.* London: Oxford University Press.

Berger, Peter L. 1981. "Speaking to the Third World." *Commentary* (October), 72(4):29–36.

Biddle, William W. and Loureide J. Biddle. 1965. *The Community Development Process.* New York: Holt, Rinehart and Winston.

Blondin, Michel. 1968. *Animation Sociale.* Montreal: Conseil des Oeuvres de Montreal.

Brager, George A. 1968. "Advocacy and Political Behavior." *Social Work* (April), 13(2):5–15.

Brager, George A. and Francis P. Purcell, eds. 1967. *Community Action Against Poverty: Readings from the Mobilization Experience.* New Haven, Conn.: College and University Press.

92   B. Lappin

Brokensha, David and Peter Hodge. 1969. *Community Development: An Interpretation*. San Francisco: Chandler.

Bruno, Frank J. 1964. *Trends in Social Work: 1874–1956*. New York: Columbia University Press.

Camfens, Hubert. 1979. "Community Development Policy and Programme: Review and Conceptual Analysis." In Chekki, ed., *Community Development: Theory and Method of Planned Change*, pp. 201–20.

Canada Department of Agriculture. 1961. *A Rehabilitation Program in the Making*. Ottawa: Canada Department of Agriculture.

Chekki, Dan A. 1979. *Community Development: Theory and Method of Planned Change*. New Delhi: Vikas.

Clinard, Marshal B. 1970. *Slums and Community Development*. New York: Free Press.

Cloward, Richard A. 1964. *Community Organization Program of Mobilization for Youth*. New York: Mobilization for Youth.

Cohen, Nathan E., ed. 1958. *Social Work in the American Tradition*. New York: Dryden Press.

Cox, Fred M. et al., eds. 1979. *Strategies of Community Organization*. 3d ed. Itasca, Ill.: Peacock.

Dasgupta, Sugata. 1979. "Three Models of Community Development." In Chekki, ed., *Community Development: Theory and Method of Planned Change*, pp. 60–75.

Dillick, Sidney. 1953. *Community Organization for Neighborhood Development*. New York: Morrow.

Dunham, Arthur. 1959. "What Is the Job of the Community Organization Worker?" In Harper and Dunham, eds., *Community Organization in Action*, pp. 463–71.

——. 1960. "The Outlook for Community Development." *International Review of Community Development* (5):33–55.

Gilbert, Neil and Harry Specht. 1979. "Advocacy and Professional Ethics." In Cox et al., eds., *Strategies of Community Organization*, pp. 95–103.

Gluskin, Alan E. and Robert Rose. 1979. "Advocacy and Democracy: The Long View." In Cox et al., eds., *Strategies of Community Organization*, pp. 305–18.

Grosser, Charles F. 1965. "Community Development Programs Serving the Urban Poor." *Social Work* (July), 10(3):15–21.

——. 1973. *New Directions in Community Organization: From Enabling to Advocacy*. New York: Praeger.

Harper, Ernest B. and Arthur Dunham, eds. 1959. *Community Organization in Action*. New York: Association Press.

Harrington, Michael. 1962. *The Other America: Poverty in the Untied States*. New York: Macmillan.

Horowitz, Irving L., ed. 1963. *Power, Politics and People: The Collected Essays of C. Wright Mills*. New York: Ballantine.

Johnson, Arlien. 1959. "Methods and Skills in Community Organization." In Harper and Dunham, eds., *Community Organization in Action,* pp. 81–85.

Kindelsperger, Kenneth W. 1960. "Community Development and Community Organization." International Workshop held at Brandeis University, Waltham, Mass., sponsored by the Florence Heller Graduate School for Advanced Studies in Social Welfare and the NASW. New York: NASW.

Kramer, Ralph M. 1975. "The Influence of Sponsorship, Professionalism and the Civic Culture on the Theory and Practice of Community Development." In Kramer and Specht, eds., *Readings in Community Organization Practice,* pp. 184–95.

Kramer, Ralph M. and Harry Specht, eds. 1975. *Readings in Community Organization Practice.* 2d ed. Englewood Cliffs, N.J.: Prentice-Hall.

Lindeman, Edward C. 1921. *The Community.* New York: Association Press.

Lippitt, Ronald, Jeanne Watson, and Bruce Westley. 1958. *The Dynamics of Planned Change.* New York: Harcourt Brace.

Lotz, Jim. 1977. *Understanding Canada: Regional and Community Development in a New Nation.* Toronto: NC Pres.

Mok, Bong-Ho. 1979/1980. "Community Work Profiles in Hong Kong." *Community Development Resource Book,* pp. 1–9. Hong Kong: Hong Kong Council of Social Service.

Morency, Marc-A. 1968. *Animation Sociale: The Experience of the BAEQ.* Ottawa: Canadian Department of Forestry and Rural Development.

Newstetter, Wilbur I. 1947. "The Social Intergroup Work Process." In *Proceedings of the National Conference of Social Work, 1947,* pp. 205–17. New York: Columbia University Press.

Penketh, Anne. 1980. "Foreign Aid Eluding the Poor." Toronto *Globe and Mail,* September 15, p. 7.

Perlman, Robert and Arnold Gurin. 1972. *Community Organization and Social Planning.* New York: Wiley.

Rabagliati, Mary and Ezra Birnbaum. 1969. "Organization of Welfare Clients." In Weissman, ed., *Community Development in the Mobilization for Youth Experience,* pp. 102–36.

Richmond, Mary. 1930. *The Long View.* New York: Russell Sage Foundation.

Ross, Murray G. 1958. *Case Histories in Community Organization.* New York: Harper and Row.

Ross, Murray G. with Ben W. Lappin. 1967. *Community Organization: Theory, Principles and Practice.* New York: Harper and Row.

Rothman, Jack, 1979. "Three Models of Community Organization Practice: Their Mixing and Phasing." In Cox et al., eds., *Strategies of Community Organization,* pp. 25–45.

Sanders, Irwin T. 1958. *The Community.* New York: Ronald Press.

Sieder, Violet M. 1959. "Developing Goals and Methods of Community Organization." In Harper and Dunham, eds., *Community Organization in Action,* pp. 135–41.

Simmel, Georg. 1955. *Conflict and the Web of Group-Affiliations.* Glencoe, Ill.: Free Press.

Smith, Muriel. 1979. "Concepts of Community Work—A British View." In Chekki, ed., *Community Development: Theory and Method of Planned Change,* pp. 47–59.

Specht, Harry. 1969. "Disruptive Tactics." *Social Work* (April), 14(2):5–15.

Spergel, Irving A. 1969. *Community Problem Solving: The Delinquency Example.* Chicago: University of Chicago Press.

Steiner, Jesse. 1925. *Community Organization.* New York: Century Press.

Terrell, Paul. 1971. "The Social Worker as Radical: Roles of Advocacy." In Weinberger, ed., *Perspectives on Social Welfare,* pp. 355–62.

Thomas, Edwin J., ed. 1968. *Behavioral Science for Social Workers.* New York: Free Press.

Thursz, Daniel. 1971. "The Arsenal of Social Action Strategies: Options for Social Work." *Social Work* (January), 16(1):27–41.

Warren, Roland L. 1963. *The Community in America.* Chicago: Rand McNally.

Webb, Beatrice. 1929. *My Apprenticeship.* London: Longmans, Green.

Weinberger, Paul E., ed. 1969. *Perspectives on Social Welfare: An Introductory Anthology.* New York: Macmillan.

Weissman, Harold H., ed. 1969. *Community Development in the Mobilization for Youth Experience.* New York: Association Press.

Woodroofe, Kathleen. 1966. *From Charity to Social Work.* London: Routledge and Kegan Paul.

4

Program Development and Service Coordination as Components of Community Practice

Paul A. Kurzman

Program development and service coordination as a model of social work community practice have their roots in the early charity organization societies and therefore may be considered the oldest theoretical approach to community practice. Focusing on the coordination of existing services and the development of support and resources for new service arrangements, it is intended to be a rational and incremental model that underscores study, planning, problem identification, initiation, and evaluation. Identifying community needs, assessing remedies, and harnessing community resources and support to address these problems has become a classic model of effective program development and service coordination activity.

Theorists of community work have seen this aspect of professional practice as involving both process and outcome goals in unison. Campbell Murphy (1954), for example, has viewed community organization as a process and skill in helping to identify and respond to areas of social need, and a field of activity concerned with agency coordination, fund raising, promotion of social legislation and coordination of social welfare activities. Murray Ross (1955) defined community practice as a process of identifying community needs and objectives and the will and resources of the community to meet them, and as the task of developing and extending cooperative attitudes and practices toward the goal of community integration. Rothman (1979) perceives program development and service coordination as closest to the social planning model, but with some mixing and phasing with the locality development model to ensure capacity building and to promote service integration.

The model presupposes neutrality, rationality, and cooperation. Issues must be amenable to mediation, objectivity should be maintained, and conflict avoided in favor of cooperative participation. In addition, this approach to practice encourages formalism, professionalism, and incrementalism. In lieu of the spontaneous and informal, arrangements should be agreed upon in advance. Instead of radical change, gradual and additive measures would be proposed; and, rather than assesssments being a lay or paraprofessional function, the technical expertise of a trained professional would be expected. While the resource coordination dimension would focus on what Rein and Morris have termed the typical process-oriented goals of council-type organizations, the program development aspect would underscore the task goals of a promotional type of organizational arrangement (Rein and Morris 1962).

Many community-based organizations perform these functions. Among them are neighborhood councils, task forces, planning committees, and advisory boards. Historically, one of these has been more influential than all the others: the community welfare council. Because all of the permutations of community agencies which address this activity cannot be described, and since the community welfare council has both historical and prototypical significance as a dominant force in the growth and development of community practice, its evolution will be discussed in depth as a case example.

Historical Overview

Arthur Dunham defines the community welfare council as "a local association of citizens, agencies, or both, which unites citizen interest and professional skill in planning for and acting on social and health problems. It seeks to determine current and emerging health and welfare needs, develop plans to meet them, and carry these plans to fruition" (1970:438). Councils have their historical roots in the development of the Charity Organization Society (COS) which began in 1877 in response to rapid urbanization and industrialization and the effects of the Great Depression of 1873. Patterned after the London Society for Organizing Charitable Relief and Repressing Mendicancy, the COS attempted to achieve some rationality in social welfare by managing the entire voluntary system based upon the most respected social science principles of the time. By the turn of the century, the COS dominated the scene, ensuring interagency cooperation and collaboration and establishing the service registration or clearinghouse concept (social service exchange) to avoid duplication and promote resource coordination. The COS was separate from the public sector entirely.

The moving force in establishment of the COS concept in America was Stephen Humphreys Gurteen, a minister in Buffalo, New York, who had studied the London model and adapted it to his community. Launched with the enthusiastic support of community leaders in business and the professions, the concept quickly spread to Boston, Philadelphia, Indianapolis, and Detroit. Based in urban, industrial communities, it stressed abolishing public relief and replacing "the existing chaos of almsgiving by systematically coordinated private philanthropy" (Lewis 1977:97). Among the key concepts embodied in the COS method and structure were voluntarism, nonsectarianism, report and survey, personal service, and, above all, interagency cooperation.

The first community welfare council was founded from these roots in 1908 and quickly was followed by others in most major American cities. Its primary, if not exclusive, function was coordination of voluntary services, and the executive usually was considered the first among equals in the local social welfare community. Right up to and through World War II, the commnity welfare councils rarely initiated or operated programs. "The council is only a coordinating body, it is not organized for social action in its own name. Problems which require professional skill are referred to the agencies where the skill is to be found" (King 1939:100). In the 1950s, the community welfare council boards moved from domination by representatives from member agencies to control by prominent, independent laymen, and the focus changed from coordination to community-based welfare planning. The growth of federated fund raising during World War II developed into permanent community chest and united funds, creating an emphasis on rational planning for agency use of these funds as an outcome measure to replace the process orientation inherent in a coordinating function. In the 1960s, what had been the National Organization of United Community Councils of America (and is now the United Way of America) significantly added "Funds" to its umbrella title. It then assumed authority to determine program goals and priorities, and to reward voluntary agencies accordingly. Even if some duplication and overlap occurred, the public emphasis now was on efficiency, planning, and willingness to respond to community priorities as determined by this new federated, supraorganization.

The community welfare councils, however, had new issues and constituencies to accommodate. The politics of the 1960s challenged the authority of the council boards, composed as they were almost exclusively of middle-class lay persons who often neither lived nor worked in the communities being served. New sources of funds were available—increasingly public—which were equal to, or greater than, those the various united funds could provide; and staff work, having become more prestigious and better rewarded, became sought after by other human service professionals trained in public health, urban planning, and public affairs. Staff positions no longer were exclusively a social work domain. The scope of service began to broaden from social welfare to human services, and as other professions laid claim to staff roles, so did citizens begin to demand participation on boards.

The most recent step in the evolution of community welfare councils has involved their move into a service role, even though they continue to perform a planning function. Their direct-service role, generally through a contract or purchase-of-service arrangement, has made their coordination function more difficult to achieve, since councils now are in a competitive stance for contracts with other voluntary agencies whom they wish to coordinate. Their planning authority in the voluntary sector also has become circumscribed by their dual role as councils *and* operating agencies, since their community-wide planning no longer could be seen as truly objective and neutral.

For those community welfare councils that merged with their local United Way, planning primarily was for the United Way organization itself and for the member agencies it funded. For councils that remained independent, planning, research, and advocacy might be community-wide in scope. These councils served as experts among local community organizations and as providers of up-to-date demographic data that could be used for community planning, priority-setting, and grant applications. Such councils became professional consultants to local groups, city-wide agencies, and even to public bodies on a municipal or metropolitan level. Nonprofit and nonpublic, they were removed from the proprietary motives of private enterprise and, to some degree, from the partisan politics of the public arena (Tropman and Tropman 1977:187; Dunham 1970).

Independent councils today, therefore, often are recognized as impartial professional experts—a blue-ribbon panel without professional vested interests. As such, they can do some jurisdictional arbitration among member agencies and plan with them according to a rational planning model. "It is the function of the planning organization," note Perlman and Gurin, "to concert the specialized activities and resources of its constituents in order to achieve goals that supersede those of the individual components" (1972:187). Councils often are criticized, however, as being mainly concerned with adjusting and improving existing arrangements rather than with imaginative long-range planning and the promotion of social change. Critics feel that community welfare councils have stayed artificially separate from government agencies and legitimate indigenous community organizations. Community groups feel that councils are increasingly less independent from the united fund-raising organization and tend to avoid controversy in order to promote consensus at all costs. Moreover, the health and welfare coordinating and planning function today is hardly the exclusive domain of the voluntary sector. As will be discussed later, the role of the public sector has enlarged since the 1930s to parallel or even to supplant that of the voluntary community with respect to service and resource coordination—especially in large urban areas of the country.

The influential Lane Report in 1939 cited the community welfare council as the *only* urban community organization to organize community resources to meet community needs (Lane 1939). However, there are now several such agencies in most cities, and many are public. They include, for example, human service departments, comprehensive employment and manpower councils, health systems agencies, urban development authorities, criminal justice coordinating councils, and municipal planning commissions. The Comprehensive Employment and Training Act, National Health Planning and Resources Development Act, Economic Opportunity Act, and Title XX of the Social Security Act are among the major pieces of national legislation that have carved out a role for new quasi-public bodies to assume a planning, coordinating role on a municipal or regional basis. Their influence over grants from the authorizing legislation gives these bodies, and the federal or state departments they represent, an influence which directly affects the voluntary as well as the public sector.

Moreover, due to the organizational structure of the public sector, and the categorical form of many grants, a new importance has emerged for the *functional* definition of community, which increasingly is transcending the geographical boundaries by which community welfare councils were established. In addition, identification and organizational loyalty in local communities by class, race, ethnicity, sex, and age frequently have begun to outweigh a commitment to geographically drawn boundaries. These contemporary realities pose obvious problems for local community welfare councils in light of their perceived program development and service coordination function.

Future alignments between voluntary social agencies and local United Ways may be presaged also by the development of the United Way of America Services Identification System (UWASIS). It is intended to aid in "developing proper directions in needs-delineating, priorities-planning, problem-solving, and service-delivery" (1972:1). The idea that UWASIS can establish overall national goals and that program identification can be relatively uniform throughout the nation is subject to debate. The Family Service Association of America (FSAA), the umbrella organization for local family service agencies, has serious reservations about the United Way's ability and authority to establish directions for program development affecting the entire voluntary sector (FSAA 1971:1). Clearly, localism and pluralism are forces which mitigate against the intentions of UWASIS; in addition, the importance of governmental planning and grant-making makes the UWASIS form of priority-setting appear somewhat unrealistic.

Perlman and Gurin have identified the forms of planning, coordination, and program development responsibility they think may be assumed by community welfare councils in view of the current stance and position of the United Way: setting minimum standards for affiliated agencies, providing information and other services, reviewing budgets and programs, coordinating existing services, organizing new services, determining priorities, and long-range planning (1972:194–96). Under current pluralistic conditions, however, voluntary agencies will be responding to many different drummers and not to the United Way alone. FSAA and the Child Welfare League of America, for example, have established their own accreditation standards for their member agencies; and budgets of United Way member agencies today are receiving more support from public funds than from the United Way itself, making review and priority-setting by the United Way more difficult to achieve. Coordination increasingly is being provided by umbrella voluntary organizations and by quasi-public bodies, making this a well-occupied terrain. Hence, achieving the goals of program development and resource coordination today may require different assumptions, and a reconceptualization of the options and the alternatives.

Conceptual Issues

A manifest assumption might lead one to accept the notion that community welfare councils, voluntary agencies, and the clients they serve all benefit from orderly program development and service integration. Such a logical conceptualization speaks to the obvious benefits that accrue to all parties through establishing a rational set of goals, adjusting them over time to changing client need, and avoiding the waste inherent in overlap and duplication of services. Such a rational model underscores the advantages of cooperation, coordination, consensus, and unity of purpose between funding and service organizations in the health and welfare sector.

Traditionally, however, more well-established voluntary agencies have tended to benefit most by such an arrangement because they have the leverage to deviate from cooperative action when they wish and usually have independent sources of status and legitimation. In addition, they benefit much more from the United Way formula grants (base allocations) which reward past fund-raising achievement than do new agencies which have commitments to meet current social needs. That is, the formula for distribution of the more than $1.7 billion collected by the United Way each year rests on the relative strength of the parties, as measured by their past ability to raise their own funds. Hence, relatively wealthy, sophisticated agencies are protected by a floor or core grant which usually represents a significant portion of United Way annual agency contributions. Smaller, newer, innovative, and more controversial agencies must first compete to be accepted as a United Way agency, must then agree to sacrifice most of their own freedom to raise funds from the lucrative corporate sector, and then compete for the residual United Way monies after formula grants are given to the more established social agencies. While distribution (reward) is supposed to be rational, impartial and objective, it is not unusual for new agencies with novel and sometimes controversial programs to find themselves bypassed in favor of the known agencies and pre-existing arrangements. The goal of self-renewal gives way to self-protection, as United Ways seek not to offend the more powerful agencies who might be able to go it alone and raise funds in competition with the United Ways' money-raising campaign.

As Perlman and Gurin note, "it is only as the basis for fund-allocation moves away from the negotiated formula to an examination of community needs that the potentialities for planning and program development begin to emerge" (1972:194). While the principle of the negotiated formula often would seem inconsistent with the manifest functions of self-renewal, this enduring rule fulfills the latent objective of the United Way—self-protection and survival. As I have noted elsewhere, "as rules reduce the 'costs' of decision-making . . . they also serve to protect the institution itself against a crisis that could jeopardize organizational equilibrium—its place within the broader social system" (Kurzman 1977:426). As Selznick states, "a given empirical system is deemed to have basic needs, essentially related to self-maintenance . . . the system develops repetitive means of self-defense, and day-to-day activity is interpreted in terms of the function served by that activity for the maintenance and defense of the system" (1961:25). The organizational unification of formally independent community welfare councils with the United Fund in most communities today—under the umbrella of the United Way of America—makes problematical the question of community welfare councils' independence and authority as the primary instrument for service coordination.

In his classic case study, John Seeley looked at the manifest and latent functions of a typical community chest (the United Fund). Among the tensions he noted were the chests' overt commitment to the concept of voluntary giving versus their tendency to push for universal giving and maximum return. Related to this was their tendency to promote their "One Gift" idea (i.e, payroll deduction plan) aggressively rather than honestly describing it, and their policy to extract money from a community rather than focus on building community services (Seeley 1957).

United Ways have been pushed recently to change the negotiated formula principle on the grounds of equity, and to begin to embrace new agencies more readily. Although little change has occured, from a program development and service coordination view, the arguments in favor of change have been persuasive. Hasenfeld, for example, argues that:

Developing [or supporting] a new agency to serve certain needs has the clear advantage of freeing the planner from the constraints of existing arrangements. These may include competing objectives of ongoing community agencies as well as tradition, and the custom of following established procedure. (1979:141)

He goes on to note, however, that overcoming such obstacles and constraints is by no means easy. Conceptually, as I have suggested elsewhere, one of the main problems is that community welfare councils and united funds, like all institutions, essentially "are social organisms that must learn to create a homeostatic relationship with their environment so that they can continue to win support and maintain stability as one planet in the orbit of the solar system" (Kurzman 1977:429).

Behavioral and Social Science Foundations

In 1967, Roland Warren surveyed the community social work literature and found marked deficiencies in references to the social
sciences; he observed specifically that important theories frequently
were neglected in the practice of community organization. Warren's
observation, while accurate at the time, fortunately does not hold to
the same degree today, given the excellent work that has been published in the past fifteen years.

Examples of behavioral and social science breakthroughs are
evident in many areas, including community decision-making theory, communications theory, reference group theory, probability
theory, and contingency management, to name but a few. Bennis,
Benne, and Chin's revised volume on planned change, issued in
1969, was an influential example of a compendium of new theoretical and methodological perspectives relevant to human service systems. Rothman's (1974) systematic and encyclopedic analysis of
more than five hundred empirical social science research studies
over a six-year period drew out action principles for program development and community planning from new social science discov-
eries. Thomas (1968) and Bloom (1969) separately explored the
behavioral sciences for new knowledge that could be applied to
community social work interventions, and Perrow (1970) explored
sociological theory for its utility and applicability to managerial and
administrative roles in community-based health and welfare organizations. Many of these studies were summarized by Rothman and
Epstein in their article on the social science foundations of community practice, in the *Encyclopedia of Social Work* (1977:1433–43).

In light of the advances in community practice through the
application of social science knowledge, one now might pose several issues that affect program development and service coordination in general, and the role of community welfare councils and
united funds in particular. I suggest three: (1) the inherent strain in
the quest for both community innovation and community integration; (2) the dichotomy that persists between rational and pluralistic
models of intervention; and (3) the tripartite tension that occurs
among the contending goals of individualism, centralism, and pluralism.

One of the dilemmas, Mayer notes, is that community welfare councils may not be the best structure through which to meet the twin goals of community integration and service innovation. Achieving cooperation and integration depends in part on an organizational leadership's adherence to these goals over others, in spite of their identification and loyalties through other memberships and community commitments. Since community welfare councils generally are not organizations that command primary membership loyality (such as churches, fraternal clubs, and trade unions), a council's reference group function may not be as binding for the voluntary board leaders as for the primary groups to which they belong. Moreover, because community welfare councils are created as intergroup organizations, social change often is feasible only when consensus can be achieved and no group member's boundaries are threatened by the proposed innovation. Therefore, such councils are more apt to become moderating, conciliatory forces than initiators of social change (Mayer 1972:103–5).

A rational model of decision-making and resource allocation is stresssed by United Way organizations. Facts are gathered about community needs, and both needs and agencies are subjected to a ranking process. Using an open systems model, United Ways state that they are committed to implementing a priority-planning process that will make possible rational and equitable decisions. However, such a process seldom takes place. First, United Ways apply the principle of "base allocation" to protect member agencies, and thus budget review does not begin with a zero base. Second, certain prestigious and influential agencies, such as the Boy Scouts, Urban League, and American Red Cross, may be informally guaranteed special consideration and therefore a protected allocation not tied strictly to the formula process. While the manifest policy of a priority-planning process may meet the United Way's latent organizational need for self-protection, and an appearance of fairness and rationality, it tends to be unrealistic and lacking in candor. In Stanley Wenocur's terms, United Way priority planning "has tended to be a costly and protracted exercise in futility" (1976:588).

Herbert Simon, in his treatise which contributed to his Nobel Prize recognition, noted that all decisions are based on both fact *and* value assertions, and therefore strictly rational choice "will be feasible only to the extent that the limited set of factors upon which a decision is based corresponds, in nature, to a closed system of variables" (1965:83). Although United Way's public adherence to a rational and factual priority-planning and allocation system may be a conflict-resistant organizational style, it generally proves neither feasible nor ideal. A problem-solving stance, structuring some uncertainty into decision-making and welcoming a collaborative process that reflects changing community values, would be more equitable and realistic. Applying Simon's insights on decision-making to the urban planning area, Davidoff cautions that "appropriate planning action cannot be prescribed from a position of value neutrality." He recommends a compromise that preserves the essence of the priority-planning concept in the context of a process that is flexible, equitable, and more likely to succeed (Davidoff 1965:331).

Simon's other major theoretical contribution to the science of organization was his clarification of the difference between "economic man" and "administrative man." The former, dominant at the time, involved maximizing benefit and outcome in each situation. Economic man strived to corner the market and control inputs and outputs in a planned and centralized fashion. The concept of administrative man, which is more appropriate in social service situations, "satisfices"—looks for a flexible and pluralistic solution that is satisfactory or "good enough." Examples of "satisficing" solutions, stated in economic terms, would be those of "sharing the market," stating a "fair price," or making an "adequate profit" (Simon 1965:xxv).

The tension among models that underscore notions of individualism, centralism, or pluralism follows from the foregoing issues in the context of contemporary America. Until recently, social welfare in this country was small, local, and voluntary. Today it is a large portion of the gross national product, increasingly public, and national in scope and organization. The organizational reference for service coordination, standards, and program planning has changed as the agencies—and their relationship to each other and to the larger social system—have been altered. Warren sees the contemporary community in two distinct frames of reference: as a horizontal system by which units are linked with each other at the local, intracommunity level, and as a vertical system by which units are linked with extracommunity units at the regional, state, and national level

(1963). Individualism, although historically a central theme in American life, inevitably has given way in part to the reality of individual and organizational interdependence, just as centralist notions have been tempered by respect for the richness of heterogeneity and difference, the reality of federalism, and the local push for community control.

Gilbert and Specht face the issue squarely. Among the three concepts of planning, central or unitary planning by government planning commissions or voluntary community welfare councils is as unrealistic as town meeting involvement of individuals and groups interacting directly. They advocate a middle-range approach—pluralistic in form—which "conceives of planning as a contentious process involving the clash of different interests in the community," but they emphasize organizational rather than individualistic competition (Gilbert and Specht 1974:178–99). Such an approach to planning and program development implicitly recognizes the role of values as well as facts; the validity of multiple loci of wisdom and authority, not of one alone; and the legitimacy, indeed the importance, of conflict as well as consensus. They suggest that the pursuit of rationality at times may itself be irrational. While facts may be the same, values may be different, and then planning decisions must rest on whose values will dominate, or what compromises among competing values will be reached as organizational interests contend in an open forum. Is there any basis, one could argue, that planning and coordination of services will be any more efficient or equitable when done primarily by a single planning council than through other new and more pluralistic organizational forms?

In this light, two contemporary contenders for this community planning and coordination function deserve mention. First, there are what Alan Pifer, a leading spokesperson for nongovernmental organizations, has called "quasi non-governmental instrumentalities" (1967:4). Independent of the traditional social welfare structure, they have authority to carry out a designated public purpose, such as overseeing publicly funded programs (Model Cities, Comprehensive Employment, Title XX). Second, there are those locality-based citizen organizations that have emerged from a movement in the community toward maximum feasible participation and community control. They vary from local school boards and community planning boards to organizational advisory committees and neighborhood councils. Eisinger defines the emergence of these bodies as the process of "control-sharing," which gives birth to a pluralistic

. . . political and administrative arrangement in which authority over policy decisions such as establishment of program priorities, service levels, and personnel choices is shared among professional bureaucrats, elected and appointed officials, and citizen representatives of geographical neighborhoods or participating client groups. (1974:459)

The contributions of social science should lead to a more sophisticated understanding of the organizational dilemmas, and illustrate the actual complexity of seemingly consensual issues such as program planning and resource coordination. They also point toward resolutions of these quandaries which may maximize goal achievement in a context that respects pluralism, the democratic process, and the values of the social work profession.

Worker Function and Skills

There are five broad areas of skills which the community developer and coordinator must begin to master: organizational skills, strategic or political skills, analytic skills, relationship or engagement skills, and administrative or management skills. Among these, the first three are the most important for successful practice and deserve further elaboration.

Organizational skills are necessary in order to develop, build, and sustain a constituency that will make an impact on a social problem. This skill includes the ability to identify problems, attain goals through program activities, and establish priorities. Organizational skills are required in order to ensure collective action that will have an impact on a social issue. Examples include the ability to identify problems, attain goals through program activities, establish an appropriate group or organizational structure, plan and conduct conferences and campaigns, and weigh multiple, competing concerns in order to help establish priorities.

Strategic or political skills are required in order to ensure collective action that will have an impact on a social issue. Examples include the ability to assess interests and commitments of parties to a transaction, identify internal and external sources of influence and power, strengthen the cohesiveness of one's constituency, and identify areas of conflict and converging interests among the parties. Implicitly necessary, therefore, are persuasiveness in both verbal and written communication, a talent for negotiation, and an ability to identify appropriate compromise positions. Moreover, analytic skill implies the ability to study a situation or problem, to assess past efforts to deal with it, and to identify additional information which might be required. In addition, the worker must be able to define a focus relevant to the central issues which incorporates an assessment of both the opportunities and the constraints posed by the context of the situation. Finally, the community worker must be able to organize and systematically deal with the range of goals, strategies, and resources which may need to be devised to solve the problem, and then specify in detail the tasks which need to be performed, by whom, and with what resources.

While no one worker necessarily will master all of these skills equally or deploy his or her talents in equal degree, these skills suggest the need for progressive mastery of a range of overlapping and interrelated skills in order to claim professional expertise. While there is frequently a degree of specialization, with some community workers deploying their mastery of verbal presentation and negotiation while others perform the critical internal roles which demand polished analytic and writing talent, supervisory and administrative positions require not only deeper mastery but a greater range and repertoire of skills as well. A conceptual capacity to see the whole as more than the sum of its parts and a creative talent for seeing beyond the obvious to the possible become demarcations for the worker who has potential for leadership within the organization and the community.

Workers with such skills would be employed by public and voluntary agencies and organizations throughout the country. These include international, national, state, and local organizations such as the United Nations, International Red Cross, the National Institute for Mental Health, the American Heart Association, a state department of human services, a state health and welfare coalition, a county child welfare administration, and municipal associations of agencies serving the aged. Agencies can be defined by field of practice (health-related organizations such as heart, lung, cancer, or kidney foundations); by commitment to race or ethnicity (a human rights commission, the Italian American League, the NAACP); by sectarian or nonsectarian sponsorship (Lutheran Service League, Catholic Charities, Jewish Welfare Board), and so forth. These public and voluntary organizations deal with issues ranging from public education to civil liberties, from child welfare to rehabilitation services.

To visualize the range of functions and activities a community worker might pursue in one of these settings, one may turn to descriptions of agency functions. For example, the Child Welfare League of America states that

[It] serves as a clearinghouse for information, knowledge and experience in the field of child welfare and is a coordinating body through which all who are concerned with the well-being of children can combine their efforts. As an accrediting and standard-setting agency, it works with agencies, community groups and individuals. It provides consultation, conducts research, develops standards for service, sponsors annual regional conferences . . . conducts surveys at the request of individual agencies or communities, administers special projects, engages in legislative research, and publishes professional literature, newsletters, and an annual directory of affiliates. (NASW 1980:33)

Similarly, the Council of Jewish Federations helps to

organize community resources to meet effectively local, regional, national and overseas Jewish needs. It serves as a cooperative association of and central clearinghouse for member agencies and acts as their instrument in dealing with national and overseas Jewish problems. . . . Its Community Planning Department conducts research on local trends in health and social welfare and aids in planning community studies and surveys. . . . The annual general assembly and regional conferences of the council bring together national and local lay and professional leaders to exchange experiences, consider common problems, and coordinate their planning and activities in welfare work and Jewish communal organization. (NASW 1980:36)

As one can see, the worker's skills and function for central tasks in these and similar organizations will involve major responsibility for program initiation and human and fiscal resource coordination. These settings, in all their variety and range, constitute prototypes for deployment of the skilled community worker.

Organizational Consequences of Change

Twenty years ago, Schottland pointed out the inability of local planning agencies to handle the impact of various emerging federal programs, and the idle hope that community welfare councils would emerge as the basic planning or program development mechanism at the local or national level (1963). A few years later, Roland Warren noted that the resulting organizational complexity of the social welfare arena made a dominant role for any one single organization, even in the voluntary sector, wholly unrealistic. The time when the community welfare council could aspire to be *the* instrument of community planning and program coordination had passed, as the texture of the organizational environment began to reflect a multiplicity of organizations exercising a planning function (1967b:401).

Unanticipated consequences deriving from new sources of public funds, the establishment of quasi-governmental planning bodies, and the emergence of agencies with advocacy as a primary focus made all past notions organizationally dated. New sources of power, sanction, and authority were challenging the status quo. This country's immigrants were beginning to reject the "melting pot" notion of a homogeneous America in favor of accenting heterogenity and difference. Not only were sophisticated theories of social conflict evolving, but many agencies were taking on social change as a primary professional function (Coleman 1957; Coser 1956; Alinsky 1969). Previous social science theories that envisioned community power in unitary terms (Lynd 1937; Hunter 1953) were being challenged by studies that gave evidence of varied loci of community power (Dahl 1961; Sayre and Kaufman 1965) which would defy the traditional elite, pyramid-of-power design (Hawley and Wirt 1968). As an outcome of the later community-based studies, other theoreticians validated these observations. Gamson, for example, noted the reasons that some efforts toward community action had failed and wrote: "Don't assume that those who are influential on some types of issues will be influential on [all]" (1965:356). Many constituencies had to be responded to within both the formal, recognized power structures (political, religious, financial) *and* the informal structure—the latter sometimes identified by race (black power), age (gray power), sex (womanpower), and neighborhood (power to the people). Each made a claim on community decision-making and resource allocation.

Rational organizations, such as community welfare councils, found they absorbed "irrationality" with great difficulty. New, informal, and homogeneous organizations refused to accept being bypassed by the formal structure simply because they did not meet established funding criteria. Following different norms of organizational behavior, they often pursued nontraditional means to achieve their ends. Efforts at co-optation at small cost, through allocation of token grants on a one-time basis, would not suffice to quiet their protest. Since other quasi-public bodies now had coordinating sanction, and alternative public sources of funding were available to new organizations, the community welfare councils found themselves in competition for authority within the voluntary sector, and their very legitimacy as first among equals being openly questioned. As Reid has noted, ultimately, unless the coordinating agency can use "its resource leverage to promote cooperative activity among service organizations, the amount of coordination resulting may be minimal" (1975:127). This goal was increasingly difficult to achieve since United Way allocations were not keeping up with public funding during the 1960s and, by 1974, the sum raised by United Way campaigns represented only 22 percent of the year's total budget for their member agencies (Levin 1977:1575).

There always had been a tacit agreement among agencies in the community not to pursue funds vigorously for controversial and, therefore, what might be perceived as organizationally divisive purposes. The most powerful agencies profited from this philosophy, since few people of power in the community felt threatened by the goals, for example, of the Red Cross or Boy Scouts. Funding for black heritage programs, legal advocacy centers, and abortion counseling clinics were an entirely different matter that could separate institutions and people with power along lines of race, sex, and religion. Moreover, the demands for inclusion by new agencies challenged the record of responsiveness of the federated United Fund and Welfare Councils, undercut the Fund's authority and stature, and implied that participating agencies might get a smaller allocation if new agencies were accommodated.

With their resources becoming only one funding option among many, and their sanction for exclusive domain of the voluntary sector in question, community welfare councils responded cautiously, indeed naïvely. By not moving toward voluntary agency accreditation, for example, which might have been an option for setting standards and reestablishing sanction, and by not shifting their allocation process to recognize the realities of consumer movements and the growing pattern of pluralism, the United Way and its councils failed to seize some of the available options. By organizational abdication, the scene was set for conflict and for change.

The Public Sector

While we have taken the voluntary community welfare council as a case example, the issues faced in the public sector are similar if not frequently the same. The question of how a program planning and coordinating agency achieves its multiple goals in a competitive and ever-changing environment poses issues that respond well to remarkably parallel conceptualizations and solutions.

Consider the municipal manpower planning council that must decide whether to delegate all responsibility for program operations to community agencies or to run some programs itself; whether to favor those agencies with the greatest experience and sophistication or to risk significant allocations to new, indigenous community organizations; whether to distribute job slots based on past performance or on future potential; whether to designate as a priority for job training those teenagers most likely to use the opportunity well, and succeed, or those teenagers who are most disadvantaged and who have the fewest alternative opportunities, but are less likely to succeed.

Similarly, should consumers (program participants) be included in significant numbers on public planning and coordinating boards, or should those with the greatest professional expertise dominate the decision-making? Should the twin responsibilities of community integration and service innovation rest with one public advisory body, or should they be separated as an inherently poor mix? In allocating funds and in providing expensive technical assistance, should one follow a principle of strict equality, or one of equity, with additional resources and outreach to institutions representing the most disadvantaged populations? To what extent, if any, should multipurpose organizations be favored over single-purpose ones? Should sectarian agencies be supported without distinction from those which are nonsectarian? When a ceiling is placed on Title XX monies, does one spread resources evenly, or is this a time to concentrate resources? When many new and innovative organizations come forward, is this a time to "zero base" program supports or even the time to add new agencies? When new procedures are promulgated, should one hold a community (public) hearing, or disseminate the new guidelines in writing, or both?

The shift of responsibility of human service programs from voluntary to public auspices during the Great Depression of the 1930s and especially after World War II made these programs federal, state, and local responsibilities for the first time. In the pursuit of rational planning, quantitative analysis and measurement were brought forward on a large scale, and power increasingly was transferred from the local to the state and national level. Program planning and coordinating agencies had to be set up to deal with familiar issues involving questions of equality versus equity. Solomon-like decisions had to be made as to whether, with limited resources, to strengthen services to abused and neglected children or to homeless and abandoned adults. What we have discussed through the case example of the community welfare council applies conceptually as well to program development and coordination agencies in the public sector, except that priorities here are often set by legislatures and elected officials. A pluralistic approach generally can be both fair and efficient, and can include different organizational actors in an arrangement for different reasons—but to accomplish the same goal.

Implications for the Future

If the United Way does not choose to adapt to contemporary realities, the implications will be far-reaching for the voluntary sector.

Community welfare councils, as an arm of the United Way in social history, clearly have been a major force in promoting program development and service coordination. If new, nontraditional, consumer-oriented social agencies bypass the United Way by seeking funds from other sources or in competition with them, not only may those who provide the core of voluntary philanthropy be disillusioned and give less, but the community welfare councils' sanction to provide coordination and program innovation may be seriously diminished. This loss to the community would not be easily overcome, even through governmental activity.

A solution stems from the application of exchange theory (Homans 1958; Blau 1964). Levine and White define organizational exchange as "any voluntary activity between two organizations which has consequences, actual or anticipated, for the realization of their respective goals or objectives" (1961:588). Cooperation among agencies in carrying out direct-service activities, for example, involves exchanges of information (social service exchanges), of clients (referrals), and of services (one provides day care for children; another, for seniors). The exchanges may be tangible (funds, technical assistance, personnel) or intangible (sanction, turf, autonomy), but they assume a pluralistic model as a given. By definition, exchange induces cooperation, participation, and coordination by respecting the principles of mutuality and organization domain.

Let us take a case in point. Perhaps the most controversial current issue involving the United Way of America with respect to voluntary community agencies is the United Way's right to a monopoly—sole access to the workplace—for charitable payroll deductions. Just as payroll deduction (withholding) is the surest, safest, most acceptable and economical form of income tax collection, so is it the most reliable and desirable form of voluntary fund raising in America. Nationwide, payroll deductions at the workplace furnish more than two thirds of United Way income, which was, for example, $1.78 billion in 1982. And figures from a recent survey made by the United Way itself showed that nearly 90 percent of local United Ways reported *no* competition at any of the business offices they solicited for contributions (Bothwell and Saasta 1979:85).

The United Way has responded to critics by defending its right to sole access as crucial to the "one gift" idea. They have insisted that a worker's payroll deduction for the United Way fulfills his or her total financial obligation to voluntary social welfare in the community. The United Way then declared an open-door policy toward admission of new agencies as members. Local United Ways, however, found that much of their energies and resources were now being devoted to "preserving a sensitive, labile equilibrium, frequently through crisis-oriented negotiating" (Rabinowitz, Simmeth, and Spero 1979:281). Tension reduction and conflict mediation quickly became overriding organizational goals. Goal displacement was taking place, and efforts toward organization maintenance were dominating their primary goal of raising funds. In the end, few new agencies were being admitted, and those that were received smaller allocations than they had expected.

The consequences were boycotts of local United Way campaigns and the formation of local fund-raising federations to compete directly with United Way at the workplace, such as the National Black United Fund, the Combined Health Appeal, the Bread and Roses Community Fund, and the Women's Funding Coalition. These new federations cited research by the National Committee for Responsive Philanthropy documenting that "profound changes in society and in the voluntary sector during the past two decades are not reflected in lists of United Way agencies, lists which read as if the civil rights or women's or environmental or consumer movements never happened" (Bothwell and Saasta 1979:85).

ADAPTATION TO CHANGE

When service coordination began to be implemented as a form of community organization and planning, it was responsive to contemporary issues. The growth of separate private philanthropies had to be monitored to see that scarce private resources were appropriately distributed to those deemed needy (and worthy), with a minimum of duplication, waste, and overlap. Important as well was the notion of maintaining an incentive for the poor to better their condition by never giving them too much, or too great a discretion over what they were to receive, or how often. Consistent with the social, religious, and economic philosophy of the day, one did not want to "pauperize" a class of recipients; one should never give cash; one should demonstrate a proper model of behavior; and one should envision the matter as a private issue to be met by private, voluntary donors rather than a public issue to be supported by government policy and public funds.

With the growth of public sector involvement first during the Great Depression of the 1930s and further after the end of World War II, there began to be a feeling that developing and coordinating programs for the poor were primarily public responsibilities, albeit in cooperation with the private sector. Expectations that government, especially through a national social policy, should be predominant grew with the Great Society programs of the late 1960s and early 1970s, culminating in the federal government's fiscal and programmatic commitment to supporting the War on Poverty, underwritten primarily by public dollars. We had come full cycle.

Present efforts represent movement toward a middle ground that would harness public and voluntary resources under new forms of collaborative public-private sponsorship. In this evolution of community practice we have witnessed the progress of an almost Hegelian dialectic where thesis and antithesis (action and reaction) have begun to move toward synthesis as an outcome. It is in this sense that we envision a pluralistic solution as a natural contemporary condition that has evolved organically from the disparate experiences—the "pushes" and the "pulls"—of the past.

At first glance one might see a pluralistic direction for community practice as an abandonment of rationality and principle. One even could envision such movement as a disarrangement of planning and coordination efforts, and regressive in its implicit denial of rational new planning models. Ultimately, one might perceive the trend as a scrapping of any commitment to service coordination in favor of a social equivalent to the economic concept of laissez-faire. However, I do not see it in these terms.

Neither the scientific precision of F. W. Taylor in the 1920s nor the anything-goes spirit of many more recent movement activities captures truth or reality. In a rapidly changing world, only programs and policies which preserve from the past *and* incorporate from the present will survive and flourish. Only an ever-evolving and maturing model will serve the interests of scientific rationalism and modern creativity in a changing world. In the framework of social science, as opposed to natural science, the very definition of rationality changes over time in an ecological context. The formality and rigidity of fixed rules and regulations—with all their precision—do not take into account the closed nature of their implicit presumptions. Efficiency is not synonymous with formality, and rationality rarely requires rigidity.

Such has been the recent American experience in both the public and the voluntary sectors. The reason that the War on Poverty was launched through new agencies (such as ACTION and the Office of Economic Opportunity) outside the existing federal departmental structure was the belief that the bureaucracy could not quickly adapt to a new and very different social philosophy. Just as Roosevelt and Hopkins established the alphabet agencies of the early New Deal (such as FERA and WPA) as separate from existing departments, so did Johnson and Schriver emulate this model more than thirty years later (Kurzman 1974; Spiegel 1968; Brager and Purcell 1967).

In the voluntary sector, community welfare councils' and United Ways' failure to respond to changing societal conditions pushed new social agencies away rather than let them in. An organizational reluctance to understand the significance of the War on Poverty, the civil rights movement, the Vietnam War, Watergate, environmental action, and the women's movement meant that organizations pursuing these legitimate social interests had to oppose the status quo by fighting for a share of the donated dollar or by establishing a competitive system.

In essence, as long as the established planning and coordinating system is *not* rational, competing, parallel organizational forms will appear. Usually, after time, their legitimate interests are incorporated or absorbed, and then opposition ends, and the planning and coordinating body evolves stronger than it was before. It achieves synthesis by balancing the organizational interests of prior participants, whose prestige, influential linkages, and historical position ensure continued support, with those who represent innovative efforts responsive to often less prestigious or less popular evolving community needs. While established agencies carry forward traditional commitments, new agencies willing to take a greater risk to serve new causes are incorporated to ensure diversity and creativity, which are legitimate community needs.

Hence, it would be a mistake to confuse a pluralistic planning model with no planning at all, or with an abandonment of planning to laissez-faire notions of "whatever will be, will be." What is needed, and is emerging, is a more open, less traditional, and less hierarchical model that recognizes the reality and desirability of change. Self-protective, unitary models of planning and coordination are giving way, frequently under pressure, to adaptive models that respect advocacy, risk-taking, and commitment to controversial causes as legitimate dimensions of healthy community life.

Planning and coordinating bodies, public and private, that wish to play a central role in ensuring the rationality of community efforts have to make certain that they establish their authority as well as maintain incentives for collaboration. Authority comes from professional expertise, recognized fairness, and broad acceptance of the right, and even the advantage, of designated organizations holding a superordinate function in a community. Incentives derive from application of norms of reciprocity which offer rewards for participation in exchange for demands for rationality in the portfolio of community programs. An example is offered below.

In Conclusion

Alternative federated fund-raising organizations are a threat to United Way's income. They endanger the organizational prestige of the United Way in the community and its authority to coordinate services—an equally important function. Following an exchange model, however, an alternative is open that might, in Simon's terms, provide "a satisficing" solution: the donor option. This principle allows workers to designate their own gift for a specific agency or agencies, whether United Way members or not. Donor option technically opens up the workplace, and early experiments in Pennsylvania show that when donor option was offered, the total amount given increased; in other words, workers gave *more* as a result (Grant 1981; Stevens 1979).

The plan has advantages. United Way does not have to absorb controversial new organizations, endanger its relationship with member agencies, endure bad publicity for being monopolistic, or expend manpower and financial resources in defending its boundaries. Innovative new organizations do not have to worry that participation as members of United Way will alter their principles and goals or force them to use scarce resources to develop fund-raising methods that are less effective and efficient than payroll deduction. Instead, organizations enter into the exchange which permits them to maintain their terrain and yet achieve their principal objectives.

A unitary model of service coordination and program development cannot be achieved through this exchange solution, but such a model probably is not desirable. Diversity and pluralism, healthy realities of contemporary renewal, are maintained by recognizing that the price of a single, closed system would be value uniformity or neutrality—and a system so rational as to sacrifice innovation. The exchange principle, in effect, sanctions establishment of protected units within the voluntary social welfare community that can serve as an advocacy subsystem. Within broad boundaries, this approach can support controversial ideas with a minimum expenditure of resources by both parties to the exchange for goal-displacing organizational maintenance and boundary defense activities. Each is able to concentrate resources on appropriate program development efforts, and in the absence of continual friction over turf is more apt to be available to the other organizationally, again on the basis of exchange, around *essential* matters of service coordination. Indeed, since new agencies *are* part of a subsystem, and their financial needs are being met, they are no longer rejected elements outside the system itself. They are therefore more likely to be responsive to planning and coordination by the health and welfare councils since *their* interests also will be served. Thus, such a solution is reached truly in the spirit of a synthesis of organizational interests.

The example of the United Way and community welfare councils has served to illustrate the historical evolution of program development and resource coordination as components of community organization practice. The changes that have taken place, conceptually and in practice, reflect reality: these models do not evolve in an ecological vacuum, but rather in response to changing conditions in the society at large. Modifications in the "melting pot" concept, the influence of social movements, changes in American mores and folkways, shifts in the loci of community power, growth of the public sector—all are factors that have impinged upon community practice. To the extent that institutions choose to resist the reality of these changes, they are changed themselves, for the need is as real for self-renewal as for self-protection. What constituted sound models for program development and service coordination, even twenty years ago, does not remain the same today, for organizations are inextricably linked to a changing environment. Those that survive and flourish are the ones that adapt while still pursuing their purpose. The goals of continuity and tradition often can best be balanced with those of advocacy and innovation through an exchange of resources and rewards among the various organizational actors.

The richness of America is in its history as a nation of immigrants, in its heterogeneity, and its tolerance of differences. Therefore, to believe that one monolithic body, public or private, can or should coordinate services in the community would run counter to what we value and wish to preserve. The irony, conceptually, is that a pluralistic planning model that may at first glance seem less rational organizationally may prove to be the most rational model of all. The historic role of the social work profession and of its community organization practitioners requires a commitment to outcome and to process goals; and, as these goals may be seen in their complementarity and counterpoint, so too we may view the paradox of program development and service coordination. As community developers and community coordinators struggle with their different roles, they enter into exchanges so that each can perform its function, over time, to complement the other. In this way, organizational experiences of the past give promise for both rationality and renewal in the future.

References

Alinsky, Saul D. 1969. *Reveille for Radicals.* New York: Vintage Books.
Bennis, Warren G., Kenneth D. Benne, and Robert Chin, eds. 1969. *The Planning of Change.* 2d ed. New York: Holt, Rinehart & Winston.
Blau, Peter M. 1964. *Exchange and Power in Social Life.* New York: Wiley.
Bloom, Martin. 1969. "The Selection of Knowledge from Other Disciplines and Its Integration into Social Work Curricula." *Journal of Education for Social Work* (Spring), 5(1):15–27.

122   P. A. Kurzman

Bothwell, Robert and Timothy Saasta. 1979. "Will the Future Pass United Way By?" *Grantsmanship Center News* (July–August), issue no. 30, pp. 85, 108.

Brager, George A. and Francis P. Purcell, eds. 1967. *Community Action Against Poverty.* New Haven: College and University Press.

Coleman, James S. 1957. *Community Conflict.* Glencoe, Ill.: Free Press.

Coser, Lewis A. 1956. *The Functions of Social Conflict.* Glencoe, Ill.: Free Press.

Cox, Fred M., et al., eds. 1979. *Strategies of Community Organization* 3d ed. Itasca, Ill.: Peacock.

Dahl, Robert A. 1961. *Who Governs: Democracy and Power in an American City.* New Haven, Conn.: Yale University Press.

Davidoff, Paul. 1965. "Advocacy and Pluralism in Planning." *Journal of the American Institute of Planners* (November), 31(4):331–38.

Dunham, Arthur. 1970. *The New Community Organization.* New York: Crowell.

Eisinger, Peter K. 1974. "The Urban Crisis as a Failure of Community." *Urban Affairs Quarterly* (June), 9(4):437–61.

Etzioni, Amitai, ed. 1961. *Complex Organizations: A Sociological Reader.* New York: Holt, Rinehart & Winston.

FSAA. 1971. "Relationship with United Way of America." *Highlights of FSAA News* (June).

Gamson, William A. 1965. "Community Issues and Their Outcome: How to Lose a Fluoridation Referendum," pp. 350–57. In Gouldner and Miller, eds. *Applied Sociology.*

Gilbert, Neil and Harry Specht. 1974. *Dimensions of Social Welfare Policy.* Englewood Cliffs, N.J.: Prentice-Hall.

———, eds. 1977. *Planning for Social Welfare: Issues, Models and Tasks.* Englewood Cliffs, N.J.: Prentice-Hall.

Gouldner, Alvin W. and S. M. Miller, eds. 1965. *Applied Sociology.* New York: Free Press.

Grant, John. 1981. "Fighting for a Piece of the Paycheck: Challenge to United Way Is Critical Issue." *Delaware Valley Agenda.* 1(23):1–6.

Hasenfeld, Yeheskel. 1979. "Program Development." In Cox et al., eds., *Strategies of Community Organization,* pp. 138–59.

Hawley, Willis D. and Frederick M. Wirt, eds. 1968. *The Search for Community Power.* Englewood Cliffs, N.J.: Prentice-Hall.

Homans, George C. 1958. "Social Behavior as Exchange." *American Journal of Sociology* 63(6):597–606.

Hunter, Floyd. 1953. *Community Power Structures.* Chapel Hill, N.C.: University of North Carolina Press.

King, Clarence. 1939. "Councils of Social Agencies." In *Social Work Yearbook, 1939,* pp. 96–101. New York: Russell Sage Foundation.

Kramer, Ralph M. and Harry Specht, eds. 1975. *Readings in Community Organization Practice.* 2d ed. Englewood Cliffs, N.J.: Prentice-Hall.

Kurzman, Paul A. 1974. *Harry Hopkins and the New Deal.* Fair Lawn, N.J.: R. E. Burdick.

————. 1977. "Rules and Regulations in Large-Scale Organizations: A Theoretical Approach to the Problem." *Administration in Social Work* (Winter), 1(4):421–31.

Lane, Robert P. 1939. "The Field of Community Organization." In *Proceedings of the National Conference of Social Work, 1939*, pp. 495–511. New York: Columbia University Press.

Lauffer, Armand. 1978. *Social Planning at the Community Level.* Englewood Cliffs, N.J.: Prentice-Hall.

Levin, Herman. 1977. "Voluntary Organizations in Social Welfare." In *Encyclopedia of Social Work*, pp. 1573–82. 17th ed. Washington, D.C.: NASW.

Levine, Sol and Paul E. White. 1961. "Exchange as a Conceptual Framework for the Study of Interorganizational Relationships." *Administrative Science Quarterly* (March), 5(4):583–601.

Lewis, Verl S. 1977. "Charity Organization Society." In *Encyclopedia of Social Work*, pp. 96–100. 17th ed. Washington, D.C.: NASW.

Lynd, Robert S. and Helen M. 1937. *Middletown in Transition.* New York: Harcourt, Brace, World.

Mayer, Robert B. 1972. *Social Planning and Social Change.* Englewood Cliffs, N.J.: Prentice-Hall.

Murphy, Campbell G. 1954. *Community Organization Practice.* Boston: Houghton Mifflin.

NASW. 1980. *Directory of Agencies.* Washington, D.C.

Perlman, Robert and Arnold Gurin. 1972. *Community Organization and Social Planning.* New York: Wiley.

Perrow, Charles. 1970. *Organizational Analysis: A Sociological View.* Belmont, Calif.: Wadsworth.

Pifer, Alan. 1967. "The Quasi-Nongovernmental Organization." In *Annual Report*, pp. 3–16. New York: Carnegie Corporation.

Rabinowitz, Herbert S., Bruce R. Simmeth, and Jeanette R. Spero. 1979. "The Future of United Way." *Social Service Review* (June), 53(2):275–84.

Reid, William J. 19/5. "Inter-Organizational Coordination in Social Welfare: A Theoretical Approach to Analysis and Intervention." In Kramer and Specht, eds., pp. 118–29. *Readings in Community Organization Practice.*

Rein, Martin and Robert Morris. 1962. "Goals, Structures and Strategies for Community Change." In *Social Work Practice, 1962*, pp. 127–45. New York: Columbia University Press.

Ross, Murray G. 1955. *Community Organization: Theory and Principles.* New York: Harper and Row.

Rothman, Jack. 1974. *Planning and Organizing for Social Change: Action Principles from Social Science Research.* New York: Columbia University Press.

————. 1979. "Three Models of Community Organization Practice, Their Mixing and Phasing." In Cox et al., eds., *Strategies of Community Organization*, pp. 25–45.

124   P. A. Kurzman

Rothman, Jack and Irwin Epstein. 1977. "Social Planning and Community Organization: Social Science Foundations." In *Encyclopedia of Social Work,* pp. 1433–43. 17th ed. Washington, D.C.: NASW.

Sayre, Wallace S. and Herbert Kaufman. 1965. *Governing New York City: Politics in the Metropolis.* New York: W. W. Norton.

Schottland, Charles I. 1963. "Federal Planning for Health and Welfare." In *Social Welfare Forum, 1963,* pp. 97–120. New York: Columbia University Press.

Seeley, John R. et al. 1957. *Community Chest: A Case Study in Philanthropy.* Toronto: University of Toronto Press.

Selznick, Philip. 1961. "Foundations of the Theory of Organization." In Etzioni, ed., *Complex Organizations: A Sociological Reader,* pp. 18–32.

Simon, Herbert A. 1965. *Administrative Behavior.* New York: Free Press.

Spiegel, Hans B.C., ed. 1968. *Citizen Participation in Urban Development.* Washington, D.C.: NTL Institute for Applied Behavioral Science.

Stevens, William K. 1979. "Charities Challenge to Monopoly of United Way." New York *Times.* May 2.

Thomas, Edwin J., ed. 1968. *Behavioral Science for Social Workers.* New York: Free Press.

Tropman, John E. and Elmer J. Tropman. 1977. "Community Welfare Councils." In *Encyclopedia of Social Work,* pp. 187–93. 17th ed. Washington, D.C.: NASW.

UWASIS. 1972. *United Way of America Services Identification System.* Alexandria, Va.: United Way of America.

Warren, Roland L. 1963. *The Community in America.* Chicago: Rand McNally.

——. 1967. "Application of Social Science Knowledge to the Community Organization Field." *Journal of Education for Social Work* (Spring), 3(1):60–72.

——. 1967. "The Intergovernmental Field as a Focus for Investigation." *Administrative Science Quarterly* (December), 12(3):396–419.

Wenocur, Stanley. 1976. "A Pluralistic Model for the United Way Organizations." *Social Service Review* (December), 50(4):586–600.

5

Planning Theory in Social Work Community Practice

Jack Rothman and Mayer N. Zald

One characteristic of modern society is the systematic attempt to use tools of rational analysis to lay out pathways to achieving future-oriented goals. As organizations, both private and public, have become larger and developed professional staffs, and as the environments they deal with have become more complex, planning and decision-making have become full-blown enterprises. Corporations, governmental agencies, social welfare agencies, community federations, and others have resorted to planning activities to gather information and chart their future courses. Rational, future-oriented decision-making is a hallmark and indeed a widely accepted definition of social planning.

In this essay we will start by examining planning broadly as a function of the modern state. We will go on to look at particular characteristics of planning in the free-enterprise or capitalist society. We will then focus briefly but more specifically on historical forces that have given rise to planning in the field of social welfare in the United States.

Having set a contextual framework, our attention will turn to the main theme, the evolution of theories of planning. We will describe the rationalistic, comprehensive model and emergent, di-

verse theoretical alternatives that emphasize processes of adjustment and the political nature of planning activity. This discussion
will be carried a step further toward practice in a consideration of
roles performed by planning professionals. We will also touch on
the knowledge base for planning. A final section will indicate some
latent functions of planning that involve social and political uses
which, while not always recognized, have tactical implications for
planners.

The Societal Context of Social Planning

In this initial section we will nest planning activity in the social
structure of society. Our questions are sociological and political
rather than normative and metatheoretical. When does planning
work? Whose goals are served by planning? What are the social and
institutional uses of planning? What are the social functions and
dysfunctions of planning? Is planning activity in the community and
welfare arena different in kind from planning in the economic sector? We do not intend to offer a sociological theory of planning but
rather to identify some of the problematics of the planning function
in society.

PLANNING AND THE STATE

As a general proposition, the growth of government and the state
apparatus in modern times has been accompanied by an increase in
planning activities (Shonfield 1965). Yet, modern societies have
varied widely in their attitudes toward national planning. Socialist
states have attempted comprehensive economic and social planning
as techniques for realizing goals of economic growth and national
development. These plans not only have established goals for specific industries, but have rationed the allocation of labor and capital.
Moreover, these plans have included large social-welfare components such as plans for housing, education, and medical care.

Obviously, the adoption of national planning is related to the ideology of ruling elites and national social structure. Comprehensive five-year plans have been adopted in Communist and socialist countries. The more fragmented or multilayered the political structure and the more the ruling elites are committed to capitalist and laissez-faire ideology, the less likely they are to attempt to adopt national comprehensive planning. Capitalist states with strong central governments are more likely to adopt "indicative planning" where specific industries are singled out for aid and development. And legislation adopted in capitalist countries may plan and allocate resources for the implementation of specific social welfare objectives such as, for instance, the subsidy of thousands of low-income housing units, or plans to establish a nationwide system of community mental health centers.

What are the results of comprehensive planning on the societal level? It is impossible to review the literature here.[1] But several general conclusions emerge. First, comprehensive planning coupled with a rationing system of resource allocation leads to systematic pathologies of production. The plans emphasize physical unit counts rather than quality criteria, and the production of inferior goods is pandemic. Moreover, there is a tendency to overemphasize the production of goods which meet raw quantity requirements at the expense of differentiated products not measured in the plan. Second, unless goals are constantly updated to record the increments in actual production, goals are rarely fulfilled. Third, comprehensive national plans have endemic problems of work incentives, labor, allocations and stockpiling raw materials to an excessive degree. Recent events in Poland punctuate these outcomes.

Over all, the information shortcomings and incentive shortcomings of national planning have led to either planning as ritual or attempts to mix market pricing systems with indicative planning focusing upon a more limited set of objectives. Yugoslavia is the prime example of this adaptive response. In spite of the vast increases in information processing capacity provided by modern computer technology and the planning theoretic devices provided by input-output analysis and other programming devices, long-range comprehensive planning eludes achievement. In capitalist societies it is not even attempted.

SOCIAL AND ECONOMIC PLANNING IN THE UNITED STATES

Although the notion of comprehensive societal planning has never been fully accepted in the United States, sectoral, policy-specific, and organizational planning is widely used. There are many examples: State prison systems develop planning models of needed facilities, taking into account projected prison populations, assumptions about crime rates, populations at risk, and sentencing policy. Forest products companies project wood-footage needs and plant seedlings now for harvesting in twenty years. Assuming market goals, large corporations project capital needs for five- and ten-year periods; moreover, large corporations have strategic planning staffs examining new product trends and attempting to project political and economic climates into the future. The Social Security Administration projects revenue needs, given demographic trends, eligibility rules, and benefit formulas. Local councils develop plans for hospital facilities. Universities attempt to develop models of projected enrollments and develop strategies for growth or retrenchment of faculty and facilities.

There is, of course, wide variability among organizations in the extent to which they engage in formal and explicit planning activities. Large organizations with larger professional and administrative components are more likely to engage in planning than smaller ones. Organizations that have longer time horizons in the procurement of resources, the development of products, or the demand for services are more likely to engage in planning than those with shorter time horizons. (It takes five to seven years to develop a new car model, while dress styles change yearly.)

Organizations with leaders trained in management-by-objectives techniques and other planning-oriented styles are more likely to engage in these techniques. And, finally, organizations that are required by external agencies to develop plans as part of their procurement or legitimation or the receipt of funds are more likely than others to engage in the production of planning documents. For instance, to receive federal grants for law enforcement activities or for community mental health centers, states and committees had to develop planning bodies and plans for services.

Obviously, there is a difference between planning and implementing plans. What kinds of organizations are more likely to implement their plans? Implementation in its simplest form (that is, the translation of plan into action) depends upon the commitment of allocating authorities to the plan. One common problem in private organizations is that the planning group may not be integrally connected to the decision-making authorities. To the extent that planning officers are removed from central authorities, their plans may be pigeonholed. The same problem occurs to an even greater extent in public organizations. Public organizations are to a large extent dependent upon decision-making bodies (legislatures, elected executives) for the establishment of goals and the allocation of resources. These are in turn beholden to constituencies composed of diverse and often conflicting elements.

Since these external interests may have different priorities for the organization and competing demands for resource allocation, we suspect it is more likely that the planning documents of public organizations gather dust or are radically modified than are those of private organizations that engage in long-range planning. Ironically, these same private organizations often express disparagement of planning for public enterprises.

In both public and private organizations the inability to attract resources from outside and the decline of slack resources within organizations inhibit planning implementation. These issues particularly have plagued planning in social welfare. Moreover, as we have indicated, in both private and public organizations, planning is part of a social and political process. It serves ends and purposes apart from its formal or stated functions of gathering information and choosing pathways to goals. Rationalist schools of planning theory have not always been sufficiently sensitive to these realities.

PLANNING IN SOCIAL WORK AND SOCIAL WELFARE

At some minimal level, planning in social work and social welfare can be said to have occurred when a person or agency, motivated by concerns for clients or beneficiaries, anticipates future needs or programs rather than responding "spontaneously" to demands.

Charity is transformed from a spontaneous response to a supplicant in need to a planned system when individuals or organizations anticipate philanthropic demand and set up rules and policies, services and organizations to respond to that anticipated need or demand. The Poor Law is thus an early instance of planning.

A caseworker can be said to engage in planning when he or she conceptualizes a goal of treatment or service delivery and anticipates or shapes alternative courses of treatment or service.

In the last century explicit planning emerged as agencies, both public and private, became aware that their ad hoc and uncoordinated efforts led to inadequate and inefficient provision of services. Sometimes clients would go to several agencies, requesting and receiving financial support from more than one source, without one agency knowing that another had helped. The community council case register movement (Social Service Exchange) began early in the century. Although these agencies may have been more effective at controlling multiple applicants (see Litwak and Hylton 1962) than they were for actually planning and implementing plans for whatever services were to be provided, the community chest and council movements represent an early attempt to assess community needs and to argue for rational decision-making in projecting the development and location of community agencies. It is important to note that once a commitment to planning emerged, a methodology was required. The development of the community survey can be seen as an emergent methodology for community planning (Byington 1911; Colcord 1939; Warren 1955).

Another early attempt at planning is found in the efforts of welfare agencies to plan for emergency relief. Whenever a major cataclysm occurs there is large-scale and sudden disruption of the goods and services available to a population. In preplanning periods individual agencies respond in an ad hoc fashion to such needs. The emergence of agencies such as the Red Cross, the development of emergency planning committees, and the legislation of federal and state loan and service provisions are all attempts to plan in advance for unforeseen disasters, to forecast need, and to develop repertoires of response.

This perspective on social welfare planning is consistent with Lauffer's definition: "Social planning refers to the development, expansion and coordination of social services and social policies" (1981:583). Lauffer goes on to state that planning is a method of rational problem-solving and that it is conducted at both the societal and the local level.

Both the community council movement and the development of emergency and disaster relief agencies are making plans for the delivery and coordination of service at the local community level. Large-scale planning has also been attempted for specific social welfare programs at the national level. The development of the Social Security system required a projection of the number and size of beneficiary claims and revenues from taxation. The planning system of Social Security has been buffeted by changes in mortality rates, changes in the economy, and political actions that have added claimants and enlarged benefit levels (Derthick 1979; Cates 1981).

Another national example of social welfare relevant planning can be seen in the development of the Comprehensive Community Health Act of 1963. Here we see an effort to use federal incentives (the federal subsidization of local services) to encourage the planning and development of mental health services in a setting close to the patient's home, the provision of outpatient and preventive services, the setting up of provisions for noninstitutional alternatives, community consultation, and local boards.

The tasks of planning in these different cases vary substantially in the complexity of the planning activity: the number of components of the plan; the time horizon of the plan (short term to long term); the locus of the planning (private local agency to national government); and in the representation of interests (client, professional, political). They differ from planning in non-social-welfare arenas not in terms of the difficulty or ease of planning but in that the values to be served by planning are those of the liberal, caring society. It is these values of a humane industrialized society that link these planning efforts to the helping professions.

These humane impulses have led to other forms of organized response to need. Settlement houses, for example, strove to change conditions of life in the neighborhood through social reform or advocacy. They, together with YMCAs and other locally based organizations, also were concerned with citizen participation, public education, and personal development of participants. Planning theory, as we shall see, reflects these various empirical crosscurrents of action and practice.

Planning Theory

Planning theory emerged as a response to the need to engage in planning activity. It arose as an answer to questons about how one ought to conduct such activity. It has been a normative exercise. For example, writers have asked what is the best way to plan. What are the limits of different kinds of planning? What alternatives are there to the standard practices? As a normative exercise, scholars have examined planning activity in specific situations as a tool of rationality and choice. They have been concerned with its limits and blind spots. Less often, scholars have raised empirical and descriptive issues: Who plans, in what situations, with what results?

Fragmentation and theoretical diversity characterize many contemporary professions, particularly those related to the social arena. Long-standing theoretical foundations have been shattered, splintering in myriad directions. In clinical psychology, as well as in social work, the pervasive imprint of Freud (and the prognostic school) has faded. Parsonian dominance has receded in sociology. Anthropologist Eric Wolf describes currents in his field following the decline of Alfred Kroeber's influence:

Social-cultural anthropologists have also split into sub-divisions, turning themselves into applied, cognitive, economic, ecological, legal, poltical, psychological, urban, or even psychopharmacological anthropologists. Area specialization has grouped anthropologists working in a particular geographical area with, say, Latin Americanists or Middle Easternists from other disciplines. Such lines of tension were deepened by opposition between older and younger members of the institutions, and between those teaching within academe and those working outside. (1980:E9)

The field of planning has not managed to escape this contemporary tendency toward fragmentation. Whereas comprehensive, rationalistic theory once held sway, it is now only one of multiple contending perspectives, and not enjoying very high repute at that. Several observers have made note of the prevailing theoretical condition. Burchell and Hughes indicate that "planning has simply become a very broad and sometimes leaky umbrella. It shelters many different kinds of people with different kinds of skills and approaches" (1979:xvii). And Branch adds: "Only bits and pieces of a general theory of planning exist today" (1978:48). Perlman comments similarly with specific reference to social work: "Social planning and community organizations are at an early stage of development. A body of propositions that relate assumptions about social reality to practice is clearly lacking. Grand theories of social change have little to offer as guides to effective practice" (1977:1411).

These circumstances create perils for those who venture to write a chapter on planning theory. We acknowledge the cluttered and incoherent state of the art, and will offer a frame of reference for analyzing existing divergences. To do this we will trace developments in planning theory by examining the earlier dominant rationalistic decision-making model and discussing factors associated with its fall from ascendancy. We will go on to explain this change in epistemological terms and to identify some of the newer theoretical schools.[2] We will focus on mainstream developments in planning theory, recognizing that thinking in social work has generally been shaped by broader intellectual endeavors. Social work variants will be pointed out.

RATIONALISTIC DECISION-MAKING THEORY

The modern era of planning theory was marked initially by a rationalistic model of decision-making, crystallized in the writings of Herbert Simon (1957). Planning was viewed as a process whereby through use of proper rules of logic an optimal solution to a problem is determined. Persons are seen as utility-maximizing beings whose relations to others are defined in instrumental terms. Classic decision-making theory involves following a task-oriented set of basic steps, including ordinarily: (1) setting a goal; (2) identifying all the alternative means of attaining the goal; (3) evaluating means in order to arrive at the single best solution; and (4) implementing the decision. Hudson characterizes the approach as examining "problems from a systems viewpoint, using conceptual or mathematical models relating ends (objectives) to means (resources and constraints), with heavy reliance on numbers and quantitative analysis" (1979:389). This may entail use of forecasting and analysis techniques such as multiple regression analysis, Markov chains, econometric modeling, and Bayesian methods. In social work planning literature the work of Kahn (1969), in particular, has been identified with procedures of rational decision-making.

Both in social work and in urban planning, the rationalistic approach has been associated with the idea of comprehensiveness. Comprehensive land use planning was the modus operandi in city planning for an extended period of time, and social work planning, according to Lane, was to entail "a progressively effective adjustment between social welfare resources and social welfare needs" (1959:65). Community chests and councils viewed their role to be that of fostering and steering comprehensive social welfare planning at the community level.

Despite, or perhaps because of, its elegance and simplicity, the rationalistic comprehensive concept has been subjected to criticism from various quarters. A variety of limitations has been attributed to the model, including limits to rational cognition, limits to analytic cogency, limits to environmental control, limits to professionalism, and limits of value dissonance.

Limits to rational cognition pertain to the amount of knowledge or information that may be gathered and digested in any decisional situation. In practical terms, far more information was required than could be acquired. The number of alternatives to be identified, documented, and weighted was legion. Technical difficulties in assembling data presented obstacles: the loss or transformation of data through aggregation or mathematical modeling; unavailability of organizational information; delays in data acquisition; faulty or falsified data; computer breakdowns, and so on. Limits to analytic cogency simply mean that what is logical may encounter fierce opposition by those who have not been consulted, or whose narrow "irrational" interests are threatened. Analytic purity is complicated by pluralism of values existing in most urban settings. Rationalism is most applicable when one can assume a unitary set of values (a general public interest), or at least a set of values that are not rancorously contentious. In other words, there are personal and organizational dynamics in formulating or implementing a decision that go beyond its intrinsic analytic features. More recently, this duality in planning has been recognized through conceptualizing "analytic" and "interactional" (Perlman and Gurin

1972) or "technical" and "sociopolitical" (Gilbert and Specht 1977) aspects of planning.

Limits to environmental control relate to the "turbulent" (Emery and Trist 1965), broader social context in which planners operate. The 1960s and 1970s were times of uncertain and shifting social, political, and economic currents, and the 1980s have shown signs of similar contextual instability. When the national or community political economy is unpredictable, the more narrow technical area of planning is subjected to unforeseen dislocations. "It is a feature of modern social dynamics that the future does not unroll incrementally but in a disjointed series of crises, breakthroughs and transformations" (Friedman and Hudson 1974:8). This has placed a high burden on the rationalist formulation.

Limits to professionalism suggest that while the planner does not have all answers, some answers do lie uniquely with other sources. In particular, it is brought out, indivduals affected by new services or facilities have a distinctive understanding of their needs and how to fulfill them. Thus families, neighborhood groups, and ethnic and racial communities are viewed as having important contributions to make to decisions concerning delivery of services. The concept of informal helping networks has come to the fore in this connection. Such networks have joined in constructive partnership with planners, both in decision-making and in the actual delivery of services at the grass-roots level. The requirement for cost constraints is another factor which has curtailed professionalism and generated increased interest in the idea of self-help networks.

A final limitation deals with value dissonance. Rationalism has been criticized by many for projecting an image of the planner as technocrat. This image is of a policy scientist or systems analyst, surrounded by printouts, engaged in model-building, standing apart from community politics, and devoid of contact with ordinary citizens. The one "best" solution arrived at by the planner in isolation through technical gadgetry is seen as imposed on hapless populations without their input or consent. "Urban renewal as urban removal" conveys the sense of this view. This critique takes rationalism to task for its failure to incorporate an element of citizens' participation into its theoretical structure, which places it in dissonance with basic democratic values.

Rittel and Webber (1973) have pointed to a significant weakness in rationalistic theory. The theory assumes problems that are definable, discrete, and responsive to purposeful manipulation. In the current scene, however, these authors tell us, planning has been obliged to deal with "wicked" problems. These elude bounded definitions, have no clear end point, suggest innumerable potential solutions, are unique and incomparable in each instance, and are enmeshed with other problems of which they are symptoms. Rationalism requires somewhat benign, docile problems. Instead, society spews forth wicked and incorrigible ones. The theory was not up to coping with this discrepancy.

According to Galloway and Mahayni (1977), the evaluation of planning theory can best be understood through application of the work of Kuhn (1970) on the structure of scientific revolutions. A paradigm develops, is articulated, and wins general professional acceptance. Later anomalies appear and a crisis ensues. Alternative competing paradigms appear. In the view of Galloway and Mahayni, the dominant rationalist paradigm broke down in the turbulent 1960s and is being superseded by other approaches.

A useful way to obtain an overview of the main theoretical orientations to planning extant today is through a schema developed by Hudson (1979). Hudson sees rationalistic theory still retaining a foothold on professional thinking, but he suggests that four alternative theoretical positions have also gained currency: incremental planning, transactive planning, advocacy planning, and radical planning. We will review each of these four succinctly. While advocated as alternatives to the rationalistic theory, these approaches contain elements of the rational model. In some ways these approaches can be viewed as other than "pure" planning models, and they overlap with concepts in other chapters of this book.

INCREMENTALISM

Charles Lindblom (1965) has been the major figure associated with the formulation of incremental planning. His analysis takes account of the political and pluralistic influences involved in planning processes. For this reason one should conceive of planning outputs as representing not the best possible rational decision but the compromise product of partisan mutual adjustment. This suggests that end states valued by the planner are not arrived at in the short run in a straight line but rather through a series of disjointed approximations. Established institutions in the community are given their due as powerful forces participating in decentralized bargaining processes, in the context of influence exchange, and with acceptance of a democratic political economy. Lindblom has characterized this planning orientation as "the science of muddling through." The planning path, accordingly, is exploratory. Rather than forecasting all the results of multiple courses, one route is attempted, the consequences are discovered and dealt with in further sequential steps.

It can be said that the formulation of incrementalism itself occurred incrementally. Simon had softened his earlier position to one of the "bounded rationality" (March and Simon 1959). Rationality no longer was required to arrive at "optimization" of decision choice. Rather, it was sufficient for a decision to be "satisficing," that is, good enough (rather than best) for the purpose of making progress toward a desired goal under known and knowable circumstances. Etzioni (1968) also suggested an adaptation he labeled "mixed scanning," which means that either of the two versions of rationalism may be employed depending on given conditions.

In the social work literature, the political realism and hard bargaining dynamics of incrementalism have been expressed by writers such as Morris and Binstock (1966) and Brager and Specht (1973).

TRANSACTIVE PLANNING

Transactive planning focuses on people rather than politics. It assumes that those who are affected by planning have the right and possess the capabilities to make significant contributions to planning decisions. The experience of people's lives is to be entered into plans through face-to-face contact and interpersonal dialogue between planner and citizen. In this way a process of mutual learning transpires whereby both contribute and benefit.

Friedmann (1973), a key spokesman for this approach, calls for decentralized planning structures that enable people to participate in social process and gain control over forces which impinge on their lives. According to Friedman, the quality of the product itself is not the main concern of planning; rather it is the quality of the lives of people who take part in, and are affected by, planning that is the central consideration. For this reason he would evaluate not the number of services delivered, the architectural design of new housing projects, or the efficiency of new transportation systems. Rather, he focuses on fundamental human impacts on people, including such considerations as their sense of dignity, values, capacity for growth, enhanced learning, ability to relate interpersonally, and spirit of generosity. In social work this approach has been articulated notably by Ross (1955) and in some of the writings of Dunham (1970).

ADVOCACY PLANNING

In advocacy planning the planner emphasizes technical or task-related functions, but places these at the disposal of minorities, the poor, neighborhood groups, and disenfranchised populations. The planner serves these groups much in the way a lawyer performs advocacy functions. One does not assume a common public interest but accepts a pluralistic diversity. The diverse interests, however, are not seen as equal. Certain interests lack the influence and financial resources to command the skills and competencies of professional planners. Advocacy planners see their role as linking up with groups with little power in order to strengthen their position in the arena of community politics.

Advocacy planning emerged as a concept during the period of urban strife of the 1960s. A major spokesman for the formulation was Davidoff (1965). A key objective of advocacy planning has been to shift planning theory from a neutral, objective stance toward social problems in the direction of normative support for social justice as an orienting precept. In the process, it has dislodged planning from its natural environment of governmental offices and board rooms and into the public domain. For example, citizens' groups have been mobilized in community protest, ordinarily with the purpose of blocking actions (urban renewal, highway construction) promulgated by planning establishments. Advocacy planning has also forged a close relationship between the planning process and the courts. Whether in planning for desegregation of schools, environmental control, or neighborhood redevelopment, more and more decisions have involved judiciary processes. Advocacy planning has not flowered in terms of widespread practice and has been criticized for emphasizing the negative role of vetoing actions without demonstrating the positive role of producing a constructive plan (Peattie 1968). In social work, advocacy planning has not been highly articulated within the framework of those who coined the phrase.

RADICAL PLANNING

Hudson tells us that there are two streams within radical planning. One entails "spontaneous activism, guided by an idealistic but pragmatic vision of self-reliance and mutual aid" (1979:390). This version has many elements of "small is beautiful" thinking, self-help, cooperative living, and so on. It entails a reconstruction of society, through many small-scale efforts which are cumulative in their impact, rather than an abrasive direct confrontation with the system. This stream is influenced by the social philosophy of John Dewey, the ecological ideas of Schumacher, Goodman's social architecture, and the humanistic writings of Illich.

The other stream takes a larger structural view of society and is influenced by the political and economic views of Karl Marx. The class structure and economic relations are perceived to be at the heart of problem definition. Planned change is generated through social movement, confrontations, alliances, and struggles. In social work writings, the radical outlook has been projected by writers such as Haggstrom (1969). One may wonder whether some of the writings of these radical thinkers represent planning theory as such or are more general theoretical notions about society. However, since part of planning involves choosing among alternative goals and structures in society, and because these positions are articulated by specialists who write on planning theory, we have included them here.[3]

A great many additional theoretical approaches to planning have been presented in the literature. A partial overview will reveal some sense of the diversity of issues that have been considered: compact policy assessment, indicative planning, heuristic and algorithmic approaches, macroeconomic policy planning, ethnographic methods, social learning theory, philosophical synthesis, sociotechnical planning, including technology assessment, impact analysis, adjunctive planning, participative planning, risk analysis, and so forth. Both the richness and inchoate state of planning theory are revealed in the listing.

Limitation of space does not allow discussion of this range of perspectives. However, two developments are of note, one substantive and the other methodological.

Although planning theory has always acknowledged an implementation aspect or phase, most of the writings have concentrated on decision-making. Only in very recent years has implementation been given a prominent place as a defined area for theoretical explications (Pressman and Wildavsky 1973; Bardach 1977; Williams and Elmore 1976; Hargrove 1975; Smith 1973). It was as though the struggles and defeats of the Great Society programs, particularly the War on Poverty, brought home to planners and policy analysts the recognition that careful follow-through is essential for the success of the most clearly formulated plan.

Several variables have emerged in implementation studies which are associated with the attainment of planning goals. Conditions identified as facilitating implementation include such variables as commitment of top leaders, organizational capacity, the commitment of implementers, and interest-group support. Variables found to impede implementation include magnitude of change, number of actors involved, alternative preferences of actors, intrinsic complexity of the plan and its timing. Although the label "implementation" may be new or different, the theoretical issues examined duplicate conceptual work in such earlier theoretical schools as planned change, organizational development, diffusion of innovations, and political science studies of governmental bureaucracies and of interest groups. Nevertheless, the recent impetus by policy science groups may generate fresh ideas and promising reformulations of earlier efforts.

As a starting point in describing the previously mentioned emergent method for generating theory, we draw on Friedmann and Hudson's definition of planning "as an activity centrally concerned with *the linkage between knowledge and organized action.*" (1974:22; emphasis in the original). In keeping with this view, one of the authors has developed a research utilization or social research and development methodology for systematically applying social science research in such a way as to construct social intervention strategies (Rothman 1974; 1980). The approach eschews a "grand theory" approach to planning but starts with more delimited planning issues or problems, such as establishing an innovative program in the community or bringing about a wider level of citizen participation in the planning process. The method proceeds through a series of steps: delineating knowledge areas that contain relevant data; determining appropriate descriptors and key words for retrieving data; evaluating, assembling, and synthesizing data; formulating generalizations concerning the phenomena under consideration; and converting descriptive propositions into prescriptive application guidelines. The methodology proceeds further into field testing and development work so that planning strategies are not only evaluated for workability but are also put into operation to facilitate practice implementation. The objective is to arrive at middle-range theory which is both tested in the user environment and "packaged" for planning practitioners in user-ready form. Since the approach has been detailed elsewhere it will not be discussed further here.

SOCIAL PLANNING ROLES

Planning roles grow out of problems or needs in the society. But the planner does not necessarily define these. The planner is not an autonomous private practitioner, but one of a contemporary breed of professionals who is organizationally based and an employee of a bureaucratic structure. It is the governing bodies of such structures (boards of directors, commissions) that typically establish policy and set the agenda. However, this often takes place in collaboration with planners, who are in a strategic position (formally and informally) to influence decisions about organizational goals.

The character of the employers of planners has shifted over the years. In the early part of the century most of the employers were voluntary philanthropic agencies including community welfare councils, community chests, and specialized agencies in fields such as housing, child welfare, health, and the like. At the same time, settlement houses provided a base for neighborhood organizing and community development. With the advent of the New Deal in the 1930s, the federal government assumed a greater role in social planning. But throughout the 1930s, 1940s, and 1950s voluntary agencies were probably the major arena for planning jobs. This situation shifted drastically in the 1960s and 1970s. Government bodies at the federal, state, and local levels took on heavy responsibility for social programs and vastly overshadowed voluntary planning activity. The political outlook and social philosophy of the New Frontier and Great Society Democratic administrations provided the impetus for this development.

The Reagan administration has put a check on this century-long trend. The expansion of federal activity in planning has been halted. Responsibility is being pushed back on voluntary agencies, private enterprise, and local and state levels of government. At this writing it is too early to predict what balance between governmental and voluntary planning efforts will be reached. One can only note that this is an era in substantial flux.

As planners carry out their roles, a variety of skills is brought to bear. Arthur Dunham (1948) engaged in an early attempt to define this area. In his view, professionals need to exert "creative leadership" around specific tasks, and also facilitate group process in collaborative decision-making. In other words, they should be able to expedite both task and process goals. For this reason, according to Dunham, they need, among other qualities, a sound knowledge of the social welfare field as well as capabilities in dealing with people.

A roughly similar twofold schema was developed in a study by Rothman and Jones (1971). It is presented in slightly abridged form below. In the *process* domain the following skills areas were identified:

A. Managing Organizational Processes
    1. Initial organizing
    2. Participation
    3. Committee technology
    4. Leadership development and training
B. Exerting Influence
    5. Coalitions and their formation
    6. Bargaining
    7. Advocate role and conflict
    8. Broker role
    9. Identifying and influencing the power structure
C. Conducting Interpersonal Relations
    10. Interviewing
    11. Use of self
    12. Leading group discussion.

More technical or task-oriented skills included the following:

A. Designing
    13. Fact-finding, needs assessment, and social-survey techniques
    14. Policy analysis
    15. Program development
B. Expediting
    16. Decision-making techniques
    17. Political liaison
    18. Legislative drafting and enactment
    19. Administrative procurement
C. Implementing
    20. Administrative role and function
    21. Fund raising and proposal writing
    22. Consultation
    23. Staff development and supervision
    24. Promotional, educational, and public relations techniques
    25. Evaluation

These are presented as fairly generic skills which should be the equipment of any planner. However, not all planning agencies or situations call for using the full array. The type of agency, its mission, and the model of planning it follows all influence planner role performance. The more politically oriented planning agencies, such as those connected to city government, may give emphasis to coalition building and bargaining along incremental planning theory lines. Agencies which are more "scientific" or "professional," such as those dealing with health matters, may give special attention to fact finding or program development in the rationalistic theory mode. Agencies dealing with consumer or racial issues may emphasize protest and conflict in keeping with an advocacy planning model. At different stages of project development one or another set of skills may come to the fore, as, for example, in moving from successful protest to program implementation. In larger agencies with abundant resources and a multiplicity of projects, staff may be able to specialize. In small agencies the jack-of-all-trades may be required. As new methods develop—nominal group process or computer-aided simulation modeling, for example—they are absorbed into the skill repertoire of planners.

Roles are related to emerging emphases in practice. A recent symposium on community social work reflected some major growth areas in the field (Root 1981). One of these is community-based services, an outgrowth of deinstitutionalization in fields such as mental health, mental retardation, and corrections. There are also increased activities in rural areas in connection with problems of ecology (water resources, topsoil erosion, and disposal of toxic wastes) and nuclear reactor construction. In addition, planning more and more reflects the intereaction of local organizations involved in competition for discretionary block grant funds.

To these may be added some fields of service that will gain greater attention in the period ahead. With an aging population, gerontology can be identified as a field requiring expanding planning. Health is another, in part in relationship to the aging phenomenon. Work-related services, including industrial social work, will likely expand as efforts to reindustrialize and enhance worker productivity are heightened. Refugee resettlement may also continue to rise in importance as an aspect of political conflict and instability. Areas which will probably decline include mental health and child welfare. The state level will become a more significant arena for social planning as will the locality.

The symposium identified certain skills as receiving increased emphasis, including needs assessment, proposal writing, and research on laws and regulations. In addition, sophisticated use of media—videotapes, recordings, and slides—for promotional purposes seems to be gaining in importance.

THE KNOWLEDGE BASE OF PLANNING

Planning cannot be said to have a specific theoretical knowledge base in the same way that other areas of social work do. Casework has drawn substantially on psychoanalytic theory or, in more recent years, on learning theory to crystallize its practice. Group work has relied heavily on small group theory and related areas from the field of social psychology. Planning has not had as firm a social science base. A wide variety of fields is able to and does feed in relevant knowledge—sociology, political science, anthropology, economics, organizational theory, as well as psychology and social psychology. In a previous work, Rothman demonstrated how systematic linkage with these varied fields can aid the development of intervention strategies (1974). Nonetheless, when Warren (1967) reviewed practitioner-oriented journals over a five-year period, he found surprisingly few references to relevant sociological literature in articles on community issues. He also discovered that research findings in key areas such as voluntary organizations or structural aspects of social problems were "virtually neglected." The situation has probably shifted in a positive direction since Warren's study was published, but the absence of systematic and concerted relationship between social science knowledge and planning theory and practice still holds today.

In a discussion of this subject, Spiro (1979) points out that knowledge for practice should have at least two components: an understanding of relevant systems (communities, organizations) and specification of particular interventions. He identifies the same array of social science disciplines mentioned here and spells out a variety of different types of contributions made by these fields: concepts, theories (or models), hypotheses and bits of information, methodological approaches, and a scientific stance.

It is our view that the greatest impact on planning theory and practice thus far has been in the realm of concepts and empirical methodology. Many social science concepts have been absorbed into planning in a way which almost seems indigenous—systems theory, bureaucracy, power structure, co-option, to mention a few. These relatively abstract notions seem to offer widely applicable conceptual tools to assist in analytical tasks. On the other hand, concrete empirical research methods have also provided helps to planning. These include statistical techniques, computer modeling, forecasting needs assessment, program evaluation, cost benefit analysis, power structure study approaches, and so forth.

The transfer of formal theories has been less common. This may relate to the breadth of planning functions and the multiplicity of relevant disciplines. There is no delimited area of social science that has been identified as one to be exploited in depth. Also, as Spiro points out, the link between the two realms is problematic, and few organized "attempts to collect, codify and digest knowledge from the social and behavioral sciences and present their consequences for practice" have been undertaken (Spiro 1979:82). It is likely that more theoretical contributions will be made in light of current trends which have seen social scientists become more applied in their interests and planners more sophisticated in their scientific training.

It should be noted that an integrated field of planning has not arisen as much because of low demand for practitioners as because of the fragmented knowledge base. For contrast, consider the training of managers and management theory. Management theory and research, too, draw upon a number of disciplines and skills. In contrast to planning, there is great demand from one large institutional system (business). Since the market for planning is heavily segmented by specific policy arenas, there is little pressure to integrate and synthesize knowledge from diffuse arenas.

SOCIAL AND POLITICAL USES OF PLANNING

Planning theory has largely been a normative exercise in which rationality is viewed as good and planning is advanced as a method or process in the service of rationality. Rational analysis is the medium for reaching desired future states. The forms of planning we have discussed, such as transactional and advocacy planning, were each developed as planning tools and were shown to have limits, either as information-gathering devices (limits of rationality) or as representation mechanisms for priority assignment and preference choice (limits of end-state and pathway preference).

Here we turn to uses of planning as an instrument of political and social control and as a ritual of justification. The emphasis is not upon planning as a rational device for the achieving of announced social ends, but as a device for maintaining power, for reaching consensus, and for justifying decisions that may be taken on other grounds.

Any social process can be used for purposes other than its manifest intent. Merton has referred to these as latent functions (1957). Three intrinsic features of planning activities lend themselves to use for other than their manifest purposes. Planning takes time, thus inhibiting current action. Planning requires explicit statement and ordering of objectives into priorities, thus it may become an instrument of conflict resolution and consensus formation. Planning leads to the generaton of written documents. These documents may serve to legitimate actions of funders and review agencies, even if the written plans are not carried out.

Planning as stalling. Any planning activity consumes time. Information must be gathered, alternatives scouted. When groups are pressing for action, yet authorities are unsure what alternative is reasonable (or whether any action ought to be undertaken), a proposal to study action alternatives and plan future steps may be adopted. The proposal to plan gives symbolic reassurance that the group's demands are being met, when in fact authorities are buying time. The results of the planning process may or may not lead to material change, but in the short run authorities buy political acquiescense.

Planning and consensus formation. When goals and priorities are clear, planning is transformed into a technical process— the efficient means to achieve ends. But where goals are not clear, where affected parties have different priorities and where authorities are loath to announce goals and priorities *ex cathedra*, the planning process may facilitate debate and the ordering of priorities. It encourages an orderly registering of preferences and a search for compromise solutions.

In a penetrating doctoral dissertation Kenneth McNeil (1973) has examined a number of local community committees and planning boards that operated between politicians, bureaucracies, and citizens in Nashville, Tennessee. These included the local zoning committee responsible for enforcing zoning restrictions, a committee to study the location and design of a new airport, the public health commission, and others. In all these areas there is room for different priorities. Bureaucrats, professionals, and citizens may value ends and means differently. The planning process, which includes the representation of different groups and a procedure for gathering evidence, holding hearings, allows a consensus to emerge. Not only may a compromise consensus emerge, but the process provides the legitimacy of due process. Losers may at least believe that they have had a chance to state their case. In this regard, planning activity takes on a quasi-judicial role in community change. Communication and consensus-building along these lines have been referred to as "process goals" in the social work planning literature (Rothman 1964).

We suspect that planning activities take on this quasi-judicial consensus formation function whenever strong competing interests confront a decision with long-range consequences and central authority is unwilling or unable to override one or another of the competing interests. The planning process in many confederated community organizations, such as local United Way agencies, resembles the quasi-judicial conflict resolution. Interestingly enough, capital allocation processes in some large corporations and in universities also resemble this process (Pondy 1964).

Documents and the planning process. Planning leads to written documents. These documents may be part of the ritual of allocation in grants economies. Kenneth Boulding has drawn our attention to the growth of the grants economy—governmental bodies, international agencies, and philanthropic foundations give grants to countries and organizations for delivery of services or the production of goods, even though the granting agency does not receive or use those goods or services (Boulding, Pfaff, and Pfaff 1973).

To receive the grant, the grantee may have to produce a plan. The plan becomes a justificatory document when the grantor must legitimate his allocation of funds. In the extreme case the grantor does not examine whether the plan is in fact implemented, whether the plan leads to any of the intended results, or whether the money is used for the original purposes. No penalty may be incurred for failure to carry out the plan. When plans are used for justification, without audit of expenditure or sanctions for failure, we can speak of planning documents as rhetorical instruments used as justificatory devices for the transfer of funds (Porter and Warner 1973; Wildavsky 1972).

There are other latent functions of planning activity. The planning process helps solidify networks of agencies and personnel who share information. In a sense, planning serves as a coordinating device, even if the formal plan is not adopted (process goals, again). Thus agencies may learn of each other's intentions and problems. Moreover, planning activity may institutionalize search and scanning activities in organizations, forcing review and reconsideration of established ways. Planning can legitimate a predetermined course of action, or justify moving ahead when there is no rational basis for a particular action path—the opposite of stalling (see Vinter and Tropman 1970 for an analysis of the uses of community studies). At this point, however, we can only speculate on these by-products of planning, since systematic evaluations of empirical cases are few and far between.

Beyond that, it behooves planning specialists to observe latent functions of planning such as these with a clear eye, both to use them in a deliberative way in practice when considered appropriate, or to defend against them when they are applied to the detriment of one's clients or organization. These functions can be seen as planning tactics that can shape the course of intervention in the service of planning objectives.

Summary

It might be said that the state of the planning art is currently at a metatheoretical level. Much of the theory is highly abstract and anecdotal in character. There is an insufficiency of rigorous literature involving systematic evaluation. There is also lack of attention to mixed models of planning. Theorists generally pursue a single model while ignoring others. Accepting the validity of mixed models, one can examine planning issues with greater refinement. For example, it would be possible to identify certain problems or areas which should be subject to controlled central planning and others which ought to be left to the free play of the market. Similarly, organizations need a mixture of planning and mutual adjustment.

In a socially and ecologically complex world, expert social planning and management by large, rationalistic bureaucracies with specialized professionals and technicians are essential elements of national survival. At the same time, the impulse of such bureaucracies, and their sponsoring governmental regimes, to become heavy-handed, arrogant, rigid, and self-serving is well known. The countervailing influence of local concerns and particular interests helps keep planning fluid and responsive to human requirements. Left alone entirely, however, the perpetual crush of pluralistic adversary pressures can lead to a neo-Darwinian nightmare of chaos and inequity. Both rationalistic-centralized and adversarial grass-roots modes of action have virtues and benefits. Their mix and interplay provide a healthy balance in the real world, at least until more ideal planning theories come into being to guide human affairs.

Notes

1. For a summary of the problems of comprehensive planning in socialist societies see Lindblom (1977).

2. We will be informed in particular by three significant articles: Galloway and Mayhayni's (1977) discussion of paradigm change in planning; Hudson's (1979) comparative analysis of planning theories; and the explication of knowledge sources for different theories by Friedmann and Hudson (1974).

3. The Hudson schema has much similarity to the "Three Models" formulation of Rothman (1979). Transactional planning has featues in common with Rothman's "locality development." Hudson breaks social planning into rationalistic (which he designates "synoptic") and incremental. He also subdivides social action, arriving at advocacy planning and radical planning. Both authors view the various approaches to planning not as competing and incompatible initiatives but as available planning strategies providing alternatives that may be used selectively in relation to given planning contexts and objectives. They both also discuss favorably the mixing of different traditions or models for particular planning purposes, taking into account the attributes of the different approaches which permit or impede combining among them.

References

Bardach, E. 1977. *The Implementation Game*. Cambridge, Mass.: M.I.T. Press.

Boulding, Kenneth, Martin Pfaff, and Anita Pfaff. 1973. *Transfers in an Urbanized Economy: Theories and Effects of the Grants Economy*. Belmont, Calif.: Wadsworth.

Brager, George A. and Harry Specht. 1973. *Community Organizing*. New York: Columbia University Press.

Branch, Melville. 1978. "Critical Unresolved Problems of Urban Planning Analysis." *Journal of the American Institute of Planners* (January), 44(1):47–59.

Burchell, Robert and James Hughes. 1979. "Planning Theory in the 1980's—A Search for Future Directions." In Burchell and Sternlieb, eds., *Planning Theory in the 1980's,* pp. xvii–liii.

Burchell, Robert and George Sternlieb, eds. 1979. *Planning Theory in the 1980's*. New Brunswick, N.J.: The Center for Urban Policy Research.

Byington, Margaret F. 1911. *What Social Workers Should Know About Their Own Communities*. New York: Russell Sage Foundation.

Cates, Jerry. 1981. "Social Security: Organization and Policy." Ph.D. dissertation, University of Michigan.

Colcord, Joanna C. 1939. *Your Community: Its Provisions for Health, Education, Safety, and Welfare*. New York: Russell Sage Foundation.

Cox, Fred M., et al., eds. 1979. *Strategies of Community Organization,* 3d ed. Itasca, Ill.: Peacock.

Davidoff, Paul. 1965. "Advocacy and Pluralism in Planning." *Journal of the American Institute of Planners* (November), 31(4):331–38.

Derthick, Martha. 1979. *Policy Making for Social Security*. Washington, D.C.: Brookings Institution.

Dunham, Arthur. 1948. *The Job of the Community Organization Worker*. New York: Association for the Study of Community Organization and Community Chests and Councils of America.

——. 1970. *The New Community Organization*. New York: Crowell.

Emery, F. E. and E. L. Trist. 1965. "The Causal Texture of Organizations and Environments." *Human Relations* (February), 18(1):31–32.

Etzioni, Amitai. 1968. *The Active Society: A Theory of Society and Political Processes*. New York: Free Press.

Friedmann, John. 1973. *Retracking America: A Theory of Transactive Planning*. New York: Anchor Press, Doubleday.

Friedmann, John and Barclay Hudson. 1974. "Knowledge and Action: A Guide to Planning Theory." *Journal of the American Institute of Planners* (January), 40(1):2–16.

Galloway, Thomas D. and Riad G. Mahayni. 1977. "Planning Theory in Retrospect: The Process of Paradigm Change." *Journal of the American Institute of Planners* (January), 43(1):62–71.

Gilbert, Neil and Harry Specht, eds. 1977. "Social Planning and Community Organization Approaches." In *Encyclopedia of Social Work,* pp. 1412–25, 17th ed. Washington, D.C.: NASW.

————. 1981. *Handbook of the Social Services.* Englewood Cliffs, N.J.: Prentice-Hall.

Haggstrom, Warren. 1969. "Can the Poor Transform the World?" In Kramer and Specht, eds., *Readings in Community Organization Practice,* pp. 301–14. Englewood Cliffs, N.J.: Prentice-Hall.

Hargrove, Erwin C. 1975. *The Missing Link: The Study of the Implementation of Social Policy.* Washington, D.C.: Urban Institute.

Harper, Ernest B. and Arthur Dunham, eds. 1959. *Community Organization in Action: Basic Literature and Critical Comments.* New York: Association Press.

Hudson, Barclay. 1979. "Comparison of Current Planning Theories: Counterparts and Contradictions." *Journal of the American Institute of Planners* (October), 45(4):387–98.

Kahn, Alfred J. 1969. *Theory and Practice of Social Planning.* New York: Russell Sage Foundation.

Kramer, Ralph M. and Harry Specht, eds. 1969. *Readings in Community Organization Practice.* Englewood Cliffs, N.J.: Prentice-Hall.

Kuhn, Thomas. 1970. *The Structure of Scientific Revolutions.* 2d ed. Chicago: University of Chicago Press.

Lane, Robert P. 1959. "The Nature and Characteristics of Community Organization—A Preliminary Inquiry." In Harper and Dunham, eds. *Community Organization in Action: Basic Literature and Critical Comments,* pp. 60–70.

Lauffer, Armand. 1981. "The Practice of Social Planning." In Gilbert and Specht, eds., *Handbook of the Social Services,* pp. 583–97.

Lauffer, Armand and Edward Newman, eds. 1981. "Community Organization for the 1980's." *Social Development Issues,* special issue of the journal, (Summer and Fall), (5):2–3.

Lindblom, Charles. 1965. *The Intelligence of Democracy: Decision Making Through Mutual Adjustment.* New York: Free Press.

————. 1977. *Politics and Markets: The World's Political-Economic Systems.* New York: Basic Books.

Litwak, Eugene and Lydia F. Hylton. 1962. "Inter-Organizational Analysis: A Hypothesis on Coordinating Agencies." *Administrative Science Quarterly,* 6(4):395–420.

McNeil, Kenneth Edward. 1973. "Citizens as Brokers: Cooptation in an Urban Setting." Ph.D. dissertation, Vanderbilt University.

March, James Q. and Herbert A. Simon. 1959. *Organizations.* New York: Wiley.

Merton, Robert K. 1957. "Manifest and Latent Functions." In Merton, *Social Theory and Social Structure,* pp. 19–84. Glencoe, Ill.: Free Press.

Morris, Robert and Robert Binstock. 1966. *Feasible Planning for Social Change.* New York: Columbia University Press.

Peattie, Lisa. 1968. "Reflections on Advocacy Planning." *Journal of the American Institute of Planners,* 34(2):80–87.

Perlman, Robert. 1970. "Social Planning and Community Organization." In *Encyclopedia of Social Work,* pp. 1404–12. 17th ed. Washington, D.C.: NASW.

Perlman, Robert and Arnold Gurin. 1972. *Community Organization and Social*

Planning. New York: Wiley.

Pondy, Louis. 1964. "Budgeting and Inter-Group Conflict in Organizations." *Pittsburgh Business Review* (April), 34(3):1–3.

Porter, David O. and David C. Warner. 1973. "How Effective Are Grantor Controls: The Case of Federal Aid to Education." In Boulding, Pfaff, and Pfaff, *Transfers in an Urbanized Economy,* pp. 276–302.

Pressman, J. and Aaron Wildavsky. 1973. *Implementation.* 2d ed. University of California Press.

Rittel, Horst and Melvin M. Webber. 1973. "Dilemmas in a General Theory of Planning." *Political Sciences* (June), 4(2):155–69.

Root, Lawrence C. 1981. "Theory, Practice and Curriculum: Issues Emerging from the Symposium on Community Organization in the 1980's." In Lauffer and Newman, eds., *Community Organization for the 1980's,* pp. 10–16.

Ross, Murray. 1955. *Community Organization: Theory and Principles.* New York: Harper and Row.

Rothman, Jack. 1964. "An Analysis of Goals and Roles in Community Organization Practice." *Social Work* (April), 9(2):24–31.

——. 1974. *Planning and Organizing for Social Change: Action Principles from Social Science Research.* New York: Columbia University Press.

——. 1979. "Three Models of Community Organization Practice, Their Mixing and Phasing." In Cox et al., eds., *Strategies of Community Organization,* pp. 25–45.

——.1980. *Social R & D: Research and Development in the Human Services.* Englewood Cliffs, N.J.: Prentice-Hall.

Rothman, Jack and Wyatt Jones. 1971. *A New Look at Field Instruction.* New York: Association Press in Cooperation with the Council on Social Work Education.

Shonfield, Andrew. 1965. *Modern Capitalism.* London: Oxford University Press.

Simon, Herbert A. 1957. *Administrative Behavior: A Study of Decision-Making Processes in Administrative Organization.* 2d ed. New York: Macmillan.

Smith, T. B. 1973. "The Policy Implementation Process." *Policy Science,* 4(4):197–209.

Spiro, Shimon. 1979. "The Knowledge Base of Community Organization Practice." In Cox et al., eds., *Strategies of Community Organization,* pp. 79–84.

Vinter, Robert D. and John E. Tropman. 1970. "The Causes and Consequences of Community Studies." In Cox et al., eds., *Strategies of Community Organization,* pp. 315–23. 2d ed.

Warren, Roland L. 1955. *Studying Your Community.* New York: Russell Sage Foundation.

——. 1967. "Application of Social Science Knowledge to the Community Organization Field." *Journal of Education for Social Work* (Spring), 3(1):60–72.

Wildavsky, Aaron. 1972. "Why Planning Fails in Nepal." *Administrative Science Quarterly* (December), 17(4):508–28.

Williams, W. and R. F. Elmore. 1976. *Social Program Implementation.* New York: Academic Press.

Wolf, Eric. 1980. "They Divide and Sub-Divide, and Call It Anthropology." New York *Times,* November 30.

6

Pluralism and Participation: The Political Action Approach

Charles F. Grosser and Jacqueline Mondros

American society, comprised of diverse social class, ethnic, racial, and religious groups, functions on the assumption that these multiple constituencies pursue their different interests within commonly accepted political, social, and economic contexts. This pursuit of subgroup interest within a common set of norms is what is meant by pluralism.

The engagement of all constituent groups in the political process is central to the efficacy of pluralism. Engagement may take place within a variety of decision-making arenas (the workplace, electoral politics, voluntary organizations) by which the nation is governed and through which resources are distributed and responsibilities assigned.

When any constituent group is excluded, the checks and balances essential for the preservation of each group's self-interest will not exist nor will the decision-making process have achieved a democratic consensus which enables it to speak for the aggregate. Groups excluded from community decision-making processes are, or come to constitute, an exploited underclass whose economic, political, and social interests are neglected or ignored.

Pluralism and participation are ways in which our society legitimates its actions, provides for social control and administrative efficiency, and attempts to ensure the rights of subgroups within the community. Participation and pluralism as used in this essay provide a framework for organizing for political action based upon the assumption that subgroup representation and social change occur as part of a social process which functions to ensure the stability of society. This stability is brought about by providing a means by which needed change takes place within existing political, social, and economic parameters.

Throughout history, attention given to establishing participation even in overtly undemocratic systems can be related to fear of the consequences of excluding some from the mechanisms of governance. Those who are excluded soon lose, if they ever had, commitment to the status quo and thereby become a threat to its existence. Over time, reversing the alienation of those excluded by bringing them into established governance becomes more difficult as the intransigence of the "ins" increases in the face of real concessions they must make; while the "outs" increasingly feel that the system has no integrity. It is at such a point that pluralism, even as a pretext, may be abandoned and communities or organizations turn from the inclusion of subgroups to their repression. The dynamics of participation, its corruption, the erosion of pluralistic and democratic decision-making, and the emergence of authoritarian rule can take place throughout the national polity and within its institutions. The process can be found at local and national levels; in voluntary associations and fraternal organizations; in the workplace and the trade union; in the churches; in social service delivery systems; and in electoral politics. It is a process endemic to democratic society.

One objective of community social work practice is to reduce the erosion of pluralistic democracy by ensuring and/or maximizing participation by citizens in the institutions and systems of society. A related goal is that of facilitating alternate channels of participation through the development of new organizations of the excluded. In both cases, a consequence of community practice is expansion of the quality and impact of participatory efforts. This is the basis upon which community social work legitimates its stance of working on behalf of the excluded by utilizing sanctions or opportunities which may have been created for other purposes and other constituencies. The rationale and sanction of such efforts relate to incorporating nonparticipating subgroups into decision-making to enhance their share of the "good life" and to maintain the institutions of our society.

Struggle within a pluralistic society (or any society for that matter) is continuous, and social conflict is seen as a continuing presence in community life. Thus, community social work involves recognizing and managing conflict in as deliberate and rational a manner as possible. However, community social workers, or any other professionals who presume to deal with social change, must come to terms with the limits of their ambitions. Social forces are beyond the control of professionals. By recognizing conflict and change as present in all human interaction, organizers can strive to influence it in directions favorable to their constituents. They can avoid confrontation when targets are clearly more powerful, choose objectives for which there are fewer declared special interests, and join more powerful movements and forces.

This perspective on conflict serves to locate decision-making in diverse places in the community, putting into operation a multiple rather than an elitist view of community power. These views of conflict and power avoid the requirement that organizers meta-phorically "push the river," a task they simply cannot do; rather, the river, like society, is in constant motion with its own turbulance, eddies, and backwashes which limit the directions in which it moves. Despite these restrictions, change takes place, and it is within the capacities of practitioners to influence this process—as it is within the capacity of pilots to navigate rivers by using forces about which they have some understanding—but not control it.

This optimism about the potential for change is not without conceptual and historical precedents. While the beginnings of social action organizing are often attributed to Saul Alinsky's People's Organizations of the 1930s, the labor movement, and the anti-war, civil rights, and student movements of the 1960s, community orga-nizing within social work practice has an earlier history. In the early part of the century, progressive settlement house leaders spear-headed reforms for better housing, good public schools, child labor legislation, and the establishment of public recreational facilities. Social action was a respectable category of service which benefited all members of the community. Social workers such as Petit, Mc-Clenahan, and Steiner, although arguing for a consensus model, were writing in the 1920s about the importance of citizen participation and the practice techniques necessary to involve people in community decision-making (Austin and Betten 1977).

The Lane Report of 1939 firmly placed the goals of community organizing within the context of the social work profession. In 1948, however, Kenneth Pray, in a paper entitled "When Is Community Organization Social Work Practice?" adopted a more conservative approach that limited community organization by moving it back toward a consensus rather than a conflict model (Galper and Mondros 1980). His thinking helped to place social action outside the profession for almost twenty years, while organizing and training schools based on the Alinsky model grew isolated from, and sometimes opposed to, the traditional social service sector. In the 1960s, under the rubric of the War on Poverty and with federal financing, social action was once again embraced by social work, as perhaps is best exemplified by the work of Mobilization for Youth (Brager and Purcell 1967).

The social activists of today, then, have available social work, Alinsky, and the movements of the 1960s as philosophical precedents to stimulate practice.

Assumptions Regarding Society

To frame a political action approach to community social work and to make our operating biases clear, four working assumptions regarding phenomena within this society which compromise constituent interests (inequality, exclusion, power, and conflict) will be described. These assumptions deserve explication because they significantly define and shape the political-action approach to community organization and, we contend, are compatible with social work's traditions.

INEQUALITY

The unequal distribution of income, social resources, services, and other amenities of life is a characteristic of our society. This maldistribution is easily documented by comparative statistics on how long people live, infant death rates, the incidence of disease, how much people earn, who is employed, who lives in inadequate housing, and who is educated. That the poor and minorities receive less of society's resources and suffer more of society's ills is more typical of American life than apple pie. Thus, persons who suffer deprivation are not seen as responsible for their fate as a consequence of personal inadequacy. Although personal inadequacies and incompetencies are as inherent in the lives of the deprived as they are in the lives of the privileged, it is the unevenness of political and economic power—not individual aberration—which defines and maintains society's underclass.

EXCLUSION

Participation in the conventional pluralistic channels of society does not include the full spectrum of citizens. The organizational affiliations of the poor, minorities, and other people at risk tend to be in primary groups. These expressive organizations (home town clubs, storefront and Pentecostal churches, social and athletic clubs) are unaffiliated and rarely interface with conventional community decision-making systems. That those who do not receive a fair share of the nation's resources are the same people who are significantly underrepresented or absent from decision-making is not accidental; the two phenomena are related and reinforcing conditions. The underrepresented do not have their needs heard or properly attended to because social resources are allocated through participatory systems in which they are not included. In turn, such neglect, underservice, and deprivation increase social alienation and decrease the opportunities for, and inclination toward participating in the conventional systems which exclude them.

POWER

Domhoff (1967) and others have documented that elitist multinational power structures control and dominate public policy in this country, particularly as it affects national affairs. Beyond this elitist superstructure, however, political power is also located differentially at various geographic levels and in numerous social institutions. This dispersal of some power permits the identification of

opportunities for relatively open decision-making within certain locations and around specific issues (Dahl 1961). The geometric possibilities for combinations and permutations—alliances, coalitions,
disengagements, and disinterest—all in continuous change, characterize much of American political and community life. This disor-
derliness, although it lacks substantive theoretical foundations,
helps to provide a viable context for a political action approach to
community practice.

CONFLICT

Finally, it is assumed that political conflict is an ongoing, normal
component of society: it is a social mechanism which characterizes
interaction and through which change takes place. That management of conflict is a fundamental component of political action
community work may be surmised from the work of Coser (1956)
and others, and such practice is part of a set of skills by which social
conflict is affected. The direction that conflict takes, its timing,
who benefits, and the nature of its resolution are amenable to influence. Professionals do not create conflict or other social processes,
but strive to understand them and utilize their knowledge in order to
facilitate desired outcomes.

Assumptions Regarding Change

What changes can reasonably be anticipated as a result of a political
action approach to community organization? Apart from the unanticipated consequences which invariably accompany all social activity, three types of change can be specified: personal growth,
acquisition of skills, and institutional and political accountability.
These changes, although modest, are not insignificant.

PERSONAL GROWTH

Individuals who are isolated, unaffiliated, with little knowledge,
and without influence, often see themselves as "objects" susceptible
to social forces and circumstances over which they have little or no

control. These self-perceptions induce destructive social and psychological adaptations such as deprecatory self-images, anomie, and fatalism. Engagement in community life through political action can be the antidote by which such individuals gain a modicum of influence over some aspects of their lives. Through this process, a consciousness raising often takes place which, among other things, enables individuals to locate the proper source of at least some of their troubles. In addition, organizational experience can provide participants with a sense of solidarity and esprit de corps. As personal growth and change occur through community participation, a person's sense of competence and self-esteem is increased. In turn, this lessens the acceptance of invidious social stereotypes, and new sources of strength and energy are found in the support of comrades-in-a-cause.

SKILLS

Participation in either an established or an alternate organization requires numerous interactional skills. Such technical skills are best acquired through a participatory experience. Modest organizing efforts which deal with relatively simple, noncontroversial problems and involve small numbers of people can give the inexperienced an opportunity to acquire important skills of citizenship. Learning how to conduct meetings, engage in group decision-making, build constituencies, and negotiate and take leadership are a few of the skills which can be acquired through organizational experience. Engaging in community organization projects also provides participants with knowledge of the way in which various community systems function and are influenced, the location of local centers of decision-making, actual and potential allies and adversaries, and the like. This knowledge can be accrued through group activity aimed at social change; once acquired it remains a personal and organizational resource. This resource may then become a source of power which will enable the unaffiliated to engage in increasingly more complicated and controversial participatory efforts.

ACCOUNTABILITY

Citizen participation is an important means of governance. The regulatory mechanisms of bureaucracies or alternate groups such as rank-and-file committees, tenants councils, or councils of beneficiaries are fundamental ways in which bureaucracies are held accountable by their service consumers. Regardless of their function, be it representation, service delivery, production of goods, public service, or mutual benefit, bureaucratic organizations tend to become deflected from their stated or mandated purpose. This deflection may result from a preoccupation with organizational maintenance, interest-group pressure, or internecine struggle. The mere presence of those for whom the bureaucracies' benefits are intended, in either mandated or alternate participatory groups, at the very least holds the systems accountable by making their decision-making visible.

An inevitable concomitant of the centralization which is a prominent aspect of urban-industrial society is the need to put into operation complex national programs at the local level. The presence of grass-roots constituencies in the process provides at least a modicum of assurance that they will receive some share of such programs.

The Role of the Worker

Given the fact that the political action approach can result in personal growth, the acquisition of skills, and institutional and political accountability, a further question remains unanswered: What can community social workers do to help achieve these results, and how does this differ from other types of community practice?

There are three roles which are frequently used by political action organizers: educator, resource developer, and agitator. These are complementary rather than discrete roles which are used intermittently by the worker in seeking to engage a community and develop organizational strategies.

In the role of educator, the organizer engages people in an ongoing dialogue which puts into perspective their life situation

(Friere 1972). As an educator, the community worker helps people to identify issues, to partialize the sources of their problem, and to speculate about possible solutions. The worker converses about power and conflict, encourages people to challenge preconceived notions, and works to unlease the potential of every community member. In addition, the community worker will collaborate with people to structure and maintain the organization, to learn techniques for holding meetings, and to understand and be able to carry out other administrative duties. It is in this role that the community practitioner helps members to become aware of their responsibilities and learn participatory skills.

The political action organizer also carries responsibilities for developing resources, and it is this role which is perhaps closest to other forms of community organization practice. The worker is a resource developer for the people by providing the resources by which the organization can operate. The resource function includes such activities as research, raising funds, acquiring staff and meeting places, drafting flyers and press releases, and other organizational maintenance activities.

The third role the political action organizer carries is the function of activist, the paid professional agitator. It is in this role that the organizer "rubs raw the sores of discontent," exposing the myths people have held about themselves and challenging them to take action in areas considered sacrosanct. In this role, the organizer is an iconoclast, but he also helps people to think and talk about the possibilities for change in power relationships. As such, he uses the Socratic method to stir people out of apathy and into action (Grosser 1973).

While the roles of educator, resource developer, and activist are common to other types of community practice, and indeed all social work methods, there are some roles which are noticeably absent from the political action model. The political action organizer does not mediate between institutions and the people, for to do so implies an impartiality which is clearly not achievable. The social worker using this approach is all for his particular constituency. Furthermore, the worker does not function as a broker between institutions and the people, for this would be fostering dependency rather than challenging people to do for themselves. Finally, the political action social worker does not advocate on behalf of the people, but through working with them helps them to advocate for themselves. In these ways, a political action worker is distinguished from the community planner or program developer who is often called upon to perform these more directive roles.

Political Action Organizations

LEGALLY MANDATED ORGANIZATIONS

Since the 1960s there has been a marked increased in requirements for citizen participation as a part of domestic legislation. Social service agencies have sought new strategies and created mechanisms to involve clients in their governance. This surge of interest in the participation of constituents has been seen in such diverse institutions as universities, churches, social service agencies, government planning bodies, trade unions, and even in the business sector. The profile of the participating constituents seems to have changed as well. Once the domain of the elite, benefactors and experts, these institutions have sought the addition of representatives of minority groups, the handicapped, women, labor, neighborhood residents, and senior citizens. The newly emerged decision-making bodies hardly look like their predecessors, such as the federated funding bodies, agency boards of directors, and health and welfare councils.

The reasons for this change in governance are not entirely clear. Certainly, the movements of the 1960s reflected the desire of the poor and the powerless to be included in policy-making and implementation. This, as we have said, is necessary for the maintenance of pluralism.

Some view the involvement of selected representatives as a form of co-optation, an effort to keep the underclass quiet. Others have viewed these sanctions as opportunities for relatively powerless middle managers and administrators to organize constituencies in an attempt to acquire influence. What is clear is that recent legislation, and the new governing mechanisms which grow out of it, gives legitimacy to constituent participation. In response, social agencies, government bodies, and other institutions have redefined their governance. Political action efforts under public administrative auspices, such as local advisory boards of public agencies, municipal neighborhood governance, or community action programs, are legally mandated organizations.

The assumption which underlies community practice under the aegis of official sponsors is that the broader the base of participation in local decision-making, the more equitable the distribution of resources will be. In addition to achieving greater equity, such efforts recruit and train a cadre of leaders for involvement in the political and social service systems. It is assumed that the presence of these leaders will broaden existing local participatory mechanisms and, by joining with elected officials and bureaucrats representing other excluded constituencies, they will be able to influence policy formulation in state and national systems.

However, efforts of this sort cannot eliminate many of the problems which beset deprived local communities. First, most community decision-making is reactive to federal and state policies over which local residents have little influence; second, the interests of one group of grass-roots consumers are not necessarily compatible with the interests of other deprived constituencies; third, legally mandated participation often exists only in areas of marginal impact. Participating in legally mandated organizations is often more useful as a means to resist further deprivation rather than a means for instituting social change. Though such modest goals are denigrated by some, we believe that the improvement or maintenance of concrete benefits such as food stamps, Medicaid, or rent subsidies are not insignificant in the lives of local citizens; if they are to be spurned, this can only be by the beneficiaries themselves.

SELF-GENERATED ORGANIZATIONS

Paralleling the development of legally mandated citizen participation programs is the continuing emergence of organizations generated by unaffiliated groups not sanctioned by law or by identifiable community institutions. These political action efforts such as neighborhood associations and minority rights and self-help organizations are self-generated organizations.

The explanatory rationale for the emergence of self-generated organizations includes the need for bonding and the desire to maximize a sense of autonomy and control. These fundamental human needs appear to have been sharpened by recent experiences with established political and voluntary institutions which as a rule do not represent the interests of the rank and file. In addition, as society increases in complexity and citizens seek to reduce anonymity and powerlessness, the need to be a part of a smaller environment becomes more salient. The complexity of post-industrial society has been increasing geometrically, and the environment is more and more viewed as dangerous, unintelligible, and beyond an individual's control. The emergency of today's self-generated organizations is not unlike the establishment of mutual-aid societies, cultural groups, and home town clubs by immigrants in the early 1900s. Within a small, self-created unit of peers, individuals can maximize their sense of well-being, autonomy, and power. The need to have an impact on the world, exacerbated by its magnitude and complexity, becomes more realizable within smaller reference groups.

There is much evidence that people's faith in the leaders, principles, and mechanisms of public and private democratic institutions has been shaken by events over the past two decades such as the Vietnam War, assassinations, Watergate, ABSCAM, and the taking of hostages in Iran. As faith is lost, ordinary citizens acquire the impulse to do things for themselves, becoming as best they can the instruments of their own destiny.

While there are differences, it should be noted that self-generated and mandated organizations have common elements. Self-generated organizations are, in the largest sense, legally mandated under the rights of free speech and assembly guaranteed by the Bill of Rights. Many such organizations receive government funding, have organizational representatives on advisory boards of other institutions, or serve in an advisory capacity to government or business. Thus, while these self-generated organizations are not explicitly mandated, their activities place them in the midst of democratic pluralism.

Organizations are dynamic in character, doing different things at different times. An organization may, in fact, begin as self-generated and become legally mandated. Many welfare rights organizations exemplify this transition. Likewise, organizations which begin as legally mandated may find they need to encourage the development of a separate, self-generated entity in order to attain particular goals. Parent-teacher and home-school associations sometimes develop parents' unions outside a school in order to organize around specific educational issues which would not be acceptable in their mandated roles. The dynamic character of organizations precludes hard-and-fast distinctions between legally mandated organizations and self-generated ones. Perhaps most important, self-generated and legally mandated organizations are related to the same struggle for inclusion in pluralistic decision-making. Therefore, we see them as variations on the themes of pluralism.

Four Organizational Strategies

We believe it is useful to categorize political action oriented organizations by the strategies used to deal with the social issues and change objections we have described. These strategies are morale building, problem-solving, function transfer, and power transfer. A morale-building strategy is one which focuses on member satisfaction, and is often related to cultural activities or common social or recreational interests. A problem-solving strategy deals with resolution of a particular issue or grievance. The function-transfer strategy deals with organizations' service failures by launching efforts to provide the service through alternate means. The power transfer mode attempts to amass sufficient influence to prevail over special interest and elitist blocs on behalf of citizens who, by virtue of their lack of collective power, have been unable to influence local decision-making.

All of these strategies may function as part of public and private participatory mechanisms or may take the form of self-generated, independent groups which are alternatives to established systems. While these strategies are not mutually exclusive, they do provide a context within which current modes of political action practice can be compared and contrasted. These strategies will help us to describe practice even though it varies enormously, and to apply some common assumptions regarding change, tactics, structure, membership, motivation, and ideology.

MORALE BUILDING

The political action mode manifesting a morale-building approach is one which focuses on increasing the level of constituent satisfaction without paying particular heed to changing the environment. This strategy assumes that people must feel good about themselves, their life style, and their environment, and that this sense of well-being will induce social behavior which will contribute to and support this feeling. Many of the goals of morale-building organizations are related to cultural activities and the maintenance of group heritage. Examples of legally mandated organizations with a morale perspective are home and school associations, retarded children associations, and regional arts councils. Activities of such groups include extracurricular parent-child school programs, olympics for the developmentally disabled, and craft exhibits. Examples of self-generated modes of morale building are senior citizen "sunshine clubs," ethnic cultural societies, and the Daughters of the American Revolution. Activities of these groups include holiday celebrations, cultural heritage fairs and exchanges, and oral history programs.

In keeping with morale-building assumptions, impetus for change in such organizations is toward self-improvement. Change objectives, when stated, are generalized and commonly related to the attitudes and behaviors of the organizations' members. For instance, a neighborhood organization looking at the issue of inferior education for children identified the problem as parents not valuing education, and the solution as changing parental attitudes. It was the parents themselves who were seen as the target for change, and as the only inducers of change. Indeed, it was thought that the inadequate educational program and the rundown, outdated school buildings were secondary to the attitudes of parents.

Tactics of this approach are almost always cooperative since conflict is viewed as destructive to the morale of the organization. The organization is loosely structured, reflecting the close primary relationship of its members who interact in a friendly and informal manner. The organizational mode is best characterized as normative, stressing shared beliefs and values and maintaining cohesion and solidarity by adherence to, and reinforcement of, these shared beliefs. Expressive benefits are clearly the central function of the morale approach.

Morale-building organizations generally do not have a codified ideology. Instead, they can be described as process-oriented in their assumption that social change comes about as people feel better about themselves. Such an organization is rarely seen as contentious by others since it does not demand institutional change. As a result, the morale-building strategy is generally well received by official sponsoring institutions which often support such efforts directly through financial support or indirectly through publicity or other forms of recognition.

PROBLEM-SOLVING

The organization which follows a problem-solving strategy is one which assumes that rational intervention and technical assistance can solve the dilemmas of disadvantaged groups. Legally mandated problem-solving organizations include local planning bodies, health planning commissions, and citizen advisory boards. Their activities encompass planning new services, integrating and coordinating existing services, or improving relationships between various community groups or institutions. These organizations are, in fact, social-planning units. Their inclusion here is relevant to the extent that their technical resources are instruments for local citizens. Self-generated organizations that operate with a problem-solving approach include community councils and chests, the Gray Panthers, and some neighborhood organizations. Activities include establishing local decision-making bodies, holding public hearings and meetings, and developing new services.

The motivation for change in the problem-solving mode derives from the discrepancy between services needed and services offered. Change objectives most often relate to instituting a specific change in the environment, such as creating a needed service or coordinating the activities of a group of local agencies. The organization may serve as a mechanism for inducing change, but such change takes the form of new behaviors by existing systems. For instance, a community council working to integrate services for the elderly may be the impetus for setting up an information-exchange network which will involve other service providers. Change tactics are largely collaborative. The problem-solving organizational mode tends to be somewhat formally structured. Members relate primarily to the task at hand, and expressive relationships between members are ancillary. The benefits to members in the problem-solving strategy are largely instrumental. Motivation for membership involvement is largely normative, based on shared beliefs regarding the problem and its solution. Organizational cohesion is maintained through the commitment that members share regarding the solution of a problem.

Generally, the problem-solving strategy lacks a codified ideology other than the belief that solutions to community problems can be rationally derived and implemented. Because problem-solving organizations articulate gaps and inadequacies in service and other discontents, they often face some opposition. However, the rationality of the problem-solving strategy calls for cooperation, and such organizations seek solutions through trade-offs and compromises when necessary.

FUNCTION TRANSFER

An organization which adheres to a function-transfer strategy assumes that unequal influence results in inadequate services and that rather than attempt to change existing systems, constituents should form their own organization which can provide the services they need. Like the problem-solving approach, function transfer is concerned with gaps and ineffective service. Examples of legally mandated organizations using a function-transfer strategy are the Natural Supports Program of the Community Service Society of New York, the Mastectomy Peer Counseling Program of the American Cancer Society, and welfare rights organizations' information and referral programs. Activities include creating support networks, providing emergency benefits, and offering peer counseling. Self-generated organizations typical of the function-transfer strategy are community credit unions, Alcoholics Anonymous, and food cooperatives. Activities within the function-transfer approach are such things as making loans and mortgages available, self-help counseling, and group purchasing.

The motivation for membership in a function-transfer organization is generally the impulse to be free of a further relationship with an inadequate service system. The change objective is the provision of adequate service to deal with the dissatisfactions of recipients. The organization is seen as the only possible inducer of change. Relationships are collaborative among members, but ancillary with external institutions. For example, a low-income neighborhood may not be getting mortgage money from local banks, resulting, among other things, in neighborhood deterioration which the function-transfer strategy tries to stem. To do so, individuals band together to form a community credit union which then offers services that the local bank failed to provide.

The structure of the function-transfer organizational mode tends to greater formalization than either of the prototypes already described; this stems from this type of organization's added role as a service provider. Membership is based on a combination of fraternal and instrumental ties. Fraternity emerges from the fact that members share common goals and ownership of the organization, while the exigencies of members being providers and receivers of service produce more formal instrumental relationships. Membership in such organizations is doubly reinforced by expressive satisfactions and material benefits derived from the achievement of shared social goals.

The ideology of the function-transfer strategy tends to be somewhat codified. The organization is likely to stress the rights of its constituency as well as the personal benefits of their involvement. Such ideology often criticizes service institutions for their failures without voicing assumptions regarding their causes. The organizations' pragmatic solution, to do it themselves, does not demand a larger ideological reference encompassing social malfunctioning. In creating alternative systems, function-transfer strategies inevitably highlight failures in ongoing institutions; consequently, they are frequently viewed as contentious. For example, the apparent effectiveness of the Guardian Angels subway patrols severely discomforts and calls forth attacks from the New York

City Transit Police while the success of Alcoholics Anonymous evokes damnation with faint praise and token support from federally sponsored substance-abuse clinics.

POWER TRANSFER

The organization with a power-transfer strategy is based on the view that society's decisions are made on the basis of power and only the creation of a powerful countervening organization can affect this process. The power-transfer organization will attempt to take decision-making from existing enclaves and place it in the hands of those most directly affected by the decision. Examples of legally mandated power-transfer organizations are health systems agencies, community block grant advisory boards, and professional associations. Activities include making decisions regarding the dispersion of hospital and medical services, deciding on the role of private investors in community development activities, and regulating professional behavior.

Self-generated organizations are represented by such groups as Chicago-based National People's Action, Nine to Five (a working women's organization in Boston), and Action Alliance of Senior Citizens (in Philadelphia). The activities of such organizations include forcing lending institutions to grant mortgages in local neighborhoods, establishing benefits for women office workers in a particular industry, and campaigning for legislative support for a "dollar-a-prescription" program for senior citizens.

The central impulse for affiliation in a power-transfer organization is the desire to change the status quo. This impulse takes many forms, such as eliminating an oppressive or hostile circumstance, seeking equity, or establishing a permanent political or economic power base. Power transfer is usually contentious, requiring condemnation of the status quo whose credibility must be negated if change is to take place. Change objectives are usually quite specific, related to the unacceptable behavior of a local institution and its consequences for the community. Organizing to acquire influence is viewed as the only way in which change can be brought about. Change tactics are conflict-oriented; collaboration is viewed as feasible only when the organization has established its power. At that point, the threat of conflict implicit in organizational strength makes collaboration possible.

The structure of power-transfer organizational modes is formal. Relationships among members are based primarily on their involvement in the organization. This is necessary to establish the discipline to acquire and utilize power and ensure that the organization can mobilize the complex, rigorous, and collective behavior of members that is necessary to engage in effective struggle. Participants tend to seek immediate benefits through successful struggle, but they may also see themselves as part of a larger social movement contributing to the creation of a better world. In power-transfer organizations, in contrast to ideological movements, these expressive rewards are secondary to the instrumental benefits gained from local victories. Power-transfer ideology is often elaborated and articulated by participants and becomes an important basis for organization building. The ideology may take the form of rudimentary social class analysis, demanding the redistribution of power and wealth. The purpose of these organizations is the reallocation of power to grass-roots constituencies, and this generates conflict. Opposition to power-transfer strategies is commonplace and viewed as a programmatic resource by the organization in that it serves to "fuel the fires of discontent" among members.

These four strategies of political-action organizing are not mutually exclusive. An organization based on power transfer will pay attention to constituent morale and in so doing, exhibit characteristics of a morale-building organization. Likewise, a morale-building organization may face an issue which can only be resolved by function- or power-transfer strategies. These perspectives are not meant to represent discrete models. They are better seen as manifestations of qualities of an organization that are highlighted at particular points in its history. For example, a self-generated neighborhood organization may fight redlining from a power-transfer perspective; operate a project which rehabilitates houses for low-income buyers as a function transfer; develop plans and legislative proposals for the rehabilitation of a neighborhood through a problem-solving strategy; and conduct morale-focused ground-breaking celebrations. In addition, this hypothetical organization may be designated as the local planning unit and thus take on a legally mandated function as well.

The variations in activity, ideology, motivation, structure, tactics, and goals represented in our model allow us to grasp the capacities of organizations, the complexities induced by multiple strategies, and the differential application of knowledge and practice skills.

We see our model helping to locate and identify the salient components of political action practice in a pluralistic society and to differentiate the changes possible through various combinations of strategies. We see expressive benefits of political action strategies facilitating people's feelings of satisfaction regarding themselves and their environment.

Attitudes and behaviors are influenced by the new organizational roles that members perform as they acquire new skills in public speaking, gathering and interpreting information, negotiating and bargaining, and confrontation. Oftentimes, these newly acquired attitudes, behaviors, and skills are transferred into social, familial, and vocational aspects of a participant's life.

Political action practice also suggests a variety of ways to obtain instrumental benefits. A morale-building approach has implications for reaching a consensus regarding acceptable norms and values, at least for the participants themselves. Function transfer and problem-solving can create benefits by way of providing new service. The power-transfer strategy suggests that holding community institutions accountable realizes instrumental benefits while helping members to feel more powerful.

DILEMMAS OF SPONSORING AGENCIES

The four strategies described here do not exist in a vacuum but operate under the aegis of some kind of formal or informal sponsorship. The sponsors may have goals which compete with the aspirations of the participants and the social worker. While this dilemma has been well-documented in other places (Brager and Specht 1973), the expectations of the sponsor have significance for morale-building, problem-solving, function transfer, and power-transfer strategies.

We have mentioned that legally mandated organizations are at times an effort to pacify a potentially powerful constituency. In these cases the sponsor may handpick participants believed to be amenable to staff manipulation. At other times, because of public financing, the sponsoring agency may be loath to participate in any action which would place its funding in jeopardy. Sponsors may also try to deflect the organization from addressing more inflammatory issues, focusing only on those areas which create little conflict. Because of these constraints, legally mandated organizations are more likely to be concerned with morale-building or problem-solving, which raise little opposition.

Participants and workers may attempt to develop aspects of the function- and power-transfer models by using such strategic skills as recruiting sympathetic individuals to the sponsor's board, by increasing public support through media campaigns, or by trying to negotiate compromises in other areas (Rothman et al. 1976). However, social workers who operate under public aegis should be aware of their vulnerability; during the twilight of the War on Poverty, programs and positions were reclassified or terminated by sponsors with the aim of neutralizing or eliminating activity that was threatening or troublesome.

Self-generated organizations which arise out of people's need to be the instruments of their own destiny often face a different sponsorship dilemma. Because of their alternative nature, self-generated organizations are more likely to be either function- or power-transfer organizations. These organizations, which often come into conflict with established institutions, may emerge from members' provincial or unrealistic expectations. In the first instance, the organization may be viewed as a vehicle for resisting change, as was the case of organizations which fought fair housing. Here the sponsor's motivations are quite reactionary (Jones 1979). In the second instance, the sponsor may have very high expectations for the organization, seeing it as the only chance for the constituency's salvation. The sponsor's anticipation of swift and global change is unreasonable. In both cases, participants and workers can use some strategic skills to overcome covert and impractical operating goals.

Taking on issues which cut across sex, race, and age lines, making use of the educating role to raise consciousness, and introducing morale and problem-solving strategies may defuse some of the provincial tendencies of the sponsors. Working out clear rights and responsibilities for the organization and its members along with short- and long-range organizational planning may bring a sense of reality to participants (Haggstrom 1969).

While it is certainly true that sponsors may have competing goals which make for added caution, the dilemmas are not insurmountable. Rather the participants must acknowledge that these dilemmas will need episodic attention through the life span of the organization. They must attempt pragmatic solutions to these difficulties, and view these situations as opportunities rather than barricades.

Summary

SOCIAL WORK

It is our view that social work community practice will continue to be a presence in American public life, fluctuating over time and certainly taking different form in the early 1980s than in the 1960s. Community work as a social work practice specialization, however, seems to have undergone a significant decline. A review of current social work periodicals and curriculum offerings at schools of social work establishes the presence of community planning and agency administration where community organization had recently been. While such activities include the development of students' skills in organizing and work with the community, their emphasis is on the rational technical rather than participatory interventions.

Community organization's presence in the whole of social work practice appears to have increased concurrent with its diminution as a specialty. Systems approaches, ecological perspectives, and the prevalence of generalist and other environmentally focused practice models represent a view of problems as deriving from both individual and social disorganization and pathology. As a consequence, providing direct service requires that social work practice encompass the ability to identify and intervene in problems whose genesis may be simultaneously social and environmental. The skills necessary for social environmental intervention include many drawn from what has historically been considered community organization. Such practice reflects aspects of all of the models discussed in this volume rather than relying on the political action approach alone.

In relation to political action organizing, current generalist programs represent a significant precedent in that they embody the premise that those whose presence is not felt will be neglected and ignored. Generalist practice makes clear, we believe, that the political action and empowerment aspects of community practice are intrinsic to the social work process. Such activities, once referred to as social action, are no longer an ancillary to practice but a fundamental element in the delivery of service.

There are still opportunities for social workers as political action workers with such constituencies as low-income neighborhood women, office workers, senior citizens, the unemployed, welfare recipients, the handicapped, and neighborhood groups; such activity is currently taking place. Certainly the values, skills, and knowledge base that social workers bring to such activities prepare them for effective political action practice. Whether or not some social workers accept such jobs depends on the availability of specialized training and the individual professional's "calling" to a type of work which is often arduous, frustrating, and at times lacking in professional status.

ORGANIZING IN A CONSERVATIVE TIME

In 1981, spokesmen for the newly elected Reagan administration and the conservative Republican Senate stated their commitment to participatory policies such as local control, community self-help, and the disposition of federal funds to the states for services provided at local levels. This is a version of the Nixon administration's "new federalism" of the early 1970s, which resulted in a severe reduction of programs and benefits for the poor.

Even fewer resources for services and benefits are being proposed by the use of "super block grants" which have virtually no categorical guidelines. By contrast, proposed tax benefits, defense contracts, public works, and subsidies for industry continue to be guided and supported by centralized federal spending programs.

The scenario for reducing and dismantling welfare state supports to the poor has been written in the language of democratic tradition, using the symbols of participation and pluralism as convenient rationales. The use of this language to justify reducing social benefits poses a number of issues for political action organizations. They will need to deny the assertion that cutbacks in social benefits are in fact decentralization and reduced public spending. To avoid becoming party to a public policy which substitutes self-help and local initiative for public services, they must utilize opportunities to serve as a countervailing force pressing for increased resources and equitable distribution.

An important aspect of political action practice is responsibility for speaking out, from the "soapbox" if necessary. The fallacious representation of welfare spending and government interference as bankrupting the nation and destroying initiative needs to be exposed as a strategy that promotes inequality and the potential for societal discord. The ideology of current conservatism misuses democratic political concepts by applying them to free-enterprise economic problems. It seems to us that political action organizations need to understand this and clearly distinguish between the economic and political systems of this country if they are to achieve effectively the modest changes and objectives they seek. Failure to do so will permit substantial numbers of rank-and-file citizens to act on their economic discontent by supporting political policies which sound like solutions to their problems but are not.

Particularly in times of political conservatism and reduced social expenditures, political action organizations need to utilize democratic, pluralistic, and participatory traditions to focus attention and counterbalance political efforts by economic institutions.

References

Alinsky, Saul. 1969. *Reveille for Radicals*. New York: Vintage Books.
_____. 1971. *Rules for Radicals*. New York: Random House.
Austin, Michael J. and Neil Betten. 1977. "Intellectual Origins of Community Organizing." *Social Service Review* (March), 52(1):155–70.
Brager, George A. and Francis P. Purcell, eds. 1967. *Community Action Against Poverty: Readings from the Mobilization Experience*. New Haven, Conn.: College and University Press.

Brager, George A. and Harry Specht. 1973. *Community Organization*. New York: Columbia University Press.

Coser, Lewis A. 1956. *The Functions of Social Conflict*. Glencoe, Ill.: Free Press.

Dahl, Robert. 1961. *Who Governs?* New Haven, Conn.: Yale University Press.

Domhoff, William. 1967. *Who Rules America?* New Haven, Conn.: Yale University Press.

Friere, Paulo. 1972. *Pedagogy of the Oppressed*. New York: Herder and Herder.

Galper, Jeffry and Jacqueline Mondros. 1980. "Community Organization in Social Work in the 1980s: Fact or Fiction?" *Journal of Social Work Education* (Winter), 16(1):42–48.

Grosser, Charles F. 1973. *New Directions in Community Organization*. New York: Praeger.

Haggstrom, Warren. 1969. "Can the Poor Transform the World?" In Kramer and Specht, eds., *Readings in Community Organization Practice*, pp. 301–14.

Jones, Delmos. 1979. "Not in My Community: The Neighborhood Movement and National Racism." *Social Policy* (September/October), 10(2):44–46.

Kramer, Ralph M. and Harry Specht. 1969. *Readings in Community Organization Practice*. Englewood Cliffs, N.J.: Prentice Hall.

Lane, Robert P. 1939. "The Field of Community Organization." In, *Proceedings, National Conference of Social Work, 1939*. New York: Columbia University Press.

Pray, Kenneth L. 1948. "When Is Community Organization Social Work Practice?" In *Proceedings, National Conference of Social Work, 1948*, pp. 194–204. New York: Columbia University Press.

Rothman, Jack, John L. Erlich, and Joseph G. Teresa. 1976. *Promoting Innovation and Change in Organizations and Communities*. New York: Wiley.

Schaller, Lyle. 1979. *The Change Agent*. Nashville, Tenn.: Abington Press.

Warren, Rachelle and Donald Warren. 1977. *The Neighborhood Organizer's Handbook*. Notre Dame, Ind.: University of Notre Dame Press.

7

Community Work and Social Work: The Community Liaison Approach

Samuel H. Taylor

During the early struggle to define community practice Robert Lane (1939:498) noted that organizations whose primary function is community work usually do not serve clients directly. In contrast, agencies which were expressly formed to serve individuals, families, and groups do work in and with communities because this activity promotes agencies' development and advances the causes of social welfare. Even before the term community organization was coined, people associated with early efforts to help indigents and the ill were keenly aware of processes that had to be carried out at the community level in order to gain support for serving those who were in need.

The earliest social service agencies were themselves the creation of organized efforts within communities, and in turn their staff members and volunteers sought to mobilize action, interpret the nature of the problems they dealt with and the services they offered, and gain support for their programs and the interests of their clients. Although most authors trace the evolution of social work community practice back to the charity organization societies and the settlements that were introduced in the United States in the latter half of the nineteenth century (Garvin and Cox 1979:51–54), direct-service agencies were already performing many of those functions, though not as their primary activity or reason for existence.

By the mid 1920s, community practice was generally associated with planning councils, coordinating and fund-raising organizations, state and local associations, and the settlements and other neighborhood-oriented programs (Heath and Dunham 1963:44–46). Mary Richmond's conceptualization of leadership and persuasive advocacy on behalf of a science-oriented, professionally skilled approach to practice with individuals and families had captured the interests and energies of social service agencies and, subsequently, the developing schools of social work. In 1929, the Milford Conference reflected the profession's focus on defining the generic aspects of social casework and educating practitioners. The generic issue was twofold; how to define the generic nature of casework apart from special attributes of practice within diverse fields such as health, schools, mental health, and so forth, and, more abstractly, to determine the generic foundations and knowledge base that should be shared by all social workers (AASW:1931). This was not a multi-method approach to practice but an attempt to elucidate core values, principles, and knowledge to which all members of the profession could subscribe. The major concern was the development of effective agency-based work with individuals and families, and less attention was devoted to changing the environment.

While this trend did not serve to eliminate the community practice functions of direct-service agencies, such functions were relegated to a secondary role. Whether this patterning was a consequence of a mutual desire for a complementary arrangement of functions or the outcome of deliberate efforts to establish domains and expertise is an interesting question. However, the outcome was that the place of community practice within direct-service agencies grew increasingly ambiguous and unclear. Agencies, through their boards, volunteers, staff, and administration, continued some community activities, usually without the status and legitimacy enjoyed by councils, planning bodies, and associations.

The direct-service arena's contributions to the advancement

of practice knowledge and skill centered more on casework and group work with only occasional published descriptions of the work of an agency dealing with a problem at the community level. It is important to realize, however, that the extent of community practice by direct-service agencies was not fully reflected in the literature. Although the Lane Report acknowledged the community practice roles and functions that direct-service agencies performed, its emphasis was on establishment of community practice as a social work method. This, in turn, implied that this goal would be best advanced by agencies which were primarily or exclusively involved with community practice (Lane 1939:496–97).

A Conflict of Interest

The early attempt of the charity organization societies both to offer direct services to clients and to serve as a locus for the planning and coordination of services offered by other agencies is a classic instance of goal and interest conflict doomed to failure from the beginning. When the National Association of Societies for Organizing Charity, founded in 1911, changed its name eight years later to the American Association for Organizing Family Social Work, this acknowledged both the move toward direct practice and the emergence of community councils and federated financing as new vehicles for community-wide planning, coordination, and funding. As Heath and Dunham concluded from their analysis of community practice at that time, "there were unmistakable signs that a direct consumer-service agency could hardly aspire to be also an objective and neutral coordinator of its sister agencies" (1963:20).

The principle that seemed to have emerged was that as social agencies developed professional staffs and focused on clients and problems within particular fields, they could not be expected to take an objective, comprehensive community perspective in terms either of relative needs in other fields or of the contributions of other agencies within their own field. The issues of perspective and objectivity were recurrent and implied that direct-service agencies could, in fact should, engage in some forms of community practice but not others. What was less clear and not dealt with was: When, and with whom, and for what purposes should service agencies engage in community practice? These questions will be taken up later in this article, following discussion of the paradoxical situation in which agencies found themselves in regard to community practice.

Recognition and Encouragement

Since the 1930s, graduate students in schools of social work have had at least some course content relating to professional involvement with communities as part of the required core curriculum. While the quality and quantity of this content and its support and reinforcement through complementary field work experiences were uneven, the rationale was a logical extension of the profession's recognition that the staff and administration of direct service agencies were and should be involved in community practice. Although there was extensive economic hardship during the depression years, by no means was there widespread understanding of social work's efforts to alleviate poverty nor a consensus that the poor and troubled deserved to be helped. Social workers and social agencies were admonished to use every opportunity to explain to citizens the nature of the problem situations they encountered and the need for help through specific forms of aid and service (Vail 1938).

In 1940, Russell Kurtz outlined the range and location of community practice. He noted that this included every social service agency in addition to, and apart from, its relationship and linkages to other agencies that were primarily involved with community practice (1940:403). This was a significant recognition of the continued expectation that agencies adopt a role in work with the community, but it assumed that this activity was aimed at assuring agency survival and development in order that clients might be helped (402).

Meanwhile, community work was still struggling to establish its legitimacy as a practice method while simultaneously endeavoring to develop a scientific conceptual framework. As late as 1959, Johnson noted:

Unfortunately, community organization method is confused, social science materials are not yet applied so that a conceptual framework can be taught; we must rely on experience to guide teaching. The agencies in which casework is the major service reflect also the stage of development of community organization theory and practice. Where there is leadership of social workers with philosophy, knowledge and experience in community organization work, young workers have a chance to develop an integrated practice of social work. (160–61)

Reflective of this integrated practice perspective, Murphy devoted two chapters of his book on community practice to line workers and administrators (1954:307–55). His approach appeared to have several purposes, namely, to label various activities as community practice, to exhort clinical practitioners and administrators to include community practice as an integral aspect of their professional roles, and to suggest new community-oriented practices as a means of addressing unmet needs. Murphy's listing included a diverse range of activities such as participating in or staffing interagency committees, liaisoning with other departments and agencies, contributing to the work of state and local conferences, collaborating with citizen groups, representing the agency at community meetings, working with professional associations to formulate policy or lobbying for change, "tying in" or maintaining an awareness of developments and trends in community life, bringing together local leadership, fund raising, interpreting agency programs and client problems and needs, lobbying for legislative change, developing resources, coordinating services and programs, and, of course, engaging in social action (327–33).

Murphy's encyclopedic listing grew out of his concern that professional education was producing narrow specialists who did not have a broad social work philosophy and conception of their responsibilities. Thus he argued that all social workers needed a community practice orientation, although only some should devote themselves to full-time involvement in community practice agencies.

Eight years later, Violet Sieder (1962) presented what has come to be recognized as a classic paper, "Community Organization in the Direct Service Agency." In it she acknowledged that though community work is a secondary method in direct-service agencies, every agency is necessarily involved in such practice. Noting that the division of roles and responsibilities appropriate for line workers, supervisors, and administrators was usually not delineated or designed in a manner that could optimally promote agency effectiveness, she argued it was crucial that the various community work functions and processes be specified and legitimated (Sieder 1962:93).

Moving beyond Murphy's listing of activities, Sieder categorized community practice in a direct-service agency into three distinct functions:

1. Interorganizational relations, including referrals, interorganization exchange, and joint agency action on behalf of its clients
2. Mobilization of community supports for the agency, its programs, financing, and ideology
3. Change of community resources, including initiation, revision, elimination or combination of services needed on behalf of the agency's clients. (1962:95)

The purpose of the agency's entry into community practice was assumed to be consistent with its predominant interest in serving and improving the wellbeing of clients. A return to a problem-oriented approach to clients was proposed as more effective than simply offering casework or group work services. Sieder deplored the tendency of many agencies to move to the sidelines of community planning, sometimes isolating their cinical and supervisory staff from such practice roles (1962:96–97).

Perlman and Gurin, acknowledging the value of Sieder's contribution, suggest that the first function, interorganizational relations, can be subsumed under the second and third functions: "Our focus there is on two major organizational tasks—*the acquiring of resources vital to the agency's operation and the redefinition of goals, functions and programs vis-à-vis a changing environment*" (1972:160). In effect, Perlman and Gurin assume a perspective more consistent with organization theory in that the community practice functions of agencies are not necessarily an additional responsibility inherent in a broadly defined social welfare mission. Rather, the community functions relate to each agency's efforts to make the most of its exchanges and relationships, such as the acquisition of needed resources and adapting to environmental changes. This perspective serves to introduce the following consideration of the questions and reservations directed toward the direct-service agency's role as a base for community work.

NARROWING THE COMMUNITY PRACTICE FOCUS

In 1929, Porter Lee argued that the time had come for social work to transfer its energies and efforts from zealous pursuit of social causes and efforts to remedy countless injustices, in favor of developing effective agency programs with an emphasis on organization technique, standards, and efficiency (1929:3–20). As Lubove has noted in referring to social work's transition:

Reformers in the late nineteenth and early twentieth centuries created an immense network of welfare organizations to care for the deprived and maladjusted. Among the consequences for remedial, preventive and constructive philanthropy were function instead of cause; administrator instead of charismatic leader; rational organization and centralized machinery of control instead of individual impulses and village neighborliness. (1965:158)

This rational approach toward work with clients suggested that a complementary relationship should develop between direct-service agencies that utilized casework as their primary method and community councils that were structured to devote their attention exclusively to the community at large and their constituent agencies. Particularly in developed urban and metropolitan areas, one can imagine the informal and formal processes of adjustment and the interagency agreements which symbolized the growing move toward structuring and patterning the roles and relationships among agencies. As councils and associations took on responsibility for orchestrating service coordination, problem identification, and mobilization of citizen and agency action for reform and change, clinical agencies and their practitioners undoubtedly felt less need to expend scarce resources in these areas.

In 1945, Kenneth Pray addressed the National Conference of Social Work with a plea for all professional social workers to engage again in social action in order to influence the basic social conditions and policies that adversely affected clients (349–50). Pray's presentation was not a call for zealous efforts at reform; his advocacy of social action was tempered by a persistently constraining focus on the latitude and discretion that professionals might employ in their activities. With reference to social service agencies, Pray posed the paradox:

It seems clear that the client-worker relationship must be held clear for service and service only . . . The process of service itself, by helping to release strength and energy in clients, which they may ultimately turn . . . toward the conscious change of social policies that affect them, may, it is true, indirectly promote social change. (1945:354)

One wonders what sanction this actually offered the social workers who sought to engage clients in working to improve their conditions. Viewing the social worker in the agency context, Pray noted that professionals in agencies that enjoyed a two-way flow of interest among board, administration, and professional staff might well take action on problems relevant to their agency's particular function and expertise, except, of course, that the social worker

is and must be the representative of a social agency, bound to operate within its policies which cannot always express his own highest ideals of service since they must incorporate, also, the differing viewpoints of non-professional sponsors and supporters. (1945:358)

In such circumstances practitioners were urged to channel their personal and professional activities through professional organizations and special-interest groups and, by implication, on their own time rather than the agency's.

Although it is ironic that Pray's call to action was so interlaced with constraints and admonitions, it is a vivid illustration of the frustration clinical practitioners experienced in their efforts to conceptualize a community practice role. If their own minimal preparation, the specialized training of community council staffs, and constraints regarding social action were not sufficient inhibitors, questions were also raised about their motives in terms of the use of community practice to further parochial agency interests and goals. Both direct-service and governmental agencies were viewed with suspicion in terms of their willingness to promote communities' interests. As recently as 1962 the National Association of Social Workers (NASW) Commission on Practice noted that:

Single purpose social agencies such as those concerned with a specific segment of the community such as children, the aged, families, transients . . . generally conduct direct services. . . . Frequently they may limit community organization functioning to predetermined specific goals usually set by the agency's official purpose and its own organizational priorities. (1962:11)

In reference to governmental departments, more serious questions were raised by the NASW Commission:

Specific objectives of the community organization services are usually set by the official mission of the chief executive officer and staff, or the responsible legislature and become organizational goals for staff to achieve. . . . They may or may not be consciously accepted by non-governmental leaders . . . These governmental auspices of community organization practice may have a high component of public promotion and co-ordination of existing governmental (and sometimes voluntary) services related to their specific mission. (1962:11)

The significant factor is that the NASW Commission on Practice felt compelled to note the influence that agency auspices, sponsorship, and interest had on the decision-making of community practitioners. While graduate schools of social work and the profession's leaders espoused values and principles such as community growth and development, self-determination, adherence to the values of the democratic process, and the use of cooperative behavior and enabling, it was implied that certain nonprofit and public agencies defined practice more narrowly in line with their organizational interests, objectives, and needs for survival. If one accepts this analysis, it is not difficult to speculate as to why the community work experience of direct-service agencies has not been a tributary source of knowledge and skill development for social work community practice. Such activity was often viewed as somewhat suspect and marginal.

THE DILEMMA OF COMMUNITY PRACTICE

During the 1950s and early 1960s, leading authors and practitioners worked to refine the role and functions of community work and to articulate the techniques, skills, and principles associated with this method of practice (Ross 1955; Lurie 1959; Warren 1962; NASW 1964). While acknowledging direct-service agencies as partners, the emphasis shifted toward identifying the unique knowledge and skills distinctive to community organization in settings primarily associated with this method (Kahn 1960; Morris 1966).

The absence of corresponding concern for development of community practice by professionals in direct-service agencies was attributable to a constellation of factors which operated in a circularly reinforcing manner. Waiting lists and a shortage of professionals focused attention on recruiting clinicians who could provide the services most closely related to agencies' primary missions. Utilization of staff for functions other than direct work with clients was hard to justify to funding bodies and citizen boards concerned with developing agency capacities and supporting new programs to meet already identified service needs.

A second major factor was that graduate schools offered most students only a passing acquaintance with community practice content, usually without the support of appropriate field experience. The recognized absence of "well-formulated concepts of process, knowledge and skills required for professional practice" (Sieder 1959:246) at the community level undoubtedly had a chilling effect on students' interest or confidence in their ability to integrate this method within their repertoire of practice techniques. Graduates entered work roles in direct-service agencies with an awareness of the social problems and stress situations that beset their clients, but without confidence in their ability to effect necessary change.

Finally, as community practice leaders moved more deliberately to marshal knowledge and establish domains, reservations were voiced again concerning the motives, commitment, and goals of direct-service agencies' involvement in the community. Reminiscent of the questions raised about the dual functions of the charity organization societies, there were expressions of concern as to whether direct-service agencies could surmount their parochial concerns and self-interest in favor of serving the best interests of neighborhoods or communities. It was assumed that community groups seeking to determine democratically their own problems and courses of action might be constrained or skewed by the predetermined agendas of direct-service agencies.

Despite these factors, many agencies continued to encourage their staffs to define their roles and responsibilities in broad terms that included activities at the community level. Often without benefit of appropriate structure, resources, time allocation, flexibility, or agency mandate, staff and administrators defined professional in ways that licensed their involvement and action on behalf of the interests of their clients and in problem areas where their knowledge and experience suggested the need for reform. Much of this activity was carried out through the establishment of ad hoc interagency committees and task forces. Agency personnel were often involved in fact gathering and problem formulation as participants in action systems sponsored by community councils. As examples, the lack of local mental health services, the need for public recreation programs for youth, and the need for temporary emergency protective care for children were situations that called for initiation and participation at the community level.

Similarly, administrators were routinely involved in interpreting agency services, public relations, fund raising, need determination, program coordination and development, and attending to the myriad exchanges and relationships that were essential to their organizations' functional interdependencies at the local, state, and federal levels. This community practice role was viewed as both a right and a responsibility. McNeil noted in 1964, while describing health and welfare councils as resources and arenas for examining the comprehensive needs of communities:

In its best definition, social administration involves community organization process and the use of methods generally identified with community organization. Thus if the administrator is to perform his functions in vital and dynamic relationship to the community, community organization knowledge, understanding and skill will be among his important tools. A central resource through a council simply facilitates and enhances their use. (8)

McNeil's reasoning takes on added significance in light of the leadership he provided over the years as a frequent spokesman for the health and welfare council sector. This legitimation of the community practice role of agency personnel as a necessary means for furthering the specific interests and aspirations of agencies and their clients serves to place the issue in perspective.

Activities and functions such as fund raising, public relations, and education are often used as a part of the community method of practice but, according to Genevieve Carter, by themselves do not constitute a conscious and responsible use of the method (Lurie 1959:46). As might be expected, there was concern that these distinct and discrete activities might be construed as the method of practice. Further, since this activity also might involve preconceived goals, administrators and clinical practitioners could be attempting to advance their organization's and/or clients' interests without being guided by two paramount goals of social work community practice: (1) reliance on, and enhancement of, the community's use of democratic process; and (2) responsibility for enabling the community to develop its own capacity to function and deal with problems.

Although the issue would recur in debates among professionals, Rothman argued that community practice could legitimately involve efforts to influence as well as enable, to be directive as well as nondirective, and community practice interventions could be aimed at developing a community's capacity and/or achieving a specific task (Rothman 1964). His rejection of the enabler role as the only guide to be used in community practice was instrumental in further legitimating and encouraging the development of community practice as one of the functions of direct-service agencies:

A useful criterion of "democratic" community organization practice within the framework of this literature would be based on whether the final decision is left to the client system. It is not the *act* of giving goal direction that may be questionable but rather the *way* it is given. Within this logic the practitioner, it would seem, may validly suggest, advocate, and stimulate, as long as the approach is a factual and rational one, conveyed without entering into personalities or invective, without expressing primarily personal motives and desires, without bringing overbearing pressure, and most important of all, as long as the final decision is left with the citizen group in which ultimate authority resides—and this lay prerogative is manifestly conveyed. There is no theoretical or ethical difficulty encountered in the practitioner's offering a suggested plan and supporting facts. The community representative group may make of this what it likes. (Rothman 1964:30)

What emerges from this discussion is that over the years direct-service agencies have been both encouraged and discouraged

from engaging in community practice. Possibly related to the inchoate development of community practice theory, in comparison to
casework and group work, most community practice authors came
close to ignoring the development of community work in direct-
service agencies. On the other hand, many clinical practitioners and
administrators, although unsure of their grasp of this method of
practice, nevertheless engaged in it both as participants and as leaders. The extent to which agency administrators and practitioners
were involved in community practice was quite variable, and undoubtedly influenced by their conception of the boundaries of their
responsibilities as professionals, the extent to which they conceived
of problems being resolvable at the community level, and the extent
to which they believed there was a role they could legitimately adopt
and perform (Johns and DeMarche 1951).

Community Liaison: The Administrator and the Practitioner

In much of the literature, reference to the community practice function associated with direct-service agencies reads as though the
agency itself is the practitioner. Little or no effort has been made to
sort out or categorize who in the agency assumes what kinds of roles
and functions and under what circumstances, toward which kinds of
goals.

Given the fact that most community practice authors have
recognized that community practice is a legitimate if not a vital
component of administration, this is not a difficult or unexpected
finding. For example, Kramer (1966) has discussed the extensive
theoretical and practice similarities between community organization and administration, and Schwartz (1977), has discussed the
need for theory development in "macro-social work." Many administrators were not only comfortable relating to the community but
also considered this an important function based on their recognition that the interface between a particular agency and other agencies and the wider community had important implications and
consequences for survival and goal achievement. Already aware of
their dependence on funding bodies, civic and business leaders, and

their working relationships with agencies, administrators could be expected to assume considerable responsibility for guiding or managing relations with significant community groups or actors.

Kouzes and Mico contend that human service organizations are comprised of three competing domains: service, management, and policy, each of which seeks to influence decisions and steer the agency in the direction of its particular interests (1979:460). One can conceive of management occupying a bridging position between the expectations of the agency's board and funding sources and those of the planning bodies, all of which are anxious to set policy and hold management accountable. In turn, service professionals seek to acquire from management the resources, autonomy, and discretion that will enable them to experience fulfillment in the pursuit of their service interests. As agencies became bureaucratized, it was natural to expect that administrators would wish to involve themselves or closely supervise their employees' relationships with coordinating and planning groups since agreements at those levels are vital to agency survival, program development, and goal-setting.

In many agencies, community practitioners were employed under administrative direction to carry out this liaison function. This linking or connecting process tended to keep administration informed about community developments and provided opportunities for influencing or negotiating interagency agreements, locating new sources of support and funding, and maintaining working relationships with other agencies.

In most agencies, a sort of informal allocation or division of responsibility evolved wherein line practitioners and supervisors were allowed a zone of freedom to define and determine their practice as long as it related more or less directly to client or service delivery matters and did not run counter to agency goals or priorities. In most instances agencies did not require practitioners to assume community practice roles, but often encouraged them when worker initiative and interest coincided around a particular problem. For example:

One of my responsibilities was the Renal Dialysis Service where I regularly encountered patients who were afraid to resume their careers because their income would make them ineligible for Medicaid. . . . They could earn enough to support themselves but not enough to cover their medical expenses . . . so they abandoned their careers to avoid becoming ineligible for Medicaid. Gradually I became intrigued by the "Catch-22" quality of their predicament and made contact with other social workers at other hospitals to determine the extent of the problem. After familiarizing myself with the legislation and regulations, I began to meet with groups of patients outside the hospital to see if something could be done to resolve their predicament. The director of social service allowed me sufficient schedule flexibility so that I could meet with professional and patient groups, and before long we formulated a specific proposal that we carried to the state legislature. Eventually we were able to influence the passage of legislation that made it possible for many of these people to go off welfare and return to work while retaining the Medicaid they so vitally required to cover their costly medical expense. (Eisenberg 1979)

It must be acknowledged that all too often, clinicians defined their roles and functions more narrowly than in the preceding example and hesitated to use their knowledge of the community and community practice, but in many agencies practice at the community level was permitted as long as it was clearly related to client problems and as long as it did not encroach on matters that administrators felt were vital to organizational survival or goal attainment.

Community Practice as a Defensive Strategy

During the early 1960s many agencies participated in the neighborhood organizing and planning activity that had been stimulated by the program goals and funding of the Delinquency Prevention and Control Act. These efforts at government, neighborhood, and agency collaboration were familiar approaches to planning, and many executives and staff had their initial exposure to working with screened and selected black leaders (Mogulof 1969).

Mobilization for Youth, the civil rights movement, and the community action programs of the War on Poverty years signaled a dramatic turn of events. Apart from the fact that the Office of Economic Opportunity's programming and funding policies seemed designed to bypass the established direct-service agencies—especially voluntary agencies (Grosser 1973:26–49; 162–65), this was an era of activism, much of which was directed at local agencies. Agency administrators who had been content to work with established leaders and nominal representation from poverty and minority communities suddenly found they were being confronted by representatives from these neighborhood and interest groups demanding to know when appropriate, responsive programs were going to be provided. This might be described as the beginning of a phase of community involvement that was largely reactive and motivated by a desire to defend agencies from their most vocal critics.

During the 1950s many agencies had been content to seek recognized business and professional leaders for their boards in order to gain the status, influence, and often the access to resources that such elites offered (Kramer 1965). Voluntary agencies sought out influential persons who could help raise funds or serve as intermediaries with federated funding bodies, while public agencies, when they had appointed boards or commissions, hoped to attract people who could further their interests with local elected officials (Ross 1955:16–21). Both voluntary and public agencies subscribed to the idea that they needed opinion and status leaders to provide legitimacy and power. Apart from token representation from racial and ethnic populations, they were totally unprepared for client and community demand for participation in board membership. Similarly, agencies were unprepared for the federal government's ambitious and pervasive requirement that citizen advisory groups be formed as a condition for receiving federal funding.

The literature reporting the purposes, failures, and limited successes of the federal government's broad efforts to inject representative democracy into the policy and decision-making of human service agencies proliferated (Yin et al. 1973). Of more importance are the ingenious strategies employed by some administrators to avoid, bypass, defuse, or block opportunities for closer collaboration with emerging community groups.

GUIDELINES AT THE LOCAL LEVEL

In 1963, Charles Schottland and Morris and Rein (1963) signaled the federal government's intention to influence a wide range of social problems by the use of program grants that also carried guidelines and both formal and informal expectations. Social service agencies as well as community councils soon discovered that in addition to needed fiscal resources there was a maze of expectations relating to the involvement of consumers and special populations, the location of programs in underserved neighborhoods, and the employment of the poor in new careers in the human services. The need for major shifts in the structure and delivery of services was accompanied by the need to establish relationships with sectors of the community that had not enjoyed such attention before.

Agency responses to the new expectations tended to vary widely, but in general proceeded at two levels: (1) client-oriented outreach and grass-roots activity, usually conducted by line professionals and/or new careerists; and (2) program development, resource acquisition, and policy formulation activities with community and neighborhood groups, usually conducted by the administrator or a staff member who had community practice expertise.

CITIZEN ADVICE AND SANCTION

As discussed earlier, Perlman and Gurin's (1972) conception of the community practice functions associated with direct-service agencies was restricted to garnering resources for the organization and maintaining awareness of environmental trends and developments that could be of significance. Indeed, administrators and their staff were often troubled by the persistently assertive stance that poverty groups and representatives of ethnic and racial minority groups presented in their dealings with agencies. The very same administrators who had successfully navigated through the networks of community, civic, political, and business leadership and power (Senor 1963) were suddenly struggling to ascertain who were the individuals and organizations that represented black, Hispanic, and Asian neighborhoods. Accustomed to negotiating with and influencing their communities' elites, they were often unable to fathom the labyrinth of social networks and relationships characteristic of racially segregated neighborhoods.

This was a critical problem for two reasons. Funding bodies, especially foundations and both federal and state agencies, often

insisted that agency grant applications be supported or endorsed by
the groups that were to receive the services and that citizen and
client groups participate in program design, operation, and over-
sight (Yin et al. 1973:6). Often, this was to be done through the
mechanism of citizen advisory boards that were to supplement the
traditional administrative boards or local government commissions.
For many administrators this seemed to be a no-win situation in that
newly emerging spokespersons and neighborhood interest groups
frequently had diverse or competitive agendas, and the established
agency boards and locally elected officials were not willing to re-
nounce their roles and authority in favor of such groups.

In some instances, among both new and old agencies, deliberate efforts and even campaigns were launched to forge new relationships to replace the neglect and insensitivity of the past.
Although those efforts were less than smooth, in many instances
forethought and persistence resulted in adjustments and then engagement:

At all of these meetings, community citizens accused us in the most severe
terms of being representative of a political system that ignored them. . . .
However, there was a quality of wishing to engage with us and test our
availability. . . . It was as if the fight had offered a major occasion for the
community to express its wish to be taken into account and acknowledged
as the major source of sanction. . . . After several weeks, the watch dog
committee informed us of a number of people who, they believed, should
be on the advisory board. (Kellam and Schiff 1966:260–61)

In contrast to the preceding example, many administrators
did not invest themselves in such processes, and the resulting frustration and recrimination were mutually felt. Advisory boards that
were handpicked for co-optability or neglected or manipulated
might have seemed a logical defensive strategy for harried administrators, but the consequences were that these agencies did not
develop new, potentially helpful and supportive constituencies, nor
did they contribute to the development of neighborhood or community capacities to help themselves to cope with social problems (Yin
et al. 1973:3–4).

Both the failures and the successes, in their own ways, sen-
sitized and socialized many administrators to the need for more
serious communication with, and linkage to, neighborhoods and

interest groups that heretofore had been ignored. Even when agencies elected to limit participation, this represented incremental if not substantive progress.

CLIENTS, NEIGHBORHOODS, AND PROBLEM-SOLVING

Although social workers in some direct-service agencies were encouraged to make visits to the homes of their clients, to keep track of and report emerging service needs, to participate in interagency efforts at coordination and facilitation of referrals, to organize and participate in case conferences and school consultations, and to educate the community about local problem situations, the trend in most clinical agencies had been toward an office-based practice that included relatively little neighborhood involvement. While this situation prevailed in many urban and metropolitan areas, a multi-method generalist orientation could be observed in rural communities where clinical workers often staffed committees, worked with local groups to develop needed programs, and so forth (Ginsberg 1977).

Mobilization for Youth in New York City served for many of the programs of the 1960s as a model that signaled the broadening role and function of the clinical social worker (Brager and Purcell 1967). Although Mobilization employed both clinical and community workers for separate functions, and at times some of its staff questioned whether it was valid even to "think of a generic practice as consisting of the application of casework or group work or community organization skills, as the nature of the problem demands" (Purcell and Specht 1967:238–39), in practice they conceded that often role and function overlapped and blurred as required by changing situations and redefinition of the problems that needed attention.

As direct-service agencies participated in the design and operation of storefront service centers, multiservice and agency centers, crisis and outreach programs, clinical social workers inevitably engaged in community liaison activities and became familiar with local institutions and the informal social helping networks in the neighborhoods they had previously "served" but had never seen.

The process itself brought many line professionals to new levels of appreciation of the impact that environmental conditions had on the etiology and prevalence of clients' problems.

In some instances, agencies hired social work community practitioners to direct or provide consultation regarding outreach, community development, and action for change. The net effect in many agencies was to provide a task-and-process complementarity that had not been a part of the work environment for many years. Even when community practitioners were not available, many line workers utilized in-service training and continuing education as vehicles for broadening their repertoire of skills and knowledge. In some agencies, the new careerist became the community worker, serving as a liaison between the neighborhood and the agency.

It is acknowledged that the use of new careerists and "outpost offices" may have served as mechanisms that protected some staff from the need to reassess and change their professional roles and helping techniques, and served to buffer more established and traditional programs. On the other hand, the cross-fertilization of ideas, methods, and practice techniques contributed to reconceptualizations of the role of line workers and their responsibilities. For many this was a period of sensitization and resocialization that led to the development of increased awareness of the social factors that affected clients' lives and needed to be changed if clients' behaviors were to be altered or their situations improved. The concept of the generic or multimethod generalist gained credibility as a reasonable and necessary alternative to shaping the client's problem to the method specialization of the practitioner.

Generic and Generalist Practice

The decade of the 1960s served to remind social work that societal forces, economic and political factors, and conditions such as poverty, racism, inequality, and dysfunctional institutions contributed as much or more to the problems of clients as did psychic or interpersonal deficiencies. Moreover, if professional social workers aspired to increase their effectiveness, a broader conceptualization of clients' problems and predicaments had to be matched by employing a more multifaceted approach to practice. Beginning in the 1960s a handful of schools of social work around the nation began to offer courses and field instruction that cut across the traditional tripartite approach to teaching practice. Unlike the 1929 Milford Conference's limited emphasis on the generic value base and principles of practice shared by practitioners in different fields and method specializations, this emerging perspective focused on preparing students to practice more than one method. What is most intriguing about this development is that it preceded the construction of theory or a body of guiding literature (Bakalinsky 1980:20).

While social work was still struggling to define and describe this new practice form, it received sufficient acceptance so that by 1972 the Council on Social Work Education acknowledged that sixty-two schools offered students opportunities to prepare for generalist practice. By the early 1970s Pincus and Minahan (1973), Goldstein (1973), Whittaker (1974), Middleman and Goldberg (1974), and Compton and Galloway (1975) had all authored practice texts formulating multi- or integrated approaches to practice.

Garvin (1976) called attention to the need for further research and critical examination of this development, while Roberts (1977) noted his reservations about the abstract nature of generalist literature, and wondered if it was sufficiently helpful to practitioners who needed to shape specific interventions and make practice decisions. These somewhat sympathetic authors seemed to support the goal but questioned the utility of the social and behavioral science foundations which undergirded such formulations. On the other side of the continuum, a number of authors seriously questioned the validity of such an approach to practice during a time when method-specific theory and technology seemed to call for greater specialization to assure public recognition of the profession's competencies and evidence of effectiveness. It has appeared to this author that the most vocal and uncompromising criticism has come from academicians more intimately involved and identified with community practice as a special method (Gilbert and Specht 1974).

This criticism by leading community practice authors is most interesting in light of recent developments within the curricula of graduate schools of social work and in the field of social welfare. During the 1960s, enrollment in community practice tracks or specializations increased dramatically, and though leveling off in the early and mid 1970s, the number of practice-oriented articles, texts, and readers available to students began to reflect the rapid development of community theory, technology, and practice techniques. By the mid and latter 1970s there was a noticeable drop-off in employment opportunities for community practice specialists and a corresponding decrease in students electing such programs. The intriguing development was that community practice courses and content remained in the graduate schools but were now aimed at direct-service generalist practitioners and generically oriented macro-practitioners who were enrolled in programs that combined administration, planning, and community content and techniques. Lauffer, arguing that community organization should remain a distinct and specialized method, nevertheless acknowledged:

The performance of community organization tasks has become increasingly legitimate within the profession and elsewhere. Such tasks are frequently performed by a variety of practitioners and administrators who do not necessarily identify themselves as community organizers. For this reason many social work educators argue that community organizing knowledge and skills are so essential to effective social work practice that all social work students ought to be taught enough of the "basics" to apply . . . wherever these are needed. . . . Its success is that everyone is doing it. (1981:172)

An irony in the development of generalist practice is that leading community practice authors have not purposefully contributed to the development of theory for generalist practitioners; in fact, the converse has occurred. Authors more directly associated with clinical practice have been involved in pathfinding the frontiers encompassing community work theory and practice within their respective theoretical formulations. One such exception has been a Child Welfare Association publication (Brown et al. 1982) presenting the collaboration of five professionals, including this author, who represented the range of micro- and macro-practice specializations. As Bakalinsky (1980:212) found after a survey of graduate school faculty teaching generic or generalist practice courses, most instructors did not have substantial macro-practice experience, had been educated as caseworkers, and therefore were not able to satisfy their own standards in terms of teaching the specifics of macro-practice, though they personally subscribed to the broadest and most inclusive definitions of practice, which included macro-interventions.

The trend toward a more holistic view of social work practice, which was revived by the community mental health movement and the War on Poverty, has persisted despite the fragile and uncertain relationships between leaders in macro- and micro-practice. Further, though the faculties of some schools of social work have struggled to develop integrated practice frameworks, organized around services and programs for populations such as the aged and the developmentally disabled or for problem areas such as delinquency or family violence, the construction of appropriate models remains problematic in the classroom as well as in the field.

Despite the relative lack of attention to the constellation of roles, functions, and skills that personnel in direct-service agencies are either called upon or should perform, it is clear that the challenges of practice require that social workers be able to recognize situations that require multifaceted interventions and, whether by themselves or with collaborative and consultative affiliations, respond to the problem (Rose 1981:152–53). Toward that end, it is necessary to reexamine the various aspects of community practice that are, can, or should be exercised by the staff of direct-service departments and agencies.

Community Liaison

A dictionary definition of liaison refers to "a bond or connecting link; a linking up; also, coordination of activities; cooperation." This definition connotes a qualitative aspect of relationship that extends community work beyond the secondary function usually ascribed to such practice when carried out by personnel from direct-service agencies. It seems to suggest, at least to this author, a flexible range of roles and activities; it does not imply that social agencies are responsible for, or even legitimated as, *the* planners or organizers of a community or neighborhood. It does suggest that within their mandated goals and areas of knowledge and competence there are multiple levels and opportunities for initiating professional working relationships with organizations and groups. Before such a practice stance can be adopted, however, agencies need to analyze the various aspects of their linkages with their communities, including current interdependencies and potential relationships. This process has often been confusing to agency personnel as well as to the community because of serious definitional problems relating to role and function. In the final section of this paper some of these issues will be discussed.

The Policy-Administration-Services Quandary

As noted earlier, the legitimacy of community practice by direct-service agency personnel has been both acknowledged and criticized, but until the recent efforts of some authors and schools of social work, relatively little attention was paid to who in the agency should do what with which groups or in which neighborhoods. This often resulted in confusion of roles that hampered the efforts of community groups, administrators, and line workers. In fact, direct-service agencies are involved in community practice at three distinct but interrelated levels and have been over the years.

During the decades when community practice authors were attempting to develop the conceptual foundations of their method in settings where its practice was primary, little attention was devoted to the improvisations and permutations which were developing within direct-service settings, often by professionals who did not claim to be community practitioners. The complexities and distinct attributes of this practice were sometimes labeled as functions rather than as a particular approach within a method.

BOARD MEMBERS AND ADMINISTRATORS

Service agencies that focus their efforts on work within particular client populations or problem areas are, of course, part of a geographic community but are more intimately and intensively associated with a network of sponsors, funding sources, agencies, constituencies, and clients that Ross (1955) has labeled the functional community. Navigating within and in concert with this ،u،، tional community has particular salience for an agency's development or survival: forging alliances, soliciting financial support, lobbying for favorable legislation or funding and negotiating service agreements. Moreover, building a favorable image in the community and keeping tabs on environmental developments that have the potential to affect programs through changing patterns of resource allocation are inherently related to knowledge and skills derived from the political, economic, and organizational sciences.

Although line staff are often encouraged to cooperate with and support such efforts, usually the principal actors are the board members and top-level administrators who are the ones charged with responsibility for defining and advancing the organization's policy and goals. Board members and administrators rarely delegate such responsibilities and, when engaging in campaigns, lobbying, fund raising, or constituency building, they weigh decisions and strategies in terms of an overall perspective that relates to their own conception of what is in the best interest of the whole organization and its clientele. Small wonder, then, that some board members and administrators conceive of their roles as analogous to the captain of a ship or the conductor of an orchestra, which suggests a conscious and deliberate use of controls and limits on staff discretion and autonomy. In such instances, agency administrators can be expected to perceive boundary-spanning community practice efforts by subordinates as having potential consequences affecting the success or failure of their own leadership.

From such a perspective it is not difficult to understand why the mandates for citizen participation and community or client advisory boards were viewed with suspicion by many administrators. Apart from the intrinsic merits of the process and the quality of advisory groups' recommendations, it was the administrator's job to incorporate these new sources of expectations and information within the networks of community support. For some, this was an unwelcome burden, while for others it was an opportunity to gain new information and forge new sources of support.

CLINICAL PRACTITIONERS

In contrast with the preceding perspective, line practitioners focus on individuals, families, and groups from a human behavior stance, viewing the community as a system that can precipitate or exacerbate the problems presented by their clients. A neighborhood and its institutions serve as factors that can either support or undercut the clinician's work.

From this perspective the clinical worker's entry into community practice is often linked either to an individual client or to a category of clients. Practitioners are keenly aware of the social stresses and dysfunctions in particular neighborhoods or communities. Overcrowded schools, inadequate and unsafe housing, poverty, crime, and delinquency are all viewed as contributory conditions which pose greater than normal life hazards. While clinicians are familiar with these problems, they are not so clear about what to do about them or how to do it. More often than not a decision to intervene at the community level evolves from a value position that guides their perception of the nature of the problem that needs their attention and even the remedial action required. For example, "health and safety codes are being ignored by landlords and they need to be pressured to improve their property"; or, "local schools have no employment counseling or training programs for teenagers who are likely to leave before graduation—the system needs to develop such a program."

While ostensibly aligned with the needs and interests of agency clientele, questions may be raised as to whether the worker's time can be made available for community intervention, and whether the proposed activity fits within an agency's priorities and goals. If the answer is yes, the clinician must recruit participants, display competency in the utilization of task group structure and process, and have strategy development and problem analysis skills. While some practitioners surmount these challenges through sheer persistence or by relying on prior training, for others the lack of agency-sponsored consultation, education, or similar support serves to discourage their efforts and lead them to lower their horizons and narrow the focus of their practice.

Though there is no research known to this author to support the contention, it appears that community practice efforts closely identified with agency problem or population domains and likely to improve the agency's image or status are more likely to receive administrative encouragement. For instance, an agency charged with counseling physically disabled persons may also support its practitioners' efforts to combat discrimination or create employment opportunities. This leads to a consideration of the third level of practice, the special project.

SPECIAL COMMUNITY PROJECTS

Over the years direct-service agencies have developed a history of designing and conducting special programs within their field of practice. These programs involve other agencies, clients, neighborhoods, and/or the general public. Often staffed by supervisors, senior professionals, or community practitioners, such projects typically have their own space and identity within the organizational structure and usually are supported by special grants, funding arrangements, or contracts. Two examples are: the family service agency that conducts programs to help families, schools, and neighborhoods become aware of, and able to take action on, drug abuse problems of teenagers; and the senior citizens counseling center that encourages other agencies to reach out to understand and serve the particular needs of the elderly. A current and controversial example is the regional center for the developmentally disabled that locates sites for group homes and then works with neighbors to gain acceptance and minimize resistance to efforts to place institutional residents into a more normal environment.

The special programs which are launched often do not include line-level clinical staff, nor is there an effort to integrate these programs into the fabric of the agency. For example, one of the goals of a mental health center with a rape counseling program is to have police and hospitals in the area provide services specially attuned to the needs of rape victims. Many of the center's line staff may be unaware of, or uninvolved in, the program's efforts to mobilize community support and change the policies and procedures of local institutions. When and if special funding incentives are withdrawn, such programs usually vanish, and their goals and working relationships become organizational orphans, relegated to token status or abandoned.

The special community project, by its nature, auspices, and staffing patterns, allows agencies to pursue their traditional goals and activities and at the same time be responsive to government or community priorities. Such relationships with citizens and agencies are not characterized by full receptivity and responsiveness to community concerns or interests in self-determination but are designed to perform tasks or achieve goals that agency administrators, funders and sponsors have already negotiated. As Brager and Specht suggest, the further the project's targets for change are from the central interests and relationships of the agency, the more likely that staff will have greater latitude to attend to issues which have salience to a neighborhood, or involve citizens in determining strategies and priorities for action (1973:190–91). For example, a mental health center that does not rely on county funding is free to allow its advocacy project to work with public housing tenants in order to achieve improved living conditions, even if this involves confrontations or efforts to engage in political empowerment. However, competition with other mental health agencies for county funds may serve to circumscribe the project's latitude and the discretionary (albeit professional) decisions of its project staff.

Such transactions can have the undesirable consequence of convincing an agency's clinical practitioners that community practice is "political" and unrewarding, while disappointed citizens feel they have been betrayed by the agency's hidden agenda which posed conflicts of interest that never could be resolved in their favor. It is such outcomes that have contributed to negative community attitudes and valuations of social service agencies and professionals, especially among poverty, disadvantaged, racial, and ethnic minorities.

In the next sections of this paper policies, structures, and practice stances will be suggested that should help agencies utilize a more reciprocally satisfying approach to community liaison practice.

Recommendations Regarding Commitment, Competency and Legitimacy

Consideration of the direct-service agency as a source for community as well as clinical practice raises questions and issues, many of which have been discussed in preceding sections of this essay. Agencies have alternately been criticized and encouraged in terms of the roles they were to perform and the purposes they might fulfill in the community. Such questioning and dialogue have been an inherent part of the development of social services in America, and the debate will continue. What emerges from this review and analysis is that the community liaison function draws particular attention because of its persistence within social service structures that are not primarily engaged in community work. At times one wonders if, at the extreme, some community and direct-service authors believe that this form of practice will disappear if ignored or neglected. Despite the unsettled nature of its environment and the absence of consistent support, the continuance of this practice suggests that it meets or fulfills important functions for agencies, clients, and their communities.

Its ascending and descending prominence in direct-service agencies suggests that community liaison as a form of practice should be deliberately examined and dealt with in each setting by sponsors, administrators, and practitioners. A profitable approach should include consideration of at least three key areas: commitment, competency, and legitimacy. Although there is an interdependence among these concepts in practice, they will be discussed separately.

COMMITMENT

Earlier discussion of community liaison suggested that administrators interact with communities for many reasons, but chiefly to garner support, manage exchanges and relationships, and to keep informed about trends and developments important to their organization or department. Line practitioners seek to intervene in terms of influencing the networks of services and the life-affecting environments which relate to their clients' problems. Special community projects often have characteristics of one or both of these approaches, but too often are dependent on special funding and limited goals. In one agency, community practice might be actively proceeding at all levels, whereas another agency participates sporadically or not at all. For example, one university hospital's social service department is well known for its insularity and avoidance of contact with the community, while another is involved at all levels and routinely contributes energy, expertise, and effort on behalf of diverse planning, prevention, and problem-solving activities.

In trying to explain these differences, it soon becomes apparent that apart from their respective sponsors' expectations, there is discernible motivation and commitment toward the community in one setting and not in the other. Stated simply, and apart from competency or legitimacy, the questions that sponsors, administration, and staff had to pose for themselves were: Do we want to . . . should we . . . take a broader, more inclusive role with the community? If so, what does this mean for us in terms of policies and then organizational structures that can help us move to this arena? As suggested by Resnick and Patti (1980), predisposing factors in or around an agency can affect its behavior; but possibly greater significar.ce should be accorded to key individuals and groups in the organization who recognize a need and decide to engage in a process of change that will enable them to perform in new arenas.

What is being advocated is that direct-service agencies must deal with an a priori question: Do we want to engage in community practice at all levels or only some or none? All too often these are default decisions. The issue is never examined, discussed, or debated, but rather a combination of momentum, compliance, and inertia resolves the issue. Commitment may be thought of as a precursor to formal policy *and* as a climate that characterizes agencies' behavior with regard to the community. In both instances it should symbolize the conscious and deliberate decision that board, administration, and staff arrive at concerning the roles and functions they will perform.

COMPETENCY

In simpler times, most administrative and community practice was conducted by social work professionals who mastered their new assignment by on-the-job, "seat of the pants" learning. Whatever the strengths and weaknesses of this model, a willingness to learn and accept new challenges was a necessary but not sufficient condition for achieving demonstrable competency. In today's complex environment, professionals must have a foundation of knowledge and skill appropriate to the tasks they are expected to perform.

What this suggests is that agencies that elect to engage in community liaison practice must also inventory the talents and knowledge of their staff, who must then proceed to acquire the education and training that will allow them to do the job the agencies have decided should be done. In some agencies, recent graduates of schools that offer generic programs may provide a reservoir of knowledge, while in other instances, basic as well as specific technical knowledge may have to be acquired through continuing education, in-service training, and the use of consultants. Most important, the preparations for competent practice need to be planned, taking into account a range of training needs, and must be appropriate for the tasks to be performed. In too many instances, early ventures into community practice have been experiences in frustration and failure which convinced participants to remain close to the practice base with which they were familiar and to leave community efforts to others.

As one would not expect a macro-educated specialist to master the intricacies of clinical practice without benefit of appropriate preparation, the same holds true for those who were educated as clinicians. Apart from the personal sense of stress and discomfort experienced by the professional, it is not ethical or fair to the client.

Without getting into the proverbial chicken-and-egg debate, another reason for attending to the competency issue is that professionals are more satisfied with themselves and their performance when they are prepared to perform at an optimal level. Successful mastery of their roles provides needed reinforcement which encourages acquisition of new knowledge and skills. Reliance on sharing experiences and the use of a colleague-consultation model may be a way of proceeding during periods when resources are limited by budgetary cuts, but a program of task and role specific preparation is more efficient and productive.

LEGITIMACY

A chronically persistent problem has characterized the community liaison approach to practice by professionals from direct-service agencies: to what extent do the public at large, various special interest groups, neighborhoods, and, last but not least, agencies whose primary function is community practice, expect, recognize, and utilize community practice efforts by the staff of direct-service agencies? As Reid (1969:182) and Levine and White (1961) have discussed, one agency legitimizes another's product in terms of perceived benefit or loss to its own goal achievement. Therefore, the community practice aspect of a direct-service agency's efforts will be evaluated by a host of community and agency actors who will question or support such activity according to their perception of its value (or threat) to their goals. It is not difficult to imagine, then, that a hypothetical family service agency which collaborates with a community council to document need and solicit citizen support for day care programs for working parents will have its efforts legitimated. However, if that same agency were to sponsor the development of a strong neighborhood council in its service area, the community council might view this as encroachment on its domain and raise objections about the legitimacy of the activity.

This suggests that direct-service agencies, their boards, and their staffs should carefully consider the issue of benefit and/or threat before embarking on a community project. Exclusive pursuit of self-interest or reluctance to engage in exchanges that are meaningful to other agencies or neighborhoods can have serious consequences.

As Lappin discussed in a preceding essay in this volume, the language and ideology of community development practice, with its emphasis on self-help, self-determination, and enabling and collaborative relationships, have great appeal. The attractiveness of community development practice to professionals and citizens derives from its promise for reliance on democratic principles and processes and its respect for the wishes and rights of participants. It is assumed, for example, that the rights, prerogatives, and best interests of a neighborhood or community will be paramount, and that the participants will experience both process and task gains. At times, when trying to enlist participants, the administrator who would not normally overpromise to a prospective employee, or the clinician who would not normally overpromise in order to hold a client, might well exhibit such behavior when operating in a new arena. In order to attract participants there may be an understandable tendency to conceal goals or interests or the limited extent to which an agency can or is willing to commit resources such as time, use of facilities, and access to staff expertise.

The preceding discussion suggests that direct-service agency administrators, the staff of their special projects, and line practitioners must forge a reputation for candor, commitment to the communities served, and a willingness to enter into exchanges that involve influencing and being influenced. To acquire legitimacy an agency must be receptive to building ongoing and responsive relationships. The legitimacy of many agencies' community practice was seriously questioned during the 1960s and 1970s when it appeared to some citizen groups and task forces that predetermined organizational imperatives defined the nature of their relationships. Agencies cannot ask for community support without negotiating acceptable exchanges that involve respect for, and responsiveness to, community norms and rights. An agency's legitimacy is ultimately forged out of its credibility, which is evidenced by its willingness over time to assume roles and responsibilities that benefit the community it has promised to serve.

References

AASW. 1931. *Social Casework: Generic and Specific.* A report of the Milford Conference. New York: AASW.

Bakalinsky, Rosalie. 1980. *Teaching Generic Practice: Social Work Educators' Experiences and Attitudes.* DSW dissertation, University of Southern California.

Brager, George A. and Francis P. Purcell, eds. 1967. *Community Action Against Poverty: Readings from the Mobilization Experience.* New Haven, Conn.: College and University Press.

Brager, George A. and Harry Specht. 1973. *Community Organizing.* New York: Columbia University Press.

Brown, June et al. 1982. *Child, Family, Neighborhood: A Master Plan for Social Service Delivery.* New York: Child Welfare League of America.

Compton, Beulah and Burt Galloway. 1975. *Social Processes.* Homewood, Ill.: Dorsey Press.

Cox, Fred M. et al., eds. 1979. *Strategies of Community Organization.* 3d. ed. Itasca, Ill.: Peacock.

Council on Social Work Education (CSWE). 1976. *Teaching for Competence in the Delivery of Direct Services.* New York: CSWE.

Eisenberg, Ken. 1979. Presentation at School of Social Work, University of Southern California.

Garvin, Charles D. 1976. "Education for Generalist Practice: A Comparative Analysis of Current Modalities." In *Teaching for Competence in the Delivery of Direct Services,* pp. 18–30, Council on Social Work Education.

Garvin, Charles and Fred M. Cox. 1979. "A History of Community Organizing Since the Civil War with Special Reference to Oppressed Communities." In Cox et al., eds., *Strategies of Community Organization,* pp. 45–75.

Gilbert, Neil and Harry Specht. 1974. "The Incomplete Profession." *Social Work* (November), 19(6):665–74.

Ginsberg, Leon. 1977. "Social Work in Rural Areas." In Green and Webster, eds., *Social Work in Rural Areas,* pp. 3–17.

Goldstein, Gerald. 1973. *Social Work Practice: A Unitary Approach.* Columbia, S.C.: University of South Carolina Press.

Green, Ronald and Stephen Webster, eds. 1977. *Social Work in Rural Areas.* Knoxville, Tenn.: University of Tennessee.

Grosser, Charles F. 1973. *New Directions in Community Organization: From Enabling to Advocacy.* New York: Praeger.

Heath, Monna and Arthur Dunham. 1963. *Trends in Community Organization.* Chicago: University of Chicago Press.

Johns, Ray and David DeMarche. 1951. *Community Organization and Agency Responsibility.* New York: Association Press.

Johnson, Arlien. 1959. "Community Organization Method and Skill in Social Casework Practice." In Lurie, ed. *The Community Organization Method in Social Work Education,* pp. 148–61.

Kahn, Alfred J. 1960. "Social Science and the Conceptual Framework for Community Organization Research." In Kogan, ed., *Social Science Theory and Social Work Research,* pp. 64–79.

Kellam, Sheppard and Sheldon Schiff. 1966. "The Woodlawn Mental Health Center: A Community Mental Health Center Model." *Social Service Review* (September), 40(3):255–63.

Kogan, Leonard, ed. 1960. *Social Science Theory and Social Work Research.* New York: NASW.

Kouzes, James and Paul Mico. 1979. "Domain Theory: An Introduction to Organizational Behavior in Human Service Organizations." *Journal of Applied Behavioral Science,* 15(4):449–69.

Kramer, Ralph M. 1965. "Ideology, Status and Power in Board-Executive Relationships." *Social Work* (October), 10(4):108–14.

——. 1966. "Community Organization and Administration: Integration or Separate but Equal." *Journal of Education for Social Work* (Fall), 2(2):48–56.

—— and Harry Specht, eds. 1969. *Readings in Community Organization Practice.* Englewood Cliffs, N.J.: Prentice-Hall.

Kurtz, Russell. 1940. "The Range of Community Organization." In *Proceedings of the National Conference of Social Work, 1940,* pp. 400–412. New York: Columbia University Press.

——, ed. 1938. *The Public Assistance Worker: His Responsibility to the Applicant, the Community and Himself.* New York: Russell Sage Foundation.

Lane, Robert P. 1939. "The Field of Community Organization." In *Proceedings of the National Conference of Social Work, 1939,* pp. 495–511. New York: Columbia University Press.

Lauffer, Armand. 1981. "Reorganizing Community Organization." *Social Development Issues* (Summer/Fall), 5(2–3):166–79.

Lee, Porter. 1929. "Presidential Address." In *Proceedings of the National Conference of Social Work, 1929,* pp. 3–20. New York: Columbia University Press.

Levine, Sol and Paul E. White. 1961. "Exchange as a Conceptual Framework for the Study of Interorganizational Relationships." *Administrative Science Quarterly* (March), 5(4):583–97.

Lubove, Roy. 1965. *The Professional Altruist.* Cambridge, Mass.: Harvard University Press.

Lurie, Harry L., ed. 1959. *The Community Organization Method in Social Work Education.* New York: Council on Social Work Education.

Maas, Henry, ed. 1966. *Five Fields of Social Service: Reviews of Research.* New York: NASW.

McNeil, C. F. 1964. "Dynamics of Health and Welfare Planning—Structures and Processes." In NASW, *Social Work and Social Planning,* pp. 1–10.

Middleman, Ruth and Gail Goldberg. 1974. *Social Service Delivery: A Structural Approach to Social Work Practice.* New York: Columbia University Press.

Mogulof, Melvin, 1969. "Federal Support for Citizen Participation and Social Action." In *The Social Welfare Forum, 1969,* pp. 86–107. New York: Columbia University Press.

Morris, Robert and Martin Rein. 1963. "Emerging Patterns in Community Planning." In *Social Work Practice, 1963,* pp. 165–76. New York: Columbia University Press.

———. 1966. "Social Planning." In Maas, ed., *Five Fields of Social Service: Reviews of Research,* pp. 185–208.

Murphy, Campbell G. 1954. *Community Organization Practice.* Boston: Houghton Mifflin.

NASW. 1962. *Defining Community Practice.* New York: NASW.

———. 1964. *Social Work and Social Planning.* New York: NASW.

Perlman, Robert and Arnold Gurin. 1972. *Community Organization and Social Planning.* New York: Wiley.

Pincus, Allen and Anne Minahan. 1973. *Social Work Practice: Model and Method.* Itasca, Ill.: Peacock.

Pray, Kenneth. 1945. "Social Work and Social Action." In *Proceedings of the National Conference of Social Work, 1945,* pp. 348–59. New York: Columbia University Press.

Purcell, Francis P. and Harry Specht. 1967. "Selecting Methods and Points of Intervention in Dealing with Social Problems: The House on Sixth Street." In Brager and Purcell, eds., *Community Action Against Poverty,* pp. 229–42.

Reid, William J. 1969. "Inter-Organizational Coordination in Social Welfare: A Theoretical Approach to Analysis and Intervention." In Kramer and Specht, eds., *Readings in Community Organization Practice.* 2d ed. pp. 176–88.

Resnick, Herman and Rino Patti. 1980. *Change from Within: Humanizing Social Welfare Organizations.* Philadelphia: Temple University Press.

214   S. H. Taylor

Roberts, Robert W. 1977. "Recent and Developing Trends in Social Work in the U.S.A." *Contemporary Social Work Education*, 1(3):3–9.

Rose, Stephen. 1981. "Reflections on Community Organization Theory." *Social Development Issues* (Summer and Fall), 5(2–3):151–56.

Ross, Murray G. 1955. *Community Organization: Theory and Principles*. New York: Harper and Row.

Rothman, Jack. 1964. "An Analysis of Goals and Roles in Community Organization Practice." *Social Work* (April), 9(2):24–31.

Schottland, Charles. 1963. "Federal Planning for Health and Welfare." In *The Social Welfare Forum, 1963*, pp. 97–120. New York: Columbia University Press.

Schwartz, Edward. 1977. "Macro Social Work: A Practice in Search of Some Theory." *Social Service Review*, (June), 51(2):207–27.

Senor, James. 1963. "Another Look at the Executive-Board Relationship." *Social Work* (April), 8(2):19–25.

Sieder, Violet M. 1959. "The Tasks of the Community Organization Worker." In Lurie, ed., *The Community Organization Method in Social Work Education*, pp. 246–59.

———. 1962. "Community Organization in the Direct Service Agency." *Social Welfare Forum, 1962*, pp. 90–102. New York: Columbia University Press.

Vail, Gertrude. 1939. "Tying in With the Community." In Kurtz, ed., *The Public Assistance Worker: His Responsibility to the Applicant, the Community and Himself*, pp. 168–98.

Warren, Roland L., ed. 1962. *Community Development and Social Work Practice*. New York: NASW.

Whittaker, James. 1974. *Social Treatment: An Approach to Interpersonal Helping*. Chicago: Aldine.

Yin, Robert et al. 1973. *Citizen Organizations: Increasing Client Control Over Services*. Santa Monica, Calif.: Rand Corp.

PART THREE

Arenas of Community Social Work Practice

8

Community Social Work Practice in Oppressed Minority Communities

Barbara Bryant Solomon

It may appear paradoxical to begin a treatise on community practice in oppressed communities with a reminder of the centrality of the individual in social work practice.[1] In theory, at least, community practice differs from casework or group work in the indirect nature of the impact on the individual. Thus, efforts to promote community well-being, strengthen community processes, or encourage community action have as their ultimate objective the improved condition or social functioning of individual residents. The concern for the individual is particularly significant when the issue is community practice in minority communities. The negative social indicators which characterize these communities—high incidence of poverty, crime, poor health, and so forth—are in reality nothing more or less than the collective description of myriad individuals in distress. Yet, in many minority groups, a higher value is placed on the collective—at least on the family or the tribe—than on the individual. From that perspective, the immediate focus of community work on the collective good should hold considerable attraction.

Despite the apparent compatibility of this value orientation of minority communities with the focus of community social work practice, the practice strategies have not been equally compatible.

For example, the mechanism for achieving the collective good in community social work practice has most often been the organization, whereas in minority communities, the most visible and effective change agents have been charismatic individuals such as Martin Luther King, Jr., and Cesar Chavez. The organizations they created were undeniably energized by the power of their personalities; and thus were quite different from the typical bureaucratic organization in which social workers practice. This characteristic may account for the fact that such organizations have found it difficult to survive the departure of their founders or to consolidate early gains when leadership has changed. Yet the reality is that to many residents of minority communities, these, and not the "establishment" agencies, are the organizations working on their behalf. Given that reality, the focus of this article is on the past efforts and future prospects for community social work practice—an "establishment" tool for enhancing community functioning.

Community practice in social work is aimed, according to several theoreticians, at reducing imbalances between welfare needs and welfare resources, utilizing a variety of individual, organizational, group, and interorganizational strategies (McNeil 1951; Ross 1955; Schwartz 1965). This definition, however, emphasizes the ends rather than the means, the goal rather than the process. Yet it is the process which generally differentiates a given profession from others seeking similar goals. A goal such as reducing imbalances between welfare needs and welfare resources could conceivably be adopted by groups as disparate as lobbyists, lay board members of a social agency, or the agency staff. In minority communities, the superabundance of such problems as delinquency, poor housing, inadequate medical services, and ineffective schools has given rise to a wide range of change efforts involving, in addition to social work, indigenous political action groups, urban and regional planners, community psychologists, health planners, and so forth, utilizing similar tactics and strategies. It is necessary, then, to identify the social work approach to community organization which differentiates it from other approaches. It is the contention here that such differentiation cannot be made on the basis of tactics and strategies employed by practitioners but on the particular assumptions guiding practice and the presence of a structured, institutionalized (in the sense of ongoing in contrast to ad hoc or temporary) delivery system.

Working Assumptions

The following assumptions appear to characterize the social work approach to community practice and are presented as the perspective from which specific community practice efforts conducted in minority communities will be analyzed:

1. Dysfunctional communities are those which do not provide adequate resources (housing, police protection, health care, medical facilities) to support the effective social functioning of its residents.

2. Minority communities are less functional than other communities due to institutional inequities which limit access to resources. Because resources translate into power, these communities are therefore essentially powerless.

3. There is a reciprocal relationship between individuals and communities, that is, functional communities support individual growth and development while functional individuals support community growth and development. Conversely, dysfunctional communities do not support individual growth and development while dysfunctional individuals do not support community growth and development.

4. Community social work practice in minority communities is aimed at reducing powerlessness of the community's residents to act collectively. This inevitably involves assessing and coping with institutional inequities.

5. Community social work practice in minority communities may involve a variety of theoretical approaches as identified in this volume; however, any approach will be implemented through a relatively stable social agency system.

The Agency Context

The social worker's function has been described as "to mediate the individual-social transaction as it is worked out in the specific context of those agencies which are designed to bring together individual needs and social resources" (Schwartz 1961:155). The social work presence in minority communities can be identified by the social agencies which have been operative within them. In addition to the traditional family, mental health, and public welfare agencies, there are also agencies which have as their primary responsibility the organization of community groups to meet some broadly defined need or to effect change in some objective social conditions, such as: community action agencies; agencies which are devoted to coordinating and planning; and agencies that provide central services, research, and fundraising, such as United Way or welfare planning councils. Although a particular approach to community practice may dictate the predominant professional skills required—political, economic, or social work—some mix is often necessary; consequently, these agencies often employ a wide range of professional staff. The social work staff of these agencies are expected not only to have a wide range of skills, but to implement certain professional values such as the belief that manipulation of the behavior of others constitutes a violation of their essential humanity.

Community organizing activities in social work practice are not confined to the so-called indirect-service agency. As a matter of fact, recent developments in the field have included attempts to break down the traditional separation of social work methods into casework, group work, and community organization. From one point of view, this separation distinguishes methods by the size of the client system in which the worker intervenes rather than by the nature or goals of the activities utilized. Morales has referred to this as social work's "constricted methods framework." He suggests that a broader ecosystems perspective in which a given problem may be approached simultaneously from a range of systems would promote social workers' understanding of the psychosocial problems experienced by Third World people, including the crippling effects of institutional racism, and the oppressive neocolonial environments in which they struggle to survive (Morales 1981:47).

This approach is reflected in direct-practice agencies such as mental health agencies, public welfare departments, family service agencies, and agencies serving the elderly which have social work staff involved in a variety of activities which might be classified as community practice, developing constructive relationships with community residents in order to link individuals and groups who need help with the services they need or collaborating with staff in other agencies to develop community awareness of some problem.

Clearly, not all efforts at producing social change have occurred due to the intervention of social agencies; thus, political action organizations such as the NAACP, Southern Christian Leadership Conference, La Raza, and the American Indian Movement have often had greater visibility and, in some instances, greater credibility as agents of major social change than have social agencies and social work professionals. It should be pointed out that this does not mean that social workers as individuals have not often made considerable contributions of their time and expertise in support of these organizations; however, this does not constitute the profession's contribution. Nevertheless, in this discussion of social work community practice in minority communities, little attention will be given to the efforts of such groups except as tactics, strategies, and theoretical perspectives developed by these groups may have influenced community social work practice.

The distinction between community social work practice and other professional strategies for effecting broad social change is not merely one of differences in credentials of the key staff involved. It also relates to differences in the priorities for reaching a solution to the problems identified. This is particularly true in regard to minority communities. For example, economic programs, such as those of community development corporations, begin with the hypothesis that most community problems in minority communities are due to the lack of access to economic resources; in other words, an increase in these resources will automatically resolve these problems. On the other hand, political approaches such as those taken by NAACP and the Mexican American Political Association are based on the hypothesis that most community problems in minority communities are due to laws and policies which place their residents at political disadvantage when compared to the dominant Anglo majority. Thus, the major activities of these organizations are political in nature, and the targets for change are laws, policies, and administrative procedures which have been identified as discriminatory and racist in origin. In contrast to these economic and political approaches, a social work approach would be based on a third hypothesis: Most community problems are due to the impotence of community residents and the lack of organized community structures through which power can be obtained and exercised in order to increase resources and close the gap between needs and resources.

Past community social work efforts to reduce this powerlessness and prospects for such efforts in the future will be the focus of the remainder of this article.

What's Different About Community Work in Minority Communities?

Having defined a social work approach to the practice of community social work practice in minority communities, the question may be asked as to whether it would be any different in other communities. Since an emphasis has been placed on closing the gap between need and resources and since the gap tends to be widest in minority communities, community organization practice in social work should logically have been disproportionately directed toward these communities. A review of social work literature, however, reveals: (1) the historical development of community social work practice emerged from, and placed emphasis, on service coordination and program planning, rarely involving minority communities and only tangentially directed toward them; (2) where community organization efforts have been directed to minority communities and non-minority communities simultaneously, results have often been less successful in minority communities; (3) the greatest impetus for increased involvement of social work in organizing minority communities has come from the federal government and has been totally vulnerable to shifts in political climate; and (4) many problems unique to minority communities have not received significant social work attention.

Massive federal programs in the two preceding decades directed considerable attention to community development in poor minority communities. Recognizing that it was not some single problem of poor housing, unemployment, or poor health care which should be the target of change efforts since these are inevitably interrelated and mutually reinforcing, it was the community's powerless condition permeating all of its institutions which was the problem to be dealt with by the community organization activity. Title II of the Economic Opportunity Act of 1964 (the War on Poverty) generated considerable social work activity in this kind of community to organize the poor so they could articulate their needs, articulate action proposals, and gain a voice in the community decision-making process which would in turn determine the weapons and the strategy in local campaigns on the nationwide war against poverty. Since these poor communities were most likely to be minority communities, there is considerable literature regarding the application of this approach to community organization from the social work perspective. Community Action Program (CAP) agencies developed under the impetus of this legislation involved community residents as nonprofessional workers in antipoverty programs with varying degrees of control by professional staff. In other instances CAP agencies acted as constituent groups, providing the professional staff with feedback for program evaluation or acting as pressure groups to influence projects' activities. This wave of "institutionalized" community organization was unprecedented but also short-lived. What the federal government "giveth" it can also "taketh away." Studies of its impact on poor, minority communities identify greater success in changing the lives of some individuals, and thereby developing more effective community leaders, than in achieving the perhaps too grandiose goal of major social change.

In some instances, there has clearly been very little or no difference in the implementation of a community organization effort in minority and nonminority communities. An example was the Chicago Areas Project. Its purpose was stated as

developing an experimental program for the prevention and treatment of delinquency in a limited number of low-income communities which for many years had been characterized by disproportionately high rates of delinquency and crime despite the ever growing number of programs, agencies and institutions established to cope with the problem. (Finestone 1972:149)

The major approach to the problem instituted in inner-city communities was the development of community committees. This approach was based on the belief that it was indispensable to recruit local leaders who would take responsibility for initiating and supporting new forms of indigenous community organizations which would promote youth welfare. Therefore, the community committees were composed of community residents who came both as representatives of other community groups and as reflective of their own personal commitment. The committees were to offer forums to provide community residents with information regarding the latest findings in child rearing and juvenile delinquency; to open up channels of communication between community residents and the larger social institutions involved in decision-making in regard to the community's youth; and to foster contact and communication with the youth and local adults.

Finestone (1972:181–185) reported that some community committees could be described as strong and others as weak. More importantly, strong committees were in communities that were almost all white whereas weak committees were in communities that ranged from 75 percent to 100 percent black, communities that tended to have higher rates of delinquency, communities in rapidly changing neighborhoods or in exceedingly homogeneous settings, such as housing projects, or in neighborhoods relatively isolated from the rest of the urban community. The weak committees were in communities which we have described as those of minorities; and community practice efforts in these communities had different outcomes than similar efforts in other low-income communities.

An excellent review of the history of community organization with particular reference to minority communities was done by Garvin and Cox (1979). Although not confined to social work approaches to community organization, their review identified the social conditions, ideological currents, and professional developments in each of four historical periods.

In the period prior to 1915, community organization as a formal specialization did not exist in social work, which had scarcely begun to emerge as a professional entity itself. The period between 1915 and 1929 was characterized by urbanization and increased antagonism toward blacks, Jews, and the foreign born. Also during this time, a growing network of welfare professionals expended considerable energy in efforts to develop a rational, systematic approach to planning welfare programs and funding welfare agencies. Essentially ignored were the repressive conditions being experienced by blacks, Chicanos, American Indians, and Asian Americans not only in the race riots and other acts of violence but in repressive legislation embodied in segregation laws, immigration restrictions, and political disenfranchisement. Community organization among these groups, if there was any at all, was indigenous in origin.

The period 1929 to 1954 encompassed the years of the Great Depression, the expansion of the government into the social welfare arena, and a major upsurge of trade unionism. Given the universal suffering of the Great Depression, remedies were based on growing recognition that there are forces in social life which transcend the individual and must be controlled by collective action through the political process. Community organization in both the larger communities and in minority communities was largely national in focus and under public auspices. Within the social work profession, this was a time of intensive efforts to conceptualize the nature of community practice as it related to social work.

Finally, the period from 1955 almost to the present was characterized by the assertion of minority groups claiming their rights. This era was strongly influenced by the civil rights movement, which was predominantly black in origin. Furthermore, it was a period of the most intensive involvement of the federal government in developing solutions to a wide range of social welfare problems; community social work practice was stimulated and encouraged by the availability of governmental support. With the erosion of such support in recent years, those activities which had been directed largely toward poor and minority communities have lessened although minority communities still tend to be a source of relatively strong interest to community workers.

In summary, then, community social work practice in minority communities, when compared with that in other communities, has been characterized by relatively infrequent utilization, generally less positive outcomes, dependence on federal funding, and failure to address minority-specific issues. Yet, despite these common experiences, minority communities are not the same; black communities are not like Chicano communities or Asian American communities or American Indian communities in regard to such factors as cultural values, attitudes toward oppression, and preferred strategies to deal with objective conditions. Furthermore, there are differences within each minority group from one community to another. For example, the Chicano communities in San Antonio and Albuquerque are not like Chicano communities in Chicago or Seattle.

Despite many similarities in the culture of the United States and Canada, their experiences in regard to ethnic communities have also been different. Like the United States, Canada has "visible" minorities—blacks, Chinese, Japanese, and the indigenous Inuit (Eskimo) and Indian groups. However, due to differences in history as well as in the cultural expression of racism (Canada's racism has been termed polite racism), Canada's minorities have come much later to the kind of positive identity that is a prerequisite if collective pressure is to change the power balance in society. Hughes and Kallen (1974) have suggested that black Canadians have been too widely dispersed geographically and internally factionalized to organize, develop effective leadership, or unite in order to take concerted action in the interest of the collective. However, late does not necessarily mean never. Recently, as large numbers of well-educated West Indian immigrants have fueled the development of more cohesive black communities in such cities as Toronto, there has been a proliferation of black organizations and newspapers.

The following discussion of community organization efforts in four minority communities—black, Hispanic, Asian/Pacific, and Indian—takes into account the North American experience and the manner in which social work has been practiced to make an impact on social functioning at the community level. It should be understood, however, that the theoretical perspectives, practice strategies, and program designs that are described will have utility for other parts of the world only to the extent that they are borrowed with full recognition of the modifying influence of history and culture.

IN BLACK COMMUNITIES

The Atlanta School of Social Work was organized in 1920 as the first school of social work in a black university with its primary objective the education of black social workers. Its first announcement of courses included not only courses in social casework, medical-social problems, economic and social theory, but also community organization. This latter course included content on publicity and finance, community organization, social programs, recreation and community movements generally (Ross 1978:435). The decade of the 1920s is extremely significant in the history of community practice in black communities since it marked the beginning of the professionalization of many social welfare activities in black communities, and an emphasis on the conditions of "the race" in contrast to the psychological emphasis that was beginning to permeate a great deal of social work among white populations.

Thus, differences in level of sophistication about community organization when blacks are compared to other minority groups may well be attributed to their history in this country. In fact, the emphasis on integration during this decade when there was still the idealism to support it as a feasible expectation, coupled with the indigenous development of leadership that preceded this period, may have made possible the development of social institutions such as schools of social work, social agencies directed toward improvement of conditions among blacks, and so on. Thus, in later years when the dream of integration no longer seemed tenable, and certainly less desirable, there were considerable resources to develop and implement other strategies aimed at improving black communities.

In 1928, Eugene Kinckle Jones wrote a seminal article detailing the social work presence in black communities. He marked its beginnings with the founding of the Committee on the Urban Conditions Among Negroes in 1910 under the impetus of George Haynes, a Fisk University sociology professor. The purposes of the committee were: to bring about coordination and cooperation among agencies and organizations for improving the industrial, economic, and social conditions of blacks and to develop other agencies and organizations, where necessary, to secure and train black social workers; to make studies of the industrial, economic, and social conditions among blacks; and to promote, encourage, assist, and engage in any and all kinds of work for improving conditions among Negroes.

Clearly, what is being described is related more to community practice than to social casework. Jones, in fact, acknowledged the social work profession's major focus on the problems of the individuals and families through therapy, education, provision of resources, or other preventive, rehabilitative, or restorative processes. However, he contended:

The Negro social worker has an *added* responsibility in the task of bringing the whole Negro group as a separate social entity up to a higher level of social status. He must show from time to time his success in securing larger opportunity for the Negro as a separate racial group. (Jones 1928:291; emphasis added)

The Committee on Urban Conditions Among Negroes evolved into the National Urban League, established in 1920 as a force both for the professionalization of social work among black Americans and in black communities and for the alleviation of many of the social problems plaguing those communities. In 1922, the League's extension secretary traveled to eighteen cities to educate local leaders of black communities to the necessity and urgency of social services among Afro-Americans and to raise funds for support. The success of these efforts is marked by the fact that local Leagues had been established in nearly fifty cities by the end of the decade. The following account graphically describes the specific community-organizing activities promoted by these early local units:

In St. Louis during the Depression . . . a major problem with which black citizens had to contend was the Depression-accelerated disintegration of their neighborhoods. Zoning laws were flouted as the properties of white absentee landlords were remodeled for maximum earning power. Barracks-like flats had been built on vacant lots against the zoning laws; city services had dwindled to near zero as street cleaning and alley clean-up were cut back and garbage collection became irregular at best. . . . When the disgust of residents of one block rose to the point that they came to the St. Louis Urban League for help, [they were] aided in forming a block unit. Eleven families met in that first effort and invited every resident of the block to membership. They formed committees specifically aimed at tackling the nuisances that afflicted them from outside and from thoughtless residents in the block itself. Committees called on the theaters, department stores and merchants whose ads and leaflets littered their lawns and streets and asked them to cease and desist. The residents took a firm and unanimous stand against postmen, ice and other delivery men, salesmen and others trampling lawns, fences and gardens underfoot. . . . Within weeks, Block Units 2, 3, 4, and 5 had been organized. One block committee made a point of demanding services from the superintendent of streets and succeeded in having the streets in its section cleaned and flushed every day. In another block, the Health Committee was particularly active, caring for each sick person and bringing group condolences when deaths occurred.

By April 1933 there were twelve block units and a federation of these was organized to coordinate action on neighborhood projects. Among the projects were the cooperative buying of coal through the League's direct contact with a coal mine operator . . . and an enlarged "lawn beautiful" contest. . . . In this atmosphere of accomplishment and group solidarity the Federation of Block Units presented to the city a six-point list of policies recommended as necessary for Black citizens to share in St. Louis' New Deal. These points included (1) removal of Jim Crow and the opening of all recreation facilities to Black citizens; (2) replacement of trees destroyed by a tornado in residential areas . . . (3) correction of violations of zoning laws . . . (4) opening of Tandy Park as an "adult only" playground . . . (5) installation of a separate children's playground . . . (6) more job opportunities for blacks.

From each block unit committees were appointed on each of these points. As a result of their follow-up pressure, [it was] reported a year later that 17,000 trees were planted throughout the city, but the first were in-stalled in Black areas; a $500,000 bond issue for two community houses for Blacks was pushed through and voted; recreation facilities were inves-tigated by the city administration and inequities were ordered corrected. By mid-1934 there were seventeen block units functioning. (Parris and Brooks 1971:222–23)

After World War II, the concern in black communities was with the elimination of legal barriers to equal opportunity which was seen as the means to eventual integration of blacks into the larger community. Thus, the development or empowerment of black communities as unique entities was antithetical to the prevailing ideology. The victories in the courts in the 1950s and 1960s, how-ever, did not merely open doors formerly closed to blacks in educa-tion, voting, and so on; it also brought forth a storm of hostile, often violent reactions from the white majority, particularly in the South. The fantasy of "all men as brothers," which had been held out as the inevitable consequences of lowering barriers to contact and under-standing, soon disintegrated. Blacks and black communities were more ready to assume that power over their lives would not be voluntarily given up by the white majority; furthermore, since inte-gration into the communities of those so visibly hostile was no longer an attractive objective and the need to improve the quality of life in communities in which blacks lived became more urgent, there was greater community support for efforts to organize in order to achieve these new goals.

Massive federal programs such as the War on Poverty, in which community organization was a central theme, gave new impe-tus to the development of a wide range of grass-roots social programs in black communities. Critics have suggested that the lack of success of many of these programs, which were heavily influenced if not controlled by social work practitioners, may have been due to the lack of emphasis on community theory and practice in social work curricula. However, as previously indicated, community organizing had been done with significant results in black communities, specifically through the work of the Urban League. Ironically, however, the League's dependence on negotiation, bargaining, advocacy, and pilot projects instead of confrontation and disruption was deemed too conservative by most militant factions of the civil rights movement that emerged during the 1960s.

The major beneficiaries of the League's activities were perceived to be upwardly mobile blacks who could walk through doors opened by efforts of the League's liberal white-labor-black-religious coalition. Thus a new thrust for the Urban League was presented to an emergency national meeting of presidents and executives of local Leagues in April 1968 by Whitney Young, the National Urban League's executive director, a professional social worker with a national reputation in the social welfare field. He indicated that though the League's commitment to interracial teamwork and an open society remained, the agency was now to direct itself to the black ghetto. This was the consequence of a growing recognition that the League's traditional strategies would "continue to benefit mainly middle-class individuals able to take advantage of opportunities and will leave the masses of black poor locked into the ghetto" (Parris and Brooks 1971:458).

In the years immediately following the announcement, the real significance of this change in the League's emphasis was abundantly clear; the League sponsored Youth Community chapters, organized domestic workers into a union in Atlanta, and developed a food-buying club aimed toward becoming a consumer cooperative in San Diego. In one city they succeeded in forcing the local government to pave streets and light them; in others, they taught classes in black history. By the end of 1968 more than thirty local Leagues were deeply involved in organizing their black neighborhood communities into black clubs and councils and forming ghetto coalitions (Parris and Brooks 1971:470).

Whereas the League's program was developing a more activist flavor, the activism embodied in most of its projects was aimed at specific targets, such as exploitative merchants, inadequate city services, and deteriorated housing. The idea was that "winning" in a confrontation with the establishment would in fact create more community cohesion and effective community leadership. However, a variety of community organization agencies were emerging with a comprehensive service orientation, primarily in response to the stimulus of federal funding. Perhaps the most widely publicized was New York City's Mobilization for Youth, which has been regarded as one of the most successful urban community development ventures (Brager and Purcell 1967; Weissman 1969; O'Brien 1975).

Launched in 1962 on New York's Lower East Side, Mobilization for Youth was a delinquency prevention neighborhood demonstration project which emphasized the organization of client groups who, with staff support, would advocate, negotiate, and confront in their own behalf. Zimbalist has suggested that much of the "new social work" of the 1960s originated in this project, including,

militant social advocacy on behalf of the disadvantaged; new careers for slum area residents; client organizations such as welfare rights groups; systematic confrontation of the Establishment by staff-supported groups of slum residents; aggressive legal services to the poor; active promotion of local neighborhood control of social institutions; subsidized employment of youth; comprehensive neighborhood-based job training and employment services; highly innovative service delivery models to reach the "unreachable"; neighborhood development and action under the aegis of a primarily federally funded, autonomous, privately incorporated structure; the large-scale local application of a formal theory of social action and institutional change, with the concomitant deemphasis of traditional social work methods. (Zimbalist 1970:123)

The community served by Mobilization for Youth was not technically a black community since the target population included Puerto Ricans, blacks, and whites. However, it is included in this discussion to contrast its outcomes with those of HARYOU, a similar project in Harlem. One of the most widely publicized community development programs in a predominantly black community was planned and to some extent implemented by Harlem Youth Opportunities, Inc. In order to solve the problem of juvenile delinquency, efforts were to be directed toward building a community with enough resourcefulness and power to manage its own affairs. Major problems of Harlem's youth—delinquency, low school achievement, and unwed motherhood—were perceived as symptoms of a wider pathology. Thus, a concerted and massive attack on the social, political, economic, and cultural roots of the pathology would be required. Although the major concern was for eliminating juvenile delinquency rather than building a better life for juveniles, it was decided that emphasis on the latter would be more likely to accomplish desired ends than would a narrow concern with delinquent acts.

Cloward and Ohlin's theory (1960), which related delinquency to a deficient opportunity system for minority and lower-class adolescents, provided the theoretical framework for the project; the specific program activities included: (1) involving the residents in efforts to solve their own problem; (2) making socially constructive activities as glamorous and self-fulfilling as socially destructive ones seemed to be; and (3) blurring the distinction between the socially conforming and the socially deviant. Originally it was hoped that the Ford Foundation would be induced to support the arts and culture component; the Taconic Foundation, the social action program; the U.S. Department of Labor, the employment program; the City of New York, the education program; the State of New York, the programs oriented toward actual or potential deviants; and the Office of Economic Opportunity, the overall administrative costs.

Unfortunately, after wrangling over the executive directorship and accusations of alleged fiscal shortages and corruption, this well-designed and potentially exciting example of community development in a black community was never implemented because the potential funding sources did not come through with their support. It is not clear why Mobilization for Youth, in a less homogeneous community, succeeded in achieving certain objectives shared with HARYOU whereas HARYOU did not. Apparently, the political and economic power inherent in HARYOU's plan for the Central Harlem community was so seductive to so many vested interests that it was beyond the skills of the professionals involved to avoid or even minimize power struggles in the pursuit of *community* empowerment—a concept far too abstract to be meaningful or to become a substitute for more tangible personal or organizational empowerment. This is a particularly difficult problem in the community development model of practice. In one attempt to differentiate community organization and community development it is stated: "In the community development context, those involved in the major effort might themselves be the beneficiaries of that effort—the result is self-help on an organized community-wide scale" (Christenson and Robinson 1980:28). However, the risks involved in having to subordinate one's own personal goals to collective goals, particularly when those involved have a history of deprivation, should be clear. An old adage in the black community is pertinent here: You don't send a hungry dog to guard the meathouse.

By the early 1970s, the federal government had funded over twenty-five hundred neighborhood service centers as components of CAP. Several hundred locally funded neighborhood centers had also been established in primarily black communities. Newsome (1973) has reviewed various studies of neighborhood centers in the United States conducted by at least five different research groups and concluded that direct services and self-help opportunities provided by these centers have been used by many blacks in these communities; on the other hand, activities aimed at increasing the effectiveness of traditional service delivery systems or activities geared toward institutional change and the redistribution of power in the community were unlikely to occur. Newsome suggests that this was due to the fact that nearly 90 percent of the neighborhood center's funding was from the Office of Economic Opportunity, and an amendment to the Economic Opportunity Act (PL90-222:1967) prohibited "certain essential but often threatening types of community organization and gives city officials the option to administer the CAP directly" (Newsome 1973:52). The continuing tension between organizing needs and organizational constraints against social work staff has led to an awareness of the need to develop an independent economic base for support of neighborhood organizations in black communities.

The recognition of the implications of dependency on funding sources on the nature of the programs developed spurred a group of black organizations to announce their intent to raise money and to win community approval to collect and allocate resources as well as evaluate a myriad of social agencies in the community. This was seen by some as a tactical error that might lead to even greater inattention to black agencies on the part of the United Way than had been given in the past. Regardless of this risk, Davis reported in 1975 that seven major fund-raising organizations were operating in the United States (one each in Boston, Los Angeles, Washington, D.C., Detroit, and Fort Worth and two in Chicago). Three others were in the planning stage. The allocative patterns of recently developed black funds, however, did not differ markedly from those of United Way:

Black fund drives can best be of service to the society by directly supporting a variety of activist movements which seek to establish community control, organization of the black community, and increased resources from governmental and private resources. At present black activists are financially incapable of working for social change because their activities so often result in a loss of support, necessitating the curtailment of their movement. (Davis 1975:156)

However, Davis also pointed out that black fund drives should not attempt to support traditional agencies and organizations supported by United Way. He argued that funds will be quickly dissipated if traditional agencies are supported, with little recognizable change in social conditions.

There are recent indications that the economic viability of the black funds may be increasing. In February 1982, IBM announced that it will permit the New York Black United Fund to solicit its workers, and Bell Laboratories in New Jersey has agreed to permit the National Black United Fund to solicit there. However, the most potentially rewarding sanction has come from the inclusion of such funds in the Combined Federal Campaign, the system of giving by federal employees.

Mogulof (1970) has assessed the extent to which five programs in black communities evolved as a response to Model Cities legislation. In all five communities, the neighborhood-dominated policy board controlled the input of recommendations to the city council. Furthermore, in all five cities, program ideas were generated in planning subcommittees that were overwhelmingly dominated by neighborhood residents; thus, the locus of power in determining how the resources of the Model Cities program were to be used rested with black leadership from the affected neighborhoods. The role of social work in these programs has not always been clear, however, since regulations merely called for some form of professional technical assistance, in a manner agreed to by neighborhood residents. However, this program demanded persons who were experts in social planning. The significance of this is best identified by the fact that planning with consequences for black communities—generally negative—has rarely included community residents in the decision-making process. The Model Cities programs gave these residents a voice for the first time in the heretofore sacrosanct area of sociotechnical intervention, the practitioners of which had been resistant to the notion that expertise may be a necessary but not a sufficient condition to bring about effective change in the objective conditions plaguing black communities.

Obviously, there are other community organization efforts in black communities involving social workers which have not been discussed here. These efforts, for the most part, have engaged neighborhoods or communities where there are large numbers of persons belonging to several racial and ethnic groups so that no single group is dominant. Perhaps most significant, however, is the fact that most of these efforts have been funded almost exclusively by federal dollars. The Nixon administration and the even more conservative Reagan administration have effectively eliminated most of the federal funding for community organization programs. This represents a considerable decline in social work's involvement in community organization efforts and a challenge to the profession to initiate ways to honor its commitment to strengthen poor and minority communities when governmental funding is no longer forthcoming.

IN HISPANIC COMMUNITIES

As indicated earlier, other racial and ethnic minorities which have experienced considerable discrimination have not had the history or the professionally trained social workers to mount the far-reaching community organizing efforts of the black group. Also, it has been pointed out that many minority groups—including Hispanics—tend to follow personalities rather than theoretical orientations, and to see major institutional change as more likely to be achieved through the mechanism of politics or economics than through social work.

Certainly, the absence of a social work presence in organization efforts in Hispanic communities cannot be attributed to the lack of organizations. However, there organizations tend to be indigenous and directed toward internal community processes. Alvarez (1971) has documented the existence of formal organizations in Mexican-American communities since the 1880s and pointed out that a 1970 directory of Spanish-speaking community organizations listed some eight hundred organizations.

Primarily, they have functioned for the preservation of the general Mexican-American way of life in that quite often they have constituted the central hub of Mexican-American activities. . . . The formal organizations also provided informational and communications networks. And finally, they have sustained by and large, the core of the philosophy that encompasses bicultural and bilingual existence. (Alvarez:213)

There is a similar abundance of organizations in Puerto Rican communities, mostly in the Eastern United States. Marrero (1974) suggested that this great network of Puerto Rican community service, civic, social, religious, and recreational groups is also concerned with

maintaining the Puerto Rican identity, culture and language; maintaining a common identity with the Puerto Ricans in Puerto Rico; rejecting any form of American racism that would divide Puerto Ricans within their own families or from other minorities in the nation; remaining the most effective vehicle for the achievement of service objectives to this community. (1974:79)

This point in the preceding reference was emphasized as an indictment, implying that the network of indigenous social programs and organizations had been developed without social work assistance.

Thus, the fact that social workers had not been intensively engaged in community practice in Hispanic communities prior to the War on Poverty is not related to a cultural distaste for organizations. It is more likely related to the fact that there has been a paucity of bilingual, bicultural social workers. A torrent of words has been written about the failure of the profession to recruit Spanish-speaking social workers—certainly a requirement if there is to be any success in organizing Spanish-speaking communities (Miranda and Kitano 1976; Delgado 1974; Carrillo 1980).

The War on Poverty and Great Society programs did, as in black communities, bring more social work community practice into Hispanic communities than ever before. Mobilization for Youth in New York's Lower East Side reached large numbers of Puerto Ricans living in that community. Its community development program sought to stimulate the participation of low-income persons in attempts to resolve community problems. Welfare rights organizations, CAP, and Model Cities programs all had some impact on Hispanic neighborhoods. However, Nixon's new federalism shut off a promising development in federal assistance programs for the development of more functional Hispanic communities.

One of the major outgrowths of the War on Poverty and Great Society programs was institutionalization of the notion that change targets or clients must be involved actively if change endeavors are to be effective. Most of the original CAP programs complied with the federal requirement by creating private, nonprofit noi governmental agencies governed by boards in which at least one third of the membership were residents of "poor" communities. However, most of the Office of Economic Opportunity delegate agencies, as well as the subsequent Model Cities program and other programs, put into operation the concept of residents' participation primarily by creating advisory councils or boards. Ambrecht, in 1972, studied seventy advisory councils in the predominantly Mexican-American neighborhoods of East Los Angeles to determine whether involvement in these councils had been maintained and had led to the acquisition of political skills, increased involvement in community activities, and the formation of indigenous leadership. She found that council membership seemed to work as a politicization mechanism regardless of the particular power configuration of the councils and regardless of the members' previous level of involvement. Furthermore, she concluded:

The politicization engendered by advisory council membership appears to be of a lasting nature. . . . It thus would appear that the process of involving previously inexperienced and politically unsophisticated individuals in advisory councils to public agencies well may portend better prospects for the development of indigenous leadership in low-income communities. . . . Moreover, the leadership likely to emerge from this process does not appear to be of an easily manipulated type. (1936:185)

Ambrecht reflects that perhaps the much-maligned War on Poverty has been dismissed too readily in regard to its impact on minority communities like East Los Angeles. Certainly there is evidence that social work agencies have not given adequate consideration to this mechanism for reducing powerlessness of individuals and ultimately the communities in which they reside.

Perhaps the most dramatic impact in Hispanic communities—at least in the West—has been made by programs utilizing Saul Alinsky's approach, utilizing as consultants organizers from the industrial areas organization he founded. Cesar Chavez and his United Farm Workers are an example, as well as the United Neighborhood Organization in East Los Angeles. Although Alinsky's model has not been identified as a social work model of community practice, it is compatible with the social work hypothesis that most problems in minority communities relate to the powerlessness of its residents to influence the organizations which control much of their lives.

Alinsky's approach includes: (1) the perception of the community as functionally related to the social, political, and economic institutions of the larger community; (2) the perception of residents as participants rather than recipients; and (3) community organization as aiming toward a redistribution of power (Schaller 1966). More dissonant with a true social work approach, however, is the lack of connection between the practitioner and any institutional base. While the confrontation tactics proposed by Alinsky may be appropriate for organizations which are not dependent upon the external political power systems for survival, a social agency utilizing such tactics or supporting such tactics in its target or client system would be highly vulnerable to economic retaliation.

The institutional sponsorship of professional social work has been a curse as well as a blessing, especially in regard to practice in minority communities. Even the direct-service agency which attempts to break out of the traditional mold may find considerable constraints. For example, an effort by a family service agency in Northern California has chronicled the difficulties in attempting to develop an advocacy program for the Spanish-speaking community (Cameron and Talavera 1976). The goals were to bring about improved use of community resources by low-income Chicanos in the area; to identify and bring about needed changes in the procedures and structures of agencies so that they could more effectively meet the needs of the Chicano population. Despite the agency's success in establishing resource centers staffed by bicultural, bilingual personnel; in creating a job-training program with a substantial budget; in convincing the Internal Revenue Service to outpost bilingual employees in two community centers to assist with tax questions; and in obtaining approval of the board of supervisors of a plan in which farm labor housing was a top priority, the agency was unable to get United Crusade funding, apparently because of the Crusade's difficulty in perceiving these activities as appropriate for a family service agency.

At the grass-roots level, however, there may be more social work involvement in Hispanic communities than in other minority communities. Perlman (1976), in a comprehensive review of sixty grass-roots groups, both urban and rural in sixteen states across the country, identified only three such groups whose origins or historic antecedents were in social work or social services. All three were Hispanic: the Guadalupe Organization in Guadalupe, Arizona; the Spanish-speaking Unity Council in Oakland, California; and the Hispanic Office of Planning and Evaluation in Boston.

It should be noted again that the lack of a social work presence in community organizing programs in minority communities does not deny significant efforts by non-social work community actors. For example, the East Los Angeles Health Task Force, which obtained the right to approve or disapprove proposed health programs in this largely Hispanic community, was an effective mechanism for program coordination and program planning in the area of health. Although social workers have been utilized at both staff and board levels, the agency has not defined its activities as social work and, most important, the social workers involved have not utilized the empirical knowledge gained from their work experience to expand the knowledge base of community social work.

In summary, then, organizing from a social work perspective has been rare in Hispanic communities. On the other hand, there is ample evidence that organization per se is not a foreign value in those communities, and some successes have been noted from utilizing different models including Alinsky's "power to the people" confrontation, and the service coordination, program planning model.

IN ASIAN/PACIFIC COMMUNITIES

As in the other minority communities, Asian/Pacific Islanders are characterized by the primacy of indigenous help systems in dealing with social, economic, and political problems. Although the number of organizations relating to these concerns is large, historically their impact has been relatively small because of their internal focus. Most important, despite the fact that there are Asian-American or Asian/Pacific Islander coalitions, alliances, and councils in the community organization arena, there is in fact much stronger commitment to separate ethnic interests than to the concept of a collection of ethnic peoples whose only commonality is their experience of discrimination in this country. Ignacio (1976) has eloquently described the difficulties in creating organizations which include such culturally diverse groups as Japanese, Chinese, Koreans, Filipinos, Samoans, Cambodians, Vietnamese, and Malaysians. Clearly, much of the impetus for organizing across these cultural groups was due to financial support from federal agencies like the National Institute of Mental Health (NIMH) that found it much easier to deal with a single group than with each of those indicated and more.

The Pacific Asian Coalition exemplifies this process. It was organized and developed with funding from the NIMH as an "advocate on behalf of Asian Americans and Pacific Island peoples for issues and concerns which affect well-being of Asian/Pacific Island peoples" (Ignacio 1976:163). Other unfunded organizations were spun off from the NIMH's organizing efforts; examples are the Asian American Council of Greater Philadelphia, Asian Americans for Human Service in Chicago, and the Hawaiian Association for Asian and Pacific People. Despite general acceptance of the need for Asian coalitions, there has been no dampening of the strong current favoring preservation of the separate national and cultural identities, and this must be taken into consideration in any organizing efforts in these communities. For example, an examination of the community newsletter of the Asian American Council of Greater Philadelphia revealed that many of its members retain their ties with separate organizations such as the Philadelphia Chinatown Development Corporation, the Japanese Americans Citizens League, the Bangladesh Association, and the Organization of Chinese Americans

(AACTION 1973). It is also clear that social workers are deeply involved in many of these groups. They tend to bring their technical skills to the service of the organizations as individuals, however, and not as professionals employed by such organizations.

The War on Poverty programs touched Asian-American communities, but to a lesser degree than black and Hispanic communities. Perhaps the most frequent organizing efforts in these communities were in the area of community redevelopment such as the HUD program aimed at revitalizing blighted neighborhoods in which many Asian/Pacific peoples resided. These organizing activities were mostly of the social planning variety, however, and much of the planning only served to reinforce feelings of powerlessness of community residents as they experienced the invitation to provide only limited input in regard to priorities for piecemeal redevelopment as, for example, senior citizens' housing or commercial office space.

IN AMERICAN INDIAN COMMUNITIES

When it comes to this country's most oppressed minority, the American Indians, not only are there very few social work programs directed toward the group but very few social workers who belong to the group and are therefore bicultural. Farris (1976) has proposed an advocacy program for urban Indians to redress this situation in which social work agencies in communities with large Indian populations would hire Indian social worker advocates. These advocates would reach out to locate the nonreservation Indian, assess his service needs, and sensitively and appropriately help if necessary:

The Indian advocate would help in the organization and supervision of Indian self-help groups, such as education, pow-wows, and social activities. He would also serve as the liaison between non-reservation and reservation Indians and their respective programs. . . . He would assist in the revitalization of tribal identities, and family and clan ties. The Indian advocate would act as a program consultant. . . . He would inform, demonstrate, and teach Indians and non-Indians, agencies and institutions about the needs and the lifestyles of contemporary Indians. It is strongly recommended that each Indian advocacy service be flexibly developed on an individualized tribal level, reflecting the characteristics of the local community's Indian population. There should also be mechanisms developed whereby program consultation, coordination and assessment could be effectively organized and implemented by permanent regional and national committees of Indian representatives from designated national Indian organizations. (Farris 1976:502)

There is no evidence that Farris' proposal has been implemented to any extent by social agencies in the communities where there is a sizable Indian population.

Other authors have promoted the idea of an ethnic agency which has special commitment to the group. Jenkins (1981) has concluded that innovative ethnic agencies in which ethnic clients and ethnic personnel predominate can provide a more accurate assessment and utilization of culture and consciousness in delivering services. The Indian Centers have been developed from this perspective. They have been funded under provisions of the Native Americans Program Act of 1974. This act provides funding for technical assistance, training, and financial support to help Indians "achieve economic and social independency by enabling them to identify their own needs; establish their own priorities; conduct their own programs to meet those needs and control the institutions and programs that affect our daily lives" (Sorkin, 1978, p. 111). These Centers include such purposes as the establishment of a continuing program which will help the American Indian help himself or to make the American Indian aware of available services in education, employment, housing, rehabilitation, alcohol treatment, and hospitalization. Although no systematic study of Indian Centers has been made, there is little evidence that they have had resounding success. However, the majority of the American Indian population still reside on reservations where social workers, when present at all, are too often the instruments of an insensitive, oppressive, federal bureaucracy.

The potential for effective social work intervention in these American Indian communities has only recently become a possibility. The Indian Self-Determination Act of 1975 reflected changing federal policy which now recognized the right of the Indian people to direct their own destinies while preserving their status with the United States government. Eddie F. Brown, a social work educator and American Indian, has indicated that although the act does not provide for a comprehensive transfer of power to tribes, it does allow for the transfer of service programs from externally imposed bureaucracies to the tribal governments (Brown 1978).

Clearly, the community social work role which this policy implies will depend on the locus of social workers. If they are located in an external system which has a formal relationship with American Indian communities and their tribal governments, their primary role could be that of advocate to ensure that resources are made available to these communities to strengthen their level of functioning. If social workers are located inside the community, that is, under contract to provide community social work service, the social work role may be that of technical assistant whose skills are placed at the disposal of the tribal government that is the employer.

Brown and Gilbert have indicated that certain specialized knowledge and skills are required if the social worker engaged in community organization activities is to be effective. This will include knowledge of socioeconomic and political forces in Indian communities, including awareness of tribal codes, federal-Indian jurisdiction, Indian law and court systems, awareness of decision-making processes, Indian problem-solving ways, and an awareness that Indian tribes are distinct entities and cannot be lumped together. Skills to be mastered include skill in negotiating with political entities in Indian communities, skill in dealing with tribal courts, coalition-building, and working with community groups (Brown and Gilbert n.d.:25–26).

Despite the fact that various Indian groups represent the largest minority in Canada, there has still been little professional social work visible in the efforts of these minority peoples to gain more control over the decisions that directly affect their lives. Cardinal, the Canadian Indian leader, points out that there is a new generation of young Indians who are working to unify Canadian Indians through Pan-Indian organizations and educational programs, inculcating pride in their ethnic heritage among Indian students, and discovering a common Canadian Indian heritage and identity that transcend their diverse indigenous backgrounds—Cree, Saultreauz, Mohawk, Iroquois, and others (Cardinal 1971). Organizational indications of this rising ethnic consciousness include the Native Alliance for Red Power and the coalition of organizations of Indian, Inuit, and Metis (mixed-blood), peoples affected by the

Mackenzie Valley natural gas pipeline, to set up a common front to bargain for settlement of land claims (Hughes and Kallen 1974). However, there is no similar mention of organizations involving social workers in roles aimed at empowering Indian communities. The deficiency may be in the reporting. However, the relevance of this issue for community social workers working with urban and reservation Indians in the United States, or social workers in other countries with large indigenous populations—Bolivia, Colombia, Australia, for example—suggest that such efforts, if indeed they are being made, should be documented and disseminated.

Assessing Community Social Work's Impact

In the description of community social work efforts in four minority communities, evidence has been provided of the utilization of each one of the practice models presented in Part I of this volume. Thus, service coordination and program planning activities were characteristically encountered in Model Cities programs in black and Hispanic communities; comprehensive community development efforts were implemented in Mobilization for Youth and partially so in the HARYOU project; political action and empowerment activities were carried out in various Urban League programs; and community liaison efforts were documented in Ambrecht's description of advisory councils utilized by social agencies in an Hispanic community. Furthermore, these efforts have included the entire range of specific tactics available to the community worker—building alliances, negotiation, boycotts, collaboration, advocacy, involving influential elites, bargaining, leadership development, pressure tactics, confrontation, and so on. However, there is no well-formulated theoretical framework from which logically interrelated principles of community practice in minority communities can be extrapolated.

It has been noted that community social work is concerned with reducing institutional inequities, and community social work in minority communities is particularly concerned with the inequities created by racial discrimination and injustice. However, there has been little systematic analysis of the effect on selection and impact of various community practice strategies when the target inequities have different sources. To illustrate, let us consider two community problems.

Community A is a white, suburban community in which the schools are inadequate due to a reactionary school board, incompetent school administration, overworked teachers, and apathetic parents. A community social worker met with a newly formed Committee to Save Our Schools and provided technical assistance to the parents who engaged in political action in order to bring about desired changes. This assistance resulted in the committee's successful utilization of negotiation and confrontation strategies to force resignation of two board members and the defeat of three others in the election. A new school board began immediately to reduce inequities in the system, which then gave the children of Community A access to educational resources.

Community B is a black, inner-city community in which the schools are also inadequate due to a reactionary school board, an incompetent school administration, "burned-out" teachers, and apathetic parents. A community social worker who went from door to door to apprise parents of the situation was instrumental in forming a Committee to Save Our Schools. However, all the worker's efforts to arouse parents, to determine strategies for dealing with school board, school administration, and teachers had to take into account the fact that responses of these key actors would be shaped by intergroup attitudes. For example, school personnel were awash in racist stereotypes of the children as less intelligent and their parents as less "moral" people who place a low value on education. Furthermore, the parents and their children had often had indications of these stereotypes in their encounters with other social institutions, and the cumulative effect led them to demonstrate the "self-fulfilling prophecy." Thus, it could be logically assumed that negotiation and confrontation would have different consequences than would be observed in a nonminority community.

Community A and Community B are different contexts for the implementation of community social work strategies. Clearly, there is a need for tested and validated hypotheses regarding the significance of the difference.

Grosser provides some insights when he suggests that community organization practice in social work has been strongly influenced by the extent to which inequities have been viewed as temporary aberrations in regularly functioning institutions or as a consequence of intentional, knowing acts on the part of individuals and institutions (Grosser 1976:10–13). The situation in Community A may be considered an example of a temporary aberration. Thus, except for an unfortunate choice of school board officials by the voters, the schools might be running well. A good school board would have hired more competent administrators who would understand how to maximize teacher performance in particular and educational resources in general. In such instances, Grosser would place the social worker in the enabler role, facilitating leadership and developing consensus in regard to the changes desired and the most effective means of bringing about those changes.

On the other hand, the situation in Community B may be considered due in large measure to the knowing acts of school officials, either committed or omitted, but based on insensitivity to cultural difference, lower expectations of student potential, and less concern about parental attitudes. In this instance, Grosser suggests that the community social worker's role should be characterized by partisanship and advocacy. The social institution must be persuaded to make concessions so that significant change becomes the price of stability. Furthermore, change must be institutionalized so that services become a permanent, enforceable right. In this inner-city school example, this translates into efforts whereby culturally and socially relevant educational practices and programs are demanded under threat of such instability as boycotting students and/or teachers (particularly effective when state funds to the school system are apportioned on the basis of average daily attendance).

Although the models of community social work practice described in Part I of this volume represent an effort to conceptualize community social work practice in a manner which generates practice principles which can be subjected to rigorous testing, the models have an additional value for those interested in community social work in minority communities. Inherent in the models is an assumption of *where* the community social work role is performed as well as *how* the performance of that role may be affected by the institutional context. Thus, the following discussion of the models explores the extent to which the models have been utilized in or have influenced (positively or negatively) minority communities.

PROGRAM DEVELOPMENT AND SERVICE COORDINATION: PLANNING

These two models of practice have been combined for discussion because of the tight connection which they have conceptually and the difficulty in separating their impact on minority individuals from that on communities. Planning and coordination *can* each occur without the other, but planning without coordination is impotent and coordination without planning lacks direction. In any event, the community welfare council or council of social agencies has been the traditional delivery system for community organization social work. There is little evidence that these councils have been effective in eliminating the inequitable access to services which characterizes most minority communities.

There is evidence that in a few cities, minorities were given some attention in the council's program development, service coordination, and planning activities. This occurred as early as 1921 (Parris and Brooks 1971). However, nearly a half century later, despite such glimmerings of minority participation, Rothman, Erlich, and Teresa wrote:

Those involved in welfare planning in the United States typically represent three categories: socially influential individuals from old families; economic influentials with private wealth or corporate managerial control; and a smattering of middle class people from civic organizations. Local voluntary organizations have excluded minority and ethnic groups as well as individuals and organizations with a "cause-oriented" outlook. (1981:13)

The explosion of governmental programs during the 1960s and 1970s—many of them directed toward minority individuals or communities—created additional social planning agencies to compete with the voluntary planning agencies in many communities. The Model Cities programs were perhaps the most influential in this regard. An in-depth study of eight cities in the Model Cities Program (with supplemental analysis of data from other studies) was published in 1974 (Washnis 1974). It concluded that the program had had significant impact on helping to achieve more effective coordination among programs as well as improving intergovernmental cooperation and program coordination. Citizen participation was perhaps the most innovative force in its impact on changing the attitudes of local officials and the ways they make decisions, and in alerting other community groups to the need to involve themselves in governmental decision-making. This is explained in some detail here despite the fact that it is not a program in which social work played a major role. However, its model of planning emphasized sociopolitical aspects of planning as well as the technomethodological (see the differentiation in Gilbert and Specht 1979), despite the fact that guidelines for the former were much more explicit. The significance of this for minority communities may be inferred from a statement contained in an ASPO workshop report:

[There is] a need for the planning agency to move substantially beyond physical planning. This type of program emphasis will require *the employment of substantially more specialists familiar with social welfare, education, poverty, job-training, and other disciplines required in solving inner-city programs.* Though the point seems obvious, it is a fact that such specialists are typically in other city agencies or are hired only on a consulting basis. Throughout the nation there are very few such specialists on the payrolls of city planning departments. (ASPO 1971:19; emphasis added)

The Model Cities program's legacy may be an increased awareness of the potential value of a social work perspective in planning for inner cities.

Traditional community councils have not developed the high level of citizen involvement necessary to reduce the level of perceived powerlessness in minority communities. Wenocur (1976) has suggested additional functions for community councils: searching out new programs and incipient organizations among low-income disadvantaged or minority segments of the community; assessing the merits of these organizations and services; and advocating their financial support within the local United Way and beyond it. Furthermore, since new low-power groups may require aggressive advocacy in pursuit of scarce resources, he argues that the council should not rule out conflict-oriented strategies, and staff should be properly trained for this search and advocacy function.

EMPOWERMENT AND POLITICAL ACTION: COMMUNITY LIAISON

Whereas the preceding two models were linked because of their complementary relationship to each other, the two models in this section are discussed together because of their often contradictory and antithetical stance toward community work with minority individuals, groups, or communities. An example is an excerpt from a progress report on a Mexican-American service project (Rothman 1971:131–39) of the Community Council of San Jose, California. An advisory committee, made up mostly of business and professional persons, was set up by the Community Council board to provide "community input." The director, however, decided not to use the advisory body or council as his major mechanism for obtaining input regarding the low-income, Mexican-American community. He would use only those who were members of that affected group as his advisers. Furthermore, he would maximize their participation in achieving the project's objectives:

Meetings were conducted among different segments of the minority community to bring out leadership; different groups accepted responsibility for various projects. The problems were defined and redefined; school dropouts, school motivation, employment, appointments to commissions, representation in city agencies, pre-school programs, each became a task organized and staffed by volunteers. The final result was that, altogether, hundreds of individuals from the community itself participated meaningfully in the execution of project objectives. (Rothman 1971:134–35)

The director in this instance had been hired to utilize the community liaison approach to community practice but insisted on initiating a political action, empowerment model.

　　　The social agency has been characterized by its expression of commitment to social change in conservative terms, and the community liaison approach often reflects this conservatism, whereas political action is a more radical approach. This perhaps accounts for the higher frequency with which social work examples of community practice in minority communities illustrate the community liaison approach (utilization of advisory councils) rather than the political action approach (promoting rent strikes). On the other hand, this should not imply that either approach may not have to be chosen on the basis of the receptivity of organizational context in which the social work practitioner operates. For example, the director of the project just described was accused of "a systematic and chronic inability to operate within the structure and function of the agency. . . . The Council cannot afford to operate with the responsibilities it has accepted and the community trust inherent in these responsibilities at the risk of relinquishing its authority to a Council employee" (Rothman 1971:137). A notice of termination was sent. However, due to pressures from the Mexican-American community, the project was granted United Way membership and funding. In a more hostile organizational environment or with a less cohesive and effective community, the project might have been discontinued and an important community resource lost. Therefore, it is necessary to be able to assess power distribution in a community accurately and skillfully apply empowerment strategies or the potential for loss is considerable.

COMMUNITY DEVELOPMENT

In 1928 Jones wrote: "The settlement house movement among colored people has never gained very great headway, although there are reputable settlement houses [in black neighborhoods] in Boston, Minneapolis and in Cleveland" (290). Although settlement houses were effective in the transition process whereby European immigrants were socialized into the American middle class, they have had much less impact on the neighborhoods of those groups we are calling oppressed minorities—the blacks, Hispanics, Asian/Pacific Americans, and American Indians.

It was only with the advent of massive federal programming in the community development field that this approach to social change made an impact on minority communities. Khinduka has stated that community development

aims to educate and motivate people for self-help; to develop responsible local leadership, to inculcate among the members of rural communities a sense of citizenship and among the residents of the urban areas a spirit of civic consciousness; to introduce and strengthen democracy at the grassroots level through the creation and/or revitalization of institutions designed to serve as instruments of local participation; to initiate self-generative, self-sustaining, and enduring process of growth; to enable people to establish and maintain cooperative and harmonious relationships; and to bring about gradual and self-chosen changes in the community's life with a minimum of stress and disruption. (1979:356)

As indicated earlier, Mobilization for Youth and HARYOU were examples of large-scale community development projects. As such, they often incorporated empowerment, political action, community liaison, social planning, and service coordination in their overall change strategy. However, most community development efforts in minority communities were not so comprehensive.

Neighborhood organizations were the mechanisms most often identified in the 1960s as the force for community development. Austin (1968) has suggested that the term neighborhood organization is too limiting since many of these organizations may be defined by many special interests with geographical location or locality as only one possible unit of interest. From the social work perspective, their most important characteristic is their congruence with the notion of a formal resource system; the social work practitioner most often encounters this system in the role of technical assistant or staff person provided by an established social agency rather than as an integral part of the organization itself. The War on Poverty and Great Society programs attempted to institutionalize such support of neighborhood organizations. However, the results have been almost inconsequential in regard to the empowerment of these communities. Austin suggests that locality is too vague a basis for attracting participation in low-income minority communities. Issues such as welfare rights or the problems of AFDC mothers, might constitute a more effective organizing principle (Austin 1968:96).

Ironically, the failures of the neighborhood action groups to institutionalize citizen participation and dramatically reform major social institutions have not diminished the value placed on neighborhoods as the focus for change efforts. The interest in informal helping networks, especially those at the neighborhood level, has been far too attractive in a period of declining economic resources and the need to seek out whatever nonmonetary resources there may be, such as social and psychological support systems. The Republican national platform of 1980 included the following statement:

The quality of American neighborhoods is the ultimate test of the success or failure of government policies for the cities, for housing, and for law enforcement. . . . We are, moreover, committed to nurturing the spirit of self-help and cooperation through which so many neighborhoods have revitalized themselves and served their residents. . . . Government must never elbow aside private institutions—schools, churches, volunteer groups, labor and professional associates—meeting the social needs in our neighborhoods and communities. . . . The duty is the focus for the lives of millions of Americans. Its neighborhoods are places of familiarity, of belonging, of tradition and continuity. They are arenas for civic action and creative self-help. The human scale of the neighborhood encourages cities to exercise leadership, to invest their talents, energies, and resources, to work together to create a better life for their families. Republican economic programs will create conditions for the birth of citizen activity in neighborhoods and cities across the land. (Boyte 1980:29)

In summary, in the majority of cases community social work practice in minority communities has been conducted in programs publicly funded at the federal level. Voluntary agencies such as planning councils and United Way which have primarily service coordination and planning functions have rarely had a major impact on minority communities. Moreover, residents of minority communities are unlikely to consider these activities as "community organization." The Urban Leagues have been the only voluntary agencies serving a predominantly minority community which have utilized community social work as the primary practice modality and whose objectives clearly relate to community development and empowerment rather than planning and service coordination. However, because social action is perceived by many in minority communities as the only activity legitimately defined as community organization, the Leagues' strategies have led to a conservative image. This image is actually the image of the social work profession. Given the fact that social agencies—public or voluntary—must reflect prevailing public opinion to a considerable extent if they are to survive, it is not likely that social work practice in these agencies will ever be able to match the grass-roots organizations in their ability to confront and attack "the system."

The greatest consequence of the War on Poverty and Great Society programs may be the legacy of grass-roots, indigenous community groups which emphasize community development and which have been able to perpetuate themselves after the disappearance of the governmental support which brought them into being. These organizations include such groups as the Pacific/Asian Coalition, funded originally by NIMH. Many have been based on the need to strengthen the functional community (in contrast to the geographical community) which has been defined by the minority group status. Thus these neighborhood- or community-based groups, defined by membership in the stigmatized collective, survive precariously in the present and with considerable uncertainty as to their future status. The uncertainty may be lessened to the extent that the new technology in social work regarding intervention with natural support systems—churches, peer friendship networks—is refined.

Conclusions and Recommendations

Theoretical models of community social work practice appear less sharply etched when the realities of practice in minority communities are considered. For example, in assessing the implementation of the various models in these communities, it is clear that their utility is based on the extent to which they either (1) empower community groups to confront the established social institutions and effectively bring about changes which reduce institutional inequality, or (2) provide for the confrontation of established social institutions by the social worker from the worker's organizational context in pursuit of the same objective. In order to make social work more secure in its own technology the following recommendations are made:

1. When the objective of a public or private agency is program development or service coordination, the involvement of individuals and groups in the target communities is imperative: inclusion of service recipients on United Way or welfare planning council committees, for example.

2. Planning bodies such as city planning commissions and regional planning commissions should include on their staffs community social work specialists with the sociopolitical skills needed to complement the physical planning skills that have been emphasized in planning agencies. Such inclusion will increase the likelihood that the concerns of oppressed minority communities will be addressed.

3. When the model utilized is political action or empowerment and negotiation, the agency should seek creative and comprehensive ways to involve community individuals and groups in confronting directly the problems of institutional inequality.

4. When the model utilized is community development, emphasis should be given to strengthening natural helping networks, the formal and informal associations which are important resources for individuals who are experiencing gaps between needs and resources.

5. When the community liaison model is utilized, every effort should be made to ensure that the community residents from whom consultation is sought represent the broad spectrum of community interests with representation heavily weighted in the direction of those who are the recipients or potential recipients of the services.

What is suggested in this analysis of the empirical reality of community organization in minority communities is that regardless of the model utilized, the major determinant of whether a community will be empowered is the extent to which individuals and/or groups in it can increase their effectiveness in dealing with societal resource systems and thereby maximize their own social functioning. The need for a more intensive level of participation and involvement of the target group stems from two conditions:

1. The social welfare agency and its staff are themselves most often reflective of the middle-class, white majority; therefore, its perspective, point of view, and value orientation are represented automatically. This, of course, is the source of institutional inequality; it is unnecessary to have individual racism or discrimination occur because the institution's myopic policies and procedures will automatically produce inequality.

2. It is only through firsthand experience of the power to change institutions that individuals increase their sense of their own capacity to affect the decisions that have an impact on their lives and thereby increase the power of the communities in which they reside.

The strong collective identity which characterizes most minority groups should serve to increase the likelihood that empowered individuals will inspire other individuals and thus further strengthen their communities. There is no more exhilarating experience for many minority persons than seeing "one of us" confront "the system" and win.

Note

1. "Oppressed minorities" refers to those in minority groups which have for reasons of physical distinctiveness—most notably skin color—been less able to "melt" into the predominantly white American mainstream. Consequently, they have been subjected to varying degrees of legalized discrimination beyond that experienced by the so-called "white ethnics" who are also minority groups in the American ethnosystem.

References

AACTION. 1973; 1974. The Community Newsletter of the Asian American Council of Greater Philadelphia.

Alvarez, Salvador. 1971. "Mexican-American Community Organizations." In Romano-V, ed., *Voices: Readings from El Grito—a Journal of Contemporary Mexican-American Thought,* pp. 205–14.

Ambrecht, Biliana C. C. 1976. *Politicizing the Poor: The Legacy of the War on Poverty in a Mexican-American Community.* New York: Praeger.

American Society of Planning Officials (ASPO). 1971. Planning Advisory Service, "The Planning Agency and the Black Community: A Workshop Report." Report no. 274. Chicago: ASPO.

Austin, David M. 1968. "Influence of Community Setting on Neighborhood Action." In Turner, ed., *Neighborhood Organization for Community Action,* pp. 76–96.

Boyte, Harry. 1980. "Neighborhood Action." *Social Policy* (November/December), 11(39):29.

Brager, George A. and Francis P. Purcell, eds. 1967. *Community Action Against Poverty: Readings from the Mobilization Experience.* New Haven, Conn.: College and University Press.

Brown, Eddie F. n.d. *A Conceptual Framework for the Study and Analysis of Indian Communities.* Monograph no. 2 in a series of monographs for social work practice with American Indians. Tempe, Ariz.: School of Social Work, University of Arizona.

Brown, Eddie F. and Betty Gilbert. 1977. *Social Work Practice with American Indians.* Monograph no. 1 in a series of monographs for social work practice with American Indians. Tempe, Ariz.: School of Social Work, University of Arizona.

Cameron, J. Donald and Esther Talavera. 1976. "An Advocacy Program for Spanish-Speaking People." *Social Casework* (July), 57(7):427–31.

Cardinal, Harold. 1971. "The Unjust Society: The Tragedy of Canada's Indians." In Elliott, ed., *Minority Canadians: Native Peoples,* 1:134–49.

256   B. B. Solomon

Carrillo, Carmen. 1980. "Mental Health Services for Minorities: Issues and Strategies." In *Manpower Considerations in Providing Mental Health Services to Ethnic Minority Groups,* pp. 11–24. Boulder, Colo.: Western Interstate Commission on Higher Education.

Christenson, James A. and Jerry W. Robinson, Jr. 1980. *Community Development in America.* Ames, Iowa: Iowa State University Press.

Cloward, Richard A. and Lloyd E. Ohlin. 1966. *Delinquency and Opportunity: A Theory of Delinquent Groups.* New York: Free Press of Glencoe.

Cox, Fred M. et al., eds. 1979. *Strategies of Community Organization: A Book of Readings.* 3d ed. Itasca, Ill.: Peacock.

Davis, King E. 1975. *Fund Raising in the Black Community: History, Feasibility and Conflict.* Metuchen, N.J.: Scarecrow Press.

Delgado, Melvin. 1974. "Social Work and the Puerto Rican Community." *Social Casework* (February), 55(2):117–23.

Elliott, Jean Leonard, ed. 1976. *Minority Canadians: Native Peoples,* 1. Scarborough, Ont.: Prentice-Hall of Canada.

Farris, Charles E. 1976. "American Indian Social Worker Advocates." *Social Casework* (October), 57(8):494–503.

Finestone, Harold. 1972. "The Chicago Area Project in Theory and Practice." In Spergel, ed., *Community Organization: Studies in Constraint,* pp. 149–86.

Garvin, Charles D. and Fred M. Cox. 1979. "A History of Community Organizing Since the Civil War with Special Reference to Oppressed Communities." In Cox et al., eds., *Strategies of Community Organization,* pp. 45–75.

Gilbert, Neil and Harry Specht. 1979. "Who Plans?" In Cox et al., eds., *Strategies of Community Organization,* pp. 337–53.

Grosser, Charles F. 1976. *New Directions in Community Organization: from Enabling to Advocacy.* New York: Praeger.

Hernandez, Carol, Marsha Haug, and Nathaniel Wagner, eds. 1976. *Chicanos: Social and Psychological Perspectives.* St. Louis, Mo.: C. V. Mosby.

Hughes, David R. and Evelyn Kallen. 1974. *The Anatomy of Racism: Canadian Dimensions.* Montreal: Harvest House.

Ignacio, Lemuel. 1976. *Asian Americans and Pacific Islanders: Is There Such an Ethnic Group?* San Jose, Calif.: Pilipino Development Associates.

Jenkins, Shirley. 1981. *The Ethnic Dilemma in Social Services.* New York: Free Press.

Jones, Eugene Kinckle. 1928. "Social Work Among Negroes." In *The Annals of the American Academy of Political and Social Science* (November), 140:287–93.

Khinduka, Shanti K. 1979. "Community Development: Potentials and Limitations." In Cox et al., eds., *Strategies of Community Organization,* pp. 356–64.

McNeil, C. F. 1951. "Community Organization for Social Welfare." In *Social Work Year Book, 1951.* New York: American Association of Social Workers.

Mapp, Edward, ed. 1974. *Puerto-Rican Perspectives.* Metuchen, N.J.: Scarecrow Press.

Marrero, Jacinto. 1974. "Self-Help Efforts in the Puerto Rican Community." In Mapp, ed., *Puerto-Rican Perspectives,* pp. 76–82.

Miranda, Manuel and Harry H. L. Kitano. 1976. "Barriers to Mental Health Services: A Japanese-American and Mexican-American Dilemma." In Hernandez, Haug, and Wagner, eds., *Chicanos: Social and Psychological Perspectives*, pp. 242–52.

Mogulof, Melvin. 1970. "Black Community Development in Five Western Model Cities." *Social Work* (January), 15(1):12–18.

Morales, Armando. 1981. "Social Work with Third World People." *Social Work* (January), 26(1):12–18.

Newsome, Moses, Jr. 1973. "Neighborhood Service Centers in the Black Community." *Social Work* (March), 18(2):50–54.

O'Brien, David J. 1975. *Neighborhood Organization and Interest Group Process*. Princeton, N.J.: Princeton University Press.

Parris, Guichard and Lester Brooks. 1971. *Blacks in the City: A History of the National Urban League*. Boston: Little, Brown.

Perlman, Janice E. 1976. "Grassrooting the System." *Social Policy* (September/October), 7(2):4–20.

Romano-V, Octavio Ignacio, ed. 1971. *Voices: Readings from El Grito, a Journal of Contemporary Mexican-American Thought*. 2d ed. Berkeley, Calif.: Quinto Sol Publications.

Ross, Edythe L. 1978. *Black Heritage and Social Welfare 1860–1930*. Metuchen, N.J.: Scarecrow Press.

Ross, Murray G. 1955. *Community Organization, Theory and Principles*. New York: Harper.

Rothman, Jack. 1971. *Promoting Social Justice in the Multi-group Society: A Casebook for Group Relations Practitioners*. New York: Association Press.

Rothman, Jack, John Erlich, and Joseph Teresa. 1981. *Changing Organizations and Community Programs*. Beverly Hills, Calif.: Sage Publications.

Schaller, Lyle E. 1966. *Community Organization: Conflict and Reconciliation*. Nashville, Tenn.: Abingdon Press.

Schwartz, Meyer. 1965. "Community Organization." In *Encyclopedia of Social Work*, pp. 177–90. 15th ed. New York: NASW.

Schwartz, William. 1961. "The Social Worker in the Group." In *Social Welfare Forum, 1961*, pp. 146–71. New York: Columbia University Press.

Sorkin, Alan L. 1978. *The Urban American Indian*. Lexington, Mass.: Heath.

Spergel, Irving, ed. 1972. *Community Organization: Studies in Constraint*. Beverly Hills, Calif.: Sage Pulications.

Turner, John B., ed. 1968. *Neighborhood Organization for Community Action*. New York: NASW.

Washnis, George J. 1974. *Community Development Strategies: Case Studies of Major Model Cities*. New York: Association Press.

Weissman, Harold H., ed. 1969. *Community Development in the Mobilization for Youth Experience*. New York: Association Press.

Wenocur, Stanley. 1976. "A Pluralistic Planning Model for United Way Organizations." *Social Service Review* (December), 50(4):586–600.

Zimbalist, Sidney. 1970. "Mobilization for Youth: The Search for a New Social Work." *Social Work* (January), 15(1):123–28.

9

The Practice
of Community Social Work
with the Aged

Abraham Monk

The "revolution of age" is one of the most far-reaching transformations sweeping the industrialized world. It is the corollary of both higher life expectancies—people simply live longer—and lower fertility rates. The net result is a proportionally higher representation of the senior cohorts: by the year 2030 the United States may more than double the 24 million persons aged sixty-five and older it numbered in 1979. It is forecast that this age group will soar to 55 million, and it may then constitute 23 percent of the population, as compared to 11 percent today.[1] Concurrent with their new demographic salience, the elderly have achieved a substantial package of social entitlements such as Social Security and health insurance programs. Retirement adds a novel dimension to their lives in the form of economically nonproducing leisure roles encompassing nearly one third of their life span. Most of these benefits are of recent vintage, however, and they have not become as firmly entrenched as the senior advocates may have expected. Originally predicated on an economy of abundance, the fate of these benefits is now subject to the ominous reality of declining resources. Policy-makers are therefore beset with the dilemma of preserving most of those entitlements while the economic base that made them possible is being eroded.

The very nature of macro-social work practice, as poignantly stated by Rothman (1978), will be deeply affected by a tightening economy and the scarcity of capital resources. As public tax-supported programs are declining in scope, macro-practice will focus increasingly on self-help and advocacy strategies, along with improved social planning and managerial efficiency. The reality of these practice modalities is more than apparent in the field of the aging.

The imperative to plan was patently manifest immediately after the passing of the Older Americans Act (OAA) in 1965. Implicit in the whirlwind of policy enactments of that decade was the assumption that governmental intervention would bring about a better redistribution of existing resources as well as a new, comprehensive system of service supports. Social planners were entrusted with overcoming the fragmentation and gaps in the services network and with creating meaningful roles for older persons. Macro-oriented social workers also embarked on campaigns to put into operation policies calling for the social involvement of senior citizens and their retention in the mainstream of community life.

The expansionist scenario of the 1960s and 1970s, however, is seemingly over, as budgets are being cut for "nonessentials" like human services, and social entitlements are being capped with inadequate ceilings. Older persons are especially hit because they find it increasingly difficult to gain access to their entitlements at all. While exercising their advocacy functions, macro social workers are also confronted with the reactions of a taxpaying population overburdened with their own economic tribulations and unwilling to consider benefits for the aged as untouchable. Talk about cutting Social Security no longer evokes irate reactions. The unthinkable prospect of reversing the direction of national policy for the elderly is more plausible than at any time since passage of the Social Security Act of 1935. Social workers in the field of aging must thus contend with a peculiar dilemma: the uncertainty of a scarcity-ridden society coupled with the demographic expansion of their client population.

260   A. Monk

Building the Agenda for Community Social Work

In the next decade the service community will have to set priorities as to what it regards as the overriding needs of older people. It will have to assess the social implications of the demographic transformation in question and sort out an agenda of critical issues. Six such issues are highlighted here because of their immediate relevance to community social work practice.

THE VERY OLD AND THE RISK OF INSTITUTIONALIZATION

The main effect of the relentless increase in life expectancy rates is the growth in the proportion of the very old among old people. Today, the 75-year or older cohort constitutes 38 percent of the 65-year and older population. By the year 2000 they will reach the 45 percent level. The number of persons 85 and older will in turn grow from 9 percent to 12 percent.[2] Because disability and chronicity increase with age, more of the very old are seriously incapacitated, and the utilization of nursing homes has increased despite efforts to create parallel, noninstitutional service options. Statistics on long-term care are already overwhelming: there are more than one million nursing home beds, and this exceeds the total number of hospital beds in the United States. While on any given day 4 percent of the aged are confined in nursing homes, the probability that an older person will end his life as a resident in such a facility is one in five. The largest number of nursing home patients are in the 85-year and older group. One out of every four people past 85 is already confined in institutional care.

As reported by the Urban Institute, between 1967 and 1977 nursing home expenditures grew 22 percent per year. While inflation partially explains this increment, it is most attributable to the greater percentage of the elderly making use of nursing homes (Scanlon 1978).

Community social workers cannot be expected to reverse that trend. Institutionalization seems to be a function of advanced age, and it correlates with the fact that a spouse is less likely to be alive as one grows old, and physical health and financial ability also decline with age. What social workers can do is introduce some rationality into the admission policies of nursing homes, and denounce and force a public examination of the gate-keeping role currently performed by nursing home operators.

If proper screening criteria were adopted, decisions concerning who will receive institutional care would rest on professional criteria, and the available beds in nursing homes could then be used judiciously. Such screening would also require community social workers to contribute to the design of the channeling services that route applicants to the right level of service, ranging from community-based programs to semi-independent living alternatives such as foster care and congregate care. In order to correct present disparities and inconsistencies in state, federal, and local regulations, policy analysis and policy development will become substantial parts of the job assignments of social workers.

Information on costs of programs, service outcomes, and utilization patterns needs to be compiled so that planning strategies and eligibility criteria can be established. The degree to which new program ideas can improve the present institutional system needs to be carefully considered. Without the information in question, collected and analyzed by the community worker, planning and reform in comprehensive long-term care planning are not feasible.

SEX DIFFERENTIALS IN LIFE EXPECTANCY RATES

The sex differential gap in mortality will continue to widen progressively over the years. There are now about 70 men for every 100 women aged 65 or over (U.S. Senate 1979). It would appear that despite the trend toward more similar life experiences for contemporary men and women, great divergence in their mortality rates remains. Because this skewed sex ratio will continue, there will be an increased incidence of widowhood, with its corollary of extended years of isolation and living alone for many women.

Widows constitute over one third of all persons aged 65 or more. They are more than half of all elderly women. Their opportunity to remarry is quite limited since they outnumber eligible males by a ratio of 4 to 1. This is compounded by the fact that males who marry after the age of 65 tend to choose a partner from a younger age cohort.

The resulting hardships for widows are self-evident: lack of companionship and lack of access to skills to accomplish tasks where division of labor according to sex has been traditionally observed. In addition, there are economic problems, such as lower standards of living among older women, partly due to their inadequate job training and inferior career opportunities during their earlier years.

Despite the euphoric exaltation and alleged effectiveness of primary support systems, most widows have lost their emotional, physical, and economic supports. Many are homebound because they have no means of transportation and are afraid of venturing outside. Community social work is and must continue to be involved in providing outreach and organizing supportive services for this large segment of the elderly population. Loneliness, as Lopata (1978) found, is the main correlate of widowhood. It is in part the result of a couple-dominated adult society that refuses to incorporate the single person. It is also the price widows must pay for their independence when they resist succumbing to the traditional roles of baby-sitter or housekeeper for their offspring. Social work will have to be responsive to the cry for independence and shape programs that explicitly meet the needs of those who choose or are compelled to adopt singlehood as a gerontological life style.

URBANIZATION AND AGE SEGREGATION

The aged are not scattered at random throughout the United States of America. They tend to be more concentrated in some areas, not so much as the result of sponsored migration or intentional segregation, but because of the ecological specialization that fosters a centrifugal movement of the young toward the urban fringes. This process, as indicated by Cowgill (1977), continued unabated during the 1940–70 period in most Standard Metropolitan Areas. As urban growth occurs, the young move to the outskirts, leaving their elders behind in the central cities. Population shifts have never shown age correlation: the young and the old go in different directions, leaving a net increase of age segregation in about 75 percent of the SMAs. The young and old go their separate ways, both figuratively and geographically.

The trend toward age segregation was corrobor d by Cantor (1976) in her study on the effects of ethnicity on life styles of the inner-city elderly. She found that Hispanic and black elderly in New York City are still part of the extended family networks, encompassing frequent contact and direct mutual assistance, but even this idyllic image is being eroded as substantially larger numbers of black and Hispanic elderly begin to live alone rather than within the traditional extended family.

Age segregation is likely to continue in the years to come, thus leading to an increase of specialized age-homogeneous communities. This is not a matter of philosophical preference but a social and demographic reality with which community planners must contend. The "age-irrelevant" society, anticipated by Neugarten (1975), will probably remain a noble aspiration whose hour may not come for at least another generation.

There are incipient signs, however, of a reversal in the geographical distancing of generations: it follows the growing disenchantment with what suburbs have to offer and the fact that many cities are being made more attractive through renewal programs. Scarcity also enters into the picture: the high costs of transportation, housing, and inflationary mortgage interest rates are limiting the capacity of the young to move away from parents. Sussman, Vanderwyst, and Williams (1976) tested the hypothetical propensity of young offspring to accept elderly relatives in their home. While he found a lukewarm level of receptivity to the prospect, there was a definite increase in readiness when it was linked to the provision of tax deductions or similar policy incentives.

Community social workers will be called upon to attend to both contingencies: if age segregation prevails, their responsibility will lie in preventing the generational fragmentation of society through the design of programs that encourage communication and mutuality among young and old. If segregation diminishes, however, the effectiveness of natural support networks cannot be sustained with nurturance of spontaneity alone. Formalized backup services (day care, respite, crisis intervention, employment, homemaking, home care) will be required to reduce the strain most likely to befall middle-aged or younger adults. Opportunities for self-help and resocialization programs will be needed to bolster the independence and self-esteem of the old.

THE REALITY OF ALONENESS

The number of elderly living alone is growing rapidly. The proportion of the noninstitutionalized aged living alone has increased from one sixth in 1960 to one fourth in 1976. The number rose from 3.8 million in the earlier year to 8 million in the latter year. The increase in single-person households among the "old-old"—the 75-year and older group—far exceeds the rates for the younger elderly; it is twice as high as the rate of the 65–74 group and three times that of the 60–64 group.

Special consideration needs to be given to the additional 5 percent of the aged—about one million—who are confined to the house and must depend on someone else to contend with the routines of daily life. An even larger number of the noninstitutionalized elderly, estimated at about 20 percent, or 4 million, are hindered by mobility or functional impairments. They need supportive services in order to get around at home and outside.

There is a presumption that the trend toward aloneness may be slowing down or even reversing because of higher rental costs, and housing and energy shortages. This in no way means a return to a familial way of life. Aloneness, coupled with the vulnerability of the very old, poses an additional programmatic challenge to community social workers: they must detect the need and stimulate new forms of communities. This is a step beyond the notion of supportive environments. They may have to assume the responsibility of promoting new patterns of residential aggregation, such as adult home residences or congregate living operating as satellites of social service agencies. Although this may be tantamount to creating new forms of total environment, or institutions in disguise, it may be the only alternative left for the "old-old" who lack viable support systems and suffer from minor disabilities.

Social workers have no right to impose gregariousness or sociability on all the elderly. It is not proven that aloneness causes depressive feelings of loneliness in all. Some may even find forti-

tude and fulfillment in their solitude, but programs need to be designed for those who wish to pull out from involuntary segregation
and reengage with the world.

WORK AND RETIREMENT

Industrial societies have subscribed to the "lineal life plan," namely,
the education, work, and retirement sequence in which people organize their existence. Bureau of Labor Statistics projections indicate
that the compression of work into the middle years may intensify in
the future (Best and Stern 1978). The proportion of the average male
life spent in the labor force will have declined from 62 percent in
1960 to 56 percent by 1990. The other 44 percent will be divided
between 26 percent at the younger end—in school—and about 18
percent in retirement. With improved health, longevity, lessened
physical demands in automated industries, better education, and a
significant reduction in the labor force participation of the young,
older workers may seek a flexible, not an earlier, retirement. New
work-sharing strategies, flexible time options, and the adoption of
forms of time release may lead to cyclical rather than linear life
patterns. It is conceivable that those cyclical life models, if generalized, may facilitate periodic reentry to the labor force, a sort of
revolving door through life. They may equip workers for leisure and
retirementlike roles long before retirement itself. Community social
workers may assume leadership in shaping lifelong learning programs and helping people to incorporate a leisurely life style in their
middle years. They may also shape opportunities for second or even
third careers.

The Uses of Theory

Inventories of critical issues, as outlined in the preceding section,
need to be interpreted in the context of valid theoretical frameworks.
Otherwise, the resulting agendas for social intervention may misin-
terpret the realities they seek to change.

Social work, like all applied professions, borrows and adapts theories with the intent to legitimize a given course of intervention, thus bridging the span that separates assessment from policy formulation and program design. The use of imported social gerontological theories is confounded, however, by the fact that they extend themselves beyond explanation into norms. These theories then tend to prescribe what aging "ought to be." They strive for utopia and sanction paradigmatic behaviors and actions, thus running the risk of forcing a rigid, ideological straitjacket on practice.

The case of the much debated disengagement theory is an appropriate example. In its initial formulations, the theory argued that older persons reduce their social activity as they give up instrumental roles and seek instead more expressive rewards. This alleged separation from obligatory forms of behavior and its concomitant turn into one's self suggests a sort of trade-off: aging individuals give up their social preeminence but gain a special sense of freedom. The critics of the theory retorted that it does not take into account the rich varieties of human experience and that it has no room for the wide coping potentialities still left intact among the aged.

Cath (1975) suspected that the idea of disengagement as a mutually freeing and partially beneficial process for the normal aged may lead to, even encourage, discriminatory attitudes and practices against the aging. Cath agreed that aging consists of a series of losses, but many older persons also have to contend with their loss-related anxieties in an environment that is insensitive and uncaring. The virtual hostility of the external environment reinforces the internal losses, thus turning the propositions of the disengagement theory into a sort of self-fulfilling prophecy. Social workers who accept a disengagement outlook may not favor the reinvolvement of the older person. They may be more inclined toward the "naturalness" of segregated, contemplative, and passive behaviors. In counterdistinction, social workers who adhere to the "activity" theory as explained by Rose (1964) may too eagerly encourage the resocialization of the older person and even the pursuit of new role identity patterns. Both are partially correct if they remain attuned to the continuous life patterns and social environment of a given individual. The danger of a universal prescription emanating from the improper use of either theory lies precisely in ignoring each individual's lifelong coping modalities.

The lessons of the already classical disengagement and activity theories are as pertinent for community social workers as they are for their clinical counterparts. Both are similarly concerned with the independence of the elderly person as a value premise.

For an elderly person, the wish to preserve independence may be a genuine expression of assertiveness, consistent with a lifelong pattern of self-sufficiency. The insistence to preserve it, even at the expense of severe hardships, may also be indicative of overcompensatory strategies aimed at neutralizing the fears of physical and mental deterioration and of altogether losing a grip on life. The ultimate denial of these impending limitations may bolster an older person's sense of self-esteem and allay death-related anxieties, but it also stands in the way of setting realistic life goals.

Independence, when coupled with deprivation, may also represent a seemingly altruistic renunciation of care by others; of not wanting to impose upon relatives and offspring and disrupt their lives. The same independence-deprivation equation may also be set in motion to produce an assortment of secondary gains such as drawing attention and provoking concern in others, usually their children.

Independence-centered anxieties in old age are also associated with the decline of power resources. From an exchange theory perspective, it is understood that older persons have little left of instrumental or symbolic value that can be traded advantageously in social transactions. Blau (1964) enumerated four generalized power resources at people's command: money, approval, esteem, and compliance. The latter would appear, according to this theory, as the only exchange benefit or reward left to the old. They must submit to the norms and demands of the most powerful to gain survival.

Emerson (1962) observed that when the exchange relationship is unbalanced the party who is more dependent, that is, less powerful, will try to correct the relation through one of four possible "balancing" strategies:

1. *Withdrawal,* removing oneself from the field as proposed by the disengagement theory
2. *Extension of power network* through new roles and associations, and by finding alternative, more gratifying sources of reward

3. *Emergence of status,* actually an increase of the power resources of the more dependent partner by reactivating old skills, symbolic prestige, public recognition, or even finding gainful occupation
4. *Coalition formation* in which the more dependent seek alliances with other dependent groups to counterbalance the more powerful member.

Macro-oriented social work interventions start from the premise that after a lifetime of work and achievement the older person suffers a considerable degree of status demotion, social and economic impoverishment, and even social rejection. The first of the four balancing strategies is the measure of last resort, used in cases of advanced disability. For the most part, macro-interventions are based upon the remaining three operations outlined by Emerson. Coalition formation appears to be the most powerful alternative, but network extension seems to be the most pervasive one. It was implicitly sanctioned by the Older Americans Act of 1965, and its implementation became the province of the expert planner.

From Expert Planning to Experienced Manager

Historically, the initial policy direction adopted by most industrial countries vis-à-vis their aged populations was one of financial support. It was assumed that if they were guaranteed a minimum income through social insurance or pensions they could then satisfy all their needs in the open market of voluntary or private services.

Elderly persons found, however, that services were insular, uncoordinated, difficult to find, and for the most part unavailable. The clamor of the late 1950s and early 1960s for better articulation of whatever services were already available and the creation of much needed services resulted in the passage of the OAA. Concurrently, the expert planning role emerged as the dominant form of community practice. It was, in fact, the cornerstone of the aging "networks," a conglomerate of state agencies on aging mandated by the OAA, and the nearly seven hundred Area Agencies on Aging (AAAs). These are the local operations more commonly designated as county or city departments of senior services. The state agencies are to design programs, coordinate services, assess the extent of need amidst an ill-defined population-at-risk, and evaluate the actual delivery of services. The substate levels of AAAs are similarly required to produce three-year plans forecasting the demand or need for services and assessing the adequacy of extant resources. The AAAs were not called to attend directly to the needs of the elderly population within their geographical jurisdiction; instead, they were to contract with local providers and monitor the implementation and quality of the services thus rendered.

The 1973 amendments to the OAA defined much more specifically the range of planning roles assigned to these novel area administrative structures. The AAAs were consequently made responsible for mounting a continuous process of planning, including the definition of service priorities and the development of a comprehensive system specially designed to improve the delivery of services. They also had to make provisions for an action program aimed at coordinating services and pooling available but untapped resources in order to strengthen or initiate new services. Given the bewildering maze of existing services, the AAAs were assigned the task of establishing and maintaining information and referral services to ensure the elderly access to such services. Finally, AAAs were authorized to enter into agreements with independent contractors or award grants for services that would fill gaps.

It is important to mention here the services included in the OAA:

1. Health, continuing education, welfare, recreational, homemaker, counseling, and referral services
2. Transportation as a means of facilitating access to other essential services
3. Services intended to encourage and assist older persons to use the facilities and services available to them
4. Services designed to assist older persons in avoiding or postponing the risk of institutionalization, including assessment and screening and home-delivered services
5. Services geared to assisting older persons to obtain adequate housing.

Funds were also provided for establishing local sites—nearly twelve thousand throughout the country—for congregate dining facilities to improve the nutritional intake of older persons. Nutritional programs actually became the pivotal factor of a rather elaborate planning endeavor: transportation had to be ensured to facilitate access to the sites, and systematic outreach efforts had to be mounted to identify the lonely, shut-in, and underserved aged. Nutrition sites, in addition to offering meals, were meant to provide opportunities for socialization and linkages to the gamut of social services. They constituted de facto intake or entry points to the service system and tested the viability of its underlying coordinative strategy.

Although the act did not encourage AAAs to engage in open class advocacy, their advisory boards had enough latitude to become interest-group representatives. The degree of pugnacious partisanship or open confrontational tactics they adopted varied from AAA to AAA, however. On the whole, there was evidence of relentless activity in the legislative domain. Assisted by planners with a bent toward policy analysis, community advisory boards took stands on proposed legislation, lobbied on behalf of their constituents, and maintained a constant watch on trends in program funding. These tasks were mostly reactive in nature, rarely exceeding the review level. Only seldom did they initiate the formulation of legislative proposals. The experiment of blending planning with coordinative and advocacy functions within public agencies initiated amidst conflicting forecasts and near universal perplexity. Would it really work?

Early critics warned that the OAA had no enforcement power and that it was vitiated by the absence of sufficient resources necessary for the policy to be carried out. The beginnings were very modest indeed. By the time of the 1971 White House Conference on Aging the administration's request for funds to finance the entire act—including services planning, training, and research—barely reached the $30 million mark. By 1980 the OAA funding exceeded $500 million, and the aging network was already placed on the political map. Binstock (1978) found no comfort in those developments, however: he contended that the OAA fostered a delusion by appearing to promise more than it could deliver and that it discouraged generic sources of social services by trying to monopolize the categorical services for the aged. Hudson (1974), in turn, stated that the OAA called for implementing an ambiguous and nearly impossible task. On the one hand it assigned to the AAAs the administrative responsibility for monitoring the existing service system, but on the other it expected them to engage in gap-filling developmental actions. The argument holding that coordinative planning and advocacy planning are antithetical, or at least pragmatically difficult to reconcile, explains the role strain and burn-out syndrome experienced by so many gerontological planners.

Estes (1979) leveled the most devastating criticism of the system as sanctioned by the OAA. She viewed it as an ineffectual symbolic gesture meant to assuage the sensitivities of middle-class older Americans. The services it generated barely touched the surface of an undetermined volume of need, and the AAAs, far from coordinating services, ended up by isolating the old from the rest of society. They also created a fragmented array of services, often in reciprocal competition, which foster the dependence of elder clients and curb their capacity for self-determination. Ultimately, the service strategy launched by the OAA fostered unequal power relationships between providers and recipients of service, the bottom line being that the new AAA bureaucracy, by siphoning resources otherwise intended for the aged, has become the real beneficiary of the generous OAA funding.

In the late 1970s Congress also began to wonder whether the OAA could deliver everything it promised. Its 1978 amendments called for the targeting of certain services and required the Federal Council on Aging to focus on: (1) program effectiveness; (2) the identification of high-risk populations, including an analysis of the number and incidence of low-income and minority elderly; and (3) alternative methods, other than categorical grants, for the allocation of funds.

Thus, the 1978 amendments introduced a more aggressive planning strategy. They required that AAAs direct 50 percent of their social service allocations to services related to access, in home assistance, and legal help. They were also mandated to design outreach strategies aimed at identifying high-risk persons. Four major planning assignments were therefore implicit in those amendments:

1. The designation of single focal or entry points in the community for service delivery, information, and referral
2. The coordination and monitoring of all programs, pol-

icies, and community endeavors that affect the elderly population, including those funded by sources outside the auspices of the OAA

3. The consolidation of service programs through more clearly defined managerial and overseeing operations

4. The operation by contract, with either a public or a qualified nonprofit agency, or an ombudsman program for long-term care facilities, to investigate and resolve complaints, and monitor the laws and statutes.

The 1978 amendments signaled the end of an expansionist era in social planning and the beginning of a more cautious managerial mandate. Social workers employed as planners in state agencies and local AAAs became more involved in scrutinizing program demonstrations and overseeing private vendors to assure proper compliance. Writing contracts in the language of management by objectives, measuring units of service, adjudicating purchase-of-service agreements, negotiating budgets, establishing quality control and quality-assurance procedures, and evaluating program efficiency became the new expertise of the macro-oriented social worker. And yet, the more traditional community practice tasks are still sorely needed to ensure the voluntary coordination of multiple services, and to enlist grass-roots support for initiating new entry points or "one-stop services" at the local level.

Coordination and Case Management

The fragmentation of public services for the aged remained unchecked through the 1970s despite the policy intent to bring about a semblance of coordination. The House Select Committee on Aging reported in 1977 that there were between 50 and 200 federal programs providing major assistance to the elderly. A year later the inventory identified with more precision 134 such programs (U.S. House of Representatives 1977). They had evolved within a process of incremental pluralism, responsive to circumstantial political agendas or demands from advocacy organizations, without having undergone even elementary tests of adequacy. Community planners have found, in fact, that:

1. Community-based services are available for only 3 percent of the total aged population, and possibly for no more than 12
percent of the high-risk subgroup.

2. Cumbersome application and exhausting recertification
procedures deter even the most determined seniors from actually
receiving services. This occurs even to those who succeed in disentangling the maze of eligibility caveats and ultimately affirm their
right to a given service.

Community social workers have become increasingly involved in efforts to assemble programs for the aging into some
cohesive package that could maximize limited resources and properly attend to the service needs of the individual. The catch-all label
of "coordination" is thus narrowly defined as specific operational
strategies such as case management and management information
systems.

Case management underscores the individual's access to an
entire service system, and it provides assurance of a continuum
from home care to institutional care. The Federal Council on Aging
defines the case manager as a caseworker with an ongoing, but not
necessarily an intensive or therapeutic, relationship with an older
person. The role is aptly described as that of a "significant other," or
facilitator and consultant for a person who still exhibits the capability of handling many life decisions but needs some help in
coping with "life bureaucracies because of the accumulation of the
vicissitudes of increasing age, not because of a single physical or
mental trauma, or a personal loss or role change" (U.S. House of
Representatives 1977:133).

Morris (1977) identifies the emergence of the case management concept as the beginning of a caretaking philosophy under-
scoring care rather than cure in its approach to the needs of
chronically impaired populations. The case manager serves a coordinating and linkage function and brings into action community-
based programs to assist the older person in obtaining health and
social supports. The structural components of case management are
somewhat standardized in their inclusion of: (1) a single-entry point;
(2) comprehensive assessment, based upon a reliable instrument
covering health, psychosocial status, financial, environment, and
social supports areas; (3) a written service plan; (4) linkage to the
service system; (5) case review and monitoring at regular intervals;

and (6) plan revision. These tasks are, for the most part, the province of a direct-service practitioner, be it a nurse or a social worker. Community social workers remain critical actors, however, in making this operation possible. They are responsible for:

1. Surveying and inventorying the service system, assessing the intake criteria and service-rendering modalities of all providers
2. Convening agencies toward the goal of adopting common assessment procedures
3. Resolving issues of funding, jurisdiction, and service contracting and negotiating waivers from state medical assistance plans
4. Designing and implementing information and referral services, monitoring client flow through the service network, assessing case-finding and discharge-planning methods and proposing uniform, simple procedures
5. Promoting and managing coordinated community-based services as an alternative to inappropriate nursing home placement.

Given the fact that case managers are still engaged in the voluntary coordination of the services of others, planners must use ingenuity in order to identify and set in motion a package of rewards or incentives that will make cooperation mutually advantageous.

6. Designing and operating centralized management information systems that collect data on clients' requests for services, presenting problems, diagnostic assessment, direct-service provision, referrals and case disposition, payments for services and billing to third parties. These systems are used for both internal auditing and external reporting. Such information systems, while assuring client confidentiality, also reflect the aggregate load and adequacy of existing services. They are the necessary foundation for program evaluation, which is another emerging domain for professional social planning.

Case management highlights the interfacing of micro and macro social work practice. It requires a complex battery of skills ranging from computer technology to grass-roots advocacy.

Social Advocacy

The aged were attracted to the political banners of a host of charismatic movements during the 1920s and 1930s, long before the passing of the Social Security Act. The 1950s and 1960s, however, witnessed the professionalization of reform and rejection of the prophetic and utopian agendas of the past. The new grass-roots organizations adopted, instead, a set of more pragmatic objectives while remaining committed to direct action and political influence. True, major organizations of the stature of the American Association of Retired Persons (AARP) and the National Council of Senior Citizens, each numbering their membership in the millions, also incorporated self-help cooperative features such as discount drug mail-order services, but advocacy continued as their primary course of action. Like all other successful advocacy organizations, the "aging" lobby underscored salient program issues that were deeply rooted in the daily life of their membership. They promoted consciousness-raising through persistent educational efforts and sought broader community coalitions with other interest groups. Some had to conceal their activities in the guise of public information programs for fear that it might otherwise jeopardize their tax-exempt status. They all maximized their effectiveness by constantly reminding elected officials that the aged are capable of delivering, on the average, 25 percent of the total vote in any given election.

The "aging" lobby made successful inroads within the decision-making circles of both major parties while remaining free of political or governmental auspice. The trend has been to constitute independently functioning local chapters connected with, but not totally subordinated to, their national headquarters. Imbued with a strong participatory and nonconformist approach to social action, some groups shied away from the trappings of professionalism.

The Gray Panthers initially made a mark of their singular nature among such associations by responding to the spontaneity of a popular upsurge and by avoiding the formal signing of members or committing themselves to organizational statutes and by-laws.

More concerned with their own survival and continuity, the mainstream of aging movements finally succumbed to the imperative of professional bureaucratization. Consequently, the emerging structures launched outreach and recruitment campaigns and enlarged their political base through coalitions and alliances with powerful occupational organizations. (The AARP established a viable partnership with the National Retired Teachers Association, and the National Council of Senior Citizens similarly linked up with the AFL-CIO.) The newer structures also generated an "intelligence base" through their own research departments and the use of sophisticated political and economic forecasting methods. Soon they were in a position to convey to policy-makers at all levels valuable information connected to the potential risks and rewards inherent in the advancement of specific proposals. As stated by Pratt, these associations gained the advantage of becoming "informants rather than only supplicants" (1976:85). They also succeeded in enlarging the policy agenda of the early 1970s and in creating a positive public atmosphere toward the initiatives voiced by the aged on their own behalf. Community social workers found a haven in the professional ranks of these mass-advocacy organizations. Their interventive tasks included fact-finding and community analysis as well as identifying potential allies, establishing informal ties with like-minded policy-makers, augmenting the power base of their constituent groups, highlighting policy agendas, educating the new leadership, and assuring a flow of information to their rank and file. They tapped the dissatisfactions voiced by senior citizens and channeled their claims and expectations to public forums such as legislative hearings and White House conferences.

Some of these professional advocates are front liners concerned with the mobilization of their indigenous clientele. Others are the promoters of linkages with external coalitions. A third subcategory identifies agenda issues and devises strategies to ensure their public legitimation as policy priorities. Whatever their specialization, advocates of the 1960s and 1970s met relatively little resistance other than indifference or callousness. The result was an unparalleled bonanza of legislative achievements. These invidious circumstances may be denied, however, to the social work advocate of the 1980s. Outspoken adversaries have now surfaced, and they warn that the aged are receiving the lion's share of public benefits. They claim that the "aging" lobby caused a distortion in the apportionment of income and human service supports and that young adults are revolting against the specter of ever rising Social Security taxes.

The promotional function of social welfare implies, in the case of the aged, the advancement of a normative standard of well-being, a quality of life that may well exceed in costs what society is willing to pay. The task of advocating for the older cohorts will then require a keen knowledge base and arguments far more convincing than were necessary for progress in the enthusiastic disposition of preceding decades. The advocate and policy analyst roles are hardly distinguishable from one another at this point.

Policy Analysis and Development

The competencies and methods required for policy development overlap to a large extent with those applied to advocacy practice. Lowy (1979) inventoried such skills and included: fact finding and information gathering, writing briefs, presenting expert testimony, conducting public information and education programs aimed at community sensitization and mobilization, organizing client groups, promoting coalitions, petitions, conferences and contacts with policy-makers, identifying viable channels of appeal, and, as the avenue of last resort, articulating protest campaigns. Although Lowy had in mind gerontological practice, his inventory draws for the most part from a generic framework.

Needless to say, policy analysis skills are predicated on an understanding of the historical, philosophical, political, and socioeconomic circumstances surrounding the provision of services and supports to the elderly population. Community practice is therefore more than just expertise on statutory entitlements and legislative provisions. It centers instead on the forecasting of possible trends and scenarios related to policy development and service provision. Two examples illustrate this point. The first concerns the debate as to whether public commitment to the aged should be channeled through categorical or block grants. The categorical support programs are specifically earmarked for special populations and leave little discretion to states and localities. The block grants provide only general guidelines and accountability procedures but return to the states and localities the decision as to who will benefit from those programs and how.

Landmark initiatives concerning services for the aged were invariably spearheaded through categorical, not block grants. The federal government and not the states or localities has been the leader and promoted most of the substantive gains in this service area. Revenue sharing is the classical case in point of a program that distributes federally collected tax revenues but was initially used by local jurisdictions to supplement law enforcement salaries and fire equipment. Human services in general were appallingly slighted. The aged were in most instances one of the last priorities. Title XX of the Social Security Act required that 50 percent of its benefits be used to support federal assistance recipients (those eligible for Aid to Families with Dependent Children or Supplemental Security Income), but it ended up excluding the vast majority of the elderly population.

The Age Discrimination Study of the U.S. Commission on Civil Rights (1979) repeatedly documented discriminatory policies and practices on the basis of age whenever age-categorical entitlements were not applied. The area of mental health services illustrates this problem. In 1975, 328 community mental health centers reported the addition of over half a million persons to their caseloads. Older persons, while constituting 10 percent of the service population, numbered only 4 percent of actual clients. This is even more appalling in light of the fact that over 20 percent of the 65 or older population have mental health problems severe enough to interfere with their ability to function on a daily basis. The Commission also found that this was not a chance occurrence but the result of deliberate exclusionary directives. In 1976, 528 community mental health centers instructed their staff that over one third of their time be devoted to consultation and services to agencies serving children, and only 5 percent of their working hours to agencies dealing with senior persons. Similar findings were reported in the areas of employment, Title XX, and so on.

The second example applies to the long-term-care field. The movement for alternatives to institutionalization started from the assumption that home care services will arrest the costly trend toward increased use of nursing homes. Field research indicates, however, that this is not a universally applicable alternative since no more than 15 percent to 25 percent of the profoundly impaired population can be maintained in their homes. Home care works only when the disability is not severe.

Community social workers, when assuming the policy analysis and development role, contribute their gerontological expertise to enhance specific proposals or devise strategies aimed at arresting their deleterious effects. At a second line of defense they revert again to advocacy and community mobilization, to bring about the pressure necessary to achieve a desired course of public action. Community social workers, in their role as policy specialists, act as consultants to community and senior action groups, as well as to health and social service agencies with a stake in the revision of policies or the design of new ones. To discharge those analytic and developmental tasks community practitioners must blend their generic macro-interventive skills with a keen understanding of the policy issues affecting the elderly population. The two case examples illustrated the fact that conventional wisdom is not enough.

Summary

The expert planning methodologies of the 1970s may prevail as the leading skills required for the 1980s as well. A report of the House of Representative's Subcommittee on Human Services of the Select Committee on Aging (1980) proposed to reduce the present functions of the aging network and have the AAAs act as advisers to both private and voluntary local services. They would also perform advocacy functions to ensure access to services, train staff, assess needs, and guide informal support systems in the provision of continuous care.

The voluntary and private sectors, consisting predominantly of multiservice centers, housing complexes, and long-term-care facilities, will increasingly depend on public contracts, grants, and subsidies, but will offer greater latitude to a variety of macro-interventive roles than does the public sector. In all instances the lack of adequate resources will frustrate and dampen the resolve of many community social workers. Others, however, may welcome this challenge to their wit and ingenuity.

A recent article on social work conceptual frameworks outlined the generic objectives of practice with the aged (Monk 1981). Most of them are especially valid for the community practitioner. They include: making service organizations more responsive to the needs of elderly peisuns; helping this population to enlarge its competence and problem-solving abilities; assisting them to obtain resources and gain access to their entitlements; facilitating an older person's social interaction and capacity to negotiate the environment and, untimately, influencing the policy formation process.

These objectives constitute a demanding agenda indeed. The tasks awaiting the community social worker are therefore complex but gratifying. Their potential role assignments will continue to expand, thus infusing greater versatility and a more profound sense of mission to the profession.

Notes

1. Demographic data for this article are from:

Statistical Reports on Older Americans, no. 3. 1978. "Some Prospects for the Future Elderly Population," USDHEW, Office of Human Development, Administration on Aging. National Clearinghouse on Aging.

CPR, Series P-23, no. 43, "Some Demographic Aspects of Aging in the United States," February 1973, no. 59, "Demographic Aspects of Aging and the Older Population in the United States," May 1976.

Developments in Aging: 1978. 1979. A Report of the Special Committee on Aging, Unites States Senate. Washington, D.C. GPO.

Projections of the Population of the United States: 1977 to 2050. 1977. U.S. Bureau of the Census. Current Population Reports, Series P-25, No. 704. Washington, D.C.: GPO.

2. Data on institutionalization are from:

U.S. House of Representatives, Select Committee on Aging. 1976. New Perspectives in Health Care for Older Americans. Report of Subcommittee on Health and Long Term Care, Washington, D.C.

U.S. Senate Special Committee on Aging, Health Care for Older Americans: The Alternatives Issue. Hearing, Washington D.C., 1977.

U.S. Senate, Special Committee on Aging, Nursing Home Care in the United States. 1974. Failure of Public Policy. Washington, D.C.: GPO.

References

Best, Fred and Barry Stern. 1978. "Education, Work and Leisure: Must They Come in That Order?" *Active Times* (Autumn), 3(3):92–107.

Binstock, Robert H. 1978. "Federal Policy Toward the Aging—Its Inadequacies and Its Policies." In *The Economics of Aging*, pp. 90–92. Washington, D.C.: Government Research Corporation.

Blau, Peter M. 1964. *Exchange and Power in Social Life*. New York: Wiley.

Cantor, Marjorie H. 1976. "Effect of Ethnicity on Life Styles of the Inner City Elderly." In Lawton, Newcomer, and Byers, eds., *Community Planning for an Aging Society: Designing Services and Facilities*, pp. 41–58.

Cath, Stanley H. 1975. "The Orchestration of Disengagement." *International Journal of Aging and Human Development*, 6(3):199–213.

Cowgill, Donald O. 1977. "The Revolution of Age." *The Humanist* (September/October) 37(5):10–13.

Emerson, R. M. 1962. "Power Dependence Relations." *American Sociological Review*, 27(1):31–41.

Estes, Carroll L. 1979. *The Aging Enterprise*. San Francisco: Jossey-Bass.

Hudson, Robert. 1974. "Rational Planning and Organizational Imperatives: Prospects for Area Planning in Aging." *The Annals of the American Academy of Political and Social Science* (September) 415:41–54.

Lawton, M. Powell, Robert J. Newcomer, and Thomas O. Byers, eds. 1976. *Community Planning for an Aging Society: Designing Services and Facilities*. Stroudsburg, Pa.: Dowden, Hutchinson, and Ross.

Lopata, Helena Z. 1978. "The Absence of Community Resources in Support Systems of Urban Widows." *The Family Coordinator* (October) 27(4):383–88.

Lowy, Louis. 1979. *Social Work with the Aging*, pp. 397–423. New York: Harper and Row.

Monk, Abraham. 1981. "Social Work with the Aged: Principles of Practice." *Social Work* (January), 26(1):61–68.

Morris, Robert. 1977. "Caring for vs. Caring about People." *Social Work* (September), 22(5):356–57.

Neugarten, Bernice L. 1975. "The Future and the Young-Old." *The Gerontologist* (Supplement), 15(1):4–9.

Pratt, Henry J. 1976. *The Gray Lobby*. Chicago: University of Chicago Press.

Rose, Arnold. 1964. "A Current Theoretical Issue in Social Gerontology." *Gerontologist* (March), 4(1):46–50.

Rothman, Jack. 1978. "Macro Social Work in a Tightening Economy." *Social Work* (July), 24(4):274–81.

Scanlon, William J. 1978. *Aspects of the Nursing Home Market Private Demand, Total Utilization and Investment*. Washington, D.C.: Urban Institute.

Sussman, Marvin B., Donna Vanderwyst, and Gwendolyn K. Williams. 1976. "Will You Still Need Me, Will You Still Feed Me When I'm 64?" Paper presented at annual meeting, Gerontological Society.

U.S. Commission on Civil Rights. 1977. *The Age Discrimination Study*. Washington, D.C.: U.S. Commission on Civil Rights.

U.S. House of Representatives, Select Committee on Aging. 1977. Hearings: "Fragmentation of Services for the Elderly." Washington, D.C.: GPO.

U.S. House of Representatives, Select Committee on Aging, Subcommittee on Human Services. 1980. *Future Directions for Aging Policy: A Human Service Model*. Washington, D.C.: GPO.

U.S. Senate, Special Committee on Aging. 1979. *Developments in Aging: 1978*. Washington, D.C.: GPO.

10

The Practice
of Community Social Work
in Mental Health Settings

Madeleine R. Stoner

History plays an important role in this paper because current community social work practice in the field of mental health is somewhat dormant relative to the broad scope of practice exercised in the ten-year period between 1963 and 1973, years in which the community mental health center movement dominated the field. This essay describes the strengths and weaknesses of community social work as it was practiced during the peak years of the community mental health decade and suggests that the best past practice is a viable model for launching future practice.

It is important to understand that selection of this period as a model does not ignore the earlier history of community work practice in mental health. Many of the earlier attempts to develop and campaign for mental health services were very significant in terms of establishing services for the mentally ill, educating the public about the needs of the mentally ill, and destigmatizing people suffering from psychological disturbance.

Although she was a teacher by profession, Dorothea Dix's crusade in the nineteenth century for the establishment of state mental hospitals thoughout the United States marked the entry of social activism in the field and has become a prominent feature of social work history. Her widely heralded political campaigns and energetic efforts to educate the public about the need for services for the mentally ill led to the nationwide network of state hospitals that still abound (Axinn and Levin 1975). Fifty years after Dorothea Dix began her work, Clifford Beers, a former mental patient, launched the state and national mental hygiene committees which spawned the mental health movement. His concentration on the need to develop aftercare services for mental patients was a manifestation of the broader progressive social reform movement of the period which emphasized the importance of the environment on the individual. Its essence was the recognition that a mental patient is a human being in need of a constructive intellectual and emotional environment (Beers 1908). It was no accident that this development of a national mental hygiene movement, comprised of lay and professional people, parallelled the rise of psychotherapy, behaviorism, and reform of social welfare (Knee and Lamson 1971).

The mental hygiene committees later became the mental health associations which continue to function as major voluntary organizations that play an important role in educating the public about mental health issues. They also follow their predecessors in campaigning for improved mental health services and legislation, in addition to their efforts to promote public understanding and reduce the stigma of mental illness. Many of the mental health associations have expanded their original purpose of providing information and campaigning for mental health services to focus on coordination of mental health programs. They have redirected much of their efforts toward work with representatives of mental health centers in most of the cities and states in which they operate. They publish newsletters, legislative briefings and analyses, and other informational material for the consumption of mental health programs and staff members. Many of the staff members of these associations are professionally trained social workers.

Sympathy and knowledge were not enough for mental health reformers of the progressive era. They recognized the vital importance of developing facilities in communities, and their primary goal shifted to the founding of free child guidance clinics for the early treatment and prevention of disease. By the 1920s, free child guidance clinics could be found in every major industrial area in the country, if not in rural areas. Social workers were a major part of this effort (Miles 1949).

In addition to the growing reform efforts in the voluntary sector, mental health planners employed at the state level also engaged in extensive social action directed toward the reform of existing services and the establishment of new kinds of care. In the 1950s, concern about the deteriorated conditions in the state mental hospitals prompted state planners to organize local constituencies which, in turn, pressured their legislators to improve conditions in the state mental hospitals and deinstitutionalize as many patients as possible. This impulse toward reform also stemmed from widespread scandals which were uncovered by investigations of conditions in the state hospitals. Some of these investigations were sponsored by state legislatures, others by the media, and, of particular interest for community organizers and social workers, many inquiries were made by volunteers who were trained by the mental health associations to serve at state hospitals.

Added impetus for reform emanated from the social psychiatry, or community psychiatry, movement which developed in the 1950s. Its stress on environmental influences and the impact of the social group on the individual was important not only in regard to understanding the etiology of mental illness, but also for purposes of treatment. Hollingshead and Redlich's *Social Class and Mental Illness* (1958), a pioneer study in the field of social psychiatry, emphasized the importance of preventive work as a form of treatment.

This combination of reform activities stemming from the voluntary sector, the public planning sector, and new developments in the field of psychiatry culminated in the formation of the Joint Commission on Mental Health at the national level which produced a comprehensive report in 1960, *Action for Mental Health* (Joint Commission on Mental Illness and Mental Health 1961). This report called for the development of a broad spectrum of services and the coordination and promotion of mental health services. Preventive mental health center legislation was a direct result of this report.

All of these efforts reflect a certain type of community organization practice which characterized the social reform impulse of early practice. Major community organization practice took place prior to 1963 when the Community Mental Health Centers Act was passed. Much of it occurred in the voluntary sector, but state planners played a critical role because of their central position with regard to responsibility for the delivery of mental health services. Community workers viewed their functions as educational and political in nature. They tirelessly worked as advocates to provide information about the need for mental health services and the rights of mental patients. They were also effective campaigners and social activists and viewed their roles as most effective when stimulating the public welfare sector to provide more and better services.

Early community organizers in the field of mental health performed several important functions which continue to be useful. Having adopted the community organization role of mediator, they acted as representatives of their communities. They engaged in political and social action, including advocacy; worked for a more rational coordination of mental health programs; and fomented public interest in the problems of the mental health delivery system. The major difference, however, between the earlier efforts and those of community workers in the community mental health centers lies in the fact that early practice was restricted to functioning outside the mental health services system. Mental health settings did not employ sizable numbers of community organizers for the purposes of education, prevention, political action, and advocacy to deal with clients or potential clients in the earlier examples. It was the Community Mental Health Centers Act which made it possible to employ community organizers in service delivery settings.

Current Opportunities for Practice

Given the problems that community workers experienced in community mental health centers, as well as the current political climate which questions the validity of all social services, and most certainly the worth of indirect services, it may appear naïve or overly optimistic to suggest that the immediate past be the basis for current practice; but, in truth, there is no stronger precedent for community social work practice in the field of mental health.

Fortunately, current opportunities for practice are not so

bleak as they would appear because of the decline of community services in mental health centers and the general retrenchment in all services. Individuals with backgrounds in community organization are well-placed in county and state mental health planning departments. Many now function as policy-makers, planners, administrators, and researchers. While this is not community organization practice at the neighborhood level in the classic sense, it is argued that such shifts in practice have been necessary in order for practitioners to be effective at the decision-making levels of the mental health system and that such work continues to have its base in a community practice orientation. What has become clear is that community organization practitioners who, in the course of their work, have developed other technical skills, such as planning, administration, and research, are in stronger positions to compete for employment in mental health settings because of their combined experience.

The county of Ventura in Southern California and Allegheny County in Western Pennsylvania operate prototypical mental health planning departments which include units for community services, research, evaluation, and training. These positions are held by people with backgrounds in community organization and planning. Both counties also sponsor a mental health advisory board which community organizers staff. Similarly, the Hall-Mercer Community Mental Health Center at Pennsylvania Hospital in Philadelphia has employed a community organizer as its director.

Some argue that these examples of current practice demonstrate a serious problem that has arisen in the field. The force of this argument is that community organizers have allowed themselves to be co-opted by the larger system in accepting employment as planners, policy-makers, administrators, and researchers rather than working at the neighborhood level as social activists and organizers. While there may be some merit to this position, it needs to be weighed against the notion that community organization can function at many levels provided the commitment to social and political change, which is a fundamental principle of community-based practice, remains intact.

Another area that remains a focus for practice is that of patients' rights. Recent examples of state legislation designed to protect and ensure the rights of mental patients have solidified the importance of patient advocacy. Many states now require mental health planning units to employ at least one patient advocate. This has largely become the domain of community organizers, some of whom find positions within mental health delivery settings while others choose to work outside the system through various human rights organizations such as community legal services, legal aid societies, mental health associations, and, in Philadelphia, the American Civil Liberties Union. Other advocacy groups have been formed by coalitions of lawyers, social workers, psychiatrists, mental patients, and former mental patients. The strength of these efforts suggests that advocacy may be the critical role for community organizers now and in the next several years.

The voluntary sector, represented by United Way planning councils and the mental health associations, remains a rich source of opportunity for community organization practice along its past lines as coordinators, activists, and information providers.

Opportunities remain in community mental health centers for classic consultation and education (C&E) services where most recent community organization activity has been located, albeit at a reduced level. The term consultation and education is fraught with ambiguity and has, therefore, come to mean different things to different people. *Consultation* was often case consultation by psychiatrists and *education* was often a lecture about the importance of mental health to local schoolteachers. Nevertheless, it was from the C&E department and its budget that community organization emanated in the community mental health centers. Typical examples of this type of activity were: (1) reaching unserved or underserved groups to make arrangements for storefront service; (2) developing links with community leaders who would serve on mental health center advisory boards or in other positions of leadership on behalf of the center; (3) organizing neighborhood and patient advisory groups; (4) establishing agency consortia to focus on problems like substance abuse, referral procedures, or school issues; and (5) organizing people to deal with environmental stresses like housing, schools, and crime. These practices, so common in the earlier years of the community mental health movement, continue to provide models for practice even though they were laden with problems and some built-in failures.

A recent study of thirty-three community mental health centers in metropolitan Chicago found that involvement in prevention programs in communities was related to organizational variables and ideological factors. Organizational support and resources for prevention correlated with a belief that prevention was relevant and meaningful. Findings from the study suggest that if staff members believe that prevention is important, the organizational support is high. The data further imply that when organizational support for prevention is high, staff belief in its importance tends to be strong. The study also explored the attitudes and beliefs of staff members holding MSW degrees, and the findings indicate that organizational support did not significantly increase the number of prevention programs in which employees with MSWs are involved. However, when the personal ideology of an employee with an MSW supported prevention, preventive practice and organizational support were comparatively high (Walsh 1982).

In the 1960s, the term "community" became the rallying cry for change in the field of mental health. Community social workers were brought into the field because of their abilities and experiences in community organizing, administration, and work with client groups. It was the first time that the profession shifted from a therapeutic role to a social reform role in service delivery. Many clinical social workers did not possess community organization training and experience, and they tended to rely on their colleagues who did, or on paraprofessionals such as indigenous workers who brought direct knowledge of their communities to the mental health centers.

In the 1980s, deinstitutionalization and chronic mental illness have become the flash points for mental health services and reform. This direction has led community organizers to focus on locating and developing community care homes or local resources that hospitals no longer provide. It has also pointed the way toward the important role which social groups play in the lives of people, and community organizers in mental health settings have been very instrumental in establishing networks of individuals who experience similar life situations. Whatever the choice of word or slogan, the meanings have much in common in their reliance on patient care in the community and preventive services. While much of this is done by therapists without community organization skills, there remains the need for community organizers to work in mental health centers as organizers and as trainers of therapists who, in addition to providing treatment, spend a good deal of time working in community development roles.

Figure 10.1. Contemporary Community Organization Functions and Settings in the Mental Health Field

Settings	Functions							
	Planning	Administration	Research	Coordination	Consultation and Education	Advocacy	Social Action	Fund Raising
National Institute of Mental Health	*	*	*	*		*		
State Mental Health Departments	*	*	*	*		*		
County Mental Health Departments	*	*	*	*	*	*		
Mental health service settings		*	*	*	*	*	*	
Mental Health Associations			*	*	*	*	*	*
Planning Councils	*	*	*	*		*	*	*
Mental health coalitions			*	*	*	*	*	*

*Types of settings that utilize macropractice skills and key functions each setting promotes

THE COMMUNITY MENTAL HEALTH CENTERS ACT

The passage of the Community Mental Health Centers Act provided the first major impetus for agency-based community social work practice in the field of mental health. Prior to the enactment of the legislation in October 1963, the field of mental health had been restricted to those social workers who engaged in psychiatric case-work. (In 1913 the first social worker was employed in a mental health setting [Nacman 1971].) The entry of community social work into the mental health practice arena was possible because of two key conceptual frameworks which were explicit in the policy of the new law. President John F. Kennedy enunciated these policies on February 5, 1963, in his historic message to the United States Congress in which he proposed a "bold new approach" to mental health legislation. In his speech the President vigorously proclaimed his belief that society would have to look for the causes of mental health and mental retardation and that "prevention is far more economical and it is far more likely to be successful" (Kennedy 1963). The President also made it quite clear that he hoped to phase out the state mental hospitals and replace them with a nationwide network of community mental health centers. This replacement of institutional care by community care became viable because of the development and refinement of psychotropic drugs which enabled mentally ill people to remain at home through a combination of drugs and outpatient care. The wishes of the earlier mental health reformers had been granted.

There were other important and innovative principles embedded in the President's speech and the ensuing legislation, but the dual emphasis on prevention and community-based practice launched the introduction of new mental health techniques and forms of practice. For community organizers the provision of indirect preventive services under the mandate of C&E services became the critical element which forged their access to this new arena of practice. C&E and the principle of prevention and community care became logical extensions of earlier consultation and education. Thus, community organizers were enabled to work inside the mental health service delivery system and carry out all of their earlier functions as well as to add new roles and objectives which were even more political in nature. They operated from a nonmedical model that sought to prevent mental illness through nonclinical services that reflected social goals rather than psychiatric ones. Such a model sought to enhance people's lives by creating opportunities through social science approaches which were not only political but organizational in nature. This meant that nonclinical services, which became community organization practice in mental health settings, were to achieve prominence in the field of community psychiatry for the first time.

As a technique of prevention, community practice in mental health settings emphasizes local and democratic control of social institutions as a means of buttressing the individual's sense of personal control through participation, and strengthening local bonds by encouraging reciprocal commitments among participants. Thus, participation is seen to be both health promoting and politically effective, contributing to the well-being of individuals and their communities (Segal and Baumohl 1981). It addresses such needs and problems as: (1) protection of the mentally ill through advocacy; (2) reduction of anomie and social isolation; (3) development of social support systems for patients and families; and (4) the therapeutic effect of social well-being. This orientation is closely associated with the field of community psychiatry in its stress on environmental influences and preventive intervention.

The community mental health center movement also emerged at a moment in history when Americans were actively concerned with problems of poverty, racism, and inner unrest. A heightened and unparalleled acknowledgment of urban and social pathology as major factors contributing to deviant behavior and mental illness occurred in society. One result of this new consciousness was the strengthening of arguments for primary prevention in the treatment of mental illness and the preservation of mental health; hence the strengthening of the role of community organizers as mental health practitioners.

It was difficult to draw upon the mandate for C&E as a framework for practice because it was extremely ambiguous and controversial from the outset. It did, however, carry with it a charge for service which was designed to bring the community into the identification of needs and the planning and direction of the new centers. The community was divided into catchment areas with geographical boundaries drawn to include a minimum of 75,000 people. Many catchment areas, however, particularly those in large urban areas, served populations up to 200,000, which the law defined as the maximum service population. This method of defining the community in itself reflected a major ambiguity in the legislation in general and, specifically, in regard to C&E or community organization services. In mandating such large population areas, the legislation contradicted its policy of establishing community-based services because it extended its service areas far beyond those of natural or functional communities, no matter what definition of community might be used. Some metropolitan areas vigorously and vocally opposed such large catchment areas, claiming that such "slicing" was artificial and actually hindered organizing in large urban areas. Other areas accepted the concept. In both instances, it is important to recall that those affluent areas that already had hospitals became recipients of grants for community mental health centers.

Practice is largely determined by the extent to which its enabling legislation is clear in its intent. It is not an overstatement to hold the view that the Community Mental Health Centers Act, in requiring C&E services, was fraught with ambiguity and suffered from a lack of clear definition and direction which had interesting implications for how community organization was practiced. Some workers seized upon the uncertainty of their situations as an opportunity to select a diverse set of approaches to their work with communities, while others perceived the confused state of the law as an obstacle to effective action. One set of approaches was highly political and fostered confrontation strategies. In New York City and Philadelphia the poor and ethnic minority groups attempted to seize control of the mental health centers and their sponsoring hospitals and universities, claiming that these institutions rightfully belonged to the communities in which they were located. Another set of approaches was extremely moderate in that workers restricted their organizing efforts to establishing coalitions of agencies with direct or indirect interest in mental health. Although both approaches were valid, any assessment of community mental health practice must take these different orientations into consideration.

Further ambiguity lay in the vagueness of what the legislation intended mental health to mean, and overriding this complexity, was the more problematic question of what community mental health meant. Finally, there was considerable doubt among a variety of practitioners as to whether community organization practice belonged in community mental health centers; while others struggled to define the correct division and balance between such community services and clinical services. As a result of this uncertain atmosphere between clinical and nonclinical practitioners, community organization in mental health settings moved in a variety of directions and, in some instances, became highly individualized and idiosyncratic, depending in large measure on the personal agendas of practitioners. The level of sophistication of community organizers also varied, with many relying upon their knowledge of theory while others behaved more instinctively. It is critical to understand that the period was one of great social unrest and upheaval which prompted people who had previously been silent and uninvolved in social issues to move into social systems with a view to changing them for whatever they understood to be "better."

What was clear, however, was that the new law attached importance to the principle of reliance upon community groups to define issues and problems and to participate in developing services. This principle of citizen participation became the rationale and basis for much community work practice that took place, no matter what the variations in mode were. It placed community organizers in neighborhoods as bona fide staff members of the mental health centers and, as such, allowed for a direct interface between the community mental health centers and programs of the War on Poverty which espoused the principle of citizen participation and maximum feasible participation. Recognizing the importance of primary prevention in the legislation, other mental health settings quickly adopted C&E types of outreach services, and community organizers found themselves employed throughout the spectrum of mental health services. Today federal and state law continues to require public participation at local, regional, and state levels, and advisory boards remain a priority for community organizers in mental health centers and regional and state mental health departments.

Sponsors and Participants

The Community Mental Health Centers Act established an intricate set of relationships and interdependencies "among the federal government, the states and the communities in which mental health centers are to be built and operated" (Bloom 1976:33). The federal government was required to write the regulations governing the legislation, establish priorities for states, demand reports, monitor programs, and provide or withhold money for the construction of facilities. However, the federal government was not allowed to disapprove state plans without justification. Similarly, the law forbade any direct control over the operation of the mental health centers.

The states were responsible for administering the act and for appointing an advisory council to assist the state administering body. Advisory councils were to be comprised of providers and consumers of services and, together with the state agency, held the responsibility for inventorying state facilities for the mentally ill and developing a state-wide plan for the creation of mental health centers throughout the state.

At the local level the community held the responsibility for finding suitable locations for mental health centers and raising the money that would be needed beyond the federal funds that were channeled through the state agency. Local communities were also responsible for assuring that their programs complied with federal standards (Bloom 1976).

Such tight interdependence between federal, state, and local government reflected an intentional policy to ensure healthy collaboration at all three levels. It did, however, pose serious questions about where the ultimate power resided and which sponsors and participants held decisive authority. Chu and Trotter (1974) argue that the Community Mental Health Centers Act was characteristic of most Great Society programs in that it was planned by professionals who tended to oversimplify problems. They argue, moreover, that the act was federally centered to ensure control. At the other extreme, some local communities argued, as in New York and Philadelphia, that the centers belonged to them exclusively and that no other body held a valid claim to determine standards or services. The rhetoric and symbolism of community control dominated this argument, and many community social workers adopted conflicting models of practice to satisfy these aspirations. A further complication arose when it became clear that the federal government abetted this confrontation by requiring that the centers offer "relevant" services, in contrast to the local professionals who wished for resources but were disinterested, on the whole, in responding to pressure that they expand their services to minorities, poor people, the aged, and other vulnerable groups. In many instances, federal officials from the National Institute of Mental Health directly supported local citizen groups in their confrontations with the centers.

An additional factor which complicated this web of entangled auspices appeared when it became clear that most local sponsors of community mental health centers were hospitals or universities which administer teaching hospitals. Adept at obtaining money for facilities and expansion, the hospitals and universities viewed the legislation, which provided funds for construction, as an expedient means of erecting new buildings. Regardless of what the future held for community mental health centers, hospitals which took advantage of capital construction money would have the benefit of expanded facilities which could be converted to other purposes if the mental health legislation were to be terminated.

This morass of participation obviated much of the "bold new approach" to community-based comprehensive mental health services because it created confusion and conflict over the important questions of sponsorship. While all concerned agreed with the principle of community participation, there was disagreement over the amount and extent of community involvement. A good deal of this could be attributed to the uncertainty in the structure of authority.

Responses of community organizers were as varied as those of the other actors within the system. As practitioners, however, they were particularly affected by the ambiguity of auspices because they found themselves caught in the midst of their own conflicts over professional accountability. On the one hand they viewed themselves as community organizers who were accountable to localities; yet they were mindful of the fact that they were required to explain and justify their activities to their employing agencies and, ultimately, to state and federal planners.

As a group, community workers were less troubled by dual accountability then would seem likely. Their tendency to view the community mental health center as a locally controlled accessible service led them to resolve much confusion in favor of accountability to the communities in which they practiced. Community mental health workers viewed themselves as *in* but not *of* their sponsoring agencies whether they were employed by hospital, university, state, or federal government. In effect, the community as client and constituent very often became the sponsor of community social workers from the perspective of the organizers.

Despite ambiguity in the legislation over very important definitions such as the meaning of community, mental health, community mental health, prevention, C&E, citizen participation, and sponsorship, community organizers managed to contribute considerably to the development of community mental health practice and to set examples which remain relevant. While their practice varied according to professional, community, and personal agendas, it is possible to discern certain classifications of practice from the vantage point of twenty years after the enactment of the Community Mental Health Centers Act.

Community Organization Practice Functions

Community organizers adopted diverse functions and identified their roles differently. They had such an unusual amount of autonomy for several reasons. Lack of definition of role and client permitted the exercise of different assumptions, values, and techniques to be determined by different types of practitioners. Diffcrences in the orientations of communities and the organizational environment in which the mental health centers were located also influenced selection of the practice mode. The debate over the importance and extent of indirect services also affected practice. Finally, some practitioners were more knowledgeable than others in applying systematic approaches to theory and practice.

Despite such an eclectic approach, it is possible to discern four main functions which community organization social workers carried out in the mental health center: (1) development; (2) services to other organizations; (3) coordination; and (4) representation. These functions did not have any order of priority; nor did every mental health center apply each one of them. These identified functions correspond to the four types of preventive activity described by Neuhring in a study of prevention in thirty community mental health centers: (1) community planning and development; (2) public information and education; (3) training; and (4) program consultation (Neuhring 1979). Neuhring did not identify the representation function, but it is a useful way of describing an important area of practice in the mental health field.

DEVELOPMENT

Development can be described as a process of reviewing existing service provisions in a community, identifying unmet needs and initiating actions to meet them, seeing where duplication exists, and trying to achieve a better match between needs and resources.

In practice this often means setting up new organizations in communities around particular needs such as housing, services to youth, single parents, the elderly, and other vulnerable populations. Community workers attempted to research and discover the unmet needs in communities, and they assumed, because they were working in generally deprived areas, that resource distribution was scarce or uneven. They acted as community watchdogs with a brief to identify possible gaps and defects in programs and services. They also attempted to persuade the churches, schools, public housing authorities, and local organizations to take action to remedy these defects. Community organizers launched tenants associations, day care centers, senior citizen clubs, youth groups, and general self-help groups concerned with social issues or specific types of mental health and conditions that would promote mental health.

To accomplish these goals of identifying unmet needs and building organizations, community workers recruited volunteers from local communities as well as other interested people who were in positions of importance related to specific issues. They also encouraged and facilitated appropriate organizations to adopt new services and programs which would fill the gaps. Whenever possible, community organizers stimulated members of the local communities or catchment areas to apply pressure to funders in order to obtain services because their role was that of enabler and facilitator in empowering people to participate in the direction of services.

Neuhring's study (1979) found that community planning and development accounted for the smallest proportion of preventive activity. It was, however, this aspect of preventive work which attracted the wide attention of community social workers and, in many instances, heightened the expectations of individuals and groups within the communities. Development activities held the greatest promise for planned change in environments characterized by poverty and powerlessness because it focused less on clients and more on system change or reform.

West Virginia University School of Social Work has adapted the strategy of community development to prevention in its work in the Appalachian region. The community development model which the school uses "posits an inverse relationship between the level of community integration and the incidence and prevalence of mental illness" (Porter, Peters, and Heady 1982). Students working on a community development project in Indian Hollow, West Virginia, for several years have found that their efforts have not been successful as a method for redressing political and economic imbalances in the community, but they did achieve significant goals in community health. The community development strategy did generate participation and affiliation as well as higher community integration. The authors of the study emphasize that such collective behavior and improvement of social structures alter life styles, reduce stress, and generally enhance the levels of physical and mental health in the vulnerable communities of Appalchia (Porter, Peters, and Heady 1982).

While not necessarily political in nature, some aspects of development activity were highly political. This was so in those instances in which organizers encouraged communities to demand or negotiate for additional resources.

SERVICES TO OTHER ORGANIZATIONS

There are a variety of services which community organizers provided for other organizations and agencies in their catchment areas. Four general types of services were made available through social work organizing efforts: (1) access to equipment and supplies; (2) information; (3) advice and consultation; and (4) training.

In acting as resources for the traditional public and private agencies as well as for the newer groups they often provided facilities such as meeting space, typing and duplicating facilities, the use of telephones, and other items needed to build or sustain organizations.

Information dissemination proved to be a vital role of community organizers. They provided information about trends in legislation, local events, how to manage funds and keep account of money, and they compiled directories of local services and organizations.

Advice and consultation focused on how to deal with officials in the governmental and voluntary sectors. Community organizers advised on the planning and development of new services, and they helped people to form new groups. Recruitment of members, definition of organizational goals, planning strategies, and something as basic as how to set up articles of incorporation were all important features of community organization advice and consultation.

According to Neuhring, much public information focused on attempts to link clients to the services of centers (Neuhring 1979). Community workers went to local groups in order to educate them about the centers and the importance of mental health and the prevention of mental illness. This was an important informational and consultation role for community organizers, but it did not preclude them from stressing those matters that were more directly concerned with the objectives of building and sustaining organizations and obtaining resources.

Neuhring found that training accounted for 21 percent of all preventive activity and was largely present in the urban community mental health centers. Training, as community workers practiced it, focused on bringing information from and about the community to the therapeutic staff of the mental health centers and to other agencies which were interested in learning how to work in neighborhoods. There was a period when most mental health agencies became interested in community development as a means of reaching more clients and working more effectively with them. To some extent, this remains true today. Neuhring also observed that training and staff development requests were greater in those community mental health centers which demonstrated evidence of medical capability (Neuhring 1979).

COORDINATION

Coordination is defined as the linkage of information and opinion between organizations and agencies. It is intended to link services and people as well as groups or organizations in an effort to exchange information on experience and policy and to formulate positions which represent the interests of many groups. Often, such linkages lead to agreements between organizations and policy changes by individual groups. Such agreements are based upon consensus, and community organizers who promote such coordination cannot exert sanctions over the linking groups. If pursued as an end in itself, coordination can often be unproductive by neutralizing the important but different values held by various organizations. However, as the by-product of the pursuit of some other objective, it can be highly valuable. This means that a group of organizations can often achieve what individual bodies would fail to do because the combination of power and knowledge can yield greater results than those of a single body. For example, once a community determines that it needs increased resources for youth services, the coordinated efforts of all youth-serving agencies in that area can achieve quicker and better results than would be attained by one or two groups, unless these happened to represent extremely powerful bases.

Given this coordinating role, community social workers established extensive involvement with coordinating and planning bodies. They also directed their efforts to the establishment of advisory boards which were characterized as coalitions of identifiable social agencies (largely providers of services) within their catchment areas, in contrast to advisory boards comprised of a mix of service providers and service consumers. The coordination function served as one check on excessive expansion of the community mental health center's services because the agency provider representatives on boards were protective of the role of their organizations in the catchment areas. In contrast, the mixed model type of advisory board, which did appear in some centers, tended to demand increased services and expanded opportunities for citizen participation in service delivery and planning.

In acting as coordinators, community organizers found it necessary to accommodate the various interest groups in their environment. This restricted their autonomy, leaving little room for activities which did not serve the center or move beyond the description of center services.

Neuhring's study suggests that coordination dominated the preventive activities of community organizers. Community mental health administrators viewed this function as useful to describe their administrative interaction with other agencies and affiliates. Those centers which were located in large systems such as hospitals or universities tended to rely more heavily on such linkages than those which were located in smaller systems, such as, for example, rural settings. Large systems used this pattern of interaction in the interest of attaining prestige and deference in the community. Such administrative interagency gaming was pursued as a means of facilitating intervention in other organizations where the centers viewed it as important to be regarded as an authority rather than as a peer among agencies in the community (Neuhring 1979).

REPRESENTATION

The representation function arose from the political imperatives of community organization which sought shifts in social arrangements in order to realize the objectives of participatory democracy that were associated with well-functioning communities. This role involves articulating the views of individuals and groups, protecting their interests, pressing for changes through negotiations, publicity, and, sometimes, confrontation on behalf of organizations and groups. The effectiveness with which this function could be carried out was affected by the extent of common ground between the organizations represented. Much representation activity was concerned with expressing the needs of the local communities to larger communities such as federal, state, and local governments, as well as other organizations and the mental health centers themselves.

Workers engaged in political action strategies which ranged from mediation or negotiation to advocacy and confrontation or conflict. These contrasting types of practice demonstrated the polarity of approaches to community work in mental health settings. This occurred because different practitioners made different assumptions and had different goals. Those who restricted their activities to coordination and mediation assumed that institutions are responsive to people and that professional roles can be most effectively discharged by acceptance of the goals of the centers. Practitioners who adopted political conflict strategies based their efforts on the assumption that center goals were unresponsive to communities which, largely minority and poor and underserved, could only be served if residents were given the necessary skills and information to gain power and make demands upon the centers.

Advocacy, an increasingly important role for community organizers in the mental health field, has two perspectives. One relates to representing the general social rights and interests of people regarding housing, schools, social services, and other social utilities. The second, and more prominent perspective today, arose with regard to the rights of mental patients. This concern came out of the more general interest in human rights that manifested itself during the 1960s.

The term advocacy means articulating, defending, or pleading a cause. Community organizers have acted in concert with lawyers, other social workers, psychiatrists, and the range of helping professionals as mental health advocates. They have also directed many of their development skills toward organizing mental patients to defend and obtain their rights on their own. Although many community organizers assume advocacy roles on behalf of client populations, case advocacy related to individual patients is a major focus for those who assume advocate roles.

Whatever function they exercised, community organizers perceived their preventive responsibilities as a means of carrying out their commitment to locality development. These activities were subject to a high degree of uncertainty about objectives with specific regard to mental health. Center administrators, state and federal sponsors, and even many community members questioned the purpose of some of these indirect community activities because they did not appear to have any clear connection to mental health services. Others perceived the value of these services as a means of creating healthy environments in which individuals and groups could exercise their well-being and functioning—the essence of preventive activity.

Citizen Participation as a Goal

Most community workers, regardless of their orientation, shared a major commitment to community involvement and citizen participation, and they attempted to demonstrate that social workers no longer had the privilege of disentangling themselves from the complex and charged issues that affect groups (Gurevitz 1969). Both the best and the worst examples of citizen participation strategies were demonstrated in mental health settings. Where communities accepted community organization principles of citizen participation, practitioners experienced success and credibility in the eyes of both the community and their employers. Unfortunately, many communities tended to refute the goals of community involvement and participation by persistently demanding direct mental health services.

In spite of these differing views about participation, community organization social workers held fast to the strategy of citizen participation, and this is a principle which continues to attract organizers. It has also become more widely accepted and expected in many communities today, although differing views about the nature and extent of participation remain. Does this mean that the strategy of citizen participation in the delivery of mental health services has become a reality?

To begin to answer this question it is necessary to ascertain what, in fact, citizen participation means. Chu and Trotter identify two meanings. One definition means bringing the services closer to where people live in order to increase accessibility to services. The other definition means integrating the services with the community so that organizations are responsive to needs and accountable to the populations served (Chu and Trotter 1974). Gilbert and Specht also identify three types of participation in which authority is shared in varying degrees. These are: (1) nonredistributive change in which people participate but no changes in organizational arrangements or authority occur; (2) token change, which offers very little influence over practical outcomes for the community; and (3) redistributive change, which includes a real shift in the organization of authority and allows citizen participants to exert a real influence on decisions that affect the system (Gilbert and Specht 1974). In the mental health field, participation has been viewed as a strategy and a method of promoting health by affirming the individual's sense of control over his environment and by strengthening local community ties.

Chu and Trotter's definition regarding accountability and Gilbert and Specht's focus on redistributive change are the aspects of citizen participation which beg for examination because of their implications for structural change in mental health organizations, as well as any other delivery system. Using these two approaches to citizen participation, it is clear that community organizers sought to achieve two related goals. One goal was to encourage the accountability of service by redistributing authority and empowering the community with respect to changes in the mental health service delivery system. Citizen participation also became a specific reform strategy which sought to reduce anomie and isolation by stimulating community bonds through community action.

While practitioners agreed on these goals, they differed in their views about their professional roles and the authority structure within the mental health service delivery system. Some viewed themselves as experts and chose to exclude clients from planning and selecting goals. Their approach to change and citizen participation was token at best. Many private acute care hospitals reflect this position. Others viewed the mental health system as rational and accountable but believed that the mental health system was restrictive. They tended to work with the community to find ways of promoting better services. They also relied on linkage and advocacy activities which continue to be prominent intervention strategies for community organizers in mental health settings. Still another group of practitioners argued that neither professionals nor organizations can legitimately serve communities because such legitimacy is derived from the community, and citizen participation in all decision-making is a prerequisite (Gilbert and Specht 1974). These professionals viewed participation as both an activity and a value; this professional stance of the political and social activist community workers in mental health centers is less prominent today.

This outline of professional perspectives about functions and goals further explains the complexity and contradictions in the design of community social work programs in the field of mental health. As a framework for understanding the nature of citizen participation and professional practice, it accounts for the wide discretion applied in the exercise of responsible community social work practice in mental health centers. Different workers incorporated different perspectives, depending upon their beliefs and values as well as on the orientations of the communities in which they practiced. It is noteworthy that many community workers adopted all three approaches to participation at different times. This type of behavior was not contradictory because different problems required different approaches.

Professional roles also varied from moderate advocacy to aggressive advocacy. Others emphasized their development, service, and coordination functions. Community workers based their selection of role and function on their particular cluster of beliefs and values concerning professionalism and the mental health delivery system, as well as on their impressions of what the community wanted. Any assessment or understanding of community organization social work practice in the field of mental health must account for this mix.

To some extent, this confusion of roles, functions, and professional values rendered citizen participation as a redistributive strategy largely a failure. While many workers sought to achieve this goal, more adopted goals which required moderate or minimal change. However, the idea of citizen participation has become broadly accepted and operates to some extent in mental health agencies throughout the United States. The model of the community health council in England is a further example of how this strategy has spread to other countries. Generally, however, citizen participation is currently directed toward minimal or token change. Redistributive participation was less a failure because of professional role confusion than because the mental health system was essentially a closed one. Neither administrative nor professional support sustained community organizers who were proponents of redistributive change. Mental health policy at the federal, state, and local levels has proved to be controlled by powerful professional and bureaucratic institutions which have used the community mental center legislation to consolidate and expand their interests. Moreover, the psychiatric profession has continued to dominate the field.

A striking example of the profession's resistance to an open system rests in the plight of the indigenous worker. Community mental health centers, along with other service delivery systems, were highly attracted to the idea of hiring untrained local people as members of their staffs. Paraprofessionals yielded many advantages to organizers, clinicians, and agencies. Structurally, paraprofessionalism was a new entry point for people who lacked training but possessed knowledge of clients and communities and demonstrated natural helping skills. Because they had such knowledge and skills they became invaluable to mental health centers since they aided clinical practitioners and community organizers by interpreting local, ethnic, and racial issues. Community organizers relied on their contacts to build community advisory boards through recruitment and dissemination of information. Their credibility within their own communities made it possible for mental health centers to rely upon them when setting up outreach centers, storefront services, and other programs in local settings such as schools, churches, and public housing projects.

Many of the paraprofessional workers proved to be highly charismatic leaders and social activists, but most tended to identify more directly with the centers and their delivery systems than did the professional community organization staff (Kupst, Redda, and McGee 1975). This strengthened those professional interests which preferred to keep the mental health system closed.

Unfortunately, the promise of career entry was never fulfilled because these workers were not placed in training grades, and career ladders never materialized. Moreover, they were the first staff members to lose their jobs when mental health funds diminished.

Despite the fact that citizen participation as a redistributive function has failed to appear, local citizens are involved in planning mental health programs, and community advisory boards are a continued requirement of the law at local and state levels. What is not clear is the extent and method of such involvement since it varies from place to place.

A study of the development functions and powers of community mental health center advisory boards cites differences between mental health professionals and community participants. The study examined the orientations of citizen board members, board chairpersons, center staff, and center directors toward functioning in eighteen community mental health centers in an urban area. It concluded that there was some agreement that boards should function to make certain that community needs are met. There were, however, basic disagreements in the way board members and professionals viewed board involvement. Community mental health center staff appeared to be stronger proponents of redistributive citizen participation than the board members themselves, with the exception of board chairpersons (Kupst, Redda, and McGee 1975). This suggests that community organizers who advocated major change were not attuned to the wishes of the communities in which they worked. It may also suggest that those community members who were more militant and did demand redistribution of power and authority did not serve on community boards because they viewed them as co-optation mechanisms.

The study also explored important demographic questions about the composition of board membership and found that most people who served on boards were nonprofessionals from varying occupations with a mean educational level of 15.8 years of schooling. Of the random sample, 44 percent lived within the catchment area and 41 percent reported that they lived elsewhere. This supports those opponents of citizen participation who pose the question of who represents the community. Neither sex, occupation, education, nor residence was significantly related to the degree of activity on the board. It is, therefore, very difficult to present a clear profile of who joins boards, who chooses to take active leadership on them, and how or why members become involved. Some members reported that they joined on their own initiative while others joined at the request of staff members.

The absence of a definitive profile of board participants adds to the complexity of assessing the outcome and practices associated with citizen participation. It also adds fuel to the fire of those who attack the goal of citizen participation by denying that it is possible to ascertain who represents a given community. It is important, however, to understand that many of the more active community participants were not on community boards.

Recommendations

As a consequence of the Community Mental Health Centers Act, planning grants were awarded in every state, and some 1,500 catchment areas were created in the United States (Bloom 1976). In the years following enactment of the law the number of centers established in these areas rapidly proliferated. Just as the numbers began to peak, Richard M. Nixon became President and set out to achieve his objective of eliminating excessive bureaucracy, which he largely interpreted as the curtailment of funds for social services. This resulted in reduced resources for mental health services as well as for most programs which were associated with the War on Poverty in the 1960s and early 1970s.

Why was such a bold and innovative approach to mental health so vulnerable? Much of the answer to this question lies in the elusive nature of preventive or indirect services. The originality of the approach itself also contributed to the fragility of the program because it challenged traditional practices and services for the mentally ill population. But all social services were vulnerable when put to the harsh tests of cost effectiveness under a conservative government, and mental health services did not fare any worse than other services because of their particular character.

Observers of the current scene claim that few roles remain for community organization social workers in mental health practice. It is now apparent that the multiplicity of the earlier C&E types of practice has shifted to direct service activities such as setting up networks and self-help groups for clients of mental health agencies, establishing referral activities, and dispensing information about services. Implicit in this shift has been a redefinition of the role and function of community organizers in mental health settings. Whereas their earlier roles tended to focus on services to the *community* as a client, present practice emphasizes services to the *agencies* as clients. It is the earlier role which exemplifies the best of community organization practice in mental health and remains a model for practitioners to maintain.

Despite its fragility, the community mental health center movement contributed to major theoretical advances about cause, treatment, and prevention of mental illness. Mental health became associated with environmental health, employment opportunity, adequate education, civil rights, and the general range of issues connected to full participation in society. The etiology of maladaptive behavior was viewed with renewed emphasis on social pathology. But the stress placed on prevention of mental illness remains the singular most important theoretical advance of the Community Mental Health Centers Act.

At the end of President Carter's administration, in 1980, the Mental Health Systems Act was passed. It would have provided for more community-based services and mandated mental health programs for specific populations of chronically mentally ill people. Community organization functions of coordination, representation, specifically advocacy, and development were identified in the legislation (U.S. Congress 1980). The law was doomed, however, because the Reagan administration's insistence on ending federal control of health and education programs by establishing block grants meant the repeal of the act.

In eliminating the mental health act, Congress placed federal funds for three programs—mental health, alcohol abuse, and drug abuse—in a block grant, and gave the states broad discretion in using the funds. However, Congress added restrictions that President Reagan had not requested by stipulating that specific percentages within the block grants be directed toward each of the three programs, including grants to community mental health centers. Under the block grant legislation, the centers are to provide comprehensive mental health services for the chronically mentally ill, the severely ill elderly, identifiable underserved populations in the states, and services related to the coordination of mental health and health care services provided within health care centers (U.S. Congress 1981). This reflects many of the objectives defined in the repealed Mental Health Systems Act. Many people regard the fact that mental health was singled out as a categorical item within the block grant legislation as a victory for mental health centers. Despite financial reductions beginning at 20 percent in the 1981 fiscal year, mental health centers can remain intact and continue to carry out many of their earlier roles.

Community organization roles and functions remain under the block grant system, but they will not be carried out on a uniform basis because each state and county law will have much discretion in this. Trends are noticeable throughout the nation, however, and planning documents in state and county departments of mental health indicate several directions.

Community services will focus more on those community systems which are most involved with the acutely and chronically disordered, such as law enforcement, public assistance agencies, and community care facilities. Services will also be increased to develop community support networks as resources for the target groups. Consultation, education, information, development, coordination, and representation services will be focused on problems related to the priority target groups. For example, community organizers will work to develop access for the chronically mentally ill to all the community services such as schools, libraries, rehabilitation, housing, and transportation. Consulting with community care facilities and coordination with private sector physicians and other health practitioners are now important community organization functions directed to target populations. Similarly, consultation, information, and education for law enforcement officials and coordination of interagency activities to assure appropriate efforts to deal with severely disordered clients have become essential community work functions.

It is also necessary to develop community services for defined groups at high risk for mental disability: abused children, elderly people, single parents, handicapped people, and victims of violence. Such programs include self-help groups, resource centers, respite care networks, parenting training, and training of peer counselors.

Advocacy remains a major community organization function. Most departments of mental health contain patient advocacy units. These are fraught with dilemmas, but they do provide certain protections for clients. Advocacy organizations which function outside the mental health delivery system are less bound by internal policies and are, therefore, in a better position to act on behalf of clients.

There will continue to be certain community organization programs which assist the overall mental health system to work with other community agencies to promote the best use of their resources to meet the mental health needs of the total community. Public information activities, especially those intended to improve access to underserved groups and to promote community understanding of mental health needs and programs, will be necessary.

Twenty years after the enactment of the bold new law, much of its rhetoric remains. The community mental health center program heightened people's expectations regarding their entitlement to service and their right to participate in the direction of service. The program provided greater access to care by establishing community-based services, despite the fact that not all who required care could receive it in the centers. It also produced some lasting innovations in primary prevention.

Community organizers, administrators, and planners would do well to examine the basis of this continued rhetoric and the expectations of individuals and groups in an effort to ensure that the new political machinery is responsive to them. During the present conservative atmosphere curtailing the role of social agencies, community organizers may have to return to the earliest models of practice which emphasized social and political action in the private voluntary sector on behalf of mental health services and clients. There may also need to be a renewal of the partnership approach to services which relied heavily upon arrangements between voluntary and statutory agencies. It is also possible that community reaction to the budget slashes for mental health services, along with all social services, will provide a role for community organizers as facilitators of political and social action against the cuts.

Opportunities remain for community organization social workers to continue their work in the areas of development, service, coordination, and representation. In addition, administration and planning hold promise for people trained in macro-practice. What remains are fewer but more focused positions. What also remains in the field of mental health is the community.

References

Axinn, June and Herman Levin. 1975. *Social Welfare: A History of the American Response to Need.* New York: Dodd Mead.

Beers, Clifford. 1908. *A Mind That Found Itself.* Garden City, N.Y.: Doubleday.

Bloom, Bernard L. 1976. *Community Mental Health: A General Introduction.* Monterey, Calif.: Brooks/Cole.

Chu, Franklin D. and Sharland Trotter. 1974. *The Madness Establishment.* New York: Viking.

Gilbert, Neil and Harry Specht. 1974. *Dimensions of Social Welfare Policy.* Englewood Cliffs, N.J.: Prentice-Hall.

Gurevitz, Howard. 1969. "The Community and Clinical Practice" in Lamb, Heath and Downing, eds. *Community Mental Health Practice,* pp. 414–29.

312   M. R. Stoner

Hollingshead, August B. and Frederick C. Redlich. 1958. *Social Class and Mental Illness: A Community Study.* New York: Wiley.

Joint Commission on Mental Illness and Mental Health. 1961. *Action for Mental Health.* New York: Basic Books.

Kennedy, John F. 1963. *Message from the President of the United States Relative to Mental Illness and Mental Retardation,* 88th Cong. 1st. sess., U.S. House of Representatives Document No. 58. Washington, D.C.: GPO.

Knee, Ruth I. and Warren C. Lamson. 1971. "Mental Health Services." In *Encyclopedia of Social Work,* pp. 802–12. 16th ed. New York: NASW.

Kupst, Mary Jo, Phil Redda, and Thomas F. McGee. 1975. "Community Mental Health Boards: A Comparison of Their Development Functions by Board Members and Mental Health Center Staff." *Community Mental Health Journal,* 11(3):249–56.

Lamb, H. Richard, Heath, and Downing, eds. 1969. *Handbook of Community Mental Health Practice.* San Francisco: Jossey-Bass.

Miles, Arthur P. 1949. *An Introduction to Public Welfare.* Boston: Heath.

Nacman, Martin. 1971. "Social Workers in Mental Health Services." In *Encyclopedia of Social Work,* pp. 822–28. 16th ed. New York: NASW.

Neuhring, Elaine M. 1979. "Preventive Activity and Inter-Organizational Factors: A Survey of 30 Community Mental Health Centers." *Journal of Social Service Research* (Spring), 3(2):285–300.

Porter, Robert A., John A. Peters, and Hilda R. Heady. 1982. "Using Community Development for Prevention," *Social Work* (July), 27(4):302–7.

Segal, Steven P. and Jim Baumohl. 1981. "Social Work Practice in Community Mental Health Settings," *Social Work* (January), 26(1):16–25.

U.S. Congress, Senate. 1980. *Mental Health Systems Act.* Public Law 96-396, 96th Cong., 2d sess., October 7.

———. 1981. *Omnibus Budget Reconciliation Act of 1981.* Public Law 97-35, 97th Cong., 1st sess., August 13, Title IX, Part B.

Walsh, Joseph A. 1982. "Prevention in Mental Health: Organizational and Ideological Perspectives," *Social Work* (July), 27(4):298–301.

11

Community Practice In Health Care

Bruce S. Jansson and Ramon Salcido

Community practice by social workers is given scant importance in the American medical system. While Americans have
pioneered medical technology, they deemphasize outreach to neglected populations, health education, planning, citizen involvement in governance of health institutions, and many other kinds of
community work. In this essay, barriers that impede social work
community practice within the American medical system are discussed as well as promising models that should be considered. Concrete examples are drawn from interviews with social workers in
hospital, public health, neighborhood health center, and regional
planning sites. In the concluding section, methods of increasing use
of community social work are discussed.

Community Practice and the Health Care System

In traditional perspectives, medical care consists of technical interventions by physicians to deal with already-developed medical
problems. Consumers recognize symptoms, seek assistance, are di-
agnosed, receive surgical or pharmaceutical assistance, follow medical regimens, and (it is to be hoped), recover. Since emphasis is

given to consumer initiative and technical services, there is little need for outreach, health education, and other forms of community intervention—much less inclusion of consumers in decision-making (Twaddle 1979:[1]-2; Rosengren 1980:ch. 4). Broadened perspectives are needed that include sensitivity to multiple causes of illness, merits of prevention, and multiple barriers to utilization of services.

MULTIPLE CAUSES OF ILLNESS

Multiple causes include not only "classic" bacterial, viral, physiological, and genetic factors, but life style, poverty, diet, malnutrition, stress, and occupational, familial, and situational factors. When multiple causes are recognized, planning is required to analyze the effects of a host of factors that precipitate illness, identify at-risk populations, and devise strategies to offset or neutralize negative factors (Rosengren 1980:ch. 4; Moos 1979). Further, it is hardly sufficient to confine "medical care" to interventions of physicians; if stress, poverty, and other factors are important, services of many professions and agencies are needed to develop multifaceted interventions. But this requires staff skilled in program development who can devise, orchestrate, and maintain complex service networks. In similar fashion, multiple causes suggest the need for grass-roots organizations (community development) that alert consumers to the importance of life style and environmental factors and engage in community activities to modify housing, work-related, and environmental causes.

MERITS OF PREVENTION

Emphasis upon community work also increases as attention is given to prevention (Boudreau 1976). To devise preventive programs, planning bodies must be established to locate at-risk populations whose members are more likely to incur medical problems than the general population: pregnant women, workers exposed to specific hazards, smokers, persons with specific genetic predispositions, the frail elderly, sexually active teenagers, persons who have suffered recent and traumatic losses, persons lacking supportive relationships, unemployed persons, and the poor. Indeed, a major task in prevention is to identify, locate, and draw into services persons who experience multiple risk factors; the infants of pregnant women who also drink heavily, for example, are far more likely than others to have birth defects.

If planning is required in prevention, outreach is needed to draw at-risk populations into service. Many consumers do not realize they are in at-risk groups—or know how to modify their life style and other factors to reduce medical risk. Access to these populations also requires cooperation between hospitals and physicians on the one hand and schools, courts, churches, and social agencies on the other. But such linkages are not emphasized if medical providers do not emphasize prevention. Consumer-oriented social action projects are also required to redress occupational and environmental factors that contribute to illness, projects that are impeded by the sheer power of tobacco, alcohol, and corporate interests in capitalist societies.

MULTIPLE BARRIERS TO UTILIZATION

In traditional medical perspectives, consumers are "rational"; that is, they recognize symptoms, seek technical assistance, and follow medical regimens. Medical sociologists have long emphasized nonrational components of medical care. Cultural, economic, and other factors influence whether specific consumers attribute importance to certain kinds of symptoms, believe health providers can assist them, and comply with medical recommendations. The importance of cultural preferences is suggested by studies that contrast orientations of different ethnic groups toward pain, optimism about recovery, trust in professionals, and beliefs about effectiveness of specific medical techniques (Twaddle 1979:22–42; Rosenstock and Kirscht 1979). Virtually all consumers use denial mechanisms at some point to discount the importance of specific conditions, but their extent and kind vary.

Many situational factors influence whether and when consumers seek assistance for specific symptoms; consumers who are poor, for example, are often deterred from using medical care when they have to make payments. Recent research indicates that many of the 30 million Americans who lack medical insurance avoid or defer utilization of medical services. Both urban and rural consumers may experience transportation inconveniences because many private physicians and hospital services are not located near them. Then, too, many physicians and hospitals engage in "patient dumping," as illustrated by a survey indicating that 60 percent of California physicians do not serve Medicaid patients (Kupcha 1979). Further, remarkable numbers of Americans do not comply with medical regimens, as reflected in the rapidly expanding literature on "compliance." It is estimated, for example, that large percentages of persons with conditions such as diabetes and high blood pressure do not use prescribed medications, even when nonuse markedly increases risk of disability or death (Kirscht and Rosenstock 1979).

Those who recognize multiple barriers to utilization are more likely, as in the cases of multiple causes of illness and prevention, to stress the need for community practice. Planning is required to identify barriers and specify consumers who are most likely to be deterred from using services. Political action is required to redress financial, transportation, facility location, and other barriers. Outreach is needed to increase access to services and to increase rates of compliance, as is involvement of citizens in governance of medical institutions to increase their visibility and credibility.

Barriers to Community Practice

An expanded concept of health care is a necessary but not sufficient condition for emphasis upon community work. Various structural, professional, financial, and technological barriers exist as well, barriers that will be discussed before analyzing factors that encourage its use.

ENTREPRENEURIAL BARRIERS

The entrepreneurial nature of American health care where hundreds of thousands of autonomous physicians and nongovernmental hospitals provide service impedes many kinds of community work. In this disaggregated and atomistic nonsystem, consumers choose their physicians, who then provide them with medical services. Lists of consumers, their medical records, records of their use of services, and other information are maintained by the physicians and hospitals that serve them, so that it is difficult for regional or governmental authorities to analyze patterns of utilization. Since there are no central registries of consumers, systematic outreach, planning, and preventive services are unlikely except as they are orchestrated by individual providers (Somers 1971). These providers, in turn, are not likely to emphasize these services even with their consumers—not only because they generally emphasize curative rather than preventive services, but because private insurance and governmental programs reimburse them only for diagnostic, surgical, and other procedures that are provided in offices of physicians, in hospitals, or in other institutions.

REGIONAL BARRIERS

Community practice is also frustrated by lack of "regionalization" of American medicine. In many European systems, health budgets are devised for geographic regions where regional authorities decide what facilities and staff are required to meet medical needs of the population. In these cases, funds and programs are linked so that regional planners who control funds can influence the nature and distribution of services (Roemer 1977).

     Regional funding accounts do not exist in the American system since funds derive from many sources that are not organized by regions. For example, private insurance companies such as Blue Cross and Blue Shield, governmental authorities through Medicare and Medicaid, and consumers each pay large portions of American medical bills. None of these funds is organized in a regional manner. Nor do funding sources operate in unified fashion. Thus, decisions by private insurance companies about coverage and eligibility are not linked to governmental decisions about coverage and eligibility under Medicaid.

Further, Americans do not link funding and programs. Insurance companies and governmental authorities reimburse private providers but seldom use funding leverage to influence their services, fees, sites of practice, or choices about whom they wish to serve (Stevens 1974; Davis and Schoen 1975). Lack of regionalization of medicine frustrates development of innovative and cooperative programs as well as planning (Ginzberg 1977). It also makes political action more difficult for consumer groups who cannot seek redress from *one* regional authority with major budget and program powers, but must approach multiple agencies at local, state, and federal levels—not to mention private insurance companies and myriad private providers.

FEE-FOR-SERVICE REIMBURSEMENT

Yet another barrier is fee-for-service reimbursement of providers in American medicine. Social work community practitioners who conduct outreach, organize community groups, build linkages between hospitals and agencies, and construct preventive programs do not perform traditional medical screening, diagnostic, and treatment services. Since governmental authorities and insurance companies fund hospitals and clinics by paying their fees for these kinds of medical services, staff who do *not* provide them must be funded through administrative overhead costs in hospitals and clinics, which, in turn, are reimbursed by insurances and governmental programs that provide a fixed percentage of their payments for such indirect costs. Such lack of direct funding of community practice services makes them residual and subject to cutbacks in times of scarce resources (Somers 1977). Fee-for-service reimbursement can be contrasted with development of budgets for hospitals and clinics that are provided by funders and that incorporate both medical and community activities.

Equally important, fee-for-service reimbursement gives physicians enormous power since many of them are not dependent upon the hospital or clinic for their income. (In many European nations licensed physicians who perform in-hospital procedures are salaried employees of the hospitals, but this pattern predominates only in teaching and public hospitals in the United States [Roemer 1977].) Further, many hospitals and clinics are dependent upon community-based doctors for their economic survival, since they obtain revenue only as these physicians admit patients—in contrast to many European nations where hospitals are directly funded by governmental authorities. One author conjectures that consumer participation in governance, even in innovative community clinics, is likely to be symbolic as long as one group (physicians) controls resources (Jonas 1978). The term "ancillary staff" often used to describe social workers, occupational therapists, and physical therapists, captures their residual status. Those ancillary staff who provide outreach and other nontraditional services that are not directly linked to ongoing curative medical services have even more precarious status.

DUAL SYSTEM OF CARE

Discussion on this point has emphasized the private physician and private insurance system of care used by the nonpoor. American medicine is characterized, however, by a dual system in which the poor are likely to use separate emergency rooms, outpatient departments, and public hospitals, as well as foreign-born physicians who give primary care services but who often lack "privileges" in hospitals. The poor tend to receive surgical services in public hospitals from salaried or contract physicians, often in tandem with medical students (Miller 1979).

The dual system of care frustrates planning efforts to develop health care programs that serve the entire population. Community organization activities often are neglected in clinics and hospitals that serve the poor. Chronic shortages of funds plague public hospitals and clinics because the nonpoor have no personal stake in them. These scarce resources are usually preempted by traditional services with resulting neglect of community and preventive services (Davis 1978).

TECHNOLOGY

Fantastic growth in medical technology has led to many obvious improvements in medical care. Mounting costs of extraordinary surgical and diagnostic techniques, however, have led some insurance and governmental funders to restrict funding of other health services. Some critics argue that medical technology in the short term has probably strengthened undue emphasis upon "the medical model" to the detriment of public health or community approaches (Reiser 1978). The development of new techniques for detecting various diseases could eventually lead, however, to community-based outreach programs. Extraordinary technical advances have also enormously expanded options available to elderly and physically disabled consumers that, in turn, have led to organization of self-help, advocacy, and service networks that provide consumers with a range of medical and community services (Goldenson 1978).

CONSERVATIVE POLICIES

In the early portion of the 1980s, drastic cuts in publicly funded programs were enacted in response to taxpayer revolts and the restrictive funding policies of the administration of Ronald Reagan. These cuts further eroded funding of preventive programs as well as regional planning projects, which many conservatives viewed with suspicion. Paradoxically, these policies may infuse new life into consumer-based social action projects that arise in response to restrictive policies.

Factors Favoring Community Practice

Were the picture entirely bleak, little purpose would be served in discussing community practice prior to major structural reforms in the American medical system. Cost, demographics, prevention, and market realities promote use of community work.

MOUNTING COSTS

The percentage of the Gross National Product devoted to medical services has risen dramatically in the last decade and now approaches 10 percent. While divided among consumers, employers, and government, costs are forcing scrutiny of medical care and service options. Indeed, a number of jurisdictions encounter bankruptcy because of rising costs of medical care of persons on public rolls, employers find it increasingly difficult to pay medical fringe benefits, and consumers who encounter major problems often find insurance coverage inadequate. Rising costs make authorities more willing to consider preventive medicine if only to cut costs, to develop service networks to allow elderly persons to avoid expensive nursing home care, and to use planning to diminish duplication and other forms of inefficiency (Fuchs 1974). Investment in expensive technology furthers the economic interests of specific hospitals which hope to attract physicians and patients, but the public ultimately pays for this technology even if it is not needed, a fact that is used to buttress the case for planning to decrease duplication and excesses (Klarman 1978).

INCREASING MULTIFACETED PROBLEMS

No demographic factor has had more profound influence on medical care than the rising proportion of elderly consumers. The elderly obviously require service networks, outreach, preventive health care, and other community services. While Americans have not developed well-conceived national strategies for assisting this population, their obvious social and medical needs—and the sheer cost of addressing them—are forcing more attention to community organization (Demkovich 1979). Innovative and comprehensive services are also needed for special populations such as abused children, battered women, rape victims, and addicted persons. As with elderly people, traditional medical services are increasingly perceived as insufficient to meet the social, financial, and counseling needs of these groups.

PREVENTION

More and more attention is given to preventive health care whether self-care by consumers through modification of life styles, early detection strategies, or modification of pollution and work-related causes of illness (Levin, Katz, and Holst 1976). While sometimes carried to faddist extremes, many theorists argue that major gains in health require substantial investment in preventive programs. (Linkages between prevention and community work have been noted in preceding discussion.)

MARKET REALITIES

In jurisdictions with an over-supply of physicians and hospital beds, such as Portland, Oregon, and San Francisco, hospitals are vigorously developing innovative outpatient and community programs to enable them to attract patients into their programs. In some cases, health facilities are conducting "marketing research" and coupling it with outreach (Nelson 1981:1). While a primary motivation in marketing is to maintain solvency, many consumers could benefit from heightened access and new outreach, program development, and planning roles could be developed for staff, as specific facilities respond to competitive pressures.

PROSPECTIVE PAYMENT SYSTEMS

Some current developments could have either an unfavorable or a favorable impact upon provision of the various kinds of community services that are discussed subsequently in this article. Thus, a prospective payment system began to replace traditional fee-for-service reimbursement when Medicare authorities received a legislative mandate in 1982 to reimburse hospitals on the basis of rates that were determined for treatment of persons with 467 defined diagnoses (Demkovitch 1983a). Each hospital would henceforth be reimbursed not according to the number of tests or services they provided for specific patients, but by an established fee for treatment of any person with that health problem. Insurance companies in some states followed suit by developing lists of "preferred providers," who received contracts with the insurance companies as they agreed to charge flat and negotiated amounts for assisting persons with specific diagnoses (Demkovitch 1983b). In some states, Medicaid authorities also began to allow their Medicaid recipients to use only those hospitals that agreed to limit charges to negotiated amounts.

This new form of reimbursement shifted power into hands of Medicare and insurance companies who now could negotiate with hospitals and insist upon negotiated or mandated levels of reimbursement. It also empowered administrators of hospitals, since they could now establish regulations over physicians to enable their institutions to compete for contracts and to retain reimbursement from Medicare.

These reimbursement policies emphasize reduction of costs of medical care and could lead to major reduction in any services that are perceived to be nonessential. Further, they can detract from services that offer a range of community and preventive services by focusing attention upon specific diagnostic categories. On the other hand, those community services that are perceived to cut costs of health care could be expanded in the wake of the new reimbursement policies. As noted in succeeding discussion, for example, preventive services, use of self-help groups, establishment of linkages between hospitals and other agencies in the community, and planning can lead to reductions in costs of services that are provided in a traditional medical model of service. Indeed, these kinds of community services could become even more important if Medicare and private insurance companies move toward prepayment models of reimbursement, where they pay consortia of providers a fixed sum for the treatment of persons at the beginning of a year. In such cases, providers will have incentives to provide a variety of preventive and community services that can substitute for traditional medical services.

Sites of Practice

While many critics of American medicine lament the lack of emphasis on prevention, outreach, and regional planning, some staff in
service and planning agencies provide various forms of community
work. As one example, data collected in a survey in 1980 of social
work directors in fifty nonprofit hospitals in Los Angeles County
suggest that a number of social work departments engage in community linkage and outreach functions.[1] Further, the social work directors did not believe that top hospital administrators were opposed to
community involvement by social work staff; while only 18 of the
50 social work directors indicated "strong encouragement," only 2
indicated opposition. On a less positive note, another survey contrasted community work activities of staff in 39 hospitals with those
in 124 social welfare agencies. The hospital-based social workers
were less likely to participate in outreach and prevention projects.[2]

A variety of health care institutions provides sanction and
staff for various forms of community work. Hospitals dominate the
health scene, accounting for 40 percent of total health care expenditures in 1980. There is also a variety of special programs. Public
health centers funded by joint federal, state, and local contributions
provide a range of diagnostic, screening, and primary care services;
about $320 million was spent on them in 1980. Funded initially
under Title 3 of the War on Poverty legislation in 1964, neighborhood health centers provide comprehensive primary care services in
low-income areas. The Veterans Administration operates 166 hospitals as well as many community clinics and counseling centers; like
public hospitals, its clientele are largely low-income patients since
more affluent veterans tend to use private insurance and nonprofit
hospitals.

Health maintenance organizations (HMOs) represent a
rapidly expanding form of medical practice even though only 4
percent of Americans belong to them. These organizations charge
enrollees a yearly fee and give consumers specified medical services during the year even if costs to the HMO exceed the annual
fee. While there are many variations among them, some studies
suggest that HMOs give more emphasis to preventive services than
hospitals and private physicians, in part because they have an eco-

nomic interest in improving the health status of their enrollees: As costs of medical service decline, HMOs can lower their annual fees and attract more consumers (U.S. Department of Commerce 1976:221–43).

A host of nonprofit agencies focus on specific populations or medical problems. The American Red Cross, the American Lung Association, the American Heart Association, the Easter Seal Society, and other associations not only raise funds to support service and research but also engage in a variety of outreach, advocacy, planning, and program development functions. The number of free clinics for women, minorities, and other groups has increased strikingly in the past two decades; many depend on volunteers but also have a core staff. Professional associations such as the American Public Health Association, local and national committees of the National Association of Social Workers, and the Society of Hospital Social Work Directors often support legislation supportive of various forms of community practice.

Social workers have long participated in the health care system. In the early part of this century, social workers assumed major roles in public health reform movements that were directed toward a host of sanitation, public inoculation, and medical insurance reforms (Trattner 1979:116–35). Health councils were formed in many jurisdictions, often under the aegis of welfare councils. Then, too, social workers developed patient service functions within hospitals, roles that soon accounted for the majority of health-related activities of the profession (Bracht 1978:3–18). This "hospitalization" of social work, however, led to the diminution of community roles, particularly when contrasted with public health perspectives of early social work reformers.

More recently, social workers have obtained important and sometimes mandated roles in various publicly subsidized programs for specific populations including renal dialysis programs funded by Medicare, programs for crippled and handicapped children, and programs for maternal and infant care. Needless to say, the ability of social workers to provide *any* services, much less community ones, is linked to efforts to retain and strengthen hospital accreditation that demands social work as well as administrative regulations by public authorities that require social work services in Medicare, hospice, and other government programs. A recent survey was hardly encouraging; one third of nonprofit hospitals in a major metropolitan county had only one social worker or even none at all or only a part-time worker, because of inadequate and insufficiently monitored standards of the Joint Commission on the Accreditation of Hospitals.[3]

In ensuing discussion, the typology of community practice that is used in the theory essays of this volume is used to analyze community work projects in the health care system. Community development, program development, social action, planning, and citizen participation projects are discussed.

Community Development

Community development is directed toward "helping people to deal more effectively with their problems and objectives, by helping them develop, strengthen, and maintain qualities or participation, self-direction, and cooperation" (Dunham 1979; United Nations Secretary General 1955). Health care is a logical vehicle for community development since all citizens have a stake in preventive health care and health maintenance. Further, health problems are less likely than mental health, delinquency, and welfare problems to be perceived as manifestations of social deviance, so broad participation can be obtained. Indeed, many argue that major strides in improving the nation's health will occur only as consumers engage personally in their own health care, an involvement that must, in turn, be encouraged by peers, families, and community residents (Pelletier 1979).

Community development activities are particularly needed in communities where health care systems are perceived as impersonal, unresponsive, or oppressive. Consumer participation in decision-making and in provision of services encourages use of health care by some who might otherwise shun it. Free clinics for women, storefront agencies in minority communities, and neighborhood community centers for alcoholics are examples of community development projects. In similar fashion, community development projects can improve recovery of patients who have suffered devastating illness. Persons who suffer from diseases widely perceived to be incurable, such as cancer, may benefit from participation in self-help groups composed of persons who *have* recovered.

But community development projects also have considerable use in the broader community. A recent project in Palo Alto, California, to modify drastically community diet, alcohol, smoking, and exercise habits made extensive use of community development by activating community groups to promote life styles supportive of health. Using foundation funds and enrollment fees, some community associations have developed health education and prevention activities—and also have sought changes in environmental conditions perceived to threaten health (Schroeder 1978; Tracy and Gussow 1976). By actively participating in consumer-oriented groups not only to receive but to promote health education, consumers supplement the negligible educational efforts of many physicians.

Three kinds of community development are particularly important in health care and are discussed in turn. Aware that there is a paucity of providers in low-income areas, the federal government provided funds for a network of neighborhood health centers that emphasize linkages with the community. Americans have evolved a host of self-help groups and alternative health care institutions. Finally, public health educators have evolved methodologies pertinent to dissemination of health education into the broader community.

BUILDING COMMUNITY INSTITUTIONS

Consumer-controlled health institutions include neighborhood health centers funded by the War on Poverty legislation that was enacted in 1964. Funded under Title 3 of this legislation, federal guidelines for the centers state:

Arrangements must be made such that the residents of the target area can participate in such decisions as the precise location of the program's services, the times they shall be available, the establishment of program priorities, matters relating to employment policy, and other policy-making responsibilities. . . . Their resident participation should occur through a community association which is comprised of representative members of the target community. (Battistoni et at. 1968:12–13).

Administrative and community staff encounter a number of issues in these centers as they try to emphasize community services. In traditional outpatient care, primary care, and hospital settings, criteria of efficiency have been developed based on the volume and unit costs of screening, diagnostic, and treatments provided by staff. These efficiency standards, often imposed on the centers by governmental funders, hardly apply, however, when outreach, consumer education, linkage, consultation, and other community activities are emphasized; indeed, centers emphasizing them appear *less* efficient than more traditional clinics, a fact that can lead to cutbacks (Davis and Schoen 1978:161–200).

Another dilemma is that extensive use of teams can also decrease efficiency since patient interviews and treatments require deliberations, negotiations, and other delays not associated with traditional doctor-patient services. Neighborhood health centers that emphasize consumer participation in planning devote considerable resources to training paraprofessionals, and, engage in other nontraditional activities, are also likely to appear inefficient.

External linkages between the centers and other health facilities can be problematic. The centers have to refer many consumers to hospitals for sophisticated testing and for surgery. But low-income patients who are recipients of multiprofessional and innovative services in community centers often encounter bureaucratic and impersonal medicine in medical centers or public hospitals, where their trust and participation in health care, nurtured in the community centers, can be erased by negative experiences.

A final dilemma is that many neighborhood health centers are approached by other funders to add drug abuse and many other services, but subsequent growth in size can lead not only to administrative difficulties but to impersonality akin to that in public hospitals. To demonstrate their efficiency to governmental funders, many of the centers have adopted endless forms and internal regulations that make innovative programming difficult.

Community practitioners who are employed by these centers, then, need to use skills to help centers develop community-oriented services when the centers are increasingly asked to conform to traditional standards of efficiency. An unexplored question

in community practice is how to develop and then justify community activities in terms of their efficiency; for example, as reflected
by use of outreach to enhance center revenue. In some cases, regardless of efficiency, community practitioners' efforts and achievements should be measured by the extent to which they improve the
effectiveness of various health care services, as well as their ac-
cessibili y to neglected populations.

SELF-HELP

Americans have developed a remarkable number and variety of self-
help groups and institutions where consumers assume major roles in
health care. The prominence of self-help—one commentator esti-
mates that there are about five hundred thousand self-help projects
in the United States—derives from many factors (Sidel and Sidel
1976). The long tradition of self-help in the United States dates back
to the origins of the republic. Consumers also need mutual support
when encountering catastrophic conditions like cancer. A more
cynical interpretation is that self-help is one method of obtaining
some consumer roles in a medical system largely impervious to
consumer participation (Sidel and Sidel 1976). In this discussion, a
distinction is made between mutual aid groups and alternative institutions.

In mutual-aid groups, consumers, often those who have
themselves experienced a specific medical condition, provide friendship, educational assistance, and other supports to fellow consumers. In some cases, assistance is given those with catastrophic health
conditions, including those with breast cancer, persons with kidney
transplants or on dialysis, or persons with multiple sclerosis (Withorn 1980). In other cases, assistance is given those with destructive
life styles, including those suffering from the effects of obesity,
alcoholism, and smoking (Riessman 1976). These self-help groups
are often organized by national groups such as chapters of the American Cancer Society. In other cases, self-help groups arise at the
local level as specific consumers seek to assist those who have
similar problems. In yet other cases, professionals organize self-

help groups as when staff in a Veterans Hospital organized a self-help group of victims of acute pain (Borman 1976).

Some self-help groups are fiercely independent of professionals and have an anti-establishment ideology. As an example, groups supportive of natural births battled obstetricians for years before relatively wide aceptance developed. Yet community practitioners can assume important roles in facilitating the work of self-help groups (Borman 1976). Selection of an initial cadre of consumers to begin a self-help project is often a crucial first step. Self-help groups also need practical supports, including referrals from providers, meeting rooms, and technical assistance. In many cases, community practitioners can assist self-help groups with political strategy, as illustrated by a community worker who helped natural childbirth and feminist groups secure policies that expand roles of midwives. When professionals themselves initiate and staff self-help groups, they assume roles within the groups to facilitate the emergence of ongoing and consumer leadership. If staff *become* the leadership, the group ceases to be self-help and resembles traditional therapeutic or educational programs.

Alternative institutions include free clinics, grassroots agencies to provide health care to specific minorities, and hospices for terminally ill patients (Davidson 1978). Unlike mutual-aid groups, alternative institutions often encounter difficult fiscal and administrative issues that derive from their need to develop and maintain facilities and paid staff, meet licensing and other legal requirements, and (when necesary) receive reimbursement from funders such as private insurance carriers (Perlman 1976). These practical realities often conflict with self-help ideology; staff in self-help institutions can be torn between maintaining independence on the one hand and seeking government funds and hospital affiliations on the other. In some cases an idealistic cadre of leaders initiates an alternative institution but is replaced, often in the course of considerable conflict, by management-oriented leaders who focus upon institutional maintenance needs.

Community practitioners assist alternative institutions in a number of ways (Miller 1977). They can asume paid positions in those institutions that have salaried staff and undertake the challenge of coupling practical administrative needs with self-help ideology. Organizers can volunteer community and administrative expertise. They can also assist with political action projects as well as educational efforts to sensitize traditional caregivers to needs of those women, adolescents, and other persons who are the primary users of alternative institutions.

HEALTH EDUCATION

Considerable attention has been given by social psychologists and public health staff to the development of methodologies for disseminating health information to consumers. As one example, research has been conducted on the use of groups, role-playing, and simulations to help consumers modify destructive health habits such as smoking (Janis 1977). This research also explores denial or coping mechanisms that prevent consumers from changing prior habits. More explicit linkage of consumer education models to community and self-help groups is needed so that consumer education by professionals is disseminated to, and used by, a range of nonprofessional persons in the community.

Program Development and Service Coordination

Program development and service coordination projects are needed because services are often marked by inaccessibility, fragmentation, and discontinuity (Spiegel and Hyman 1978). Inaccessibility occurs when consumers do not use services because of their location, hours, or fees—or when consumers lack knowledge of services or resist using them. Fragmentation occurs when consumers do not receive a range of needed services that use contributions of many professions and agencies. Financial barriers, absence of referral mechanisms, and other factors can foster discontinuity for victims of cancer and other illnesses where consumers need a sequence of medical, physical, homemaking, counseling, and occupational therapies. Outreach, service network, and linkage strategies represent three community practice approaches to these problems in the medical service delivery system.

OUTREACH

Interviews with staff in many service settings suggest that outreach is minimal in American health care even in neighborhood health centers and maternal and infant care projects where at-risk populations are served. In many centers, staff hired to do outreach are instead pressed into a variety of aide and translation functions *within* facilities. In one center, a minority social worker, recruited to increase use of the clinics by foreign-speaking populations, discovered that medical and nursing staff were annoyed when these consumers did increase their use of the clinic and began to refer many of them to the county hospital.

An outreach strategy is to send staff from a facility to meetings of neighborhood community organizations, churches, and social agencies to provide health education and information about available services and the intricacies of health programs. Or outreach staff can be used to enhance the visibility of a facility by providing community services such as helping public housing residents set up food cooperatives or engage in other forms of community development. "Health fairs" are used by health facilities or community-wide civic associations where volunteer medical and agency personnel offer a range of educational and health care services to community residents.

A number of health facilities are now using marketing approaches not only to identify unmet community needs but to use the mass media to advertise services. The medical profession has not traditionally sanctioned advertising, but these forms of outreach are more likely as hospitals and clinics believe they *must* seek patients in order to survive. As in the case of needs assessment, many private physicians perceive outreach that increases use of hospital outpatient departments or neighborhood clinics as competing with them by drawing patients from their private practices (Flower 1981).

DEVISING SERVICE NETWORKS

Health care in the United States is largely delivered in facilities and offices that emphasize time-limited and highly specific services. Some providers, however, are developing more complex service structures, as illustrated by hospitals that purchase community residential facilities that incorporate homemaker, recreational, and counseling services (Jennings 1981; Schlenker 1980). At higher levels, health services are incorporated in some jurisdictions into broader "human resources" departments where, most ambitiously, health services are systematically linked with other services (Murphy 1977).

These complex service structures are emerging for a number of reasons. The proportion of elderly persons is increasing, and combinations of services are needed for them. Service networks are also used as a cost-cutting strategy and are likely to become more important as rising medical costs lead governmental authorities to favor facilities that demonstrate cost effectiveness. If the frail elderly are provided with community supports and timely medical assistance, for example, many of them can delay or avoid resorting to nursing homes. Administrators of service networks can, in short, experiment with program alternatives because, unlike specialized institutions, they possess multiple capabilities (Schlenker 1980).

Many barriers frustrate construction of service networks. A tangle of separate governmental programs, each with different eligibility requirements, makes consolidation difficult. Management problems reach the point that some human resources departments are unwieldy bureaucracies. Hospitals and other facilities often lack required management capabilities to orchestrate service networks.

LINKAGE STRATEGIES

In most cases it is not possible to place "under one roof" a range of health services, so increasing attention is given to building consortia of agencies and services to offset fragmentation and discontinuity in services. Linkage options extend from ambitious efforts to develop joint programs to modest projects to promote joint referral policies. Other options include pooling staff and resources for specific projects, agreements about service priorities to reduce duplication, and systematic exchanges of case consultation and information (Barrett 1979). The importance of linkage strategies is suggested by a recent survey that indicates 67 percent of hospitals engage in the sharing or pooling of resources (Barrett 1980).

Linkage strategies are reflected in programs devised to assist specific populations including victims of rape, battering, child abuse, and drug overdoses where it is particularly obvious that short-term acute services cannot suffice either to meet short-term legal, financial, or mental needs or to help victims cope with problems months or even years after the event (Litwak and Rothman 1979). In loose coalitions of social and medical agencies, referral networks are established so that constituent agencies agree to give prompt service to victims and to evolve agreements concerning which staff assume lead roles.

A problem with this approach is that often there is no "case manager" who follows the consumer through the network, monitors progress, and intervenes when the consumer leaves services prematurely. In some cases a new agency is set up (for example, an agency for victims of rape) that uses loaned staff or volunteers to provide service. At a more modest level, health agencies use loaned staff, as illustrated by a hospital that obtained staff from a community mental health center to provide counseling to women contemplating abortions and that stationed protective service staff from a child welfare office in the emergency room.

Community practice workers who develop linkage approaches often use conflict management and negotiation skills. When participants believe that there is "an uneven exchange," that some obtain greater monetary or prestige rewards than others, for instance, linkage is likely to be resisted. Leadership struggles can occur, since some agencies may fear that those who assume initiating or leading roles will receive undue credit. Linkage projects are sometimes resisted when they require agency staff to be supervised by staff in other agencies or to cede "control" over staff to relatively autonomous or new programs (Cook 1977; Levine and White 1961).

Political or Social Action

The politics of medicine prior to 1965 was dominated by provider groups, most specifically the American Medical Association. As chronicled by a number of historians, the AMA developed its strength through a community political action strategy that linked grass-roots organization with county, state, and national organizations in the early part of this century (Numbers 1979). While dissidents in progressive and depression eras favored government regulation, the AMA was militantly against governmental participation in financing health care. Passage of Medicare and Medicaid over strenuous lobbying of the AMA somewhat diminished its influence, but physicians' and hospital associations continue to exercise enormous power in national and local arenas.

Community organizations that seek changes in health policies encounter a number of obstacles in addition to opposition to governmental controls by providers. There is considerable "buck-passing" among local, state, and federal authorities regarding policy-making and funding so that it is often difficult to obtain support from *any* level. When approaching local officials, organizers are often told "that's the responsibility of state officials," but the latter often defer to local or federal authorities. Many health care institutions and financing mechanisms are relatively impervious to external pressure so that it is difficult to obtain changes in coverage of private insurance companies, prevent providers from denying non-emergency service to low-income consumers, or influence policies of nursing homes. Nonetheless, community practitioners often try to modify current policies by mobilizing constituencies to seek policy changes for specific interests or populations by forming coalitions in the broader community.

CONSTITUENCY BUILDING

If coalitions mobilize diverse interests, constituency strategies are directed toward activating specific interests whether populations (blacks in Harlem), disease types (renal dialysis patients in California), or institutions (free clinics in Ohio). Constituency mobilizing can foster dramatic successes, particularly if there is broad public sympathy. At the national level, for example, subsidies to renal dialysis patients were added to the Medicare program partly because advocates wheeled patients who were on dialysis into legislative chambers and then proceeded to disconnect them from the machines to the astonishment of legislators.

Social work practitioners confront numerous challenges when they engage in constituency building. In some cases, considerable effort is required to convince specific interest groups that they should organize. It was only when free clinics in one state realized they shared common interests in licensing and reimbursement matters that they were willing to fund and hire a lobbyist who advocated their cause in the state capitol. Communication and logistic factors impede success when seeking to establish regional or state-wide coalitions of local groups. In some cases marked cleavages exist within constituencies. Community workers in the Hispanic community often find it difficult to secure support for expanded public programs, since relatively affluent Hispanics use private physicians and insurance, and often have little interest in medical care of low-income Hispanics who use public programs.

An example of constituency building was a project in California to modify state statutes pertaining to Medicaid.[4] A social worker in a renal dialysis unit noted that patients who sought employment often suffered a net loss in income when their earned income made them ineligible for Medicaid, a program that had covered a large portion of their dialysis expenses. Such working patients not only suffered an income loss, but devastating psychological setbacks as well when they were forced to leave their jobs. Social work staff took the initiative in rallying the hemodialysis community of patients, providers, and relatives as well as the general public through use of mass media. Behind-the-scenes contacts with experts in the state's Department of Health were used to define technical and legislative proposals and to develop data to counter contention from top officials that the proposal would be overly costly.

COALITIONS

Coalitions have been used extensively to modify policies regarding closures of public hospitals, state funding cuts in Medicaid, and numerous other issues (Alford 1975). Coalitions vary widely in structure and membership. Some are led by volunteer professionals while others are dominated by providers, as when unions of health care employees spearhead efforts to fight cutbacks and terminations. Some are tightly organized and visible, as when representatives issue joint proclamations to media. In other cases, including some cases when organizers encounter marked resistance in hospital and legislative settings, coalitions are loosely organized and rely upon "behind-the-scenes" strategy. In a case study of Congressional health care politics Redman (1973) documents how he and allies maintained loose communication and a low profile in order not to mobilize powerful interests against their proposal to establish a corps of doctors in areas with a shortage of doctors. Since they feared others could perceive this proposal as linked to controversial proposals such as national health insurance, they wanted to use behind-the-scenes influence at strategic points to avoid opposition from conservatives.

A number of factors diminish the success of coalitions in health care. Coalitions that are headed by union personnel and other health care staff can be perceived as serving their own interests rather than those of the general public. The technical nature of many medical decisions requires coalition participants to invest considerable time in data collection and technical analysis to the detriment of other organizing activities. Even when they possess considerable expertise, it is difficult to document the effects of specific policies upon the health of consumers. In a detailed study of coalition building in Chicago when the Welfare Council sought support for construction of a satellite public hospital on the South Side, Banfield (1961) documented difficulties of the Council in demonstrating that the satellite would improve the health status of residents. In this case, opponents were able to arrest momentum by raising technical objections. The Council also found its coalition strategy stymied by divergent interests of potential members, which is another obstacle to use of coalitions. While many professionals and some hospitals wanted a new public hospital on the South Side, some civil rights leaders feared it would encourage patient dumping by local non-profit hospitals since many of them routinely referred low-income consumers to public hospitals.

Planning

Planning projects are used to identify an array of program objectives and policy and program options, choose preferred objectives and options, and develop proposals. While they can be conducted in any setting, considerable attention has been given regional and governmental planning, an area where Americans have lagged when compared with many European as well as Canadian systems. Voluntary planning through welfare councils as well as local health planning and hospital councils was present in the 1940s and 1950s, but rested upon voluntary compliance with planning recommendation (Sheps and Madison 1977).

There were preliminary if ineffective efforts at planning before landmark legislation in 1974. Hill-Burton legislation in the period of 1948 to 1974 offered federal subsidies for hospital construction provided it was in compliance with mandated state plans. The legislation did not affect the location of existing facilities, however, and was often bypassed when hospitals used private funds. In 1965 Congress passed the Regional Medical Program to encourage local program planning and in-service training regarding heart disease, cancer, and stroke. Medical schools usually assumed leadership in the health planning consortia that followed, even though they included providers and consumers. Few funds were provided for the program, however, and planning was further impeded by lack of detailed federal guidelines and the low priority given to the projects by many medical schools. Most resources went to in-service training and pilot projects. Emphasis upon cancer, stroke, and heart disease also detracted from planning about larger issues in local health delivery (Sheps and Madison 1977).

Recognition of the need for stronger local planning led to passage of the Comprehensive Health Planning Act of 1966 that provided federal support for new public or private comprehensive health planning agencies in local and regional areas. Though given a broad mandate, the work of these agencies was generally disappointing.

The most ambitious planning legislation yet considered by the Congress was passed in 1974 when the National Health Planning and Resources Development Act established local Health Systems Agencies (HSAs) to review (and veto if needed) applications for federal funds for special projects, engage in extensive data collection about local health needs and resources, and make advisory recommendations to state planning agencies regarding expansion of hospitals or purchase of technology. The legislation also mandated HSA to use persuasive powers to encourage greater attention to preventive services and coordination of services. Formation of boards with more than 50 percent consumer representation was also required, ones that were to have extensive representation of physicians, hospitals, and other providers.

While an innovation, HSAs have had marginal effect upon the American health care system (Fisher 1980). HSAs could be set up as public or nonprofit agencies with final designation in each of 218 regions designated by federal officials. Support of the 1974 legislation by providers was partly conditioned upon limitations placed upon HSAs. They were given limited seed money for new programs, no power over Medicaid and Medicare programs, advisory rather than veto powers regarding facility expansion, and virtually no regulatory powers over private physicians or hospitals (Demkovitch 1979a). As with War on Poverty agencies in the 1960s, providers have often been able to use their resources to dominate local elections by proposing and supporting consumer slates supportive of their interests. HSAs have been under attack by Congressional conservatives and have not had sufficient resources to accomplish even their limited mandate (Demkovitch 1979a). Many conservatives hope to eliminate the HSAs altogether.

While Americans have been reluctant to institute regional planning, a number of submodels of planning have been employed extensively, often in clinic and hospital settings. These submodels include needs assessment, logistic advocacy, and strategic planning.

NEEDS ASSESSMENT PLANNING

An extensive methodology has developed in public health and epidemiology to facilitate analysis of health needs and resources in geographic areas. There are many data sources pertinent to rates of mortality and morbidity, utilization of health resources, and distribution of services (Jonas 1977). Needs assessment techniques are used to study the extent to which new services are required, to estimate the demand for proposed services, and to determine the oversupply of beds and services. While there is considerable disagreement about roles of stress, physical inactivity, diet, pollution, and other variables, progress has been made in identifying clusters of variables that place persons in high-risk categories (Antonovsky 1979).

Use of needs assessment is illustrated by the development of a project by a social work director in a hospital to assess community need for an outpatient "clinicare service" for elderly consumers (Flower 1981). The director of the hospital marketing department asked the social work director to assume a major role in exploring feasibility of a hospital department to provide primary care and needed referrals. Marketing and social work staff developed a series of successive surveys and meetings and found a large number of elderly persons within a mile-and-a-half radius of the hospital who did not have primary care physicians and had considerable interest in the possibility of a community clinic. They determined that extensive use of the clinic was likely if vans were available, the elderly were not subjected to long delays, and the clinic surroundings were attractive. The director concluded that social workers possess interpersonal, group, and outreach skills to assume large roles in marketing strategies.

LOGISTIC PLANNING

Planning at all levels of the health care system is needed to troubleshoot operating programs when they fail to achieve stated objectives. Rivalries between different professions and specialties, financing or reimbursement issues, and lack of defined program objectives often frustrate implementation of programs. Logistic planning, then, is directed toward use of task forces and committees to examine organizational and financial factors that impede success of a program and to clarify and weight program objectives.

An extended case study of logistic planning is provided by

Tichy when he examines internal and community operations of a neighborhood health center over a period of ten years (Tichy 1977). Operations of the center were complicated by shifting external expectations. In early years, federal authorities wanted innovative and extensive use of community programs, outreach, and advocacy. Policy environment of the center changed dramatically, however, as federal authorities placed more emphasis on efficiency and provision of traditional services. Continuing planning was needed to help the center adapt to a turbulent policy environment. Tichy advocates greater use of planning to assess logistic factors, to explore unanticipated consequences of specific organizational arrangements, and to develop service objectives in the context of external realities.

ADVOCACY PLANNING

Central emphasis is given in advocacy planning to development of political strategies to promote policies and programs to assist low-income, minority, or other powerless groups. Those who use this model perceive health care as dominated by a series of special provider interests as illustrated by Alford's description of health care politics in New York City. He argues that physician and hospital interests continue to mobilize vast political pressure whenever regulatory proposals are advanced (Alford 1975).

Advocacy planning is illustrated by the work of an Asian American social worker's attempts to obtain representation for Asians on the governing board of an HSA. The project required analysis of legal mandates, analysis of intricacies of appointing and elective processes, analysis of sources of support within and outside the HSA, and planning of a community-based strategy to alert officials to the problem. Attorneys assisted in identifying legal mandates and preparing the group for possible court action. The social worker was able to conduct the project in this case as part of her employment in a neighborhood health center, but many advocacy projects use volunteer staff because employers are reluctant to allow their staff to engage in social change projects.

STRATEGIC PLANNING

Strategic or long-term planning is often needed so that health facilities and programs can chart a course in the turbulent and competitive health care environment (Steiner 1979). Strategic planning involves task forces or committees that estimate population, financing, and other contingencies in a five-year or other time frame, examine likely competitors, and develop alternative program options.

An example of strategic planning was a planning project by directors of social work of neighborhood health centers in a metropolitan health department. The social workers analyzed kinds of patients likely to use the centers and developed staff projections in the context of numbers of patients with demonstrated need for social work services. They made an inventory of staff and functions, projected required additions in staff increments during a five-year period, and identified new programs for social work staff. The social work plan was adopted as a model for other professions in the health department and increased support for social work in the department.

CONSUMER PARTICIPATION

A number of rationales have been made for involving consumers in the governance of health care institutions (Campbell 1979). First, consumers can offset traditional medical perspectives when they possess expanded notions of health care that include prevention of health problems, advocacy, and outreach. Second, consumers have a stake in shaping priorities and programs in the health care system, since they are the ultimate users and funders of medical services. Finally, citizen participation can make health care institutions more receptive to the needs of specific groups in the community.

Nonprofit hospitals have used consumers in governance since the latter portion of the nineteenth century. Consumer participation requirements were included in legal mandates of neighborhood health centers and HSAs. Consumer participation has been impeded, however, by the highly technical nature of medical care; physicians and hospital administrators question the ability of consumers to make informed choices about complex issues, particularly those bearing directly upon medical services and priorities (Greer 1976). Even when formally included, consumer representatives can be overwhelmed by complex information that is often not translated into terms understandable to laymen. A recent study of HSA boards suggests, however, that voting patterns of consumers and providers on key medical issues are not dissimilar (Grossman 1978).

Participation is also impeded in many settings by lack of clear definition of powers of boards as illustrated by uncertainty about whether consumers have advisory, veto, consent, or decision-making power with respect to choice of staff, grant proposals, budget decisions, program-review functions, and program development. It is also frustrated by lack of definition of organizational objectives in many clinic and hospital settings, so that decision-making is confused and choices ill-informed (Greer 1976).

Most hospital boards are composed of community elites, but there has been conflict in many neighborhood health centers and other community clinics over board composition. As an example, health care professionals in one Hispanic organization were pitted against indigenous residents who charged that they did not implement election procedures specified in their charter. In many HSA elections, health care providers mobilize support behind consumer representatives perceived to be friendly to them, even to the point of persuading hospital workers to vote for provider-endorsed slates. In one instance, a community group withdrew from participation because they lacked resources to compete with physician and hospital providers (Checkoway 1980).

As staff to boards, social work community practitioners use conflict management and negotiation skills to fashion and maintain boards that develop indigenous leadership that reflects perspectives often ignored in policy deliberations. In the process, they must decide whether and how to advocate inclusion of representative of groups that are systematically excluded.

Reform Strategies

How can use of various kinds of community work for health care be enhanced? Strategies are needed to foster funding and ideological changes, visibility of specialized community work services, regional approaches, and development of theory useful to those who provide community work in settings where staff are not accustomed to it.

BASIC REFORMS

Major structural and ideological changes in the American health care system are required if community work is to become integral to it; such changes include regionalization of American medicine, greater emphasis upon program rather than fee-for-service reimbursement, and development of medical institutions that serve rich and poor alike. Challenges to traditional medical perspectives are needed so that more emphasis is given to multiple causes of illness and multiple barriers to utilization of services. Community organization also needs to be linked to prevention; since Americans place emphasis upon prevention, they are more likely to mandate staff to engage in outreach, community education, and advocacy.

FUNDING AND VISIBILITY OF COMMUNITY WORK

When discussing funding and visibility of community practice, it is important to reiterate current realities. Specific staff are seldom designated as community organization staff nor are outreach and other community functions usually identified as program items in budgets. In many cases, some community work is performed by direct-service staff who are also deluged with requests for clinical services.

In the absence of specific and earmarked funding, community work is likely to remain a residual service. One strategy could be to develop national funding of a corps of community work staff to be affixed to a variety of public health agencies, neighborhood health centers, and hospital facilities. Alternatively, legislation could require that Medicare, Medicaid, and private insurance payments for institutional overhead include specific earmarked sums for community work staff. These direct or mandated funding strategies are not likely to be successful in an era of scarce resources, however. Accreditation standards of various health institutions could also be modified to require provision of specialized community work services.

The ultimate objective of these funding, mandating, and accreditation strategies would be to elevate community work to the status of other medical specialities. Only as a range of medical staff perceives community organization to be a legitimate specialty, one with funding and mandate supports, will they widely support it in various institutional settings. An objective of those strategies would be to obtain designation of certain staff in health institutions as community practitioners. Some facilities currently have "health education" staff, but this title is not sufficiently broad to include the variety of submodels discussed here (Somers 1977).

Several problems should be noted in designation strategies. In some settings there is sibling rivalry between public health and social work staff for community functions. Further, official designation of some staff as community workers could allow remaining direct-service staff to believe *they* do not need to engage in community work. Still, it is difficult to obtain dramatic increases in the volume of community work if mechanisms are not found to heighten the profile of staff who provide it.

REGIONAL OPTIONS

In addition to bolstering community work within specific institutions, its advocates might consider regional options where community work staff are concentrated in settings external to hospitals and community clinics. Many health problems and services function apart from major hospital settings, including those associated with nursing and convalescent homes, school-based programs, and primary care services of private physicians. An institutional strategy that made hospitals and community clinics the locus of most community work services could ignore these broader health issues. Two logical candidates for pools of community work staff are the present network of public health clinics and regional planning authorities such as HSAs. While now preoccupied with traditional screening and diagnostic procedures, public health centers are logical candidates because they provide grass-roots services and are imbued with public health ideology that is consonant with planning, outreach, and prevention (Bracht 1978).

The disadvantage of locus in public health centers is that they lack a broad mandate to coordinate services; indeed, private health providers have restricted the scope of public health in the United States precisely because they feared public health centers would compete with them. Because HSAs have a mandate to engage in planning and coordination, they offer another possible locus for community practice staff. Even more than public health, however, they have precarious funding and policy status in American health care, as illustrated by the efforts of conservatives to dismantle them in the early 1980s.

ACHIEVING COMMUNITY WORK MANDATES

The preceding discussion suggests that community work is deemphasized in many settings. More attention needs to be given to programmatic assertiveness by community work staff; that is, to methods of obtaining sanction or mandates for services that would not normally be given to them. Traditional community organization literature emphasizes practice techniques for staff who occupy already-designated community work positions. In health care, staff must often *create* a mandate, sometimes as they also assume major direct-service functions. Development of appropriate theory is needed to assist practitioners in obtaining and maintaining mandates. Put differently, community workers need to market their functions to decision-makers in hospitals, clinics, and other settings.

In obtaining mandates, many practitioners appear to utilize formal clearance and ratification strategies. In the former case, they obtain formal sanction prior to initiating a project, as in the case of the social worker who developed a needs assessment to determine if a hospital should have a clinic for primary care of elderly consumers. In other cases, staff engage in certain forms of community work *prior* to written or formal clearance and *then* use the precedent and, one hopes, positive outcomes to persuade decision-makers that even more community work is warranted. While this approach may appear devious, interviews with social workers in health care suggest that it is commonly used. Indeed, community work staff who enter employment in many health settings expecting to receive clear mandates can become disillusioned.

In great measure, a community practice mandate must be earned in the course of a succession of activities. In one case, a social worker in a neighborhood health center developed power as she undertook public relations and advocacy tasks as she successively engaged in various outreach, health education, and advocacy projects—power that in turn led top administrators to perceive her as an indispensable community resource in a turbulent environment. This respect subsequently led to formal enhancement of her community roles as well as decreasing the effort of a competing public health worker to undermine her community roles. (Although she was a graduate of a specialized community practice program, the worker began the job with little more than a mandate to engage in patient aide and translation functions within the institution.) In many cases, community social work practitioners have to accept positions where community functions are only partially defined and where a major challenge is to evolve them.

Clearly, however, key decision-makers are unlikely to formalize or accept community work functions if they do not believe they serve the institution, so practitioners need to market their community knowledge and skills by showing that they can serve important public relations functions, enhance consumer utilization, and reduce conflict between departments within health care settings. Indeed, persons who provide community practice expertise can sometimes obtain support from key decision-makers by applying their skills *within* their institutions. Hospitals and community clinics, for example, are akin to communities since they are composed of different interests, experience conflict, and try to resolve competing priorities. A conceptualization of community work in health settings is worth considering, then, that encompasses both external (community) and internal (institutional) roles.

In some cases, key decision-makers may develop sufficient confidence in specific staff to allow them to engage in important external functions, but only when they perceive them as able to participate in internal planning and other activities. Ultimately, however, this confidence stems not only from skillful interpretation of positive benefits for the institution and consumers by community workers, but demonstrated competence. Verbal or written defenses or rationales are no substitute for demonstrated effectiveness and payoff for the institution and its consumers, particularly when medical and administrative staff have had little prior exposure to public health models of health care. The social work community practitioner, like traditional medical specialists, needs to be seen as a valuable member of the medical community, someone who provides needed supplements to traditional medical services in community outreach, linkage, planning, and development functions.

In both internal and external roles, community staff have to wrestle with important ethical dilemmas. They may dislike policies in institutions that hire them, including those that preclude provision of preventive services or that discriminate against low-income populations. When should organizers indirectly engage in activity by "planting" reform agendas in community groups or providing them with crucial inside information? When they do not engage in efforts to modify distasteful policies, they cast a vote for existing institutions, but overly assertive workers run the risk of losing confidence of key decision-makers who may have only gradually entrusted them with community roles.

Summary

Despite its promise, social work community practice exists at the fringes of the American medical system. Few major American health institutions or clinics invest major resources in outreach, linkage, and other strategies discussed in this article. Interviews with many social work staff in a variety of health care settings suggest that much of current community work occurs not because of high-level mandates but through unsolicited initiatives of staff. Further, there is relatively little activation of American consumers in broader issues of health policy; while numerous national health insurance proposals have been advanced, policy discourse has generally been limited to politicans, governmental officials, providers, and selected trade unions supportive of major reforms.

Continuing work is needed to define alternative models of community practice in the health care system, including the five major models discussed here. Theory is also needed that facilitates development of community work mandates in settings where key decision-makers are not familiar with, or supportive of, it.

In the earlier part of this century, many social workers assumed major roles in the community-oriented public health reform movement. Hospitalization of social work health functions, however, has sometimes led to preoccupation with patient clinical, financial, and discharge roles. Perhaps it is time for community-oriented theorists, researchers, and practitioners to supplement these direct-service roles with a range of community activities.

Notes

1. Findings derived from a survey of hospital social work departments conducted by Bruce Jansson, June Simmons, and Candyce Berger in Southern California in 1980.
2. Findings derived from a survey of social work administrators in Los Angeles County, conducted in 1979 by Bruce Jansson and Samuel Tayor; not previously reported.
3. Findings from a survey of hospital social work departments conducted by Bruce Jansson, June Simmons, and Candyce Berger in Southern California in 1980.
4. Interviews conducted by the authors with Kenneth Eisenberg and Michael Cervantes in 1982.

References

Alford, Robert. 1975. *Health Care Politics*. Chicago: University of Chicago Press.
American Public Health Association. 1981. *Washington News Letter,* February.
Anderson, Wayne F., Bernard J. Frieden, and Michael J. Murphy. 1977. *Managing Human Services*. Washington, D.C.: International City Management Association.
Antonovsky, Aaron. 1979. *Health, Stress, and Coping*. San Francisco: Jossey-Bass.

350   B. S. Jansson/R. Salcido

Banfield, Edward C. 1961. *Political Influence*. New York: Free Press.

Barrett, David. 1980. "Multihospital Systems: The Process of Development." *Health Care Management Review*, 5(1):49–50.

Battistoni, Kenneth J. et al. 1968. *Neighborhood Health Centers*. Ithaca, N.Y.: Center for Housing and Environmental Studies.

Borman, Leonard D. 1976. "Self-Help and the Professional." *Social Policy*, 7(2):46–47.

Boudreau, Thomas J. 1976. "Taking a New Perspective on Health in Canada." In *Proceedings of National Leadership Conference on Health Policy*, pp. 30–33. Washington, D.C.: National Journal.

Bracht, Neil F. 1975a. "Public Health Social Work: A Community Focus." In Bracht, ed., *Social Work in Health Care*, pp. 243–60.

———. 1975b. "The Scope and Historical Development of Social Work, 1900–1975." In Bracht, ed., *Social Work in Health Care*, pp. 3–18.

———. 1978. *Social Work in Health Care*. New York: Haworth Press.

Campbell, Lenore A. 1979. "Consumer Participation in Planning." *Social Work*, 24(2);159–60.

Checkoway, Barry. 1980. "The Struggle for Consumer Control: Champaign-Urbana." Paper presented at annual meeting of the American Public Health Association.

Cook, Karen S. 1977. "Exchange and Power in Networks of Interorganizational Relations." *Sociological Quarterly*, 18(1):62–82.

Cox, Fred M. et al., eds. 1979. *Strategies of Community Organization: A Book of Readings*. 3d ed. Itasca, Ill.: Peacock.

Davidson, Glen W. 1978. *The Hospice*. Washington, D.C.: Hemisphere.

Davis, Karen and C. Shoen. 1978. *Health and the War on Poverty: A Tenure Appraisal*. Washington, D.C.: Brookings Institution.

———. 1975. *National Health Insurance*. Washington, D.C.: Brookings Institution.

Demkovitch, Linda. 1979a. "Health Planning Agencies Face Threat from Deregulation." *National Journal*, 11(17):687–90.

———. 1979b. "Seeking Alternatives to Nursing Homes." *National Journal*, 11(51–52):2154–59.

———. 1983a. "Who Says Congress Can't Move Fast: Just Ask Hospitals about Medicare." *National Journal*, 15(45):2314–16.

———. 1983b. "PPO—Three Letters That Form One Answer to Runaway Health Costs." *Natonal Journal*, 15(22):1176–77.

Dunham, Arthur. 1970. *The New Community Organization*. New York: Crowell.

Fisher, George R. 1980. *The Hospital That Ate Chicago*. Philadelphia: Saunders Press.

Flower, Martha. 1981. "Market Research and Social Work." Paper presented at annual meeting of the Society for Hospital Social Work Directors.

Fuchs, Victor. 1974. *Who Shall Live?* New York: Basic Books.

Ginzberg, Eli. 1977. "The Many Meanings of Regionalization in Health." In Ginzberg, ed., *Regionalization in Health Policy*, pp. 1–6. Washington, D.C.: U.S. Department of Health, Education, and Welfare, Public Health Service.

Goldenson, Robert M., ed. 1978. *Disability and Rehabilitation Handbook.* New York: McGraw-Hill.

Greer, Ann L. 1976. "Training Board Members for Health Planning Agencies." *Public Health Reports,* 91(1):56–61.

Grosser, Charles F. 1973. *New Directions in Community Organization: From Enabling to Advocacy.* New York: Praeger.

Grossman, Randolph M. 1978. "Voting Behavior of H.S.A. Interest Groups: A Case Study." *American Journal of Public Health,* 68(12):1191–94.

Jaco, E. Garth, ed. 1979. *Patients, Physicians, and Illness.* New York: Free Press.

Janis, Irving. 1974. *Decision Making.* New York: Free Press.

Jennings, Mary. 1981. "Life Care: An Opportunity to Participate in Your Hospital's Planning." Paper presented at annual meeting of the Society for Hospital Social Work Directors.

Jonas, Steven. 1977a. "Data for Health and Health Care." In Jonas, ed., *Health Care Delivery in the United States,* pp. 40–69.

———, ed. 1977b. *Health Care Delivery in the United States.* New York: Springler.

———. 1978. "Limitations of Community Control of Health Facilities and Service." *American Journal of Public Health,* 68(6):541–43.

Kirscht, John P. and I. M. Rosenstock. 1979. "Patients' Problems in Following Recommendation of Health Experts." In Stone, Cohen, and Adler, eds., *Health Psychology,* pp. 189–215.

Klarman, Herbert E. 1978. "Health Planning: Progress, Prospects, and Issues." *Milbank Memorial Fund Quarterly,* 56(1):78–113.

Kupcha, Dorothy A. 1979. "Medicaid: In or Out of the Health Mainstream?" *California Journal,* 10(5):181–83.

Levin, Lowell S., Alfred Katz, and Eric Holst. 1976. *Self-Care: Lay Initiatives in Health.* New York: Prodist.

Levine, Sol E. and Paul White. 1961. "Exchange as a Conceptual Framework for the Study of Interorganizational Relationships." *Administration Science Quarterly* (March), 5(4):583–601.

Lewis, Jim. 1982. "How the Health Revolution Will Affect Most Californians." *California Journal* (November), 13(11):403–06.

Litwak, Eugene and Jack Rothman. 1979. "The Impact of Organizational Structure and Linkage in Agency Programs and Service." In Cox et al., eds., *Strategies of Community Organization,* pp. 249–62. Itasca, Ill.: Peacock.

Miller, Alfred E. 1979. "The Changing Structure of the Medical Profession in Urban and Suburban Settings." In Jaco, ed., *Patients, Physicians, and Illness,* pp. 239–59.

Miller, Merlin. 1977. "Organizing the Consumer Cooperative." In Cox et al., eds, *Tactics and Techniques of Community Practice,* pp. 174–81. Itasca, Ill.: Peacock.

Moos, Rudolph H. 1979. "Social Ecological Perspectives on Health." In Stone, Cohen, and Adler, eds., *Health Psychology: a Handbook,* pp. 523–49.

Murphy, Michael J. 1977. "Organizational Approaches for Human Service Programs." In Anderson, Freiden, and Murphy, eds., *Managing Human Services,* pp. 193–229.

Nelson, Harry. 1981. "Doctors Vie for Patients in Portland." Los Angeles *Times,* March 21.

Numbers, Ronald L. 1979. *Almost Persuaded: American Physicians and Compulsory Health Insurance.* Baltimore: Johns Hopkins University Press.

Perlman, Janice E. 1976. "Grassrooting the System." *Social Policy,* 7(2):4–20.

Pelletier, Kenneth. 1979. *Holistic Medicine.* New York: Dell Books.

Redman, Eric. 1973. *The Dance of Legislation.* New York: Simon and Schuster.

Reiser, Stanley. 1978. *Medicare and the Design of Technology.* New York: Cambridge University Press.

Riessman, Frank. 1976. "How Does Self-Help Work?" *Social Policy,* 7(2):41–45.

Roemer, M. 1977. *Comparative National Policies on Health Care.* New York: Decker.

Rosengren, William R. 1980. *Sociology of Medicine.* New York: Harper and Row.

Rosentstock, Irwin M. and John P. Kirscht. 1979. "Why People Seek Health Care." In Stone, Cohen, and Adler, eds. *Health Psychology: a Handbook,* pp. 161–81.

Schlenker, Robert F. 1980. "The Future Health Care Organization." *Health Care Management Review* (Spring) 5(2):69–74.

Schroeder, Elaine. 1978. "Organizing Nonsexist Health Care for Women." In Bracht, ed., *Social Work in Health Care,* pp. 261–70.

Sheps, Cecil G. and Donald L. Madison. 1977. "The Medical Perspective." In Ginzberg, ed., *Regionalization and Health Policy,* pp. 18–19.

Sidel, Victor W. and Ruth Sidel. 1976. "Beyond Coping." *Social Policy* (September/October) 7(2):67.

Somers, Ann R. 1971. *Health Care in Transition: Directions for the Future.* Chicago: Hospital Research and Educational Trust.

——. 1977. *Health and Health Care: Policies in Perspective.* Germantown, Md.: Aspen Systems.

Spiegel, Allen D. and Herbert Hyman. 1978. *Basic Health Planning Methods.* Germantown, Md.: Aspen Systems.

Steiner, George. 1979. *Strategic Planning.* New York: Free Press.

Stevens, Rosemary. 1974. *Welfare Medicine in America: A Case Study of Medicaid.* New York: Free Press.

Stone, George C., Frances Cohen, and Nancy E. Adler, eds. 1979. *Health Psychology: A Handbook.* San Francisco: Jossey-Bass.

Tichy, Noel. 1977. *Organizational Design for Primary Health Care.* New York: Praeger.

Tracy, George S. and Zachary Gussow. 1976. "Self-Help Health Groups: A Grassroots Response to a Need for Services." *Journal of Applied Behavioral Science* (July/September), 12(3):382.

Trattner, Walter. 1979. *From Poor Law to Welfare State.* New York: Free Press.

Twaddle, Andrew C. 1979. *Sickness Behavior and the Sick Role.* Boston: Hall.

United Nations Secretary General. 1955. *Social Progress Through Community Development.* New York: UN Bureau of Social Affairs.

U.S. Department of Commerce, National Technical Information Service. 1976. *Trends Affecting the United States Health Care System.*

Withorn, Ann. 1980. *Social Policy* (November/December), 11(3):23.

12

The Practice of Community Work in Child Welfare

Geoffrey L. Pawson and Terry Russell

The purpose of traditional child welfare services is to support, supplement, or substitute for the care of children (Costin 1979:7–8). Despite the extensiveness of such services, up-to-date accurate statistics on the number of children served and the costs of such services do not exist. Drawing upon a number of reports from a variety of sources using discrepant definitions, Kahn (1977:101) estimated that in 1975 one million to three million children in the United States were receiving child welfare services through foster care, institutional placement, adoption, juvenile court, and inpatient psychiatric care. Nearly eight million children received social services through Aid to Families with Dependent Children (AFDC) in 1981 (U.S Department of Health and Human Services 1982:4). Current and accurate data are lacking for other countries as well. The most recent estimate of Canadian child welfare services was that nearly eighty thousand children were in need of protection in 1977 (Canadian Council on Children and Youth 1978:1), and when all Canadian child welfare programs are considered, it is estimated that 1.35 percent of the total population of children live in out-of-home placements under the care of some child welfare agency (Johnson 1981a:47).

These statistics reflect a narrow view of child welfare within the larger arena of services to children. If child welfare is viewed more broadly in terms of concern for the well-being of all children, then other issues arise. These include concerns involving the disproportionately high incidence of infant mortality among minority groups across North America, the growing number of teenage pregnancies, the rising suicide rate among youth under eighteen years of age, the increasing number of admissions of children to psychiatric facilities, the educational disabilities of an expanding number of school dropouts, and similar concerns.

In our opinion these broader problems are societal responsibilities and those who work with children need to become active in promoting change. Children are unable to act in concert on their own behalf due to their social, psychological, and economic dependency. While society already takes an interest in the protection of children and the promotion of their well-being, there is significant variation in the levels of concern and action taken on their behalf. Different states and provinces allocate varying amounts of their resources to meeting the educational, health, recreational, and social service needs of children located within their boundaries, and this varies again within local jurisdictions. The challenge to social work is: to what extent will the profession work to involve citizens, interest groups, organizations, and governments in a commitment to enhancing the lives of children and protecting their interests?

Historical Involvement in Child Welfare

The development of services to children passed through three overlapping phases from the seventeenth to the early twentieth century. These include laws emanating from Puritan times, the refuge managers, and the child savers (Lerman 1970:3).

The Puritan era was characterized by legislation that defined moral prescriptions for the behavior of children. To maintain these behaviors, a system of punishment was established which included the death penalty for crimes such as cursing or "smiting parents," rebelliousness, or denying the Scriptures as the infallible word of God (Powers 1970:9). Children who were delinquent or dependent were assumed to have inherited the moral inadequacies of their parents. To correct these deficits, stern discipline was required (Betten 1973:2). As a result, the care of dependent, neglected, and delinquent children was characterized by rigidity, suspicion, and hostility from the outset, and this has continued in various ways up to the present time.

In regard to children, the Puritan era was notable for Colonial America in terms of its importation from England of the Elizabethan Poor Laws (1601). This legislation decreed that dependent, orphaned, and criminal children were the responsibility of the local parish or municipality. Indenture and almshouse programs were established. Indenture was the forerunner of foster care, while the almshouse was the ancestral beginning of institutional care (Mayer, Richman, and Balcerzak 1977:28). Juvenile delinquents were handled by judicial process as adults before the law, and houses of correction were used to contain these young people until the late nineteenth century when juvenile reformatories were established (Powers 1970:10).

The refuge manager period emerged in response to concerns about the quality of life for children within the almshouse environment. These concerns emanated from some members of the judiciary, newspaper reporters, socially aware politicians, and enlightened citizens who tried to encourage communities to recognize the plight of children in the public institutions of that day. In response, private orphanages were established by religious organizations, guilds, and philanthropic groups (Zietz 1969:51–58). Concurrently, large public orphanages were established to care for the increased numbers of children who were homeless due to the cyclical problems of war, famine, and economic depression that plagued the nation. Citizen groups pressured governmental authorities to assume moral, legal, and operational responsibility for these residential care programs (Abbott 1938:3).

The popularity of institutional care during the nineteenth century was not confined to dependent children; private residential schools for upper-middle-class youths were also very popular. This created a rationale for residential care which extolled the redemptive qualities of institutional life (Gill 1974:70). These exaggerated claims were challenged, and a controversy arose regarding the merits of institutional care versus foster care for dependent children (Rothman 1971:35). Wolins and Piliaven (1964:3–35) have documented various aspects of the debate, focusing on the efforts of humanitarian leaders in the mid-1800s such as Charles Loring Brace and Charles W. Birtwell.

The controversy stimulated the development of the era of the child saver. This was a period of discovery of the problems surrounding poverty. The child-saving era traces back to the early 1800s when many middle-class women became concerned and involved with the plight of deprived children, perhaps due to the prevailing attitude that it was a woman's role to watch over their interests (Platt 1970). The work of these early child advocates, in concert with legislators and community groups, resulted in the establishment of juvenile courts, child labor laws, birth registration, universal education, mandatory school attendance, standards for children's institutions, and schools of social work.

During the 1800s there was a sharp debate about the causes of poverty and, subsequently, the handling of indigent families. The Social Darwinists such as Herbert Spencer and Andrew Carnegie argued against charity on the basis that indigent people were morally inadequate and to provide any kind of help would weaken the moral fabric of society. In contrast, economist John R. Commons, novelist William Dean Howells, Brown University President E. B. Andrews, and author Henry George argued that war, famine, urbanization, depression, and immigration were some of the direct causes of poverty (Betten 1973:4). It was during this period that the charity organization society (COS) and the settlement house movement evolved in North America. The COS tended toward the Social Darwinist approach and provided in-kind help and counseling only to the "worthy poor." The settlement houses, which introduced a Christian viewpoint to the environmental argument, both initiated and supported legislation to promote the well-being of families.

If one studies the community practice efforts of the COSs and the settlement houses, it is clear that both were intricately involved in community change. The process involved dynamic individuals assuming leadership roles and actively working to build powerful community constituencies. From their work, social and financial networks were established at local, state, and national levels on behalf of children and their families.

Turning first to the COS, Rev. Henry Solly was active in the Charity Organization Society in England, and he espoused the concepts of scientific philanthropy. As a result of his personal charity, novels, sermons, activity in men's clubs, and public lectures, Solly established the Garden City movement (Woodroofe 1975). Similarly, in 1881 Mary Richmond developed a constituency of 9,000 contributors in Philadelphia, which was the largest such effort in the United States at that time (Rauch 1975). During periods of attack by the press Richmond could defend the position of the COS, namely, to provide help only to the deserving poor, because of strong community backing. In Canada, the COS also had its champions. Charlotte Whitton was a flamboyant and controversial figure who actively worked to develop scientific charity. Partially as the result of her work, the Canadian Council on Child Welfare was established in 1920, and the mandate of the Council was similar to that of the Children's Bureau in the United States (Rooke and Schnell 1981).

Using similar community support networks for different purposes, Julia Lathrop's efforts typified the style of work used by leaders of the settlement house movement. She was appointed as first chief of the new Children's Bureau in Washington. Her informal constituency of resource people "included college women (Association of Collegiate Alumnae), clubwomen (Daughters of the American Revolution, General Federation of Women's Clubs, Chicago's Women's Club), suffragists (Cattand Shaw of the National American Women's Suffrage Association), philanthropists (Rosenwald Foundation, Russell Sage Foundation, Elizabeth McCormick Memorial Fund), social welfare experts (National Council of Charities and Corrections), scholars (Small, Mead, Dewey, et al. at the University of Chicago)" and others (Parker and Carpenter 1981:61). It was the power of Lathrop's support networks that facilitated her work toward reducing infant mortality, establishing birth registrations for children, enforcing new child labor legislation, and similar achievements.

As the COS and the settlement houses continued their work on behalf of families and children, other specific programs were instituted to care for and protect children. Beginning with Charles Loring Brace, the New York Children's Aid Society introduced the placing-out system which resulted in obtaining free foster care in rural environments for about one hundred thousand children between 1854 and 1929 (Kadushin 1967:355–63). Similarly in Canada, Dr. Thomas Barnado led a movement which placed more than eighty thousand children from England's poorest areas with Canadian farm families (Bagnell 1980). This system proved to be controversial because many of the children were exploited. As a reaction to this, Charles W. Birtwell in Boston began using free homes that were selected specifically to meet the needs of individual children, thus reversing the expectation that children meet the families' need for cheap farm labor. Later, Martin Van Buren Van Arsdale initiated the practice of paying foster parents to board children through the State Children's Home Society in Indiana. By 1923, thirty-four states had adopted this practice (Kadushin 1967:361).

The Great Depression of the 1930s stimulated a new form of community involvement and participation at the federal level of government in Canada and the United States. The concept of the mother's pension had been adopted in 1909 by the First White House Conference on Children. The advancement of this proposal was spurred by voluntary agencies insisting that economic hazards to a large number of families could only be handled by government action. By 1933, a wide spectrum of voluntary agencies supported and worked collaboratively to obtain legislation that embodied the concept of a national Social Security program (Pumphrey and Pumphrey 1973).

With the passage of the Social Security Act of 1935 in the United States, the federal government responded to the pressure and assumed the major role for assuring the financial care of families and the elderly. Canada followed this lead, and federal unemployment insurance was introduced in 1940 followed by family allowances in 1945. Later, both Canada and the United States government continued to expand income security programs by including medical services. Again, this came about through pressure from wide sectors of the local, national, and international community. For example, Social Security recommendations were included as a part of the Atlantic Charter of 1941, and in 1944 the International Labor Conference in Philadelphia adopted income security and medical care as major programmatic recommendations which would be advocated (Statistics Canada 1976:5–14).

After 1935, global planning conferences and position statements based upon research reports became a means of stimulating community services and legislative change. For example, the Beveridge Report (1942) in England and the Marsh Report (1943) in Canada laid the philosophical guidelines for social program reconstruction. In the United States, new programs were built into the various entitlements within the Social Security Act, or were designed to be adjuncts to this act, such as the National School Lunch Program (1954), federal funding for social services for Aid to Dependent Children (1956), and the extension of child welfare services to rural areas.

Demonstration projects became popular in the 1950s and 1960s as a means of testing new programs or stimulating interest in innovative service delivery systems. For example, area projects designed to involve citizens in solving their own commuity problems were demonstrated in New York and Ohio in the 1950s (Santiago 1972:76); the St. Paul Family Centered Project attempted to demonstrate the value of intensive social work services to a limited number of multiproblem families (Geismar and Ayres 1959); the Gray Areas Program funded by the Ford Foundation tried to improve inner-city schools; and the Henry Street Settlement Community Action Program attacked delinquency problems on Manhattan's East Side (Santiago 1972:77).

With the advent of the Economic Opportunity Act (1964), social work community practice shifted away from its association with program development, and many social workers assumed a reform approach to broader concerns such as empowering the poor and the consumers of social services. Welfare rights organizations became vocal and persistent vehicles for change in communities across the nation (Axinn and Levin 1975:249).

The period 1960–1975 was one of social turmoil. The family, church, school, business, labor, and government came under extreme stress as young people challenged the basic principles upon which these institutions were founded. Community programs for youth in transition circumstances proliferated as agencies and community groups moved to develop crisis centers, youth hostels, drug therapy units, storefront medical and legal services, drop-in centers, employment, and other programs responsive to newly emerging needs. These services were not limited to the children of poverty or multiproblem families; rather, these programs were open to youth from all socioeconomic levels. Despite the fact that a cross section of people in local communities was involved in initiating and supporting these novel programs, they were not able to survive the funding cutbacks of the 1970s.

Many traditional child welfare services for children moved

toward community-based programs during this period. Large insitutions for children waned in favor of increased reliance on foster care; those that survived did so by offering specialized services for emotionally disturbed, delinquent, or handicapped client groups that were less easily cared for in communities. New pharmacological developments spurred interest in deinstitutionalization of children with serious behavior problems, and this posed new challenges for community social work which was struggling to gain community acceptance. For children in the care of the state a variety of community-based programs developed, including specialized foster care, group homes, and day care which served as alternatives to traditional foster homes or institutionalization. In many instances social workers found themselves interacting with community agencies and institutions, such as the public schools, to obtain needed services and programming, while at the same time they were meeting with community groups and neighbors who were suspicious and hostile toward this trend.

Evaluation of the effects of the social interventions of the 1970s has proved ambiguous. The War on Poverty was judged not a success, and major programs such as Head Start still did not deal with many of the problems of poverty and multiproblem families. Delinquency continued to increase as did many other social problems. This resulted in widespread misunderstanding about the purposes and effectiveness of programs. This certainly laid the foundation for cutbacks in funding for social service programs.

Recently, new research is more optimistic. For example, Piper and Warner (1980–81) in their review of the literature, suggest that Romig (1978) has identified distinguishing factors for successful residential care. Further, they suggest that in addition to individual work with youth, community social work practice may be a crucial factor in the success of treatment programs located in the community. Deinstitutionalization should include careful collaborative planning with local agencies to assure that vital services and complementary programs for youth are actually available. In addition, neighbors and community groups need to be aware and involved if they are expected to accept or support these programs.

In 1979, the world celebrated the International Year of the Child. This celebration was designed to renew interest in meeting children's needs and upgrading the standards of living for children.

Paradoxically, the decade of the 1980s ushered in worldwide financial problems which threatened existing services and created an uncertain future for child welfare. It is frightening to read the call from the Child Welfare League of America for urgent action because "Fiscal Year 1983 looms as a disaster for children and their families" (1982:1). Budget cuts in a range of programs have occurred and more are being planned. If these take place, they will cripple or effectively dismantle major programs and threaten to undo concepts of social responsibility for children that were painstakingly developed over the past fifty years. Community social work can play a dynamic role in counteracting these forces through refocusing interest on children, the most vulnerable of the nation's citizens.

Community Organization Issues and Problems in Child Welfare

This section delineates some of the issues and problems of social work community practice in the field of child welfare. The examples focus on the roles of community workers, leaving strategies of implementation to the final section of this paper.

SOCIETAL AND POLITICAL ATTITUDES

The first general attitude arises from the sociolegal status of children in countries that follow the British legal tradition. Over the centuries four concepts have emerged that guide legislative, judicial, and administrative approaches. Although these concepts do not have the power of law, they symbolize and guide societal expectations relating to family matters and the care of children by parents and legal guardians. Included are: *patria potestas*, or the power of the family to protect its cultural, religious, and social integrity from outside interference; *parens patriae*, or the power of the state to intervene in family matters in exceptional circumstances; *the best interest of the child*, which places the onus of responsibility on the state to protect the interests of the child above all other interests; and a newer concept, *the child before the law,* which demands special legal protection for children in civil and criminal matters (Canadian Council on Children and Youth 1978:10–16).

The application of these concepts in law and social practice guides decisions made on behalf of children. The current debate revolves around traditional attitudes regarding the sanctity of the family versus the need for protection of children, children's rights, and the support of families with financial allowances and needed services. These three concepts receive endorsements in special circumstances, but many people still believe that they undermine the strength of families as independent social units.

The second societal attitude involves the traditional stereotype of family roles. North American society still believes that the father is the breadwinner and the mother is the caretaker of children, and that only this model is the highest form of family life (Costin 1979:1–8). Success in fulfilling these traditional family roles is often used as a major measure of success by society. Consequently, programs that seem to alter or support changes in traditional family structures are viewed suspiciously. Advocates of such attitudes seek to maintain the status quo and often limit the creative development of needed services designed to meet current social realities, such as the prevalence of mothers who hold full-time jobs.

The third community attitude that must be considered in developing services is the skepticism associated with large-scale professional or bureaucratic efforts to intervene in family problem situations. Privacy in family matters is highly valued. There is a reluctance on the part of public funders to develop comprehensive and/or universal programs unless they are clearly supported by a majority of the general community. At this point the public does not appear to understand or enthusiastically support such programs even if the obvious beneficiaries would be children.

Since governments in both Canada and the United States are major funders of child welfare programs, the politics of child care is a major factor that must be considered in creating, designing, or implementing programs. Boles (1980:344–49) argues that a comprehensive child and family policy is not likely to be developed due to the divisiveness between various local, regional, and national interest groups. Howe (1978) has reservations about the usefulness of legislative advocacy to benefit "devalued" members of society since legislators tend to reflect the majority's value system and are not likely to champion or support the interests and welfare of those viewed as deviants. Child welfare continues to have some degree of appeal based upon the need to protect the young; family programs have less support unless various sectors of society can perceive that they will derive particular benefits.

The slow development of day care services in North America provides an example of the effect of community and political attitudes on service development. The popularity of day care in Canada and the United States has changed according to historical circumstance. During World War II, day care was highly regarded, and governments actively supported these programs since they allowed mothers to work as part of the war effort. Following the war, money was withdrawn from day care, and it was not until the 1960s that renewed interest developed. A number of groups pressed local, state, and the national government in the United States to implement this service; included in these groups were the National Committee for the Day Care of Children, social work and educational authorities, the National Association for the Education of Young Children, the Association for Childhood Education International, and the Black Child Development Institute (Lansburgh 1977:142–43). These efforts, along with the philosophical thrust that came from the War on Poverty, resulted in day care services designed for actual or potential welfare recipients, emphasizing the opportunities that day care offered for preventing or correcting social and economic disadvantage.

Ruderman (1968) studied attitudes toward day care, using a sample of community leaders associated with social service programs. Their attitudes were that day care should be used for children with special needs; concern was expressed that wider application would encourage more mothers to leave home responsibilities and go to work. Lansburgh (1977:144) suggests that negative attitudes toward day care are built upon concerns related to weakening the integrity of the traditional family through the establishment of communal child-rearing practices. As the result of conflicting public opinion, President Nixon vetoed comprehensive day care legislation, while Presidents Ford and Carter used their influence to have such bills withdrawn before they were passed (Boles 1980:355–57). In Canada the establishment of day care is the responsibility of the provinces. Although incentives are available through cost-shared federal programs, there has been limited growth.

Analysis of these concerns within the context of the four social attitudes discussed earlier reveals the complexity of community practice. It would appear that a sizable portion of the population feels that universal day care would seriously jeopardize the integrity of the family. Intervention by the state is viewed as unwarranted despite evidence to the contrary. The underlying rationale is predicated on the belief that such programs are not in the best interests of families. Further, they are seen as professional and bureaucratic interventions that will change traditional concepts of family roles. However, for welfare families, these programs are viewed differently. Since they are designed to keep people off the welfare rolls, day care programs directly serve the community's interest. Also, it follows that these children will benefit due to the enriched environment attributed to these programs when compared to the dreary stereotype of welfare family life. Specifically, there is hope that day care can, through education and socialization, interrupt the chronic cycle of poverty, dependency, and problems that characterizes future generations reared in welfare households.

Community practice emanating from day care settings will have to perform a variety of important functions. Of utmost concern will be identification of community need, community-based research for planning services and mounting effective public education programs. Facts must be kept before the public if they are to appreciate the increasing number of women who are working. It is projected that women who work will be 62 percent of the work force by 1990 (Child Welfare League of America 1981:61), and this poses potential hazards for children unless quality, low-cost day care is readily available.

Another task of community practitioners will be to advocate improved standards and monitoring of day care programs. A scandal of any magnitude would provide considerable ammunition to those opposed to the concept of day care. Also, practitioners need to develop local networks of individuals, groups, associations, and agencies that can form firm coalitions and take clear positions on day care issues. Simultaneously, vertical networks need to be established to collaborate with state and national governments in order to supply information and lobby so that both bureaucrats and politicians are informed about, and responsive to, changing local needs (Brager and Specht 1973:20).

Kramer and Specht (1969:9) define community as a range of collectivities including neighborhoods, cities, regions, or nations, as well as social, racial, and political subgroups. In child welfare, there are three overlapping communities. The first includes special-interest groups and associations that advocate for children who possess common characteristics, such as foster children, adoptive children, and delinquent children. Second are the groups of adults associated with the child welfare network, who may or may not be formally organized, such as single parents, those receiving public assistance, parents of delinquent, psychotic, or emotionally disturbed children, as well as parent or teacher groups for developmentally-disabled, learning-disabled, or hearing-impaired children. Finally, professional organizations, employee associations, and voluntary societies should function as active local and national subgroups to promote the concepts of enlightened child welfare.

All too often community practice in child welfare has not received the support, legitimacy, and commitment of agency professionals. It is not enough to treat the child and ignore the family, neighborhood, and societal conditions that contribute to such problems in the first place, and then fail again by neglecting to make the public aware of the problems and the need for adequate levels of quality services. All too often the blame is placed on sponsors and funders, who may in fact be unaware of local conditions.

Increased efforts to intervene at the community level will also serve to highlight some interesting differences in both goals and approaches. As Brager and Specht (1973:171–87) have noted, the sponsors of community practice often have a profound influence on the type of change processes utilized by practitioners and on the purposes of their activity, and this may serve preconceived organizational interests as well as clients.

Deinstitutionalization of residential centers for children is a useful example. This issue emerged in the 1970s, and three basic arguments are evident in the debate. The first suggests that institutional care is an abdication of community responsibility (Coughlin 1977); the second argues that institutional care is an infringement on the legal and civil rights of children (Kenniston and the Carnegie Council on Children 1977:193); and the final argument holds that institutional care is a needed resource in the continuum of child care services (Reid 1974b).

In social work, if community practitioners are hired by a children's rights organization, then the position of the sponsoring organization and the practitioners will probably reflect an activist role which may result in organizing parent groups, funders of service, and the general public to promote the provision of community care programs, or it may be one part of a larger plan to focus attention on a range of issues concerning children's rights. However, if a community practitioner is hired by a family service agency, the purpose of the intervention may be directed toward such changes as improved residential services, greater parental access to their children, quality discharge planning using children's natural homes or augmented community resources, or the provision of family support services.

In contrast, if the practitioner was hired by a residential center, then the role might involve public education, organizing parents to support the provision of effective placement, or negotiation with funders to provide needed residential resources or adequately financed contracts for services. The purpose defined by the residential center may be organizational survival. This purpose may also be held by the practitioner, but it is likely that there are other legitimate motives, such as assuring that institutions have the resources to care for and effectively rehabilitate the complex and stubborn problems presented to them by referral sources.

Clearly, there are trade-offs relative to the needs of the target community and the sponsor that need to be considered. Community practice requires a professional objectivity about the issues being debated based on knowledge and understanding of all arguments and interests. Ultimately, social work community practitioners must commit themselves to a position that reflects the suggestions and ideas of the target community, and this may necessitate the development of opportunities to encourage community suggestions, advice, and conceptions of their best interests; at times this may result in a healthy tension as the exchange of ideas and viewpoints educates all parties to the process.

GOALS

The goals of each party are important considerations. Etzioni (1961:6) defines goals as a desired state of affairs, while Thompson and McEwan (1958:23–31) view goals as means of defining relationships. In terms of community practice in child welfare, there are four sets of possible goals, including the goals of the community, the goals of the sponsor, the goals of the practitioner, and the goals of actual or potential clients. It is possible to have congruence, partial congruence, or incongruence of goals depending upon how the stated purposes are interpreted or whether hidden agendas are exercised by all four parties. In all cases, goals limit the types of relationships and interventions which are possible.

The impact of goals can be exemplified in relation to "black-market" babies. Adoption is a highly regarded child welfare program that usually occurs through authorized public or private adoption agencies in Canada and the United States. However, in some United States jurisdictions, the use of third-party intermediaries is allowed or not specifically prohibited. This allows physicians, lawyers, or others to arrange adoption placements that are legalized through the courts in return for remuneration. However, this system is open to abuse. Entrepreneurs are often able to charge wealthy couples exorbitant prices for desirable babies if they are unwilling to undergo screening or wait for a child to be available. Also, charges have been made that "procurers" locate pregnant women by waiting outside pregnancy-testing laboratories. These young women, usually teenagers, are pressured to give up their children at birth in return for payment. Further, it has been reported that there are baby farms where pregnant females are paid to live, or young females are paid to become pregnant providing they release their children for independent adoptions (Meezan, Katz, and Russo 1978:4–9).

In analyzing these problems within the context of goals, it can be argued that public apathy toward abuse of independent adoptions is based on lack of goal specificity. The decision of the natural mother to give up a child for independent adoption is felt to be a matter of choice in jurisdictions where this is legal. Consistent with this concept, the social goal of achieving permanency for illegitimate or unwanted children has been achieved, and the adoptive parents in "purchasing" a baby have indicated their desire to be good parents. Since the courts legalize the procedure, the best interest and legal rights of the child are assumed to have been assured.

Zald (1963) suggests that goals help focus attention on areas of concern. The most interested groups probably will be adoption agencies and child advocacy groups. Their common goals will be to have all adoptions processed through licensed adoption agencies in order to limit abuses often associated with independent adoptions. But this may not be a common community goal. Independent adoptions are a means of quickly solving the social and financial problems of the birth mother; changes in the adoption requirements may seriously limit the financial interests of procurement intermediaries; and doctors, lawyers, and others would have to channel their activities through social agencies, which may create conflict between these professions and social workers. Goal conflict leads to confusion, and the result is a tendency to avoid issues that are seemingly insolvable.

Young (1966) suggests that goals help to facilitate planning. Community social workers can document the problems through service data and research while building linkages among concerned services agencies and governmental leaders as a process of stimulating action. Such a process is slow at first and practitioners have to have dedication and fortitude to remain in a planning role. As consensus grows about goal desirability, however, joint and collaborative planning proceeds with increased momentum.

VALUES AND PURPOSE

A great deal has been written about the relationship of values and purpose in the profession of social work and how this relationship forms part of a constellation distinguishing this profession from other disciplines (Bartlett 1958). Siporin (1975:61–90) details these relationships at considerable length, noting the intricacies of these two areas. The application of values and purpose in clinical practice is usually relatively clear, but the application of these areas to community social work is more diffuse. However, if community social work operates as part of the social work discipline, then it follows that the philosophy of social work must hold for this form of practice.

It is not possible to detail the application of social work values and purposes in community practice within the constraints of this article. Let it suffice to trace the application of the values of dignity and worth to community practice since they are central to social work philosophy.

The issue of transracial and ethnic adoption and foster care is a major issue in child welfare across North America. The major elements of the debate involve the lack of a sufficient number of homes to accommodate children of various races and the concern of minority groups that adoption or foster care in transracial homes removes children from their cultural identity and heritage.

Community workers involved in this issue are subject to a variety of dilemmas. Practice knowledge suggests that permanency is a major factor in the development of children; similarly, cultural identity is integral to the development of personality. To reconcile these two areas, a variety of new endeavors are being attempted. These include new efforts to develop homes within racial groups where there are shortages, arranging for cultural involvements for those minority children living in transracial homes, cultural exchanges between foster or adoptive parents and minority community leaders, and forums to heighten awareness about the need for homes from particular racial and ethnic groups.

If a community practitioner is hired to locate and develop interracial homes by an indigenous organization, the issue of "standards" must be addressed. For example, in Canada, native leaders are adamant about the need to discontinue transracial care for native children, and they have charged that this is a form of cultural genocide (Johnson 1981). Also, it is the feeling of natives that white "standards" for foster care or adoption cannot be applied to them because those expectations are culturally inappropriate.

In terms of the value of dignity and respect, the issue is

complex. Practitioners must decide who is the target community and what are the desired goals. If ethnic children are the target community, then decisions must be made as to whether dignity and respect for children are best accomplished in transracial homes of higher socioeconomic standing or whether it is more important to have children placed with people of their own race or culture, sometimes in poverty situations. On the other hand, if potential Indian foster parents are the target community, then the question becomes how to maintain their dignity and respect while helping them to meet standards. In most cases, the definition of community is ambiguous, and the practitioner is torn between conflicting values. Confounding this issue are the cultural background and racial identity of the professional. If this person is from a minority group, knowledge of indigenous community customs and standards will be useful, but these concepts must be synthesized with values and purposes of the sponsor, the best interests of children, and professional objectivity.

The guidance provided by the philosophy of social work is often unclear due to the magnitude and complexity of the issues. Dignity and worth are guiding concepts that need to be carefully applied to hard decisions. Although they set limits on the practitioner and provide general direction, these concepts are not as clear as they are in the companion practices of casework and group work.

Approaches to Community Practice

Theoretical models are well defined in social casework and group work, but they are less clear and developed in community work. Nevertheless, if community practice is to develop within social work, then theoretical formulations are needed to provide guidelines and a means of conceptualizing the work of the practitioner.

In this section five approaches to community practice are discussed, including planning, community development, community liaison, program development and coordination, and political empowerment. Our emphasis is on practical application of these approaches. Examples are used to illustrate the types of strategies used by practitioners with subsequent discussion of each model.

PLANNING

Ross suggests that the impetus for social planning is dissatisfaction within a community about a particular condition (1955:135). Gilbert and Specht (1977:1), however, contend that in most situations social plans are developed and implemented by experts who often rely on their own conception of community well-being.

In child welfare, the relationship between a child, the child's parents, and the community is a triad that requires support to maximize the potential of the relationship. This interdependency experiences stress when the types of support that society must offer are nontraditional since parents and communities are highly protective of the sanctity of the family. Community desires to preserve the traditional meaning of family present severe barriers to legislative reform, and few politicians are willing to challenge such opinions even if they are cognizant of problems that require attention.

Hibbard (1981:557–65) argues that a new social planning paradigm rests on cultural pluralism, and although there is a range of viewpoints as to how it should be applied, the common element is the displacement of authority for planning from experts and elites to those involved in social interactions. Social planning interventions must include the various individuals and groups that will be affected as well as the larger community that may be indirectly involved.

Boles (1980:344–59) traces the development of comprehensive day care legislation in the United States. Despite three separate bills introduced in the Congress and Senate, day care is still thought of as a program for the poor based on the assumption that it will facilitate their obtaining or maintaining employment. Boles concludes that legislation providing such care to a range of different people may be possible if programs are federally guaranteed under a specific funding formula, but the responsibility for program design and administration must rest with local providers and consumers.

This allows for local differences within a pluralistic society; also, it strongly indicates that services for a range of families are likely to follow a path of incremental development.

The basic strategy of the social worker in community planning for children and families may be to support an incremental growth of services rather than fight for universal programs. As communities have opportunities to consider the benefits of programs available in other jurisdictions, citizens can be encouraged to initiate their own efforts to obtain such services. In order to minimize local resistance, practitioners should promote the establishment of quality programs that are not perceived as radical innovations. Further, efforts should be made to involve a range of potential consumer groups in planning forums that allow people involvement in designing the types of programs they are ready to utilize.

The community practitioner needs to maintain a short- and a long-term perspective in social planning. For example, new ideas in child welfare and family services can be introduced through attempts to prompt agencies and community groups to establish new programs. Although these may be rejected in the short term, the ideas that are planted may germinate later.

The potential for planned change based upon empirical data, internally consistent approaches, and trial or pilot applications is clearly evident. However, the practitioner must encourage participants to include as part of the strategy a variety of contingency plans, since what seems a logical and rational case of action to planners based upon their knowledge and perceptions may not be perceived as valuable by constituents with limited information or different needs. This suggests that community education and public relations are vital factors in the planning process. Mechanisms to educate the public can include widely circulated factual documents, public forums, conferences, community advisory groups, and other forms of constituency involvement. These mechanisms inform citizens, clarify issues, and encourage inputs that can serve to revise proposed plans in order to increase their acceptability.

Local citizen groups and their representatives should be given opportunities to exchange ideas and express their attitudes. Even planning at regional and federal levels should offer the opportunity for communities to control what happens in their jurisdiction. This does not assume that local area management is most beneficial for clients; rather, it assumes that an incremental approach based on local control is most productive in the long run, and encourages development of a variety of programs that reflect local attitudes and customs.

COMMUNITY DEVELOPMENT

The major emphasis in community development is the process of community building where the organizer creates an identification of common interests through stimulating and facilitating community awareness and involvement and the growth of citizen leadership (Brager and Specht 1973:27). Many of these concepts have evolved in rural areas or undeveloped countries, and they have been translated, with some difficulty, to urban areas within North America (Grosser 1973:204).

An example is the case of Sandy Bay, an isolated Indian village in northern Saskatchewan, Canada. In the past thirty years, the social fabric of this community has been devastated by change due to the village's location in a resource-rich area of the province. As a result of outside intrusions, traditional patterns of mutual help through extended families and neighborhood networks began to deteriorate, and children were particularly vulnerable. Previously, children were an accepted community responsibility; if parents could not care for their children, another family provided for them.

In the early 1960s, Sandy Bay was accessible only by air or overland through the bush. Local services were provided by an outpost nurse, a policeman, and a priest, all of whom were residents in the community. When children were neglected or temporarily abandoned, a provincial child welfare worker was contacted by radiophone to come up and investigate the problem. In many cases, children were temporarily removed from the village until parents returned or family disputes were resolved. This system was extremely expensive and not particularly effective.

Because the village was identified as having some of the worst social problems in the area, a community development project was planned for Sandy Bay by the Department of Social Services. Social workers began flying into the village and staying for several days. Initially they slept in an abandoned building because of the lack of housing, but this inconvenience was necessary in order to meet the local people and become familiar with village customs. It became clear quite early in the process that the only formal group in the community was the local chapter of Alcoholics Anonymous (AA), whose members met nightly at the recreation center. Workers joined this group every evening and noted that both children and adults came to the recreation hall to talk with this group.

Gradually, the subject of protective services was introduced by the social worker, and the group was asked to consider alternatives to the present system of care. A child care committee was formed after extensive deliberations lasting several months, during which the expectations and responsibilities of the proposed committee were examined in great detail. Finally, the committee developed both an approach to the problem that included identification of children requiring protection within the village and a resource network utilizing extended family members and neighbors (Soiseth 1970:8–9).

The Minister of Social Services for Saskatchewan formally recognized the work of the group with a plaque that was hung in the local recreation hall. Further, one member of the committee was authorized to serve as a resident child welfare worker, under the authority of existing legislation, and he was provided with an identification that indicated his status and legal authority in child welfare matters. From this small beginning, Sandy Bay residents went on meeting and set up day care services, a group home for older adolescents, foster care, and an alcohol treatment unit. The University of Regina, through its School of Social Work, was an active participator and resource for the community and made a film, *We Can,* designed to show other communities how they might proceed to resolve problems based on the Sandy Bay experience.

This example indicates the importance of developing goal congruency and consensus in a problem area. Although the community social worker, sponsor, and community were highly committed to instituting workable programs for children, it can be argued that a range of other factors helped to stimulate this interest. For the community practitioner, the existing system of care was inadequate, and there were indications that its child welfare policies and services were contributing to family breakdown rather than strengthening family life in Sandy Bay.

With the Department of Social Services serving as sponsor, both political and financial benefits were apparent. The multitude of social problems in the village were well known, and these difficulties were adding fuel to an ongoing controversy about exploitation of rural natives living in resource-rich areas of the province. If changes could be facilitated, it was anticipated that both the village and the wider community would benefit and in time there could be increased support and public responsiveness to these concerns.

In terms of the community, the villagers were most anxious to keep their children at home, but there was a sense of powerlessness. The group of AA members who formed the first child care committee were committed not only to performing designated child care functions but also to aggressively attacking the alcohol problem within the village. The skills they learned about obtaining resources and collaborating to institute programs carried over to a range of other problem areas.

Part of the strategy used by the community worker was the use of symbols. These included the plaque from the Minister and an identification card for the villager designated as a child welfare worker. The importance of these symbols is evidenced by the fact that the original plaque still hangs in the recreation hall, and when the indigenous child welfare worker lost his wallet in a canoeing accident, he immediately informed the community worker that "his card had drowned." A new one was quickly issued.

One major strength of this model rests on the community identifying common concerns. Application of this practice approach in child welfare is particularly appealing due to the high priority most people accord to serving those who require special protection. Also, this approach stimulates the transfer of power to community members, which means that they experience a sense of regaining control of decisions regarding the welfare of their children. This can be a powerful motivating force.

COMMUNITY LIAISON

The role of working with communities through direct involvement of agency staff, usually administrators, has been identified as a legitimate community practice function. Murphy (1954:308–9) listed a variety of community interorganizatinal activities, while Sieder (1960) expanded on this aspect of agency operations by focusing on mobilization of support for agencies and development of community resources.

Brager and Specht (1973:223–30) indicate that an executive can offer important resources for boards such as knowledge, reports on communication with staff and other agencies, and assistance in decision-making.

Although social agencies are capable of producing positive community relationships, it is inherent in the approach that there is a need to balance the needs of clients with the needs of organizations. If the equilibrium tips in either direction, programs can be seriously affected and jeopardize the credibility of an agency or have a deleterious affect on clients.

The development and growth of a residential treatment center in Saskatchewan, Canada, reflect one aspect of the comunity liaison approach. In 1964, a change of provincial governments resulted in the closing of the only residential treatment center in the province due to questions about its cost effectiveness. Within two years, a large number of emotionally disturbed children were being placed in treatment centers located outside the province. A newly appointed Director of Child Welfare was most interested in reestablishing residential treatment services. When this interest became known, a professional social worker moved to mobilize professionals and citizens so that a proposal was presented that was formally accepted by the Minister of Social Welfare within two weeks.

The strategy of the social worker in developing the original proposal evolved through discussion with a variety of people who were already familiar with the attitudes of government or who had worked in the residential care field. Key variables appeared that needed to be dealt with in the proposal. First, the Minister of Social Welfare was a Mennonite farmer who highly valued rural life for raising children. The previous center had been located within a city neighborhood whose residents had opposed the program. Second, the new government was suspicious of civil service staff based on its perception that these people did not support the government and therefore should not be entrusted with developing the program. Third, although the government was receptive to reestablishing residential treatment services, it wanted to maintain tight fiscal control in order to prevent spiraling costs. Based on this information gathered from knowledgeable people, an ad hoc group decided to locate the center in a small rural setting outside a major city. This met the requirements of the Minister while facilitating the program's ability to obtain needed professional services.

In developing community support, the community worker recruited a few respected community leaders who were well known to the government for their political support. This group also was a source for the agency's first board of directors, and their involvement alleviated the government's concern about funding a service that was in opposition to its political ideology. This type of board was not fully representative but was a rational response to the realities of the environment (Pfeffer 1972:226).

The proposed program was based on plans for a facility that would care for twelve children, and there was no attempt to conduct a survey of needs since it was already known that the demand clearly outstripped the allocated resources. By beginning small, it was hoped the program would grow over time as its worth and the need for its services were demonstrated.

Another strategy was careful timing of the project. The organizer submitted the proposal early enough to have special project money allocated by the beginning of the new budget year. Although the government agreed only to a per diem rate and monthly advance payments, this provided sufficient cash flow to arrange a mortgage on some property, refurbish the residence, and hire staff. All of this had to occur within three months, due to concern that prolonged delay or debate over the project, or other requests for programs, would jeopardize the new service.

The community worker operated as the center or linking agent of an informal system that was backed by a loosely organized board. Major interorganizational involvements focused on the public funder, and the Department of Social Welfare was kept constantly informed about developments in order to coordinate efforts.

From this small beginning, the population of the center expanded to eighty children in ten years, and a range of programs was established including group homes, specialized foster care, special education facilities, summer facilities, and wilderness programs. The first board of directors was highly committed to the program. Over time, the board became educated about the purposes of the center, and appropriate committees were appointed to set policies and oversee agency operations.

In analyzing this example within the context of the community liaison approach, the initial requirements of interorganizational involvements, mobilization of support from the community's leaders, and obtaining resources were all met. It is clear that the service was designed to suit the requirements of the government but in such a way that the integrity of the program was not violated and a needed service was initiated.

The strengths of the community liaison approach include rapid application of ideas for services based on predetermined goals. Since the goals are specific, citizen and consumer involvement can be selective, thereby creating the potential for a committed and cohesive organization. This in itself facilitates the effectiveness of the model in selected situations.

The basic weakness of this model is that it usually does not allow for a high degree of widespread community participation. By developing an organization of like-minded citizens the potential for constructive criticism may be thwarted, thereby creating the possibility that the program will not meet the needs of particular groups in the community. Further, organizational goals may become so parochial that they do not take into account other community needs or recognize the importance of collaborative action within the network of agencies. However, community liaison can produce change for community benefit as long as the weaknesses are recognized and safeguards such as advisory groups and interagency collaboration are maintained.

PROGRAM DEVELOPMENT AND COORDINATION

Litwak and Hylton (1962:566) give three reasons for agencies to enter into formal linkages with other organizations: interdependence, information gathering, and monitoring the allocation of resources. Evan (1971:33–45) goes further, arguing that agencies use other groups as sources for new ideas, while Reid (1964:420) points out that sustained interorganizational relationships and cooperation lead to coordination.

Community practitioners can achieve coordination in a variety of ways. Two examples illustrate this point. In 1970, the Commission on Emotional and Learning Disorders in Children (CELDIC) completed a national study of Canadian children entitled *One Million Children*. Six national voluntary agencies and one international agency agreed to sponsor the study, and funding for this ambitious undertaking was provided through a combination of federal, provincial, and foundation grants, and contributions from the business community. Provincial and territorial organizations brought thousands of people together to consider the present state of children's services in Canada. Service agencies, advocacy groups, associations, and concerned citizens shared a variety of program information with each other in small gatherings that were conducted across the nation. This involvement provided a means of heightening public awareness, developing interorganizational linkages, and redefining the needs and programs required by children in various communities and regions. Also, the meetings provided a forum for informally evaluating existing service delivery systems.

From the work of CELDIC, local and national coalitions formed and pressed government for expanded resources based on their revised sense of what needs existed. This would not have occurred if there had been no opportunities to build relationships and share information. No national solutions were instituted, given the federal structure of Canada, but a variety of services strengthened, and new resources were made available through governmental and private sources. In fact, the report has provided a philosophical foundation for a decade of service development.

The second example involves the establishment of Mobile Family Services in Regina, Saskatchewan, an agency that was developed as a coordinated effort involving the city police, child welfare, family social services, and mental health agencies. The initial collaboration of these agencies was directed toward obtaining federal and provincial funding to launch innovative programs appropriate for the changing life style of youth during the 1960s. The project involved hiring young people to operate a twenty-four-hour crisis telephone program with appropriate follow-up services. Though it has been argued that the youth were co-opted, the service that resulted was beneficial to the children who were served and did help agencies to move toward more flexible modes of service and greater recognition of the need to coordinate their efforts. As the youth crisis subsided and the special funding was withdrawn, the original agencies agreed to continue the project in expanded form through existing agency budgets. The expanded services included child abuse, emergency child welfare and social assistance, social service participation in emergency police calls involving suicide and domestic disputes, and emergency services. To achieve these ends, further professionalization of the service resulted, and the original emphasis on youth participation ensured the move toward quality programs and fostered the coordination of efforts among the participating agencies.

Analysis of these two examples suggests that collaboration can lead to coordination and heightened interest in particular issues that are of common concern. In these instances, collaboration stimulated and encouraged agencies to review and adapt their policies and practices in order to provide services in a more effective way. The basic strategy of the community practice involved bringing agencies together around specific issues and arranging various community forums to encourage the design of new resources, assessment of existing services, and collaboration with integrated service delivery systems.

Use of the model assumes that there is enough goal consensus to support mutual collaboration. This is an ideal that is seldom maintained over time since disequilibrium can occur if strong agencies become sources of power unto themselves. This can lead to organizational inflexibility, which is usually the condition which prompted the original coordination effort. Also, the coordination effort can be sabotaged in the initial stage if organizational domains are threatened or agency resources are usurped. Nevertheless, this model holds considerable potential for community social workers, providing that common objectives are self-evident or can be developed.

POLITICAL EMPOWERMENT

Generally, political empowerment occurs through some recognized authority delegating power to a particular group for specific purposes or through groups assuming power based on interest, expertise, or other resources.

In the child welfare field, the use of political empowerment as a community practice strategy has been very limited. Children and youth do not usually have an organizational base on which to build, and society does not expect the young to act as an organizational force nor does it accept them when they behave as if they are a force. Children in need of protection, often by definition, do not have parents or a concerned community who are perceived as having power. Consequently, outsiders—concerned citizens and professionals in child welfare—have unwittingly contributed to this problem through projecting a sense of powerlessness upon these children, their families, and their immediate community. As a result, political empowerment as a community social work strategy in child welfare has received only minimal emphasis to date.

Political empowerment requires commitment to a common central ideal. This is usually accomplished by adopting values that provide the ideology underlying the organizational activity (Katz and Georgopoulos 1971:356–66). In child welfare the usual ideological focus is protection of children through the provision of the best possible services. Rather than work to empower the children and families who are most centrally concerned, social workers have tended to institutionalize programmatic solutions, and through professionalization, they lose sight of the political character of their activity (Corwin 1972:472–75).

In children's services, the moral question is seen in the protective attitude of society toward children. Economically, child welfare services are highly dependent on public or private funding since it is not possible or socially desirable for children's programs to compete in an open-market system. Political problems are always in the background, and protective services, for example, are known to be poltically volatile. Consequently, professional groups often are empowered to handle difficult child welfare matters. At no time are child welfare services autonomous from the environment in which they operate. Traditionally, the legitimacy of child welfare has been derived from the community at large that has expectations about the need to protect and care for children caught in situations that expose them to serious risks not of their own making.

Child welfare social service agencies must deal with environmental complexity, which is defined as risk, dependency, and interorganizational relationships (Osborne and Hunt 1974:231–46).

In most communities attitudes toward child welfare are extremely conservative and services are dependent on public or charitable sources. Consequently, there has been extreme caution in developing approaches which are unusual or innovative. There are seldom any "risk" programs undertaken which are not first legitimized by strong endorsements from national associations. Thus, the majority of essential child welfare services are legitimized by the general community, but service providers do not often gain or even seek legitimacy from client populations or citizen groups.

Experimental programs which utilized community workers with gangs of youth have successfully transferred some power to client groups in some instances. However, this has usually been an exercise in short-term process rather than the basis of lasting change. Youth street organizations have a transitory membership which is not suited to continuing organizational responsibility or evolution. Nevertheless, the strategies of political empowerment can have an impact when they form the basis of youth work.

Probably the most significant uses of political empowerment in child welfare services to date have involved the empowerment of parents to act on behalf of their children. The parents of children with specific handicaps such as mental retardation, learning disability, and autism have become powerful forces over the last decade as child advocates, fund raisers, and service providers. Parent-dominant organizations have been especially powerful in the development of community-based alternatives to institutionalization.

These parent empowerment organizations are usually begun as parent-professional-community partnerships. The development of the political action approach usually passes through three stages. First, a group of concerned citizens take collective action to develop an organization that will advance their interests. Second, funding problems are addressed. At this point, the political action model is often in jeopardy, since allocation of funds for specific projects often diverts the attention of the group away from more universal issues. Many groups stop at this point, and they place all of their energies into building a specific service, such as a school for retarded children. It can be argued that the provision of funds for projects is a conscious co-optation of the group by funders in order to divert the attention of the members away from more global issues.

The final phase emerges when the empowered group recognizes the range of needs that are not being met due to their involvement in providing direct services. At this point, members reassume the role of advocates. Many examples are evident, such as schools for retarded children that were operated by parents being turned over to public authorities. This frees the group to direct attention to new endeavors, often with the specific objective of starting services and then turning them over to others to operate. This form of the political empowerment model has great potential since members are usually highly committed advocates who are free to and willing to develop a strong power base.

Finally, political empowerment in child welfare is an important issue arising among certain racial and ethnic minorities, most notably blacks and the North American Indians (Cardinal 1977; Hudson and McKenzie 1981; Johnson 1981a). Criticisms have been made of cross-racial adoption (Sanders 1975), the lack of appropriate foster care, and the need for provision of treatment services on reservations (Simon 1973). In Canada and the United States, ethnic and racial interest associations are extremely concerned about child welfare services which they describe as a form of cultural genocide. The disproportionate numbers of Indian children who are in the care of child welfare authorities is cause for concern (Candian Council on Children and Youth 1978:130–5). There is little doubt that child welfare services will become an integral part of the Indian rights movement in the years to come. Community practice strategies which empower communities to care for their children will be an essential part of this movement.

References

Abbott, Grace. 1938. The Child and the State, vol. 11: *The Dependent and Delinquent Child, the Child of Unmarried Parents*. New York: Greenwood Press.
Axinn, June and Herman Levine. 1975. *Social Welfare: A History of the American Response to Needs*. New York: Harper and Row.
Bagnell, Kenneth. 1980. *The Little Immigrants: The Orphans Who Came to Canada*. Toronto: Macmillan of Canada.
Bartlett, Harriet M. 1958. "Toward Clarification and Improvement of Social Work Practice." *Social Work* (April), 3(2):3–9.

384 G. L. Pawson/T. Russell

Betten, Neil. 1973. "American Attitudes Toward the Poor." *Current History* (July), 65(383):1–5.

Beveridge, Sir William. 1942. *Social Insurance and Allied Services*. New York: Macmillan.

Boles, Janet K. 1980. "The Politics of Child Care." *Social Service Review* (September), 54(3):344–62.

Brager, George A. and Harry Specht. 1973. *Community Organizing*. New York: Columbia University Press.

Canadian Council on Children and Youth. 1978. *Admittance Restricted: The Child as Citizen in Canada*. Ottawa: M.O.M. Press.

Cardinal, Harold. 1977. *The Rebirth of Canada's Indians*. Edmonton: Hurtig.

Child Welfare League of America. 1981. *Child Welfare Planning Notes*.

———. 1982. *Urgent Bulletin* (an open letter to member agencies).

Cohen, Nathan E., ed. 1960. *The Citizen Volunteer: His Responsibility, Role, and Opportunity in Modern Society*. New York: Harper and Row.

Corwin, Ronald G. 1972. "Strategies of Organizational Survival: The Case of a National Program of Educational Reform." *Journal of Applied Behavioral Science* (July/August), 8(4):451–80.

Costin, Lela B. 1979. *Child Welfare: Policies and Practice*. New York: McGraw-Hill.

Coughlin, Bernard J. 1979. "Deinstitutionalization: A Matter of Social Order and Deviance." *Child Welfare* (May), 61(5):293–301.

Etzioni, Amitai. 1961. *Complex Organizations: A Sociological Reader*. New York: Holt, Rinehart and Winston.

Evan, William M. 1971. "The Organization-Set: Toward a Theory of Interorganizational Relations." In Mauer, ed., *Readings in Organizational Theory: Open-System Approaches*, pp. 31–45.

Geismar, L. L. and Beverly Ayres. 1959. *Patterns of Change in Problem Families*. St. Paul, Minn.: Greater St. Paul Community Chest and Councils.

Gilbert, Neil and Harry Specht. 1977. *Planning for Social Welfare*. Englewood Cliffs, N.J.: Prentice-Hall.

Gill, David G. 1974. "Institutions for Children." In Schorr, ed., *Children and Decent People*, pp. 53–88.

Grosser, Charles F. 1973. *New Directions in Community Organization: From Enabling to Advocacy*. New York: Praeger.

Hasenfeld, Yeheskel and Richard A. English, eds. 1975. *Human Service Organizations*. Ann Arbor, Mich.: University of Michigan Press.

Herman, Paul, ed. 1970. *Delinquency and Social Policy*. New York: Praeger.

Hibbard, Michael. 1981. "The Crisis in Social Policy Planning." *Social Service Review* (December), 55(4):557–67.

Howe, Elizabeth. 1978. "Legislative Outcomes in Human Services." *Social Service Review* (June), 52(2):173–88.

Hudson, Pete and Brad McKenzie. 1981. "Child Welfare and Native People: The Extension of Colonialism." *The Social Worker* (Summer), 49(2):63–66.

Johnson, Patrick. 1981. "Indigenous Children at Risk." *Policy Options* (November–December), 2:47–50.

Kadushin, Alfred. 1969. *Child Welfare Services.* New York: Macmillan.

Kahn, Alfred J. 1979. "Child Welfare." In *Encyclopedia of Social Work,* pp. 100–114. 17th ed. Washington, D.C.: NASW.

Katz, Daniel and Basil S. Georgopoulos. 1971. "Organizations in a Changing World." *Journal of Applied Behavioral Science* (May–June), 7(3):342–70.

Kenniston, Kenneth and the Carnegie Council on Children. 1977. *All Our Children.* New York: Harcourt Brace Jovanovich.

Kramer, Ralph M. and Harry Specht, eds. 1969. *Readings in Community Organization Practice.* Englewood Cliffs, N.J.: Prentice-Hall.

Lansburgh, Terese W. 1977. "Child Welfare: Day Care of Children." In *Encyclopedia of Social Work,* pp. 134–46. 17th ed. Washington, D.C.: NASW.

Lerman, Paul. 1970. *Community Treatment and Social Control: A Critical Analysis of Juvenile Correctional Policy.* Chicago: University of Chicago Press.

Litwak, Eugene and Lydia F. Hylton. 1962. "Interorganizational Interdependence, Intraorganizational Structure." *Administrative Science Quarterly* (March), 6:395–420. Reprinted in Hasenfeld and English, eds., *Human Service Organizations: A Book of Readings.*

Marsh, L. C. 1943. *Report on Social Security for Canada.* Ottawa: Edmund Cloutier Printer.

Mauer, John H., ed. 1971. *Readings in Organizational Theory: Open-System Approaches.* New York: Random House.

Mayer, Morris Fritz, Leon H. Richman, and Edwin A. Balcerzak. 1977. *Group Care of Children: Crossroads and Transitions.* New York: Child Welfare League of America.

Meezan, William, Stanford Katz, and Eva Monoff Russo. 1978. *Adoptions without Agencies: A Study of Independent Adoptions.* New York: Child Welfare League of America.

Murphy, Campbell G. 1954. *Community Organization Practice.* Boston: Houghton Mifflin.

Osborne, Richard N. and James G. Hunt. 1974. "Environment and Organizational Effectiveness." *Administrative Science Quarterly* (June), 19(2):231–46.

Parker, Jacqueline K. and Edward M. Carpenter. 1981. "Julia Lathrop and the Children's Bureau: The Emergence of an Institution." *Social Service Review* (March), 55(1):60–77.

Pfeffer, Jeffery. 1972c. "Size and Composition of Corporate Board of Directors: The Organization and Its Environment." *Administrative Science Quarterly* (June), 17(2):218–28.

Piper, Edward and John R. Warner, Jr. 1980–81. "Group Homes for Problem Youth: Retrospect and Prospects." *Child and Youth Services,* 3(3/4):1–11.

Platt, Anthony M. 1970. "The Rise of the Child-Saving Movement." In Herman, ed., *Delinquency and Social Policy,* pp. 15–20.

Powers, Edwin. 1970. "Crime and Punishment in Early Massachusetts, 1620–1692." In Herman, ed., *Delinquency and Social Policy,* pp. 8–12.

Pumphrey, Muriel W. and Ralph E. Pumphrey. 1973. "Private Charity in the Twentieth Century." *Current History* (July), 65(383):29–32.

Rauch, Julia B. 1975. "Women in Social Work: Friendly Visitors in Philadelphia, 1880." *Social Service Review* (June), 49(2):241–59.

Reid, Joseph H. 1974a. "From the Executive Director." *Child Welfare League Newsletter* (Spring), 4(1):1.

———. 1974b. "From the Executive Director." *Child Welfare League Newsletter* (Summer/Fall), 4(2):4.

Reid, William. 1964. "Interagency Coordination in Delinquency Prevention and Control." *Social Service Review* (December), 35:418–28.

Romig, Dennis A. 1978. *Justice for Our Children*. Lexington, Mass.: Lexington Books.

Rooke, Patricia T. and R. L. Schnell. 1981. "Child Welfare in English Canada, 1920–48." *Social Service Review* (September), 55(3):483–506.

Ross, Murray G. 1955. *Community Organization: Theory and Principles*. New York: Harper.

Rothman, David J. 1971. *The Discovery of the Asylum—Special Order and Disorder in the New Republic*. Boston: Little, Brown.

Ruderman, Florence A. 1968. *Child Care and Working Mothers: A Study of Arrangements for Daytime Care of Children*. New York: Child Welfare League of America.

Sanders, Douglas. 1975. "Family Law and Native People," p. 14. Unpublished background paper prepared for the Law Reform Commission of Canada.

Santiago, Letty. 1972. "From Settlement House to Antipoverty Program." *Social Work* (July), 17(4):73–78.

Schorr, Alvin L., ed. 1974. *Children and Decent People*. New York: Basic Books.

Sieder, Violet M. 1960. "The Citizen Volunteer in Historical Perspective." In Cohen, ed., *The Citizen Volunteer: His Responsibility, Role, and Opportunity in Modern Society*. pp. 41–58.

Simon, Bill, Jr. 1973. "The Social Conditions of Indian Reserves in Eastern New Brunswick." Unpublished report prepared for the Union of New Brunswick Indians.

Siporin, Max. 1975. *Introduction to Social Work Practice*. New York: Macmillan.

Soiseth, Len. 1970. "A Community That Cares for Children." *Canadian Welfare* (May/June), 46(3):8–10.

Statistics Canada. 1976. *Social Security National Programs: A Review for the Period 1946 to 1975*. Ottawa: Statistics Canada.

Thompson, James D. and William J. McEwan. 1958. "Organizational Goals and Environment: Goal Setting and an Interaction Process." *American Sociological Review* (February), 23(1):23–36.

U.S. Department of Health and Human Services. 1982. *Quarterly Public Assistance Statistics: Jan.–Mar. 1981*. Washington, D.C.: U.S. GPO.

Wolins, Martin and Irving Piliavin. 1964. *Institutions or Foster Family: A Century of Debate*. New York: Child Welfare League of America.

Woodroofe, Kathleen. 1975. "The Irascible Reverend Henry Solly and His Contribution to Working Men's Clubs, Charity Organizations, and 'Industrial Villages' In Victorian England." *Social Service Review* (March), 49(1):15–32.

Young, Robert C. 1966. "Goals and Goal-Setting." *Journal of the American Institute of Planners* (March), 32(2):78–85.

Zald, Mayer N. 1963. "Comparative Analysis and Measurement of Organizational Goals: The Case of Correctional Institutions for Delinquents." *Sociological Quarterly* (Summer), 4(3):206–30.

Zietz, Dorothy. 1969. *Child Welfare: Services and Perspectives.* New York: Wiley.

13

The Practice of Community Social Work in Third World Countries

Kenneth L. Chau and Peter Hodge

Similarities in the social and economic problems confronting developing countries are such that they are often viewed as a somewhat homogeneous Third World; the differences in their histories, cultures, and political systems are such, however, that to search for common elements of community social work practice among them is an impossible task. Consequently, the authors have chosen to narrow the task and focus on those parts of that world—primarily Africa and Asia—with which they have had direct experience.

Community social work in Africa and Asia is similar to that in England and the United States in that it began under religious-vocational sponsorship. It differs, however, in that its early development was influenced by colonial policy and practices.

Missions, particularly Christian ones but also those of the Hindus and the Buddhists, were the pioneers. The major aims of these missions were evangelism and conversion, but it was soon realized that the amelioration of the whole condition of the lives of their converts was inseparable from the main object. Thus, education and conversion were intertwined.

Because so many of the developing countries of today were the colonies or mandated territories of yesterday, the colonial relationship was the context for a number of the early experiments in community practice. In many cases, the colony was also the mission field for the evangelizing outreach of the churches of the colonizing country; thus the community development efforts of the missions became intertwined with the community development efforts of the colonial government.

The fashionable anticolonialism and antimission stance of the 1960s is now proving to have been extreme and unbalanced in its criticism. A new climate of restraint and objectivity is making possible a fresh examination of that period of history in an attempt to draw up scenarios for the future. Thus, as a backdrop for the analysis of current practice in developing countries, the background and the context within which community practice developed will be reviewed.

The Earliest Process and Evaluation

In the United Kingdom colonies and dependent territories, the concept of community development originated "in the search for a program to compensate for the limitations of the conventional school system, and to enable education to provide for the progressive evolution of the peoples" (United Nations 1956:13). One of the earliest attempts to devise such a program was for the British West Indies, in response to the social and economic difficulties that followed the emancipation of the slaves in 1838. The details of a scheme of organizing and conducting day schools of industry, model farm schools, and normal schools were set out in a dispatch of 1847 from the Privy Council Office, London, to the Governors of the West Indian Colonies (Curtin 1972:191–209). Curtin suggests that the aim was to create a docile and semiskilled working class through an educational system heavily biased toward industrial education. The long-term hope, stated in the document, was to promote work habits for a settled and thriving peasantry that might in time develop the elements of a native middle class, interested in the protection of property and able to take part in the conduct of local affairs.

Missions. Christian missions had also evolved programs and methods for the education and betterment of their converts. One strategy was to create separate Christian communities in which converts might live free from the influences of a "pagan" environment. The Basle Mission in West Africa, for instance, created exclusive mission compounds, "salems," where young converts were taken to live away from their homes and separated from parents and village elders. The Basle Mission also gave practical craft and vocational training, and taught in the vernacular. The Moravian Mission in East Africa also created social communities of elect souls, self-supporting and sufficient unto themselves, and used artisans as lay missionaries.

Much of the criticism of the missions has centered upon their tendency to uproot converts from tribal society, and thereby to inculcate a rejection of indigenous culture and preference for urban, Western ways of life and the encouragement of bookish learning and aspirations for white-collar jobs. Oliver refutes this criticism of detribalization, however, pointing out that the missions intended to work within the framework of the tribal system. This is evidenced, he claims, by the missionaries' patient, almost hopeless, study of tribal languages and their insistence that education should be given in the vernacular (Oliver 1952:180).

The separated communities were also criticized for preventing native converts from serving as models and exerting religious influence upon the families and kin to which they belonged. There were exceptions, however. Modern research is revealing a subtle and highly differentiated picture of mission interaction with the process of social change. The Scottish Presbyterians, for example, with their abiding faith in the value of education, tried to create a middle-class elite. This was a sharp contrast to the attempts of many Catholic and Dutch Reformed Church missionaries to produce a rather contented Christian peasantry (Strayer 1978:2).

The mid-Victorian debate over pure missionary activity for conversions versus indirect evangelism through creating Christian communities to promote true religion, agriculture, and lawful commerce (Livingstone's notion of a legitimate trade to supplant the slave trade) arose in relation to the problem of freed slaves and how they were to be rehabilitated. The use of community building as a practical demonstration of the new way of life for converts extended to providing economic means of survival in the wilderness in territory beyond colonial administration. After the end of the slave trade, and after the partition of Africa, the debate reemerged as "missions and education" (Oliver 1952:26).

Industrial education. The popular American solution to the problems of missions and education was the industrial education for black Americans, developed in Hampton, Virginia, and Tuskegee, Alabama.[1] Emphasizing simple forms of trade and manual training and elementary agricultural work, the education at Hampton Institute was considered to be relevant to the needs and conditions of black Americans who would be returning to their own communities (King 1971:6). The basis of Tuskegee's appeal in Africa was its educational formula to fight urbanization, and its school life that was to compensate for a backward home and provide practical instruction (48).

The Hampton and Tuskegee model of industrial education had great effect on Indian and African education for the first three decades in the twentieth century. The first World Missionary Conference in 1910 at Edinburgh recommended that missionaries, especially those from Africa, pay particular attention to Tuskegee and Hampton. In India a Commission of Inquiry recommended that the missions develop the concept of the village school as a community center to provide education that could meet the needs of village life and the challenge of illiteracy (Village Education in India 1920:ch. 8). In America, the needs of black American communities had been defined as sanitation, health training, improved housing, and increased industrial and agricultural skills (Jones 1917:81). The instrument for rural betterment was to be the adaptation of education to the needs of the pupil and the community. Adaptation appropriate to Africans could be best embodied by schools teaching what Jones called the "Simples" of health, home life training, industry and agriculture, and recreation (Jones 1922:16–37).

The concept of an adapted education was taken up by the missionary societies of America and Europe, and became the official policy of the British Colonial Office where, in 1923, an Advisory Committee on Native Education in Tropical Africa formulated broad principles to serve as the basis of an educational policy to be recommended to the colonial governments and administrations. As the first of a series of documents often regarded as the original foundation of modern community development, the Memorandum is worth quoting:

Its aim should be to render the individual more efficient in his or her condition of life, whatever it may be, and to promote the advancement of the community as a whole through the improvement of agriculture, the development of native industries, the improvement of health, the training of the people in the management of their own affairs, and the inculcation of true ideals of citizenship and service. It must include the raising up of capable, trustworthy, public-spirited leaders of the people, belonging to their own race. Education thus defined will narrow the hiatus between the educated class and the rest of the community whether chiefs or peasantry. (Colonial Office 1925:4)

Two important principles of community and social development were stated: first, the promotion of the advancement of the community as a whole; and second the requirement of all government departments to work together closely in developing relevant policy. Encouragement of voluntary educational effort through cooperation between government and other education agencies was to be promoted "since education is intimately related to all other efforts whether of Government or of citizens, for the welfare of the community" (Colonial Office 1925:4).

The London Advisory Committee, reconstituted in 1929 to scrutinize education in all of the British colonies and dependent territories, extended "education" far beyond the sphere of the conventional school system, and to a great extent determined the emphasis that was placed on community development as an *educational* process (United Nations 1954:3).

In 1935 the Colonial Office made two important recommendations of strategy: (1) to set up in each territory a pilot project to experiment with a comprehensive and intensive program of rural betterment; (2) to experiment with a team of technical officers and missionaries, to try to combine efforts in a single, unified program (Colonial Office 1935:21).

Demonstration centers and pilot projects have been a common feature of community social work. The missions pioneered this strategy and reconfirmed its value as an approach in rural community development in 1928 at the Jerusalem meeting of the International Missionary Council. The Council's statement contained what appears to be the first official usage of the term community development. Until then the process had been given a variety of labels: community consciousness, advancement of the community as a whole, rural betterment, rural reconstruction. The 1928 statement set down the aims of community development afresh and listed the agencies for the process: (1) the family and the home, preserving all of permanent value in the indigenous family systems yet renewing them and giving major attention to work for women; (2) the church, fellowship and building, ministering to the whole life of the whole community; (3) the school; (4) voluntary organizations, both economic and social, since all such organizations afford rural people an opportunity for training in self-government; (5) government (International Missionary Council 1928:291–92).

During the years of the economic depression of the 1930s, what was achieved in community development was limited and scattered. In India there had been a variety of experimental projects in rural betterment: those of Tagore at Sriniketan, West Bengal (Dasgupta 1963); Hatch at Martandam, Travancore, present-day Kerala (Hatch 1949); Gandhi at Sevagram near Wardha in present-day Maharashtra. Each of these worked in its own way; however, each was uncoordinated with the others and tended to die when the pioneer direction was withdrawn. The whole program of community development enunciated by the Jerusalem Conference remained on paper, and was never seriously put into practice.

In Africa it was not until World War II and the urgency of mobilizing for the war effort that specific programs were suggested. One of these was the teaching of literacy. A subcommittee of the London Advisory Committee, working on the problem of mass literacy and adult education, examined the success of the Chinese and Russian mass education movements and recognized the importance of adult literacy as an essential means of achieving all-around progress.

Mass Education in African Society, a report which identified mass education as a problem of special importance and urgency, was the starting point in the evolution of community development as an arm of government policy (Colonial Office 1944). The new policy was not a break with the former tradition and policy of community education, but a speeding up of the process, with the aim of getting people everywhere "to be aware of, to understand and take part in, and ultimately to control the social and economic changes which are taking place among them" (Colonial Office 1944:13). The report advocated the project or campaign method as means of application to particular communities, with specific and limited objectives. To provide the necessary drive to make a campaign successful, the appointment of a local Mass Education Officer was recommended rather than relying on an officer distantly connected with the activities from a provincial or district headquarters.

The end of World War II was followed shortly by the attainment of independence by India, Pakistan, Ceylon, and, in 1948, Burma. The focus upon Africa for the execution of British plans for community development was reinforced by these events. In November 1948 the British Secretary of State for the Colonies sent a dispatch on community development to the governors of the African Territories containing what was to be regarded as an authoritative definition of the process, and to make clear beyond all doubt that community development was to be regarded as one of the central features of the African policy of the British Government. Community development was not regarded as something new, but more "the intensification of past plans for development by means of new techniques; its main novel feature [resting] in the great emphasis which it places on the stimulation of popular initiative" (Colonial Office 1955:50).

The Secretary concluded that community development programs had not progressed since 1944, largely due to an absence of activity and involvement among a number of the relevant departments of government. He saw an officer specializing in community development, especially trained for the purpose, as a member of a provincial team, such a team being the main operative unit for the purpose of planning and executing community development programs.

At that time social workers played little part in community development. The few social workers—their training for colonial territories had not begun until 1943 in Jamaica for the West Indies, and in the same year in London for African territories—were appointed to social welfare departments operating in urban areas (Simey 1946:197; Hodge 1970:35). British territories in South and East Asia were then under Japanese occupation. The first school of social work in India, the Tata Graduate School, was established in Bombay in 1936. Earlier, however, training of the pioneer YMCA workers in rural reconstruction had included some elements of community practice to enable the workers to promote social betterment in the villages through educational and recreational approaches (Pande 1967:66). In China, community practice evolved from mass education for literacy and rural reconstruction programs (Cheng-Su Wang 1942–43:105).

Because of the overwhelming needs of the rural population, community practice stressed literacy, primary health care, the promotion of cooperatives and credit unions. It therefore attracted and required the skills of anthropologists, adult education and literacy teachers, agronomists, agricultural extension workers, nutritionists, maternal and child welfare workers, and only marginally social workers with community organization expertise. Social work remained confined, at least in British territories, to remedial measures to deal with one specific social problem or another, such as the care of orphans, of juvenile delinquents, and the prevention of prostitution in growing towns and cities.

The British Colonial Secretary in his 1948 dispatch was anxious to make a clear distinction between community development and social welfare. West Indian experience had shown, unfortunately, that social welfare departments were used as "handy administrative dustbins in which to get rid of inconvenient governmental functions that could not be tidily attached to any of the existing departments" (Simey 1946:192). The first explicit manifestations of community practice which linked social welfare and community development were the community centers and community halls set up in towns and villages, with the staff trained locally in short courses on community organization and development (United Nations 1953:15).

Kinship-based organizations. In the cities and urban centers in Asia, community practice and its manifestations reflected the work of village-based kinship associations and religious bodies as well as the influence of missionaries and colonial governments. Such organizations, until the early 1960s, provided urban dwellers with many of the early forms of community practice programs. As large numbers of people from rural areas and neighboring countries migrated to urban centers, indigenous and kinship-based benevolent organizations, such as the Kaifongs in Hong Kong and the Kongsi in Singapore, were set up to provide for the protection, care, support, and integration of the migrant groups, many of whom were overwhelmed by city life (Wong 1971). Much of the cultural values of mutual help and humanitarian feelings for one's fellowman that these indigenous organizations subscribed to, are themselves manifestations of what present-day community practice seeks to foster.

It was through the initiative of these organizations that the growth of many self-help, mutual aid, and other early programs of community improvement were promoted in the cities.

A Contemporary Scene

Once the arena of rival Western colonial powers, developing countries in the Third World are today a center of rapid social change. Overwhelmingly agricultural and rural, many of these countries have to contend with a low gross national product amidst rising expectations. Though hopeful about the potential for growth and modernization, they are often beset by immediate problems such as overpopulation, poverty, environmental deficiencies, and political metamorphosis.

The practice of community social work in contemporary Third World countries must be seen in the context of the dramatic changes that took place in the history of these nations in the first half of this century. With the collapse of the social, political, and cultural orders that occurred in this period, the transformation that took place was accelerated by the growing impact of Western political, economic, and technological influences. Much of the aspirations and energies of these countries was channeled in the direction of fostering a sense of national identity and economic sufficiency. However, it has become clear that independence from colonial domination involves more than political independence, and that national progress requires more than modernization and economic growth.

The conditions of these nations are wrought with many internal contradictions. The fruits of modernization did not eliminate an inequitable distribution of power and wealth. The urgent call for people's participation in social change, whether as rhetoric or as honest policy, did not raise basic human rights and the welfare of individuals remained subordinate to national productivity and political security. The early programs of community practice did not contribute very much to the kind of community development that the United Nations defined as:

[the] process by which the efforts of the people themselves are united with those of governmental authorities to improve the economic, social and cultural conditions of communities, to integrate these communities into the life of the nation, and to enable them to contribute fully to national progress. (United Nations 1960:1)

What resulted was, in Frank's words, "the development of under-development" (Frank 1969).

National development strategy, which had economic growth as the primary objective, did not help to close the social and cultural lags in countries that had recently gained independence. People's participation remained an empty shibboleth. But the strategy of social development, adopted by the United Nations for the Second Development Decade, is now gaining a wider acceptance and has made greater impact on community practice in these countries today. Paiva provides a conception of social development:

The goal and substance of social development is the welfare of the people, as determined by the people themselves, and the consequent creation or alteration of institutions so as to create a capacity for meeting human needs at all levels and for improving the quality of human relationships and relationships between people and societal institutions. In this process we have to deal with the fact that human and natural forces are constantly intervening between the expression of needs and the means to attain them. (1977:329)

As this quotation highlights, the target of social development is institutional change, and its purpose is embodied in the general goal of improved human welfare. The primary values of social development are equality (versus inequality), cooperation (versus competition), and collectivity (versus self-orientation) (Gil 1976). Ideas such as these underly the practice of community social work in developing countries and are reiterated in the themes of regional conferences and workshops organized by international organizations.[2] These ideas have been put into practice by a growing number of voluntary organizations which have taken it upon themselves to organize communities to bring about an involved interest in matters affecting their lives.

Thus, today's community practice in the Third World is linked to programs for national progress. It emphasizes two interrelated features: (1) popular participation and a reliance on the people's initiative; and (2) the provision of services to encourage self-help. It also differs from prior community practice which, often based on an educational process, focused on human resource development and neglected institutional change, and has been found to be an inadequate response to the demands of contemporary conditions.

The adoption of a social development perspective within community practice recognizes the importance of creating new institutions or changing existing ones. As transformation takes place in the institutions, disruptions of certain traditional life patterns become inevitable. New community resources and programs are needed to replace or supplement the traditional ones.

Community practice in Third World countries is increasingly taking on a broader perspective. In the first place, pressures are applied to community practice to contribute to national development objectives. Many of these objectives are political in nature and intent, emphasizing community integration, social stability, and responsible citizenship. These objectives often cause concern among social workers in the West who, on ethical grounds, worry about sacrificing the "private good" to the "public good."

Second, national development objectives call for cooperation between the government and the voluntary sector engaged in community practice. The argument for such cooperation is that in the Third World massive social problems cannot be dealt with in the absence of popular participation and joint efforts of government and voluntary civic organizations.

Third, measures that have to be employed adopt a developmental outlook and often are aimed at a relatively large portion of the population. The emphasis on community-oriented social provisions necessitates community practice taking a positive role "in transforming social structures, participating in the development of social policies, and developing grassroots people's institutions for popular participation in national development" (Desai 1976:1–2).

This, then, provides the setting and the context for the analysis of contemporary community practice in the developing countries, especially the urban areas of Asia.

Issues, Problems, and Tasks

A wide range of political, social, and economic issues and problems has confronted community practice in these Third World countries. These problems have their roots in the fact that for generations people have endured poverty, been excluded from decision-making, handicapped by backwardness in technology, and frightened by climates of political uncertainty.

ISSUES AND PROBLEMS

In the process of rapid development and social change, the people in these Third World countries have had their aspirations raised to a level which their achievements cannot satisfy. As these aspirations are frustrated, either because of inadequate personal means or because resources are denied to them, their increased level of frustration further aggravates the problem. In community practice, public recognition of a problem does not automatically lead to programs for its solution or stimulate collective social action. These responses occur only when people affected by the problems take the initiative, or when those who are concerned with the welfare of the affected group take leadership to seek solutions or to get the people organized. Until this happens, the problem remains and continues to affect adversely the lives of the people. This kind of situation is not uncommon in many of the countries in Asia where, traditionally, government decision-making processes and policy machinery are so centralized that local bureaucracies become corrupted and insensitive. Although there are benevolent elitists who try to speak for the deprived and the disadvantaged, the sad fact is that many genuine concerns become bottlenecked in the bureaucratic process and ignored.

When economic concerns took precedence over other social concerns, community practice in the rural sectors of developing countries focused on problems of ignorance, sanitation and hygiene, illiteracy, and training for handicraft or agricultural production. Issues such as exploitation of the poor, especially of the small farmers and the fisherfolk, have prompted the initiation of simple self-help cooperatives and credit unions. It has been this tradition of self-help and mutual aid, along with charity from the rich, that has enabled village and clan groups to survive so many adversities.

In urban centers, however, the nature of problems takes on a different character, shaped as they are by rapid industrialization and urbanization. Major problems confronting community practice in the cities include the following: (1) the deterioration of social relationships, which become characterized by anonymity, ineffective communication, conflicting standards of behavior, and loneliness; (2) the deficiency of social provisions, especially those of housing, education, traditional support networks, environmental sanitation; (3) the worsened conditions of certain disadvantaged groups, such as the aged and the handicapped; (4) the absence of community identity or cohesion.

TASKS AND PROGRAMS

Two major types of programs have been developed in response to these problems: one focuses on providing services and facilities, the other on developing the people's capacities to fend for themselves.

In the development of services and facilities, the tasks that engage community practice are those connected with the inadequacy of social and welfare provisions, such as for cultural, social, and recreational needs; housing provisions for low-income groups who are relocated because of urban development or natural disasters; provisions for environmental improvement; and various other services of an educational and developmental nature. Such programs and services are directed at the perceived needs of the community as a whole or for specific, usually disadvantaged groups. They are provided through neighborhood-level projects of voluntary organizations or through a chain of community centers, neighborhood halls, and other official or semiofficial institutions. These specific social tasks engage the community practitioners in studying the community and its needs; educating the community residents through information dissemination and developing local information networks. They are also engaged in policy and program analysis; in coordinating services; and promoting, planning, and implementing new ones; and mobilizing local resources of money and manpower. These social tasks seek to foster public understanding or awareness of the deficiency of present provisions, to mobilize support or demand for new provisions, and to develop collaboration between organizations and disciplines.

A second broad category of programs and tasks is community- or resident-focused. The primary interest of such programs lies in educating the community for self-help and mutual-help initiatives; and in developing the capacities of individuals and groups, especially deprived ones, for enhanced community participation and social relationships. When a specific need of a disadvantaged group is at stake, the social task may be one of problem-solving. Dependent upon how the specific issue is perceived and how concerned the particular group is, the tasks involve organizing people, bargaining and negotiating with relevant authorities, and mobilizing for collective social action. When the issue at stake is of a broader nature—such as community cohesion or social relationships—the dominant social tasks of community practitioners are usually those of organizing residents' groups, helping members to set priorities for community needs, building leadership and allies, and mobilizing for community self-help initiative.

The thrust of these programs has been to provide for the basic needs of the people and to foster self-reliance and mutual help. The tasks that engage the community practitioners tend to be process-oriented, geared to the acquisition of methods and skills which, some might argue, only enable them to tinker with the system while the roots of the problems remain unconfronted.

Sponsors, Participants and Goals

A host of factors interact to determine the nature of the needs and issues for which a program of community practice is or is not initiated and, if initiated, who is involved and with what goals.

SPONSORS

In most Third World countries, the influences that shape the nature and the scope of community practice come from two significant sources: the policies and funding of voluntary organizations, and the social and welfare policies of governments and the attitudes of their officials.

In some of these countries, the relegation of social welfare activities to indigenous philanthropy has led to the mushrooming of voluntary organizations, with local governments limiting their activities to the provision of certain urban-based remedial services and efforts to fulfill a coordinating role (Hodge 1980:97). Such voluntary agencies, in addition to instituting various social programs, pioneered in community development and self-help initiatives and used a range of strategies including social action (Leung 1978:142). The official attitude toward some of these strategies led to a change in government policies toward social and welfare services and to the adoption of an increasingly active intervention stance that, in effect, supports only those programs that are consistent with national priorities and social policy decisions. Such changes in attitude dictate the direction in which community practice is to move, and create situations in which only consensual collaboration will ensure official backing and support. An increasing measure of social control is being felt by community practitioners.

Simultaneously, there has been a trend toward increasing dependency on government funds for community improvement projects, necessitated by the gradual withdrawal of overseas sources of support which voluntary organizations had relied upon. In combination, these changes have forced voluntary organizations to reexamine their roles, functions, and orientations to practice. At the same time, many governments have begun to support new forms of constituency-based organizations with the aim of involving community residents in local affairs. This has been a deliberate process of politicization of the people as a means of strengthening the governments' sociopolitical functions in the name of development and stability. As would be expected, these trends are having a serious impact on both the selection of participants and the goals of contemporary community practice.

PARTICIPANTS

Neither the historical development of community practice nor the factors that shape it suggest any uniformity by which participants are selected for involvement in community programs.

At a time when governments were relatively nondirective and when indigenous organizations were pioneering with early forms of community development, the practice of community social work was largely undefined, guided by vague and ambiguous expectations, and subject to the interpretation and ideological inclinations of its practitioners. Under those circumstances, the selection of community participants usually revolved around the pivotal actor— the community practitioner—with the participants or beneficiaries of the programs taking on a secondary role.

To the extent that local leadership is developed and responsibility delegated, citizen participation becomes more active when circumstances demand that issues, goals, and activities be redefined. Analyses of community practice (to be discussed in later sections) indicate that the goal of citizen participation is assigned a different meaning in keeping with the different orientations to practice adopted by government and voluntary organizations.

When governments commit resources to community development there is a tendency for participants to be limited to specific sectors of the population and specific low-income communities. In Asia, this situation tends to be intensified as governments increasingly attach a functional role to community practice. It is not unusual to find, for example, that community practice is used as an administrative tool for implementation of bureaucratic or national policies such as community building in Hong Kong; advancing democratic socialism in Singapore; implementing national development goals in the Philippines; nationwide implementing of the Panchayati-Raj pattern of rural development in India; and promoting the Saemaul Undong or new village movement in Korea. In these situations, where community practice is seen as a form of political control or is used for advancing political party policies and combating political opposition, citizen participation tends to be restricted to those who are acceptable to the government.

In Singapore and Hong Kong, for example, urban community centers and community development programs are based on ideologies which emphasize consenus-collaboration-integration and provide recreational and leisure outlets for children and youth plus some simple self-help projects for the deprived. A study conducted in these two communities revealed that in Singapore, local people appointed to the management committees of the community centers were screened by government officials, and managers were chosen because they were known to be sympathetic to the goals of the People's Action Party (Riches 1973:116).

In the community centers in Hong Kong, appointment to the members' council was influenced by staff members, and the warden was the person responsible for running and managing the center (Riches 1973:118). In both cities, the dominant activities of the warden and the staff were in the promotion of outlets for children and youth. Obviously, the bulk of community practice is not confined to community centers nor is it entirely for the purpose of catering to children and youth. An element of social control underlies most if not all of these community programs.

Where community practice is used for political or bureaucratic control, the levels of the government involved and the types of structures and mechanisms used are, as a rule, very explicit. The nurturing and creation of intermediary or quasi-official structures as an institutionalized strategy for community improvement have significantly influenced practice in these countries.

As changing social conditions have made traditional kinship-based organizations less effective in meeting the social needs of their communities and government, social agencies have suffered the consequences of corruption and insensitivity of staff. Failure of communication (Hong Kong Commission of Inquiry 1967) and a lack of integration between the government and the people (King 1975) have led many governments in Asia to seek new forms and strategies for community organization practice. What has developed are known as intermediary organizations. These are programs sponsored by the government, overseen or coordinated by bureaucrats. Membership to these organizations are directly appointed by the government or selected by procedures which contain elements of an election process.[3]

With national integration and development as major goals, these intermediary organizations are part of the governmental infrastructure. Because they involve collaboration between some citizens and some government officials, they represent a fresh approach to community practice and can serve as a useful bridge between the government and the grass roots.[4]

Social workers have been employed by intermediary organizations but have not had a major role. In India social work is found at the block level (a block consists of about one hundred villages) but it is one of many extension specialities—social education, welfare of women and children, and Panchayats were the most common subject matter specialities—using social group work and community practice skills. The training and recruitment of community development workers were separate from the university-based schools of social work, and "constructive workers" were another distinct group trained for community work in the Gandhian institutions.

Elsewhere, in Ghana, Uganda, and the Philippines, for example, social work and community development students were educated and trained together in the universities' departments and schools of social work or in training institutes set up by government ministries responsible for community development. The relationship between social work and community development was still exploratory and had not matured (Biddle and Biddle 1965:ch. 13). Not until the late 1960s and early 1970s did community practice of the Saul Alinsky school appear under interchurch sponsorship in East Asia and in church projects in Manila, Seoul, Singapore, and Hong Kong. Through church patronage, lessons acquired from Latin-American experience were adapted for use in Korea and the Philippines. Community practice was manifested in labor education, welfare rights for squatters and slum dwellers, and work projects for the unemployed.

The priorities, functions, and activities of these organizations are largely prescribed by state policy which is formulated by the central government. Despite this concentration of power in the government, some useful cooperative initiatives have been made between local governments and rural villages, resulting in small-scale physical improvements and provision of services that benefit village populations. In the huge housing estates and new towns (newly developed housing conurbations) of Singapore and Hong Kong, these intermediary organizations have been helpful in coping with emerging difficulties such as the need of a population of strangers to establish a new community. Intermediary organizations also provide channels for residents to discuss problems of housing block maintenance, cleanliness, and security, and the need for social and recreational resources.

Despite such successes, government support of community practice through these intermediary structures has been criticized as a strategy of controlled mobilization and participation. Based upon a study of the records of these intermediary organizations, Seah (1975:7–8) has charged that they have acted as social control agents by: amplifying government policies, keeping government officials informed of grass-roots demands and opinions, and assisting governments in preempting the influence of organized opposition and pressure groups. Given this interpretation, such community practice is seen as political and functional. To the extent that the central government has assigned the planning and direction of community improvement efforts to political departments, social welfare activities have been relegated to a residual function, and community practice by the voluntary sector plays little more than a follower role. A management circular on community building issued by the Hong Kong Government Secretariat (1977:4) documents the disenfranchisement of voluntary social agencies:

Since the aims of the voluntary agencies often differ from those of Government in community building, it is not considered practical for them to be represented on the various coordinating committees. Nevertheless, they should be encouraged to participate, by way of consultation, discussion and occasional attendance of meetings as appropriate.

POLITICAL PATRONAGE

That community practice expresses or is made to reflect the policy and ideology of governments is clearly the situation in Hong Kong and Singapore. This practice is even more blatant in certain other countries where the heads of government choose to patronize and personally back a particular program for community improvement.

A recent case in point is the Saemaul Undong of Korea. This

new village movement, a product of the 1970s, was stimulated by a speech by the former President, Park Chung Hee, to provincial governors recommending self-help as the answer to rural poverty. The movement began shortly thereafter when the government provided each village in the country with 335 sacks of cement, its use to be determined by villagers. After government evaluation of each village's use of the cement more was provided to those villages that had made good use of their original shipment. By 1973 all villages had been accepted into the Saemaul movement and were undertaking various kinds of community improvement projects. Previously, lip service was paid to rural development, but now local officials could be held accountable for any lapse in village progress, and Saemaul leaders were allowed to bypass local officials and report directly to national authorities (Miller 1979:70).

Expanded Saemaul training institutes and propaganda seem to have convinced people that rural prosperity stems from community self-help, cooperation, and diligence. However, rural expectations have been heightened, but not necessarily satisfied, and many country people still seek their fortunes in urban areas. Rural-urban migration has been slowed down, however, and at the end of 1977 the average income of a farm household was slightly higher than that of the average urban household. The rural environment has been changed within a decade, and an attitude engendered that poverty, after all, is not insurmountable (Hoon 1981:44).

History has shown that political patronage and official backing led to other community improvement accomplishments. Ghana, in Africa, enjoyed success in its program in the 1950s, largely because of the patronage and backing of Dr. Kwame Nkrumah's administration following his election in 1951. In Asia, community development in the Philippines gained crucial support from the charismatic President Ramón Magsaysay. In India, supposedly because of his friendship with Jawaharlal Nehru, Albert Mayer's work at the Etawah Pilot Project in Uttar Pradesh (Mayer 1958) was used as a model, and with U.S. aid, applied on a nationwide scale (Pande 1967:71).

Political patronage, the government's increased intervention in community affairs, the assumption of a growing responsibility for coordination and overall social provision for community building, the relegation of the voluntary agency to advisory levels of participation, the establishment of intermediary organizations, the recruitment of progovernment leaders, and the overhaul of social service objectives in keeping with the aims of development and security, all serve to define the goals and participants of community practice and limit the role of nongovernment sponsors at the neighborhood level.

Models of Practice

Several dominant themes presented in the foregoing discussion serve to shape practice and influence the choice of approaches:

1. Economy-oriented focus: enhancement of economic sufficiency
2. Social goals focus: promotion of social relationships and a sense of social responsibility
3. Service-oriented focus: improvement of social provisions and community facilities
4. Social integration and stability focus: advancement of community integration and stability.

Not all these themes appeared simultaneously in the history of community practice; their prominence at a given time was contingent upon particular problems, demands, and situations, and the ideologies, values, preferences, and goals of sponsors.

ECONOMY-ORIENTED FOCUS

Economic self-sufficiency is the theme that underlies most of the early community programs in rural sectors and in some cities of Third World countries. The programs were usually in the form of training opportunities to teach the villagers a craft, skill, or trade; the construction of facilities such as electrification or improved irrigation; or self-help, mutual-aid projects such as simple cooperatives or credit unions to protect the poor from middleman exploitation. Based on a tradition of self-help, this approach was predicated on the assumption that economic self-reliance would lead to improvement in the standard of living.

SOCIAL GOALS FOCUS

Promotion of social relationships and social responsibilities has been based largely on the desire of governments to maintain social stability. This theme was especially prominent at the time when nation building was the main objective of many Third World countries. By providing social, cultural, and recreational programs through community centers, this approach attempts to shape the development of citizens, especially children and youth, in the direction of preferred social goals such as cooperation, community consciousness, and social responsibility. By supporting neighborhood groups, indigenous leaders, and volunteers; by sharing resources and collaborating with other organizations in joint projects at the neighborhood level; and by encouraging citizen participation in community or environment improvement and self-help programs, it was expected that a community spirit or sense of neighborliness would result and that harmonious social relationships and a sense of social responsibility would emerge.

SERVICE-ORIENTED FOCUS

The third theme, involving improvement of social provisions and community facilities, has found expression mainly in the programs of community practice carried out by voluntary organizations, civic bodies, and church groups.

Dependent upon the progress of a particular program and the ideology of the sponsor, the approaches adopted have ranged from those that anchor their work in the development of grass-roots groups and neighborhoods for mutual-aid initiatives to those that promote the interests of disadvantaged groups through social action. The former approach emphasizes raising the social consciousness and self-confidence of people. It assumes that the solution of problems and improvement of social provisions must be a task shared by the people or neighborhood and the relevant authorities. The ideology of this approach gives primacy to consensus and collaboration. Through self-help initiatives such as neighborhood-level projects, communities are helped to increase their problem-solving capacities and to contribute toward the improvement of their environment.

In contrast, the social action approach, based on the ideas of Christian socialism and the quest for justice, is predicated on the assumption that disadvantaged groups lack the skills or the capacity to deal with the power of the administration that discriminates against them. Thus, the assumption is that organizing disadvantaged groups around their particular concerns will empower them to "work the system" and to bring about desired policy changes. The use of advocacy through confrontation and conflict has produced some measure of success, resulting in certain changes in policy and provisions for the disadvantaged groups. These efforts were not without their costs in terms of the maintenance of independent community practice.

SOCIAL INTEGRATION AND STABILITY FOCUS

In advancing community integration and stability, the emphasis has been on establishing and strengthening channels of communication. Predicated on the assumption (and painful experience) that ignorance breeds discontent which, in turn, often upsets social stability and community integration, it is understandable why many governments, especially those of Singapore and Hong Kong, have focused so much on bridging communication gaps between the people and the authorities through extensive use of official and sponsored intermediary structures. The importance attached to closing the communication gap can be documented through the directives issued by these governments. In Singapore, for instance, the following objectives have been listed for the residents committees: (1) to promote a better channel of communication between the residents and the various authorities so as to enable the authorities to obtain feedback information and find solutions to the problems of the housing estates residents; (2) to promote better social order and security; (3) to promote a sense of neighborliness and social harmony among residents.

In Hong Kong, the government's city district offices, which are responsible for intermediary organizations such as the mutual-aid committees, are required to: (1) develop the widest possible contacts with groups and individuals in the district; (2) supplement the government's information efforts with personal explanations and the use of mass media; and (3) advise the government on public opinions and needs. Thus, the function of disseminating information to residents is clearly political and is enmeshed in a range of educational and propaganda activities designed to ensure community feedback and control, to co-opt local leaders, and to manipulate public opinion, through various intermediary structures.

From the perspective of the political leadership, this process yields an enhanced sense of common identity that provides the basis for political integration. All these efforts purport to achieve a process of "administrative absorption" whereby articulation of the views, discontent, or conflicts is localized through established systems of official and intermediary channels.

The foregoing analysis suggests some basic differences and similarities in the approaches to community practice. A degree of similarity is discernible in the practice approach adopted by governmental agencies for community improvement. The emphasis on enhancing individual capacities for social relationships and economic adequacy in the programs of community practice by departments of social welfare, and the reliance of political departments on closing communication gaps and promoting a common identity among citizens, serves to promote social and political goals. Both rely upon processes of civic education, socialization, co-optation, and provision of services. Although the adoption of an overriding goal (community building, for example) is no guarantee of uniform interpretation and implementation of programs at the operational levels of different government departments, at more abstract levels these departments do complement each other's efforts. These complementary forces are strengthened by a centralized process of policy formation and goal-setting which, in turn, support a comprehensive and integrated approach to social development, a direction toward which community practice in some Asian communities (especially Hong Kong and Singapore) is moving.

In applying community practice in order to achieve social development, the voluntary sector tends to be more diversified, having dealt with issues and problems of a magnitude and scope broader than capacity and communication enhancement. This is to be expected, given the wider perspective and greater flexibility these agencies have exercised in responding to new situations. Thus, no single model seems to dominate the practice of community social work in the voluntary sector, even though the approaches adopted tend to emphasize the strengthening of grass-roots and indigenous groups for neighborhood-level self-help and political action for change. It should be recognized, however, that the use of social action was not divorced from a commitment to social change objectives, but followed earlier efforts to strengthen the confidence of citizens in the social institutions of their countries.

A matrix of broad issues is at play that has favored the use of certain approaches and strategies but not others. Real as they are, these issues lead to a series of questions that community practice cannot afford to ignore. The first relates to a trend toward increasing dependency on government funding as voluntary organizations are faced with shrinking overseas support. Whether this dependency will eventually limit community practice to serving official efforts to maintain social stability (perhaps at the expense of social justice) is not known. If so, some may perceive it as an ethical issue; the authors suggest that this is not the case, for as an ethical issue, a free choice of alternative value preferences is implied. In the Third World, people tend to settle for social and political stability and a better economic future. The use of aversive or disruptive strategies for the advancement of minority interests may be less of an issue in times to come. The present-day need, however, is to establish community stability and to combat anomic individualism so that the process of nationalism can be hastened. No individualism can be possible without first establishing a solid national foundation.

A second factor to be considered is the sociocultural religious imperatives ingrained in the attitudes, beliefs, and value orientations of persons in Third World countries. There is the Buddhist idea of oneness, the Taoist idea of harmony with nature, the Confucian concept of relationship and authority, as well as the Islamic concept of brotherhood and mutual help. All these ideas provide bases for certain preferred behaviors which restrict the ways by which a problem can be resolved. From a Western point of view, many of these behaviors may be considered as fatalistic and passive, especially when it comes to the process of change. Instead of adopting an approach which results in others (persons or external environment) being changed, most Asian people seek change in themselves in order to harmonize with the external environment and the persons around them. Because of this, Asian people are believed to show greater tolerance for their adversaries.

If this is a valid observation, what implications might it have for community practice? For example, to what extent should the strategies and techiques of community practice be adapted to these imperatives? Should change efforts be directed toward enhancing the person's adaptive and coping capacities? If, however, change efforts are applied to systems external to the group concerned, would such strategies tend to further frustrate or alienate the group which community practice seeks to help? Are there other approaches and strategies which could be used?

A third factor is the political-economic realities which impinge upon planning in Third World countries. The issue is whether and to what extent such factors should comprise the humanitarian concerns of social work community practice. This issue becomes exaggerated for some whose myopic perceptions of their colonial heritage breed attitudes of suspicion toward all governments. In Third World countries, where a unity of minds and efforts is essential to the solution of massive social problems, the lack of an atmosphere of faith and trust impedes collaborative efforts between governments and the people. In many circumstances, what has been at issue is the notion of popular participation which some community practitioners have attempted to impose upon the citizenry in situations where participatory democracy is not at stake, not called for, nor even resisted.

If real meaning is to be derived from the experiences of community practice in Third World countries, these questions must be addressed honestly, realistically, and unemotionally.

Success and Failures

Observers often disagree on what is and what is not a successful outcome in developing countries, because they disagree on goals and outcome criteria. Despite this disagreement, achievements can be identified that most people would rate as successful. The provision of certain services and facilities for community improvement has been expanded and improved, and changes in some policies and programs have benefited large populations. New programs have been implemented for disadvantaged groups such as the aged and the handicapped. Some community groups living in deleterious conditions have organized to press successfully for relocation to better living environments. Increasing numbers of interest groups are coming together to form coalitions, advance legislation on behalf of labor, industrial welfare and safety, public education, abortion, consumer protection, rent control, and public housing. Channels have been provided for redress of grievances and review of public policies and plans, and many authorities have become more responsive to public complaints. Authorities have established mechanisms such as working parties and planning committees to begin work on the comprehensive development of education, the provision of rehabilitation services for handicapped persons, and other areas of need.

While these achievements are good, doubts have been expressed as to whether they advance the fundamental goals of social development. People have questioned whether such achievements have built up the inner strength of their communities or furthered the integration of diverse groups into the community. Some observers are doubtful that citizens are sufficiently self-reliant in coping with daily problems of living. Question is raised about the extent to which neighborhoods and grass-roots organizations take part in mutual-help efforts or take an interest in what their governments do. That is, are they real participants? Some are skeptical that new channels of communication really facilitate two-way communication between people and the administration or that policies take into account popular wishes. Instead, they allege that what occurs is a top-down flow of information, policies, and influences from the administration to the people and that there are no horizontal linkages of different neighborhoods and the community as a whole.

References to document allegations of failure are easy to find. A severe critic of the Indian program argued, for example, that it failed because the educational element was sidetracked and separated from it. An attitude change was considered an essential prerequisite for the sustained adoption of any new technology which people were to be persuaded to follow (Karunaratne 1976:117). Holdcroft (1978) argued that an inability to arouse popular participation has plagued most community development programs in the world—not just the developing ones. For instance, the shift from state government direction to village Panchayat planning and implementation in India in 1959 did not succeed because, although the people were involved through their labor, they were never real participants (Karunaratne 1976:117). A more universal criticism of community development is that such programs were inefficient in reaching economic goals. In many countries, they were not even able to alleviate food shortages and extreme poverty.

In urban areas, critics assert that small-scale incremental changes such as the ones already mentioned are made in the interest of the sponsor and the status quo, and not for basic social change and the benefit of the people; and that community practice is inefficient in eliminating social problems and social inequalities.

These criticisms have a ring of truth. For although community practice has recognized the importance of the development of self-reliance in communities, early interventions produced a network of services that in the end did not eliminate social problems and inequalities. Thus, in the recent past, community practitioners have come to believe in the significance of citizen involvement as a prerequisite for community improvement and have sought opportunities to promote popular participation. But this does not seem to be working either. Today's critics blame the people and the cultural imperatives for their apathy and simultaneously accuse the socially elite of pursuing their self-interest.

Needless to say, debates of this kind are scarcely productive: for it is the basic difference in the ideologies and yardsticks used to measure the success of community practice that is at issue. In fairness, it is accurate to say that changes and improvements have been made in government machineries and policies as the result of the persistent and progressive efforts of some community practitioners. Without the backing of governments and their commitments of resources, without the growing patronage and responsiveness of enlightened bureaucrats and technocrats, many of the improvements in public services and facilities could not have been possible. Perhaps what is needed is the reformation of community practice to take into account the unique conditions in developing countries.

The experience of community practice in the rural and urban programs of the Third World countries can provide several useful lessons in such a reformulation. First, the concept of overall community improvement was difficult if not impossible to translate into effective campaigns. When community betterment became the concern of many separate departments of government, it soon became the responsibility of none. To begin with, finding a home base for community development proved difficult. As a ministerial portfolio it was linked with health, or agriculture, or local government and cooperatives, or social welfare. The creation of a separate ministry did not survive the early disenchantment with the process or the political decline of a powerful patron. Creation of a separate ministry multiplied the problems of coordination among government agencies.

Second, the struggle for resources for community development programs precipitated interministerial and interdepartmental competition. Technical departments, especially Agriculture, were reluctant to allocate any of their resources for projects over which they had no control. Coordination of a number of departments proved to be most successful at the district level. A district officer, as administrative head of the district or chief executive of an elected district council, had the authority and could give effective leadership, but this was dependent on personal attributes—experience, maturity, political skill—as well as on the office itself.

Third, although the neighborhood base of community practice was a logical choice, the agents of the process were usually not sufficiently powerful to induce change. Because they lacked the power to confront vested interest groups in rural areas, their search for consensus and allies led them to associate with the elite and reinforced traditional paternalistic authority in the villages. Conflict approaches in urban situations seem to have had very little effect. It was the impact of political powers rather than community practice that fostered the growth of self-reliant or intermediary local institutions. Short-term, self-help projects have done little to promote community planning, sustain participation over time, or develop new social institutions, which in the long run are the only effective instruments for betterment. In Kenya, however, the very success of self-help projects led to tension with government agencies that felt pressured to match the efforts of the communities (Wallis 1976:195).

What does this lead us to? A certainty amidst doubts and confusions, perhaps. A challenge and further questions.

Scenarios for the Future?

The certainty is in the irony that community practice is getting weaker. The fragility of community practice increases as the impact of political power intensifies. As this happens, it becomes more difficult for community practitioners to apply their ideals. This is not meant to be a defeatist's view, but a challenge to community practice. The question is how to face this challenge in Third World countries where priority tends to be given to political and social stability.

If a scenario is to be constructed, it must first of all recognize that community practice has only a limited role in solving social problems and inequality. This is a fact which practitioners in Third World countries have ignored in the past. The goals of social development require concerted efforts to generate needed resources. Eliminating inequalities and raising the quality of life require joint efforts and cooperation between the government ministeries and the voluntary sector. Uniting the voluntary sector with the government is warranted if for no other reason than to create an environment and atmosphere that generate a spirit of working together. Increased financial backing of voluntary efforts in community improvement is important. But government support through subvention need not be a paternalistic orientation toward voluntary and intermediary organizations. A genuine sense of partnership must be fostered.

Second, it is unnecessary to polarize the maintenance of social stability and the advancement of social justice as competing ideologies. No doubt, the two ideologies are different, but the ultimate goal for both approaches is the advancement of the community and national progress.

Third, community practice must take steps to define its mission in order to define its parameters. In view of the wide-ranging scope of activities that have been included under its rubric, community practice in the voluntary sector must redefine its role and function, and reexamine its focus and direction of practice. A case in point is those countries where traditional areas of concern, such as grass-roots organizing, are becoming absorbed into, or taken over by, official and intermediary institutions. Community practitioners in these situations serve their function well if they prepare local residents for election to these organizations, organize and mobilize local people to vote for delegates and to use their local communication networks to foster an interest in the well-being of the neighborhood. Voluntary organizations, on the other hand, might well consider moving into wider policy issues and planning, assuming certain watchdog functions alongside their traditional developmental and educational roles. Efforts at social development and social change will be effective only if they are backed by legislative provisions, policy reviews, and planning that reflect popular inputs.

Future scenarios for community practice must also resolve two dilemmas: the concept of permanence and the relationship between community practice and social work. The establishment of intermediary institutions has certain advantages, but the question remains as to whether they should be perpetuated. In the rapidly changing conditions of Third World countries people become highly mobile, and their interests and concerns often are centered around the workplace and special interests rather than the neighborhood in which they live. Groups are likely to come together to work on specific issues or problems, and then disintegrate. People in cities are no longer bound, as were their counterparts in rural sectors, by geographical boundaries or lineage groupings. Would it not be more strategically appropriate for community practice to follow the motions and events of the people, and adapt its method of approach accordingly instead of trying to perpetuate structures that may be functionally obsolete?

The linkage of community practice with social work has been tenuous, though traditional. In light of the political nature of the issues, is the existing social work value framework of community practice adequate and appropriate for the political functions of community practice? Should community practice remain a component of social work or should community social work be just one element of community practice?

Community practice in developing countries has now come to a point where it can and should stop emulating the basic models of practice rooted in a political philosophy of participatory democracy that is only an illusory image in the Third World. Although the approach (or approaches) being used in Third World countries may bear resemblance to aspects of the models of practice enunciated in the first section of this volume, the approaches are more a product of the realities of the situation than a conscious theoretical eclecticism. Social work and community practice educators must reappraise their experiences and attempt to formulate approaches suited to the unique conditions and requirements of these countries. Some suggest that community practice theory taught in schools in Third World countries bears little relevance to local conditions and needs (Midgley and Adler 1978). The uncritical praise bestowed on grassroots movements and the myopic condemnation of government actions should give way to more objectivity on the part of community practitioners and educators.

Notes

1. Hampton Institute, founded in 1868, developed education and training that would avoid the traditional alienation of the educated man from his own people. Hampton Institute had a largely white staff whereas Tuskegee Normal and Industrial School had an entirely black staff. Both institutions were expressions of a political and educational compromise, conciliating white opinion in the South and disavowing political ambition for the blacks and abandoning their quest for higher education.

2. See, for example, the following reports of regional and international conferences:
International Council on Social Welfare. 1971. *New Strategies for Social Development: Role of Social Welfare.* Proceedings of the XVth International Conference on Social Welfare, September 6–12, 1970, Manila, Philippines. New York and London: Columbia University Press.
International Association of Schools of Social Work (IASSW). 1974. *A Developmental Outlook for Social Work Education.* A report of a seminar on maximizing social work potentials for family planning and population activities, November 5–15, 1973, Singapore. New York: IASSW.
———. 1975. *Education for Social Change: Human Development and National Progress.* Proceedings of the XVIIth International Congress of Schools of Social Work, July 6–9, 1974, Nairobi. New York: IASSW.

———. 1976. *Asian Social Problems, New Strategies for Social Work Education.* Proceedings of the Third Asian Regional Seminar on Development of Teaching Resources and Interdisciplinary Communication, August 25–30, 1975, Hong Kong. New York: IASSW.

———. 1977. *Social Realities and the Social Work Response: The Role of the Schools of Social Work.* Proceeding of the XVIIIth International Congress of Schools of Social Work, July 13–17, 1976, San Juan, Puerto Rico. New York: IASSW.

United Nations Economic and Social Commission for Asia and the Pacific, and International Council on Social Welfare. 1977. *Methods and Techniques of Promoting People's Participation in Local Development,* a report of a regional workshop held on December 9–22, Bangkok, Thailand. Bangkok: UN Economic and Social Commission for Asia and the Pacific.

United Nations Economic and Social Commission for Asia and the Pacific, Social Welfare Development Centre for Asia and the Pacific, and International Council on Social Welfare. 1977 *Philippine Study Tour of Barangays.* Bangkok: UN Economic and Social Commission for Asia and the Pacific.

3. The term intermediary body in this article is used differently from the same term identified in the British study, *The Future of Voluntary Organizations,* generally referred to as The Wolfenden Report. That report considered the relationship between government and the voluntary sector in Britain and focused substantial attention on the role of coordinating organizations which it termed intermediary bodies. The report rejected the commonly used words "coordinating and coordination" because the number of senses in which they are used impedes a clear understanding of the work of such organizations. The Wolfenden Report defined intermediary bodies as those which are intermediary between different voluntary organizations and provide "support for voluntary organizations individually and collectively, and in reconciling the inherent tensions between the autonomy of individual organizations and planning for the pursuit of common objectives." The term specifically excludes organizations which provide direct services to individuals and groups. See *The Future of Voluntary Organizations: Report of the Wolfenden Committee* (London: Croom Helm, 1978) p. 100.

4. Examples of these intermediary organizations are: the Barangay of the Philippines, the Zila Parishad of India, the Citizens Consultative Committee of Singapore, and the District Board of Hong Kong. In essence, these institutions are each made up of a three-tier structure. In India, at the village level there is the Village Panchayat, elected by all adult members of a village. For blocks of 100 villages there is a Block Panchayat Samiti, made up of the presidents of village panchayats, to be the chief body for the formulation of plans for the whole block, and a Zila Parashad, at the district level, which reviews and coordinates the work of the blocks within its district. The parallel to this, as in Hong Kong, is the Mutual Aid Committee-District Board-City District Committee, and, for Singapore, a series of residents committees, management committees of community centers, and the Citizens Consultative Committee, all under the coordination of the Members of Parliament of the particular constituency. It should be noted, however, that where the Zila Parishad of India was the product of Panchayati-Raj, a scheme to shift state government direction to village Panchayat planning and implementation, the structures in Hong Kong and Singapore are not designed to devolve authority.

References

Biddle, William W. and Loureide J. Biddle. 1965. *The Community Development Process.* New York: Holt, Rinehart and Winston.

Colonial Office. 1925. *Education Policy in British Tropical Africa.* London: HMSO.

——. 1935. *Memorandum on the Education of African Communities.* London: HMSO.

——. 1944. *Mass Education in African Society.* London: HMSO.

——. 1955. *Social Development in the British Colonial Territories.* London: Colonial Office Miscellaneous No. 523.

Commission of Inquiry. 1967. *Kowloon Disturbances 1966.* Hong Kong: Hong Kong Government Press.

Curtin, Philip D., ed. 1972. *Imperialism.* New York: Walker.

Dasgupta, Sugata. 1963. *A Poet and a Plan.* Calcutta: Thacker Spink.

Desai, Armaity S. 1976. "The Report on the XVIIIth International Congress of Schools of Social Work." Paper presented at the International Conference on Social Welfare, 1976; quoted by Katherine A. Kendall in *The Social Realities and the Social Work Responses* (New York: International Association of Schools of Social Work), p. ix.

Frank, A. G. 1969. *Capitalism and Underdevelopment in Latin America.* New York: Monthly Review Press.

Gil, David G. 1976. "Social Policies and Social Development: A Humanistic-Egalitarian Perspective." *Journal of Sociology and Social Welfare,* 3(3):242–63.

Hatch, D. Spencer. 1949. *Toward Freedom from Want.* London: Oxford University Press.

Hodge, Peter. 1970. "A Historical Note on Social Science Courses for Overseas Students at the London School of Economics." *Hong Kong Journal of Social Work* (Winter), 5(1):34–41.

——, ed. 1980. *Community Problems and Social Work in Southeast Asia.* Hong Kong: Hong Kong University Press.

Holdcroft, Lane E. 1978. "The Rise and Fall of Community Development in Developing Countries, 1950–65: A Critical Analysis and an Annotated Bibliography." Michigan State University Rural Development Paper No. 2.

Hong Kong Government Secretariat. 1977. *Management Circular 1/77 [on] Community Building.* Dated February 22.

Hoon, Shim Jae. 1981. "Self-Help, Seoul Style." *Far Eastern Economic Review* (July), 113(29):44–45.

International Missionary Council. 1928. *Report of the Jerusalem Meeting of the International Missionary Council* (the Christian Mission in Relation to Rural Problems), vol. 6. London: Oxford University Press.

Jones, Thomas Jesse. 1917. *Negro Education: A Study of the Private and Higher Schools for Coloured People in the United States.* Washington, D.C.: GPO.

——. 1922. *Education in Africa: A Study of West, South, and Equatorial Africa.* New York: the African Education Commission.

Karunaratne, Garvin. 1976. "The Failure of the Community Development Program in India." *Community Development Journal* (April), 11(2):95–118.

King, Ambrose Yeo-chi. 1975. "Administrative Absorption of Politics in Hong Kong: Emphasis on the Grassroots Level." *Asian Survey* (May), 15(5):422–39.

King, Kenneth James. 1971. *Pan-Africanism and Education: A Study of Race Philanthropy and Education in the Southern States of America and East Africa*. London: Oxford University Press, Clarendon Press.

Leung, Joe C. B. 1978. "The Community Development Drama in Hong Kong: 1967–77." *Community Development Journal*, 13(3):140–46.

Mayer, Albert et al. 1958. *Pilot Project India: The Story of Rural Development at Etawah, Uttar Pradesh*. Berkeley: University of California Press.

Midgley, J. and Z. Adler. 1978. "Community Work Teaching at Schools of Social Work in Developing Countries." *Community Development Journal*, 13(3):131–39.

Miller, Matt. 1979. "Saemaul Movement: From Bureaucratic Fancy to Simplistic Philosophy." *Far Eastern Economic Review*, 104(20):66–70.

Oliver, Roland. 1952. *The Missionary Factor in East Africa*. London: Longmans, Green.

Paiva, J. F. X. 1977. "A Conception of Social Development." *Social Service Review*, 51(2):327–36.

Pande, V. P. 1967. *Village Community Projects in India: Origin, Development and Problems*. London: Asia Publishing House.

Riches, G. C. P. 1973. *Urban Community Centres and Community Development, Hong Kong and Singapore*. Hong Kong: Centre of Asian Studies, University of Hong Kong.

Seah, Chee Meow. 1975. "Whither the City-State: Challenges of Security and Stability." In Chee Meow Seah, ed., *Trends in Singapore; Proceedings and Background Paper*, pp. 3–35. Singapore: Institute of Southeast Asian Studies, Singapore University Press.

Simey, T. S. 1946. *Welfare and Planning in the West Indies*. London: Oxford University Press, Clarendon Press.

Strayer, Robert W. 1978. *The Making of Mission Communities in East Africa*. London: Heinemann Educational Books.

United Nations. 1953. *Series on Community Organizations and Development, Country Monographs, United Kingdom Dependent Territories*. New York: UN.

——. 1954. *Methods and Techniques of Community Development in the United Kingdom Dependent and Trust Territories*, a study prepared by S. Milburn. New York: UN.

——. 1956. *Special Study on Social Conditions in Non-Self-Governing Territories*. New York: UN.

——. 1960. Community Development and Economic Development, Part 1: *A Study of the Contribution of Rural Community Development Programs to National Economic Development in Asia and the Far East*. Bangkok: UN Economic Commission for Asia and the Far East.

Village Education in India; the Report of a Commission of Inquiry. 1920. London: Oxford University Press.

Wallis, Malcolm. 1976. "Community Development in Kenya: Some Current Issues." *Community Development Journal*, 11(3):192–98.

Wang, Cheng-Su. 1942; 1943. "Rural Reconstruction and Education in China; Village Education in China." *Overseas Education* (October) 14(1):1–7; (January) 14(2):60–66; (April) 14(3):102–7.

Wong, Aline K. 1971. "Chinese Voluntary Associations in Southeast Asian Cities and the Kaifongs in Hong Kong." *Journal of the Hong Kong Branch of the Royal Asiastic Society,* 11:62–73.

Index

432   Index